PSYCHOLOGY OF MOHAMMED
INSIDE THE BRAIN OF A PROPHET

BY
DR. MASUD ANSARI

WASHINGTON, D.C.

MAS-PRESS, 2007

Ansari, Masud

PSYCHOLOGY OF MOHAMMED
Inside the Brain of A Prophet

Printed in the United States of America

Mas-Press
P. O. Box 57374
Washington, D. C. 20036

ISBN 978-1-4276-1729-3

ACKNOWLEDGMENT

The author wishes to expess his most sincere appreciation and gratitude to Dr. and Mrs. Thomas Reid who generously donated their scholarly insight to edit this book. I will be forever grateful to them.

CONTENTS

CHAPTER SEVEN. WERE MOHAMMED'S INSPIRATIONS GENUINE?

CHAPTER EIGHT. THE MENDACIOUS STRATEGIES OF MOHAMMED'S PROPHETHOOD

CHAPTER NINE. EXILE AND MASSACRE OF THE JEWS FROM MEDINA

PREFACE

This book should be read almost as if it were a work of fiction. It deals with a religion and with events in the life of a man who claimed to be its prophet, both of which are far from truth and credulity to a rational mind. This book will unveil the self-serving nature of the self-proclaimed prophet as exemplified in the Koran and *hadith*. Mohammed, through his book, the Koran, both tried very hard to make realities out of unrealities. He fabricated a preposterous metaphysical faith designed to appeal to the baser instinct of pagan Bedouins. It began on the Arabian Peninsula and then, by bloody conquest, spread throughout the Mid-East, northern Africa and even into Spain. If anyone should ask why more than one billion of the world's population follows this absurd creed and accepts Mohammed as a prophet, I would refer them, *inter alia*, to the works of two distinguished scientists: Richard Dawkins, *The Selfish Gene*[1] and Susan Blackmore, *The Meme Machine.*[2]

It is not the intention of the author to delve into the definition of *religion* because it would be impossible to find one that would be acceptable worldwide. I am writing this book to analyze and expose the psychology of the creator (Mohammed) of the religion called Islam; the despicably crafty methods he used to achieve his ambitions; the spirit and principles of Islam; and the drastic and destructive impact of that religion on Muslims' minds in particular and the world in general.

Religion should transcend human ethics, generate a sense of spirituality, and establish principles to guide human behavior along paths of peaceful, caring coexistence with one's fellow man. But no phenomenon in human history has caused as much bloodshed and

---

[1] Richard Dawkins, *The Selfish Gene* (Oxford: Oxford University Press, 1976).

[2] Susan Blackmore, *The Meme Machine* (Oxford: Oxford University Press, 1999).

fratricide as religion. One of many examples: at the beginning of the sixth century a Jewish king, Dhu Nowas, after having defeated the Christians of Najran and having conquered their land, dug an enormous trench which he filled faggots and burned twenty thousand Christians alive. During the Crusades, Christians and Muslims butchered each other for 300 years; each side called it a Holy War. Crusaders committed themselves with solemn vows and in the thirteenth-century were granted full Indulgence, i. e. remissions of all punishment for sins committed in their quests and an assurance of direct entry into heaven. The battle cry of Christians, Pope Urban II urged, should be *Deus volt* [God wills it]. In a like manner, Muslim theocrats called fighting against Christians, Holy War *(Jihad)* against infidels and promised Muslim fighters a paradise with houris (virgin girls) among other delights in return for their deaths in battle.

The Thirty Years War (1618–48) eventually involved almost all of the European powers and they were all convinced that they were fighting for a Holy Cause. The actual cause of these wars was the attempt of the Habsburg controlled Holy Roman Empire to impose Catholicism on Protestant principalities such as Sweden and the Netherlands. The war affected the lives of the 500 million or so people who were then living on the earth, and that of their descendents.[3]

Historians have written that in Brandenburg, Mecklenburg, Pomerania, the Palatinate, Wurttemberg, and parts of Bavaria, civilian population losses may have been 50 percent or more. Art, science, trade, and industry declined.[4] Whole cities, villages, farms, and much property were destroyed. It took almost 200 years for the German territories to recover from the effects of the war.

For 1400 years Jews and Muslims have been killing each other, the Muslims believing that they are following a sacred edict. Many of the tragic conflicts in the world today are rooted in long-standing religious differences and animosities. Even within a certain religions such as Islam, intramural differences have caused Sunnis and Shi'as to massacre each other for hundreds of years and Irish

---

[3] J. V. Poli Sensky, *The Thirty Years War*, trans. Robert Gvans (California: California University, 1971), p. 9.

[4] *Americana Encyclopedia,* 2003 ed., s.v. "Thirty Years' War" by H.G. Koenigsberger.

Catholics and Protestants have been at each other's throats for over a century.

Homo sapiens, is a Latin term meaning a wise or knowlegable man. But in actuality many times we simply ignore our innate wisdom, believe in superstitions and easily become the victim of impostors. Where religious ideas are concerned, we often become narrow-minded and ethnocentric because we naturally tend to identify religion with our heritage or with those conventional forms of religious behavior that we observe in our own communities. We simply believe the religious faith that our parents have chosen for us is the best and even thinking about the authenticity of that faith is profane. The new-born mind is a blank slate upon which all the environmental and cultural elements that are prevalent in our milieu, including our religious beliefs, are copied.

The ubiquitous characteristic of religion is "sacred power." What is the nature of this "sacred entity" that we unconsciously inherit from our forefathers? If all the multitude differences of worship are eliminated, then the only remainder will be the common denominator of an unseen power, sanctity. If we remove sanctity from religion, then what remains will be superstition. In other words, sanctity plus superstition makes religion; religion minus sanctity makes superstition or myth. Therefore, sanctity is an attribute peculiar to religion. Sanctity is a man-made invisible power that man must live in contact with it or be condemned to chaotic experience where there is no foundation for reality.[5] In the *Elementary Forms of the Religious Life* (1912), Emile Durkheim (1858–1917) writes, "The division of the world into two domains, which include everything that is sacred in one and everything that is profane in the other, is the characteristic feature of religious thought." For Durkheim, sanctity is not an intrinsic status. Sacred is an appellation conferred by human beings on other persons, places, or things. This has been expressed as the vague and undefined Mana of the Melanesians; the Kami of primitive Shintoism; the fetish of the Africans; spirits possessing some human characteristics, that pervade natural places and animate natural forces; the Sutras and impersonal principle of Buddhism; Tao Te Ching and

---

[5] *Encyclopedic Dictionary of Religion,* 1979 ed., s. v. "Sacred and the prophane," by "V. T. Johnson."

the Analects of Confucius, the Vedas and Upanishads of Hinduism, the gods and goddesses of the Greek and Roman Pantheons, the essence of Judeo-Christian faiths, the preposterous content of the Muslim's Koran echoing the power-hungry, lascivious thoughts of Mohammed who presented himself as a prophet of God. It is this invisible sacred power which generates obedience and reverence, awe, and fear in the mind of whomever becomes the follower of a particular religion.

The difference between a sacred power and that which is almost powerless is, according to the Dutch scholar Gerardus Van der Leeuw, what distinguishes the sacred from the profane. When elaborating on sacred power, der Leeuw points out that a unique characteristic of sacred power is the fact that it evokes an ambivalent response. He believes that sacred power awakens a profound feeling of awe which manifests itself both as fear and as being attracted. There is no religion whatever without terror, but equally none without love.[6] The author of this book rejects Van der Leeuw's characterization of religion insofar as its application to Islam. Throughout passages of the Koran, one can rarely find a verse indicating Allah's "love" of his followers. Rather, the bloodthirsty Allah of Islam, among other threatening verses, clearly states: "Many of the jinns and human beings I have made for Hell," (Koran, VII: 179); "I have only created jinn and human beings that they may worship me" (Koran, LI: 56) and "I shall assuredly fill hell with *all* of you" (Koran, VII: 17, XXXII: 13).

A truly 'sacred power' condemns evil and cruelty and embraces good and truth. In other words, in all religions sacred power, God, and truth are virtually synonymous. Plato said goodness, knowledge and truth are interrelated and since the goal of knowledge and truth is goodness, therefore, the goal of knowledge is also goodness. Gandhi believed that the truth is higher than God.[7] Every religion teaches that rejecting the faith means turning away from truth. The sacred power turns evil and cruelty into good and truth. Plato, in *Eu-*

---

[6] Gerardus Van der Leeuw, *Religion in Essence and Manifestation,* 4 vols. trans. J. E. Turner (New York: Harper and Row, Publishers, 1963), 2: 48.

[7] Hendrik M. Vroom, *Religion and the Truth,* trans. J. W. Rebel (Michigan: Grand Rapids, 1989), p. 139.

thyphro also proposes the same idea, that what makes an action right is simply the fact that it is commanded by God. But, Socrates asks him' "Is something right because God commands it or does he command it because it is right?" *Euthyphro* replies that, of course, God commands it because it is right and it is against the nature of God to command cruelty.

Most theologians would tend to agree with this norm. However, some writers including Soren Kierkegaard do not agree. As an example, Kierkegaard believes that the God's command to Abraham to sacrifice his son Isaac (Genesis 22) is not just. In the Koran, Allah orders Muslims to kill the cursed people mercilessly (Koran, XXXIII: 61). The interesting point in this verse is that Allah not only commands Muslims to kill the cursed people, but they have to do it mercilessly and because it is the command of God it should be taken to be the "truth."

Women may not resist sexual abuse and the Koran commands that the men who abuse them get off free.[8] Believing in such cruelty makes a person good Muslim; rejecting it arouses the wrath of Allah and condemnation to Hell. To be religious and have faith is to believe without asking questions such as an explanation of Mohammed's trip to seven heavens on an animal similar to a donkey. This fantasy cannot be tested because God is invisible and invisibility is the sacred characteristic of Him. Thus blind faith protects a religion from rejection.

Contrary to science, which will not validate any theory until it is tested, religious injunctions are considered to be "sacred" and demanding proof will be "profane," liable to punishment and hell-fire. In Islam, questioning the ascendance of Mohammed to seven heavens is considered "apostasy" and the punishment of an apostate in Islam is death.[9] Whatever has been discussed above boils down to the fact that in order to be a true believer all of the ludicrous and illogical precepts found in "sacred" books should be considered absolute truth and any doubt leads to hell. Thomas Moore brilliantly explains that,

---

[8] Blackmore, *The Meme Machine,* p. 190.

[9] Hassan aHMoujudi, *Ezdevaje Daem va Ezdevaje Movaqqat,* Farsi Edition (Tehran: Moujudi Publications, 1370), p. 85.

"Spiritual intelligence requires a particular kind of emptiness, a sophisticated ignorance, an increasing ability to forget what you know and to give up the need to understand."[10] Just as DNA is passed from generation to generation, so religion passes from parent to offspring. In his book, *The Selfish Gene,*[11] Richard Dawkins for the first time proposed the theory of transmission of ideas through culture. Many authors after Dawkins followed his lead by devoting entire chapters to the subject. In countless lectures for the past two decades, Dawkins has strongly suggested that God is a meme and religion is akin to a viral transmitter.

The recurrent pattern of social behavior defines a culture. John Teske quotes a number of scholars that as a result of their scientific studies they have come to the conclusion that both our cognitive and emotional lives may be locatable socially rather than individually; *between* rather than inside persons. Vygotsky and Luria also believe that even our thoughts and memories are dependent of our social life.[12] The ideas of "belief in life after death" and "hell-fire" are self-perpetuating unconsciously because of their physical impact.[13] The reason that religions with all of their weak points became successful was that their litany and doctrines were passed down from one person to another throughout the long history of humanity; at first orally, then in hand-copied manuscripts and, finally, in printed books and via the perorations of TV evangelists. That is why they have been with us for thousands of years, and why millions of people's lives are controlled by ideas that are preposterous as well as historically inaccurate.

Having analyzed the psychosocial mechanism of religiosity and how religious faith transfers like a cultural virus from generation to generation, now we have to understand that though all religions sprang from the same psychological compulsion, none of them is more inane than Islam. It is not too much to say that if Islam had not

---

[10] Thoms Moore, *The Soul's Religion* (New York: Harper Collins Publishers, 2002), p. 17.

[11] Dawkins, *The Selfish Gene,* pp. 92, 192.

[12] *Ibid,* p. 195.

[13] *Ibid.*

developed as one of the major world religions, civilization would have evolved with less bloodshed and to a higher level than it is today.

Finally, one author writes: "The five oldest and most trusted Islamic sources don't portray Mohammed as a great and Godly man. They reveal that he was a thief, a liar, an assassin, a pedophile, a womanizer, a rapist, a mass murderer, a pirate, a warmonger, and a scheming and ruthless politician. It's hardly the character profile of a religious leader."[14] I am writing this book with the sincere aim of helping the Muslims of the world understand the base origin of the god they worship and, hopefully, persuade them to stop throwing away their lives on such horribly misanthropic precepts such as *jihad*. It is also my hope that this book will help the non-Muslims understand the nature of Islam and alert them to the implacable, vicious and endless menace of *Jihad*.

---

[14] Craig Winn, *Muhammad, Prophet of Doom* (Canada: Cricket Songs Books, 2004), p. XIV.

CHAPTER ONE

A SHORT ACCOUNT OF THE LIFE OF MOHAMMED, FOUNDER OF ISLAM

Paradise is under the shade of swords.
Mohammed Sahis al-Bukhari, Vol. IV, N. 7.

Prophets are more evil doers than professional liars, because the former commit crimes on the pretext of divine authority, but the latter only fabricate falsehoods of their own making.
Masud Ansari

It is not the intention of this book to go fully into the details of the life of Mohammed, but in order to understand how an ambitious Arab camel driver was able to establish one of the most successful organized world-wide religions, by means of the sword, terror and guile, we must take a brief look into his origins and at those individuals who influenced his early thinking. To understand Islam and the Koran, we first have to shed light on the life of its author. Over the centuries, thousands of biographies of Mohammed have been written. This short biography is based on information gleaned from the works of the most reliable authors who have written about Mohammed, both Muslim and non-Muslim.

The author will try to show how the mores of the clans and tribes that lived in and around Mecca, the birthplace of Islam in the early years of the seventh century, influenced Mohammed's character. Analysis of the works of Islamic historians shows that the chief philosophy governing the creation of the Islamic empire, which at its apogee stretched from India and China in the East through Southeast Asia and the Mediterranean to Spain in the West, was "the ends justify the means," and the chief tactical instrument was terrorism.

The Birth of Mohammed

There is no agreement on Mohammed's precise date of birth. It has been estimated as sometime between 567 and 573 CE. The most commonly accepted time is the autumn of the year 570 CE, the Year of the Elephant.[15] The infant was born in Mecca, the Holy City of Islam on the western side of Arabian Peninsula. At the time of Mohammed's birth, Mecca was inhabited by followers of the traditional Arabic idolatrous religion as well as adherents to the religion of Abraham (Koran, II: 130).

Mohammed's father, Abdullah, belonged to the clan Hashim, a sept of the Quraysh tribe. He married a woman named Amina, the daughter of Wahb, who belonged to the Bani Zuhra tribe. They named their only child Mohammed, a name derived from the root *hamada,* meaning 'the praised.'

The Quraysh tribe during the previous two centuries had risen to undisputed pre-eminence in Mecca. They controlled, in so far as the nomadic nature of Arab life permitted, all civil, military, and religious matters.

Mohammed's Childhood

It is a historic certainty that Mohammed was the first and only child in his family. Mohammed's father, Abdullah, died while on a business

---

[15] In this year, Ashram Abraha, an Abyssinian Christian viceroy in San'a (Yemen) of the King Negus (Najashi), of Abyssinia, had driven out the Jewish Himyar rulers because at the beginning of the sixth century a Jewish King, Dhu Nowas, had fought the Christians of Najran and had burned, twenty thousand of them in an enormous cave transformed into a furnace. Then, he led a big expedition and a number of elephants upon Mecca, with the intention of destroying the ka'ba, in order to spread Christianity among the Arabs. His mission was a failure and his army was destroyed in so sudden a manner, as to give rise to the legend embodied in the 105th Sura of the Koran, known the chapter of Elephant, or (Sura Al-Fil). This chapter of the Koran says, a shower of the stones, thrown by flocks of birds, destroyed the strong army almost to a man. The reader should be aware of the fact that the above-mentioned miracle is performed by the idols which were kept in Ka'ba, before the advent of Mohammed. This fable indicates that the whole contents of the Koran are as preposterous as the above-mentioned myth.

trip to Medina either during his wife's pregnancy or shortly after her delivery. At that time, the city of Mecca was considered unhealthy for infant children and it was customary for the Mecca nobles to employ a wet-nurse chosen from one of the neighboring nomadic tribes to nourish their infant progeny. The men reasoned that their wives, without the distraction of suckling infants, would dedicate themselves more assiduously to their pleasure and bear more children. Their infant children would benefit from the pure desert air and, away from the filth of the city, thrive in the black tents of the Bedouin. Thus the infant Mohammed, shortly after his birth, was placed with a Bedouin wet-nurse named Halima. She was a slave belonging to his uncle Abu Lahab and came from the clan Bani Saad, a branch of the great tribe known as the Hawazin. Halima was encamped near Mecca and had been brought, along with other lactating women, to take care of Meccan infants.

Mohammed's infancy and part of his childhood was spent with Halima among the Bani Saad clan. When Mohammed was two years old, his foster-mother, Halima, weaned him and took him back to his mother.

Amina was delighted with the healthy and robust appearance of her child but, because Mecca was still deemed insalubrious, she ordered Halima to take him back to the desert hoping that he would continue to thrive there. Even though the epileptic seizures that were to plague him later in life were not yet manifest and he appeared healthy, Amina's insistence on taking the child back to the desert beyond the usual term of suckling indicates that she believed he suffered from some constitutional delicacy.[16] At the end of his fourth year, however, a strange event occurred that greatly concerned his foster-mother. This event is palpable proof that Mohammed was from childhood subject to emotional disturbances.[17] Koelle quotes Ibn Ishaq as follows: One day a friend of Mohammed asked him for an account of an event that occurred during his [Mohammed's] childhood. Mohammed explained it thusly: "Once, while my foster-brother and I were tending the cattle in the desert, two men clothed in white and bearing a golden wash basin filled with snow came toward me.

---

[16] S. W. Koelle, *Mohammed and Mohammedanism* (London: Rivingtons, 1972), p. 40.

[17] *Ibid.*

They split open my body, took out my heart, cut it open, and removed from it a black clot, which they threw away. Then they washed my heart and body quite clean with the snow and one said to the other, 'Weigh him against ten of his people' and, when he did so, I outweighed them. Then he said, 'Weigh him against a hundred of his people' and again I outweighed them. He continued, 'Weigh him against a thousand of his people;' and when I outweighed them, too, he said, 'leave him now: for if thou wert to put his entire people onto the scale, he would outweigh them all.'"[18] Tabari refers to the same story as told by Mohammed on another occasion. He quotes Abu Dharr al-Ghaffari who asked him, "How did you first know with absolute certainty that you were a prophet?" Mohammed answered this question as above with some minor differences.[19]

Some historians have written that when Mohammed was ranting about his visionary travel to the sky, he mentioned that the above incident took place before Gabriel flew him to the sky.

Halima also refers to the same subject, as follows: "Some months after our return home, when Mohammed was tending our lambs behind the tents with his foster-brother, his foster-brother came running to me and said, "Something has happened to Mohammed!". My husband and I ran to Mohammed and found him standing with his face livid. We took hold of him and asked him what the matter was. He said, 'Two men in white clothes, came and threw me down and opened up my belly and sought something in it; I know not what.' So, we brought him back to our tent." Guillume[20] relates this incident to verse one of *Sura* XCIV which states: "Did we not open up your breast?"

Halima continues: "When we brought him to our tent, my husband said to me, 'I fear this boy is plagued by evil spirits, so must take him back to his family before makes a problem for us.' So, we picked him up and took him to his mother. Upon seeing us, she exclaimed, 'Why have you brought him back to me, when I asked you

---

[18] Koelle, *Mohammed and Mohammedanism,* pp. 43–44.

[19] At-Tabari, *The History of at-Tabari* (Ta'rikh al-rusul wa'l muluk), vol.6 (New York: State University, New York Press, 1988), p. 75.

[20] Alfred Guillume, *The Life of Muhammad, A Translation of Ibn Ishaq's Sirat Rasul Allah* (New York: The Viking Press Inc., 1926), pp. 33–34.

to keep him longer?' I answered, 'God has allowed my foster-son to grow up; I have done my part and he is now five years of age. I am afraid lest any misfortune should happen to him, so I have brought him back to you.' Amina rejoined, 'That is not the reason. Tell me the exact truth.' She persisted until I told her all that had happened. Hearing this, she said to me, 'No demon has any power over my son; he has a great future before him. However, leave him with me, and return safely to your tent.'"[21]

It can be inferred from these accounts that the robust but emotionally unstable boy, like some other emerging prophets, had an acutely sensitive nervous system and showed signs of what was probably an epileptic seizure.[22] Some historians have written that whenever Mohammed was in the throes of the "falling sickness," he pretended it to be a trance caused by the angel Gabriel bringing him revelations from Allah. Mohammed's explanation of his fits was that he was overwhelmed by the splendor of Gabriel's appearance.[23]

Koelle considers this alleged event in Mohammed's childhood of great importance to anyone attempting to assess Mohammed's claim to divine revelations. According to Koelle, it proves that the hysterical paroxysms from which he attributed his prophetic call did not result from the visit of an angel bringing him divine revelations, as believed by Muslims, but were the result of a neurological disorder that first became manifest in his childhood. Just as in his mature age he allegedly was able to retain the memories of the "revelations" revealed to him during his epileptic fits, so after that attack that occurred during his childhood (as related by his Bedouin nurse and himself), he was able to recollect disordered fantasies occurring during a paroxysm as if they were objective realities.

The disorder from which he suffered has been called *hysteria muscularis* by his medical biographer Sprenger. Supposedly, such attacks closely resemble common epileptic fits but differ from them inasmuch as the victim remains cognizant during the paroxysms, which is not the case in classical epilepsy. Sprenger maintains that

---

[21] Koelle, *Mohammed and Mohammedanism,* p. 30–41; Guillume, *The Life of Muhammad,* pp. 71–72.

[22] R. F. Dibble, *Mohammed* (New York: The Viking Press Inc., 1926), pp. 33–34.

[23] Humphrey Prideaux, *The Life of Mahomet* (London: 1723), p. 58.

Mohammed's hysterical ranting and visionary fantasies were obviously involuntary, and yet they emerged from within his own psyche, just as one's dreams come involuntarily, but originate in the subconscious mind. The nature of both phenomena is purely subjective.[24] Modern psychiatric doctrine might find Sprenger's hypotheses improbable, to say the least.

Muir characterizes the attacks that alarmed Halima, as fits of a nervous nature that conjured (according to Mohammed) visions of inspiration.[25] I shall deal in detail with the psychobiology of Mohammed's so-called "revelations" in *Sura* seven under the rubric of "Were Mohammed's Inspirations Genuine."

When Mohammed was six years old, his mother took him to visit relatives in Medina. After a month, she decided to return to Mecca. About half-way back, when they reached a spot called Al-Abwa, Amina fell sick, died, and was buried there.[26] The little orphan was carried back to Mecca by Um Aiman, Amina's Abyssinian slave girl. She left him with Mohammed's eighty-year-old grandfather, Abd al-Muttalib. Although he himself was dying, Abd al-Mutallib (whose nickname is said to have been Shaiba,[27] meaning "white hair") took charge of the orphan. This guardianship came to an end two years later when Abd al-Mutallib passed away. Abd al-Mutallib, before his death, had assigned the guardianship of his orphan grandchild to Abu Talib, Mohammed's paternal uncle, a dealer in clothes and perfumes. Abu Talib was neither the eldest, nor the richest of his family, but he was the noblest and most hospitable. Abu Talib loved his orphan nephew so much that he gave him precedence over his own children and would never allow a meal to begin without his presence. The only certain historical fact written in the Koran is that Mohammed grew up as an orphan in very poor circumstances (*Sura* CXIII: 6). This *Sura* says, "Allah made the poor orphan prosperous."

---

[24] Quoted in Koelle, *Mohammed and Mohammedanism,* pp. 41–42.

[25] William Muir, *Mahomet and Islam* (London: Darf Publishers Limited, 1986), p. 7.

[26] *Ibn Hisham,* p. 107; *Ibn Sa'd,* p. 73.

[27] M. TH. Houtsma, T. W. Arnold K., Rasset and R. Hartmann, eds. *The Encyclopedia of Islam,* vol. 1 (London: Luzac & Co., 1913), p. 52; at-Tabari, *The History of at-Tabari,* vol. 6, p. 9.

When he was about twelve years old, his uncle Abu Talib took Mohammed on caravans trading between Mecca and Syria, Yemen and, occasionally, Egypt, Abyssinia and Persia. Mohammed became familiar with the peoples of the Byzantine Empire and holy monks who sought out their salvation in solitude in the desert. Undoubtedly, these mercantile journeys widened the mental horizons of the aspiring youth, afforded ample inspiration for his developing mind, and provided him with an opportunity to become acquainted with various classes of men and learn how to deal with them.[28] On these journeys he came into contact with scattered settlements of Jews as well as the Christians of Syria. Mohammed lost no opportunity to inquire into the practices and tenets of the Syrian Christians by conversing with the monks and clergy whom he encountered.[29]

In Syria, Basra was a great center of Christianity and a monk called Bahira, who was well versed in Christian Scriptures, lived there. It is said that Mohammed learned a lot of Christian principles from him. Muslim writers and hagiographers (in particular the late traditionalists), without any historical foundation, have twisted the facts and made a legend of these visits, contending that the interest taken by the monk in the youthful stranger, arose from his having accidentally perceived the so-called "Seal of Prophethood" in the very place between Mohammed's shoulders where it was to supposed to appear according to legend.

Prior to his journeys with his uncle, Mohammed had been exposed only to isolated pockets of Jews, but now he had a chance to observe the workings of a wholly Jewish community; their rites of worship, dietary taboos, etc. He also became familiar with Christian rites and social customs; the churches with their crosses and images, baptism, and other rituals of their faith. These religious customs contrasted sharply with the gross idolatry of Mecca. Many writers have claimed that the religious education Mohammed received on these trips inspired his zeal for religious reform of the idolatrous Arabs in Mecca.[30]

---

[28] Koelle, *Mohammed and Mohammedanism,* pp. 43–44.

[29] Muir, *Mahomet and Islam,* p. 21.

[30] Tor Andrae, *Muhammed: The Man and his Faith,* trans. Theophil Menzel (New York: Harper & Brothers, 1960), p. 38.

Many writers have ascribed Mohammed's knowledge of the principles and traditions of the Christian faith, which he often displayed during his life, to his conversations with the monk Bahira. They had frequent discussions on matters of religion, in the course of which the teachings of the monk must have influenced Mohammed against idolatry. In later years, on subsequent visits to Syria, Mohammed had further encounters with Bahira.[31]

Was he ever a true religious evangelist inspired to reform idolaters? Did any of the Christian principles that he might have learned from the monk Bahira guide his behavior, especially after he gained power in Medina? The reader can draw his own conclusions after we examine more fully his acts as recorded by eye witnesses and the so-called "revelations" as written in the Koran.

The Youth of Mohammed

When Mohammed was in his late teens, Abu Talib assembled the tribes around Mecca to repulse the Negus Abyssinians. Mohammed was forced, for the first time, to face the dangers of war. Nervous, impressionable, and sickly, he could not stand the sight of the battlefield, so he ran away. This cowardly behavior exposed him to the ridicule of his associates.[32]

When Mohammed was in his twenties he used to attend a fair held annually at Okaz, a three day trip from Mecca. At this fair he met Jews and Christians, and, no doubt, learned some of their religious philosophies.[33] In later years, he used to brag that he had met Cross, the bishop of Najran, and had learned from him the all-embracing faith of Abraham.[34]

---

[31] Washington Irving, *Washington Irving's Life of Mohammed,* Charles Getchell, ed. (Massachusetts: Ipswich Press, 1989), pp. 20–21.

[32] Sprenger, *Vie et Enseignement de Mahomet,* quoted in Andre Servier, *Islam and the Psychology of Musulman,* trans. A. S. Mose-Blundell (London: Chapman and Hall Ltd., 1924), pp. 45–46.

[33] Muir, *Mahomet and Islam,* p. 16.

[34] *Ibid.* p. 16.

One time, during one of these fairs, a typical Bedouin war broke out between the tribes of Kinanah, relatives of the Quorayshites, and a neighboring tribe, called Beni Hawazin. Mohammed was caught up in one of the battles, but he did not evince any signs of courage or bravery. He busied himself in gathering up the enemy's arrows as they fell, and handing them to his uncles. According to Muir, "physical courage, indeed, and material daring, are characteristics which did not distinguish the prophet at any period of his career."[35]

Mohammed's youth passed without any other important incident. At one period he was employed, as were other Arab youngsters, as a shepherd.[36] When he preached in Medina he used to refer to this employment, saying that all prophets engaged in the same menial work at one time or another. This was true, no doubt, of Moses and David, but not all his forerunners (as he termed them).

When Mohammed reached the age of twenty-five years, Abu Talib suggested that he should start earning a livelihood for himself.[37] At this point, about 595 CE, fortune knocked at Mohammed's door and his luck changed dramatically. The widow of one of the leading merchants in Mecca named Khadija had taken over her dead husband's business and was now a wealthy, dignified Qurayshite merchant woman in her own right. Khadija was forty years old, had been married twice and had several children. She hired Mohammed to manage her trading caravans that carried merchandize to Syria in exchange for goods to sell in the Meccan markets. For three years Mohammed traveled with Khadija's camels and served her honestly. On these expeditions, Mohammed revisited Syria and met more monks, clergymen and other Syrian Christians. One can assume that he grasped any opportunity to inquire into the practices and tenets of the Jews and Christians who fell in his way.[38]

The empty and seemingly endless deserts of Arabia, where Mohammed herded sheep and goats in his youth and where wandering Bedouins lived out their lives, engendered many superstitious

---

[35] *Ibid.*

[36] *Ibn Sa'd,* p. 97f.

[37] *Ibn Hisham,* p. 119f.; at-Tabari, *The History of at-Tabari,* 1, 1127f.; *Ibn Sa'd,* p. 82f.

[38] Muir, *Mahomet and Islam,* p. 21.

fantasies. Their Arabian minds were engrossed with all kinds of fantasies of magic and mythical creatures such as *jinns,* demons, *ifrit, shaytan, ghul, gog* and *magog,* angels and so forth. In the evenings, the caravans would halt and, while sitting round a campfire, tales of encounters with these fancied entities were spun. The youthful mind of Mohammed would have no doubt absorbed those superstitions and beliefs in imaginative creatures. Later on, when he started his prophetic career, he inserted this nonsense into the Koran as "revelations" of Allah.

In contrast to the tales of the Bedouin, in Syria and Yemen everybody was preoccupied with monotheism. Everywhere, in the bazaars, in the churches, in the streets, in the gardens and public baths, people proclaimed the verity of their particular version of God. Sectarians preached in public places, proselytizing the truths of their faiths and condemning the heresy of others. Jews of all sects, Christians, Nestorians, Monophysite Copts, and Gregorians fought each other in the name of their particular faith. They all believed in the Bible as God's Divine Truth, but each sect interpreted it to their own end.

In Arabia, Mohammed observed much the same situation but without the commonality of monotheism. Most of the Arabs were poor: petty traders, butchers, blood-cuppers, wine-sellers, peddlers, smiths, and slaves. They had no organized community or prescribed religion; no priests or churches. Arabs belonged to various sects and each believed that the others were heretics. Thus, the superstitious beliefs of the desert people and the philosophies of the urban Christians and Jews were woven together in the mind of the young ambitious cameleer.

The public preachings of the Jews and Christians in Mecca began to weaken the faith of the Arabs in their idol-gods. The old idolatry became less and less attractive. It became apparent to Mohammed that Arabia was ready to embrace an organized religion. Why, then, should he not introduce himself as a new prophet?

Many scholars, such as Brockelmann, claim that Mohammed's "acquaintanceship with biblical material was, to be sure, extremely superficial and rich in errors. He may have derived some of his "divine revelations" from the Jewish legends of the Haggadah, but probably was more influenced by the Christian teachers who acquainted him with the Gospel of Infancy, the legends of the Seven

Sleepers, the saga of Alexander, and the other recurrent themes of medieval world literature."[39]

First Marriage with Khadija

Khadija's wealth increased as did the reputation of her young manager, but Mohammed's material fortunes did not improve. He remained a bachelor longer than was customary among his people, probably because of his penury. Gradually, Khadija grew fonder and fonder of her loyal manager until finally, despite the fifteen year difference in their ages, she offered her hand to Mohammed. Mohammed accepted her proposal and they married. This incident was a major turning point in the early part of Mohammed's career. Now, instead of being her employee, Mohammed became the master of both Khadija's person and her estate. And now, being equal in wealth to the most prosperous men of the city, his ambitious mind began to entertain thoughts of becoming a political entity.

A psychoanalyst has suggested that the subconscious longings of an orphan for a mother's affection, might explain Mohammed's attachment to the older woman. Mohammed used to say that Khadija was the best of all the women of his time, and that he would live with her in peace and tranquility in a house built of reeds.[40] Mohammed's marriage with Khadija opened the door to a brilliant future for him. It gave Mohammed that position in society which he craved, freedom from the cares of daily life, comfort, and a mutual love that never faltered over the twenty-five years of their marriage. His wife managed their wealth so he had no need to concern himself with material activities. From being an impoverished member of a great family, earning his livelihood in the hard service of others, he became a person of dignity and importance. Khadija was evidently an Arab lady of remarkable intelligence and sexual attraction. With these attributes,

---

[39] Carl Brockelmann, *History of the Islamic Peoples* (New York: G. P. Putman's Sons, 1947), pp. 16–17; C. H. Becker, *Christentum und Islam* (Leipzig: 1907); K. Ahrens, "*Christlichem im Koran,*" ZDMG, LX (1930), pp. 15–16.

[40] Maxime Rodinson, *Mohammed,* trans. Anne Carter (New York: Pantheon Books, 1971), p. 51.

she maintained an effective ascendancy over her husband and succeeded in keeping him from marrying other wives as long as she lived. However at her death, even though he had long ceased to be a young man, Mohammed indulged without restraint in a revel of sexual debauchery, taking a multitude of wives.[41]

The great Syrian historian Ammianus has said that both the male and female sexes dream of abandoning themselves to the Arabian practices of love. Also, a scholar of the Talmud, Rabbi Nathan declared that nowhere in the world was there such a propensity towards fornication as there is among the Arabs. Rabbi Nathan also observed that, if all the sexual license in the world were divided into ten parts, then nine of these would be distributed among the Arabs and the tenth would be enough for all the other races.[42]

Contemplating Prophethood

Observing that different sects of Christians in the Mideast, as well as the Jews, were uncompromisingly divided, Mohammed came to the conclusion that nothing would be more likely to attract a party loyal to him and fulfill his ambitions than founding a new religion with himself as its prophet. "Where religion exists," says Machiavelli, "it is easy to introduce armies and discipline, but where there are armies and no religion it is difficult to introduce the latter."[43] Mohammed, a poor insignificant shepherd boy and camel driver, who was lucky enough to have a wealthy wife, was smart enough to know this theory before Machiavelli expounded it; he recognized that the short cut to obtain power over his fellow Arab citizens was via the path of a new religion. He had neither a legitimate claim by birth nor an army to obtain power, but he could pretend to be a prophet to all who

---

[41] Koelle, *Mohammed and Mohammedanism,* p. 47.

[42] S. Kraus, "Geschichte: Griechen und Romer," in Von S. Funk, W. A. Neumann und A. Wünsche, *Monumenta Talmudica, unter Mitwirkung Zahlreicher Mitarbeiter hrsg,* vol. 1 (Vienna and Leipzig, Orion: 191), p. 57, quoted in Rodinson, *Mohammed,* p. 54.

[43] Niccolo Machiavelli, *The Prince and Discourses* (New York: Ransom House, Inc., 1950), p. 147.

would listen. And, the time was ripe for the emergence of a new prophet among the Arabs.

For several years after his marriage, Mohammed continued in commerce, visiting the great Arabian fairs, and making distant journeys with commercial caravans. Among Khadija's relatives, there were persons who possessed knowledge of Judaism and Christianity and perhaps subscribed to some of their beliefs and observed some of their rituals. Undoubtedly, they influenced Mohammed in the formulation of his religion. Among these people were Khadija's cousins, Othman and Waraka ibn Naufaul. Waraka, an aged scholar and Jewish convert to Christianity, most likely had much to do with the beginning of Islam.[44] Waraka was a Hanafite, a monotheistic religious sect, and is said to have been acquainted with the religious tenets and sacred scriptures of both Jews and Christians and even copied or translated some parts of the Old and New Testament into Arabic for the first time.[45] It was said that he even knew the Hebrew language.[46]

The Hanifites practiced the faith of Abraham, a kind of Judaism stripped of all ritual observances that did not require any interpretive manipulation of scriptures. It was from the womb of this Hanifite sect that Islam was born. Mohammed himself used to say that he was a Hanifite, kindred to those known as such in Mecca, Taif, and Yathrib (Medina). "Hanif" means a monotheist and a hater of idolatry.[47]

From Waraka, Mohammed is supposed to have garnered much of his knowledge regarding the writings, and traditions of the Mishna and the Talmud. Therefore, when Mohammed was fantasizing the Koranic verses, he must have remembered what he had learned from Waraka. His knowledge of both Jewish and Christian doctrine that he acquired from all sources was most superficial, as will be seen. He misinterprets the dogma most flagrantly in the Koran.

---

[44] David S. Margoliouth, *Mohammed and the Rise of Islam* (New York: Books for Libraries Press, 1972), p. 42.

[45] *Ibn Hisham,* p. 143f.

[46] Rodinson, *Mohammed,* p. 73.

[47] Clement Huart, *A History of Arabic Literature* (London: William Heinemann, 1903), p. 33.

It is exceedingly probable that Khadija, in talking with Waraka on familial matters, learned of and sympathized with the views and aspirations of the Hanafite sect. When she was informed of her husband's strange visions, she no doubt turned to Waraka for guidance. As Khadija herself was favorably disposed towards Hanafism, it is highly probable that, along with Waraka, she exercised her influence to encourage her husband to don the mantle of a prophet. Mohammed was already a prominent member of Arabian society due to his wife's wealth, rank and influence. When his cataleptic fits and visions became common knowledge, he came to be viewed in an entirely new manner—that of a man claiming to be God's apostle. Thus, he became acceptable to those patriots and reformers who were seeking to rid Arabia of its superstitious beliefs and worship of idols.[48]

Mohammed started this religious period when he was about forty years old. He began to spend an increasing amount of time on Mount Hira in a form of solitary devotional prayer and meditation, called *tahannuth* (penance). Khadija knew that whenever he went to Mount Hira, he underwent a spiritual experience that completely rejuvenated him.

The full support of Khadija finally encouraged him to impertinently pretend to hear God's revelations as spoken by the angel Gabriel. Accounts of these visitations are recorded by Muslim writers and are also alluded to in certain passages of the Koran. The Arabs call a night during the month of Ramadan *Alkader* (divine decree). About 610 CE, on that night, according to Koranic twaddle, angels descended to earth and Gabriel brought down the decrees of God. As Mohammed said:

> Gabriel, as I was sleeping, came to me in a human form and displayed a silken cloth covered with written characters. "Read!" said the angel. And I replied, "I know not how to read!" He pressed me tight and almost stifled me, until I thought that I should die. Then he let me go, and said, "Read!" I said, "What should I read?" Only saying that in order to free myself from him, fearing that the might repeat what he had done to me. He said: "Read in the name of the lord who has created all

---

[48] Koelle, *Mohammed and Mohammedanism*, p. 48.

things; who has created man from a cloth of blood. Read in the name of the most Bountiful, He who teaches by the pen teaches man what he knew not. (Koran, CXVI: 1–5)

I recited it, and then the heavenly messenger announced, "Thou are the prophet of God and I am his angel Gabriel." Thereafter, he hesitated and departed. I woke up, and it was as though these words had been written on my heart. There was no one of God's creation more hateful to me than a poet or a madman; I could not bear to look at either of them. I said to myself, "Your humble servant is a poet or a madman, but Qu*raysh* shall never say this of me. I shall take myself to a mountain crag, hurl myself down from it, kill myself and find relief in that way."[49]

Following this fancied incident, Mohammed pretended that he had fallen into a state of distress, unsure whether he was a contemptible poet or a possessed man. While still pretending anxiety because of "revelation," he entered Khadija's chamber and told her the story. Khadija believed him and said, "You must rejoice. Never would God confuse you. You do well by your kindred and you deserve to be trusted by God." Then, Khadija sent Mohammed to Waraka saying, "Listen to my husband and tell us your thoughts." Mohammed himself quotes his conversation with Waraka as follows:

"'He questioned me and I told him my story. He said, 'This is the *namus*[50] that was revealed to Moses. Ah! If I only were young! If only I could be still living when your people drive you out! I said to him, 'Will they drive me out?' He answered, 'Yes. No one who has brought what you bring has ever failed to make enemies. If your time had come in my lifetime I would have helped you with all my strength'"[51]

The zealous concurrence of the learned Waraka is said to have had a powerful impact and assuaged any doubts in the mind of Mohammed.[52] Naturally, the first to accept Mohammed's message

---

[49] Tabari, *The History of at-Tabari,* vol. 6, pp. 70–71.

[50] Tabari, identifies *namus* with Gabriel, but Rodinson believes it was the Greek word *nomos,* meaning law, which was the name given to the *Torah* and the Pentateuch revealed by God.

[51] *Ibn Ishaq* in Guillume, *New Light on the Life of Mohammed,* pp. 7, 27, 59, quoted in Rodinson, *Mohammed,* p. 73.

[52] Washington Irving, *Washington Irving's Life of Mohammed,* p. 29.

were the people of his own household, beginning with his wife, Khadija. The second was the freedman Zaid ibn Harith, his adopted son and servant, who may have played a great part in informing Mohammed about Christianity, a faith quite widespread amongst the Kalb tribe to which he belonged. The third was his cousin and son-in-law, Ali, the son of Abu Talib.

The fourth and the first outside his family to join Mohammed's faith was Abu Bakr, a distinguished, rich merchant two years younger than Mohammed, who was his best friend and close neighbor. Abu Bakr always remained unconditionally loyal to Mohammed. His superior judgment and wisdom exerted a moderating influence on Mohammed's decisions and brought great help and repute to his cause. Abu Bakr's original name was "Attiq ibn Uthman." His nickname, "Bakr" means "virgin" and, coincidentally, his daughter Ayesha was the only one of Mohammed's wives who married him as a virgin girl. Abu Bakr brought many of the younger men of Mecca into Islam, including some from the most powerful clans.

Preaching in Mecca

Mohammed's public preaching began three years after he allegedly received his first "revelation." Until then his message remained mainly within the circle of his family. On his first public appearance as a prophet, the people laughed at him, ridiculed his pretensions and called him a liar and teller of old fables. He often complains of this in the Koran. The reactions of the Qurayshites and the people of Medina to his divine pretensions were quite agonizing to him. As he passed by groups of people, they would point at him with distain and call him a half-wit or insane creature possessed by the devil.[53] They sneered at him exclaiming, "Behold the grandson of Abd al-Motallib, who pretends to know what is going on in heaven!" Some who witnessed his epileptic-like fits associated with mental ecstasy merely considered him insane and offered him medical attention; some declared that he was possessed of a devil, while others

---

[53] Muir, *Mahomet and Islam,* p. 43.

charged him with sorcery and magic and deceit.[54] The negative re-action of those whom he most expected to listen to him and adopt his new faith was so overwhelming that over and over again he con-templated suicide.[55]

> "No knowledge have they of such a thing, nor had their fathers. It is a grievous thing that issues from their mouth as a saying. What they say is nothing, but falsehood." (Koran, XVIII: 5)
>
> "It may be you who will kill yourself with grief that they do not be-come believers." (Koran, XXVI: 3)

It would appear from the references noted above that Mo-hammed's biographers have mainly dealt with the external manifes-tations of his pretensions and they have avoided delving deep into his psyche. He certainly knew what he was saying and what he was planning in order to fulfill his ambitions. As long as he was residing in Mecca, he bore all affronts without any apparent resentment; preached to all sorts of people, from the wealthiest and highest born to the lowest of the homeless, without condemning any and courte-ously received visitors of all classes. None of the insults discouraged him from attempting to achieve his self-imposed goal.

In the first years of his career, he placated the great men with flat-tering praise; to the poor he gave gifts and alms. In this way, he suc-ceeded in attracting all classes of people to his new faith. For many years he had planned to satisfy his power-seeking ambitions by pre-tending to be the chosen ambassador of Allah and now, in his forti-eth year, he believed the time had come to set his plans into motion.

At the expense of his 40,000 *dirham* fortune (which had dwin-dled down to 5,000 *dirhams* by the time of *Hijra*), Abu Bakr suc-ceeded in converting five other youths to Mohammed's new faith. Despite his hard efforts, secret preaching, and private solicitation, in the first three or four years after Mohammed's self-proclaimed

---

[54] Irving, *Washington Irving's Life of Mohammed,* ed., p. 40.

[55] Muir, *The Life of Mohammad* (Edinburgh: John Grant, 1923), p. 44; Subhash C. Inamdar, *Muhammad and the Rise of Islam* (Madison Connecticut: Psychologi-cal Press, 1959), p. 110.

prophethood, the converts to his faith amounted to a mere forty-four persons: thirty-five men and nine women.[56]

The main arguments that he used to delude the people were promises of rewards in heaven and threats of punishment in hell. The rewards were designed to fulfill the day dreams of the Bedouin Arabs and the punishments were tailored to terrify them in the event that they did not comply with his ambitious agendum. The rewards for obeying him were chiefly visions of a Paradise, which he cunningly framed to satisfy the longings and dreams of the Arabs to whom he preached.

Arabia is an arid country; the scorching heat and dryness of the land, plus the difficulties to marry imposed by tribal custom, have always made Arabs fond of rivers and waters, cooling drinks, shaded gardens, tasty fruits and attractive women. All of these dreamt of fantasies were promised in abundance to the True-Believer who worshipped the Allah whose divine promises and precepts were revealed by His Prophet Mohammed. The believers, the virtuous, the devout, the martyrs, the repentant souls, those who have suffered in the cause of Allah and have been ejected from their homes will go, as Allah has promised, to Paradise as a reward for their deeds in this life. These good people will reside in an eternal Paradise to which death has no access. In this Paradise, gardens will bloom in full glory and bear delicious fruits, fountains will gush forth wine and rivers of honey flow interminably. According to verse 15, *Sura* XLVII of the Koran:

> "Here is the representative of the paradise which the righteous have been promised: there shall flow in it rivers of incorruptible water, rivers of milk forever fresh, rivers of delectable wine and rivers of clearest honey. Clusters of fruits whose season is not limited, especially dates, grapes, and pomegranates, as also all that the soul of man could desire or the eye could delight in are there in abundance and within easy reach."

If writers are still wondering whether he was a true prophet who was receiving revelation from higher metaphysical sources or an im-

---

[56] *Ibn Ishaq*, quoted by Koelle, *Mohammed and Mohammedanism*, p. 85.

postor who was deceiving his fellow citizens by pretending to receive revelations from the sky in order to rule over them, it is apparent that Mohammed himself was completely aware of what he was saying and doing in order to achieve his goals.

Koelle, one of those scholars who believed Mohammed suffered from hysteria has written, "Men of Mohammed's hysterical disposition are often found to have such an unexpected amount of strong will and quiet resolve, bordering on stubborn obstinacy, that their whole souls become absorbed in their aspirations and they seem more possessed by their ideas than possessing them."[57] In the next sections, I will analyze his importuning and the psychobiology of the symptoms he produced while pretending he was receiving revelations.

As long as Mohammed and his converts abstained from publicizing their religion or abusing the traditional idols of Ka'ba, they were safe from persecution by the Qurayshites. But, when the followers of the new faith exceeded forty persons and they began to proselytize their new religion, they became a threat to the conservative inhabitants of Mecca. Prior friendship or even blood relationship was of no consequence in alleviating the growing animosity toward the self-proclaimed prophet. For example, one of the worst critics of Mohammed's cause was one of his uncles, Abu Lahab, and, more importantly, his wife, Omm Jemil, who had great influence over her husband.

Mohammed maintained that both Moses and Jesus Christ were prophets sent from Allah, but that the Jews and Christians had corrupted the Holy Scripture, both the Old and the New Testaments, and that he was sent to purge these corruptions, and restore the law of Allah to the purity in which it was first delivered.

Although Mohammed never depicted himself as a superman or a miracle-worker, the opponents of Mohammed demanded proof of his allegations that he was in communication with God. They pointed out that Moses, Jesus, and the other prophets performed miracles in full view of the people to prove their divine connections; therefore, he should show similar proof. Unable to do so, he countered this demand with several answers. On one occasion, as the Koran indicates, Allah told the skeptics, "What greater miracle could they wish

---

[57] Koelle, *Mohammed and Mohammedanism,* p. 52.

than the Koran itself; a book revealed to an unlettered man; so elevated in language, so incontrovertible in argument, that the united skill of men and devils could compose nothing comparable. What greater proof could there be that it came from none but God himself? The Koran is a miracle." (Koran, II: 23; X: 38; XI: 13; XVII: 89) The first two verses (II: 23 and X: 38), say, "If you are in doubt as to what we have revealed . . . produce a *Sura* like them. . . ." The third one (XI: 13), says, " . . . bring ten *Suras* like them. . . ."

Mohammed, to explain his inability to perform miracles, modestly portrayed himself as a "warner:"

> "Say: I have no power over any good or harm to myself except as Allah willeth. If I had knowledge of the unseen, I should have multiplied all good, and no evil should have touched me. I am but a warner, and a bringer of good tidings to those who have faith." (Koran, VII: 188)

At another time he told the people, that he was only a man sent to them by Allah to preach to them the rewards of Paradise, and the punishments of hell. (Koran, XVII: 94) The Koran represents Paradise as a place of extreme beauty, sinless, absent of pain or sorrow, and replete with sensual fulfillment. He describes the delights of Paradise, the eternal abode of the pious and martyrs, as follows:

> "Having rivers of water without corruption, and rivers of milk, the taste whereof changes not, and rivers of wine delicious to those who drink; and rivers of honey clarified." (Koran, XLVII: 15; XVI: 31, 32)
> "Around them shall go eternal youths as handsome as pearls with goblets and ewers and a cup of flowing wine which does not cause headache or dizziness." (Koran, LVI: 11–38, 88–91) ". . . . And girls with black eyes and swelling breasts of the same age as themselves." (Koran, LXXVIII: 33) "And made them virgins, darling of equal age for the fellows of the right (Koran, LVI: 37, 38) . . . No man or jinn has touched them."

Naïve and literal interpretation of these descriptions made the plundering Bedouin tribes into an army that was eager to sacrifice itself. It was not faith in God, but the lure of a fancied paradise, avarice and unbridled carnality that led the army of Islam from victory to victory and converted Islam from a religion into organized crime. The Bedouins, who knew nothing but the poverty-stricken life of the desert, were prime targets for anyone who offered an escape from their misery, even if it meant death to attain it. Therefore, they accepted Mohammed's drivel as revelations from God.

A *hadith* says:

> "Narrated Anas ibn Malik: The prophet said, 'Nobody who dies and finds good from Allah (in the hereafter) would wish to be back to this world even if he were given the whole world and whatever is in it, except the martyr who, on seeing the superiority of martyrdom, would like to come back to the world and get killed again (in Allah's cause.)'"[58]

Just as Mohammed framed his promises of the rewards in heaven to appeal to the sensual appetites and desires of those to whom he preached so, in contrast, he described the grievous punishments in hell waiting for those who would not believe in him. Hell was described as a burning, odiferous, and fiery place. In Hell, the unbelievers and infidels drink nothing but boiling sulfurous water; nor do them breath anything but exceedingly hot winds (such as those commonly found in Arabia). They would dwell forever in a continual fire with a coverlet of black hot smoke and eat nothing but briers and thorns and the fruit of the tree *zacon* (a most bitter fruit) which would remain in their bellies like burning pitch. To add to their misery, molten lead would be poured into the ears of some select sinners.

On another occasion, he told the Arabs that when Allah gave His Apostle Salih the power of miracles, the people still vilified him and the other prophets and for that reason Allah destroyed them all. (Koran, VII: 73–79; VI: 61–68; XXVI: 141–159; XXVII: 45–53) Later on, he said, those whom Allah had ordained to believe, will believe without the necessity of seeing miracles. Those whom Allah had not ordained to believe would not be converted to the Faith and were therefore expendable. (Koran, VI: III and 125) But this excuse did not satisfy some Arabs and caused several of his followers abandon him. He complains repeatedly of this in the Koran. However, when he escaped to Medina and became a political power in that city, he began to sing another tune.

---

[58] Muhammad Muhsin Khan, *Sahih al-Bukhari* (Cambridge: Cambridge University, 1975), Hadith IV: 42, 52, 6, 53.

The Migration of Muslims to Abyssinia

For about the first three years after Mohammed's "revelations," his converts abstained from coming forward and proselytizing their new religion, so they did not provoke the hostility of other sects. But, when the number of converts to the new faith reached forty and they began to promulgate their faith, and especially when Mohammed began to revile the traditional gods, the non-believers became aggressive; hostility broke out between them and the followers of the new faith. This, at times, became intense and physical.

When, Abu Talib, Mohammed's uncle was alive, he came under great pressure from the authorities in Mecca to turn over his renegade nephew to them. He was not happy with Mohammed's choice of career but, nevertheless, he and his Hashimite clan continued to protect him. Because of this continual hostility, Mohammed left his residence where he was surrounded by irate neighbors and took refuge in the house of a disciple named Arkam, a wealthy young man of about twenty-five years, who owned a large house near the center of Mecca. Arkam's house was a safe refuge for Mohammed and he made it the center of his activities for about a month, preaching to his followers as a *Warner.* Although he had changed houses, he was still under the protection of his uncle, Abu Talib.

Shielded by his uncle, Mohammed's own life was secure but his converts, mostly slaves and other low-life, were vulnerable to persecution and possible death. There was nothing Mohammed could do to protect them in the lawless state of Mecca so, in the fifth year of his preaching, he sent fifteen of his converts to Abyssinia, where they were received and protected by the Christian ruler, the King Najashi (Negus). Later on, the rest of the Muslims joined them and eventually they numbered all told, about eighty men and twenty women. The period of this exile is called the "First *Hijra*" (flight) to Abyssinia, which lasted three months, as distinguished from the second *Hijra,* the flight of Mohammed from Mecca to Medina in 614 CE.

Hamza and Omar Adopt Islam

The fourth year (614 C.E.) of his preaching was a lucky year. While he was living in Arkam's house, Mohammed acquired two converts and, by doing so, increased credence to his claim to prophethood. One of these was his uncle, Hamza. The other was Omar ibn Khattab (the second Khaliph).

These conversions came about as follows: One day Abu Jahl, chief of the Beni Makhzoom tribe, met Mohammed in the street and rudely derided him. Shortly thereafter, Mohammed's uncle, an athletic man of great physical strength, while returning from hunting met a woman who had observed the incident and she described it to him. Hamza was not yet a believer in Islam, but he was pledged to protect his nephew. He furiously pursued Abu Jahl to Ka'ba and gave him a severe beating. Afterwards, he declared himself a convert to Islam and became one of its most zealous and valiant adherents, to the extent that he lost his life in the battle of Uhud in the cause of Islam. Naturally, when it became known that Hamza, the strongest man of the Quraysh and protector of his nephew, had adopted Islam, Mohammed became less of a pariah.[59]

The other convert was Omar, Abu Jahl's twenty-six year old nephew. Omar was a fierce, aggressive man and a confirmed enemy of Islam. One day, he set out from his home with the intention of killing Mohammed. On his way, he met a Muslim from his own clan and told him about his plans. The man told him that he should first talk with his sister, Amina, and her husband, Seid, who had become converts to Islam. Omar could not believe it. He went to his sister's house to confront her and confirm this and during the course of conversation, became so impressed by his sister's faith that he, too, became a convert. Like Abu Bakr, Omar later gave his daughter, Hafza, to Mohammed in marriage. The conversion of Hamza and Omar added greatly to Mohammed's prestige.

The conversions of two such powerful men as Hamza and Omar to the faith gave Mohammed courage leave Arkam's house and

---

[59] Tabari, *The History of at-Tabari,* vol. 6, p. 104.

again rely on his family and his increasing flock of believers for protection. When the Qurayshn learned that Mohammed's companions
had found rest and shelter in Abyssinia; that Omar and Hamza had
converted to Islam; and that Islam was gradually spreading amongst
the tribe, they resorted to the drastic measures. In the seventh year
of Mohammed's proselytizing, they placed Mohammed and his entire clan under a social ban. Under the relentless leadership of Abu
Jahl, a decree was issued forbidding any of the Qurayshite tribe from
marrying with Mohammed's adherents and banning any intercourse, even commercial dealings, with them until Mohammed was
delivered up for punishment.

Deaths of Khadija and Abu Talib

For three years the ban remained in effect and Mohammed was
forced to conduct his preaching covertly. Abu Talib intervened and finally the ban was lifted during the last year of Mohammed's residence in Mecca (620 CE). But the same year brought Mohammed
the greatest sorrow of his life. Within a few months of each other, his
faithful wife, Khadija, and his lifelong protector, Abu Talib, passed
away. He could not replace his uncle, but he soon replaced his deceased wife with two wives. One of them, Ayesha, was a six-year-
old child, the daughter of his faithful follower, Abu Bakr. Khadija had
passed away at the age sixty-five and Ayasha was only six. Therefore, there was a fifty-nine year difference in age between his deceased wife and his new bride! Since he could not immediately
consummate his marriage to the six-year-old child, two months after
Khadija's death he married Sawda, the widow of Sokran, one of his
followers who had fled into Abyssinia.

The death of Khadija, closely followed by that of Abu Talib, who
had been not only an affectionate relative, but also a staunch de-
fender and powerful protector, renewed the persecution of Mohammed by his fellow tribesmen. Unable to preach his religion any
longer in Mecca, he set out with Zaid, his adopted son, to seek
refuge in Taif, a small walled town inhabited by the Thakeef tribe in
a fertile area forty miles east of Mecca. Taif was a stronghold of idolatry and its inhabitants were as hostile as the Meccans. They re-

acted to Mohammed's preaching by flinging stones at him. With much hooting and yelling, the people of Taif chased Mohammed and Zaid through the streets, pelting them with stones. Blood flowing from head wounds, Mohammed and Zaid were driven from the town and, greatly dejected, they set out to return to Mecca.

Later on, Mohammed bragged that when they had stopped for the night in the Valley of Nakhla, between Mecca and Taif, and he was immersed in reciting the Koran, a passing company of invisible creatures called *jinns* stopped and listened to him. Mohammed told this superstitious fabrication (variations of this story were common throughout the Mideast long before the time of Mohammed) to illustrate that although he and his doctrines might be rejected by some men, they were held in reverence by other creatures who were not visible to human beings. This incident is explained in the forty-sixth and seventy-second *Sura* of the Koran. Thenceforth, Mohammed declared himself as being sent for the conversion of the invisible creatures as well as of the human race.[60]

The Flight to Medina

Mohammed's future in Mecca became more and more tenuous after his rejection in Taif. Deprived of Khadija, his generous benefactress, and Abu Talib, his efficient protector, he soon became an outlaw in Mecca. But in midst of this hopeless despair there came, in the year 620 A.D. a glimmer of hope.

In that year, a group of seven or eight men, all but one from the Khazraj tribe, came from Medina to Mecca on a pilgrimage. Mohammed seized the opportunity to meet them and expound his new religion to them. They were impressed by his personality and responded to him positively for two reasons. According to one of the pilgrims, Ibn Ishaq, there were many Jews in Medina who were fighting against the Arabs. They [the Jews] believed that a prophet would soon appear to help them conquer the pagans. The pilgrims saw Mohammed's cause as one which might persuade the contentious

---

[60] Washington Irving, *Washington Irving's Life of Mohammed*, p. 57.

Arab tribes of Aws and Khadraj to unite against the Jews. At the end of their pilgrimage, they returned to Medina, meditating on this possibility.[61]

At the traditional time of pilgrimage in the summer of 621 CE, the seven men from Medina with whom Mohammed had spoken the preceding year returned to Mecca bringing five more men with them. This group of twelve represented most of the Arabs of Medina, ten from the Khazraj and two from the Aws, and they sought Mohammed's council about their local problems. Following a conversation with Mohammed, they became converts and promised to accept Mohammed as their prophet, obey him and abide by the principles of his religion. This meeting occurred in Akaba, on the road between Arafat and Mina and later became known as "The First pledge of al-Akaba," or the Pledge of Women, because it involved a promise of loyalty but without an obligation to fight.

When the pilgrims left Mecca to return to their native city, Mohammed sent with them a trusted Muslim called Musab ibn Omeir,[62] who was well-versed in the Koran. He was one of the exiles, returned from Abyssinia, who could teach the Koran, instruct in Islam, and also keep Mohammed informed of the political situation in Medina. This missionary was so successful that at the next pilgrimage (June 622 CE), seventy-three men and two women came from Medina to join with Mohammed in Mecca. This party of seventy-five met with Mohammed secretly by night. Mohammed's uncle Abbas, though still an idolater, spoke with them, telling the pilgrims that Mohammed was prepared to live among them, if they would pledge to protect him. The chief of the group of pilgrims, al Bara ibn Maroor, replied that all were willing to give their allegiance to Apostle and would protect him as they would protect their own women. This pledge be-

---

[61] John Bagot Glubb, *The Life and Times of Muhammad* (New York: Stein and Day Publishers, 1970), p.143.

[62] Musab ibn Omeir closely resembled Mohammed and was his personal standard-bearer. In the battle of Uhod he was killed before the eyes of Mohammed and therefore his enemies thought they have killed Mohammed himself. This caused Mohammed's enemies to shout the news about his death, which threw complete disorder into the Mohammedan ranks.

came known as "The Second Pledge of al-Akaba" and paved the way for the *Hijra.*

News spread among the Meccans of Mohammed's agreement with the pilgrims from Medina. His bitter enemy, Abu Jahl, suggested that he be stabbed to death simultaneously by several people, to avoid a vendetta by his followers against one particular group. As relations worsened between Mohammed and the leaders of Mecca, he instructed most of his followers to emigrate from Mecca to Medina, until finally only he, Abu Bakr, and Ali remained in the city. His Meccan enemies presumably knew Mohammed's plan to escape to Medina, and realized that he might become a dangerous enemy if he became a leading politician in Medina. Therefore, they tried to keep him in the Mecca and planned to assassinate him. According to legend, Ali slept in Mohammed's bed, and as the murderers approached, Ali slipped out of bed and escaped without harm.

Mohammed, accompanied by Abu Bakr, secretly escaped from Mecca and proceeded to a cave in Jebel Thaur, not far south of Mecca, and remained hidden there while the Quraysh searched for them. After two days, when Abu Bakr's son reported that the search for him had slackened off, Mohammed left the cave and arrived safely at Medina. An early Medinan verse of the Koran (IX: 40) confirms the story of the cave:

> If you do not aid him, God had already aided him, when the unbelievers expelled him with only one companion; the two of them were in the cave, and he was saying to his companion: "Grieve not, verily God is with us. . . . ."

Mohammed's flight from Mecca to Medina, the *Hijra,* was later adopted as the first year of the Islamic era. It was the turning point in his career and in the history of Islam. It happened in the 12th of the month of Rabi'al-awwal, (July 16, 622 CE). Those Meccan followers of Mohammed, who emigrated from Mecca to Medina, were called *Mohajirun* (emigrants). Those who resided in Medina and joined Islam were called *Ansar* (helpers).

The political situation in the city of Medina was the primary reason for inviting Mohammed to the city. In contrast with Mecca, which was dominated by one tribe, the Quraysh, the three thousand people of Medina were divided into two Arab tribes, the Aws and the

Khazraj, and three Jewish tribes, Bani Nadhir, Bani Kainkaa, and Bani Quoraiza. Like Mecca, the city of Medina lacked a central government. A destructive vendetta had been going on for many years between the two Arab tribes and the Jews.

The tribes of Medina desperately needed a single authority to unify them. Some scholars believe that the Jews, who were mainly engaged in agriculture and handicrafts, were culturally and economically superior to the Arabs, and for that reason, the Arabs disliked them.[63] Therefore, the most important task for Mohammed in Medina was to create a political environment favorable to his followers and somehow rid Medina of its domestic strife. To accomplish these ends, he repealed the old, loosely drawn tribal agreements and replaced them with a new document called the Constitution of Medina. This constitution included stipulations about waging war, paying blood ransom, and ransoming captives. The document also stated: "Whatever difference or dispute between the parties to this covenant remains unsolved shall be referred to God and to Mohammed, the prophet of God." The unwritten eventual goal was to make Islam a world religion and an empire ruled by Mohammed.

Obviously, God is an unseen spiritual entity and no one but Mohammed can see or have any contact with Him (according to Mohammed). Therefore, the powers that are ascribed to God are directly given to Mohammed. In other words, it can be said that "God" throughout the Islamic scriptures is used as a euphemism for "His Apostle."

However, the unification of the community of Medina did not proceed without conflict or tension. Not only was there turmoil between Jewish and the Arab tribes, but distrust and tension also arose between the Medinian *Ansar* and the *Mohajirun,* those Meccan converts to Islam who had emigrated to Medina. Moreover, some Medinian Arabs pretended to accept Islam but inwardly remaining pagan and had no intention of surrendering any political power or social prestige to Mohammed. These ostensible converts were called *monafiqun* or "hypocrites" and their leader was Abdullah ibn Ubay,

---

[63] Martin Forward, *Muhammed: A Short Biography* (Oxford, England: One World Publications, 1997), p. 17.

an ambitious tribesman who, before the arrival of Mohammed, had almost succeeded in establishing himself as king in Medina.

In order to weld friendly ties between his followers from Mecca and the converts from Medina, Mohammed appealed to their belief in the old Arabian tradition of "brotherhood." Unfortunately for the Jews, this brotherhood, according to the Koran, occurs only between faithful Muslims (Koran, XLIX: 10), and not Muslims and non-Muslims. The verse 51 of the fifth *Sura* of the Koran says:

> "O you who believe! Take not the Jews and the Christians for your friends and protectors. They are but friends and protectors of each other. And he amongst you that turns to them (for friendship) is of them."

Relations with the Jews of Medina were of prime concern to Mohammed. The constitution of Medina granted religious freedom to the Jews but demanded their support for Mohammed, should it be needed. However, the Jews expected their next prophet to spring from the House of David as foretold in their Holy Book, not from the Quraysh or any other Arab tribe. Therefore, they refused to believe in Mohammed's alleged divine inspirations.

In order to appease the Jews, Mohammed first tried to win them over by making concessions to their religious rituals. For example, in conformity with Jewish custom, he ordered his followers to turn their faces toward the city of Jerusalem when praying. Mohammed's visionary "Night Journey" to Jerusalem had made this city central to the Islamic faith as well as the Jewish. Prescribing Jerusalem as the direction of prayer was a cunning strategy to attempt to connect the new religion with the other Semitic faith. Next, learning that the Jews fasted on Yom Kippur (the Day of Atonement) which is the tenth day of the Hebrew calendar month Tisri, he proclaimed a Muslim fast to be held on that same day. He even called it *Ashura,* an Arabic variation of its Jewish name *Ashur* (the fast of the tenth).

But none of these attempts at accommodation worked, so Mohammed reverted to his tried and true *modus operandi* and proclaimed that he had "received a revelation from Allah" commanding him to face Mecca instead of Jerusalem when praying (Koran, II: 136–147). He also changed the Day of Atonement observance into the month-long fast of Ramadan. He denounced the Jews as deviants from the true faith and falsifiers of the Holy Scriptures that he had received from God.

Although Mohammed labored to solve the political and religious problems created by the migration, the problem of subsistence of the new emigrants was easily resolved. Mecca had been a city of commerce: farming was impossible in the arid desert. Fortunately, Medina, about 250 miles to the north, was an agricultural society, and gained its livelihood chiefly from growing dates and cereal grains. The émigrés had little trouble finding work and supporting their families. At one time the Jews had had total political control of Medina and perhaps it was they who introduced agriculture to the region, as they did in other parts of Arabia.

A Man of the Sword

Without deceit and sword, Islam would have been stillborn.
Craig Winn, *Prophet of Doom*, p. IV.

In Mecca, after a decade of preaching, only fifty men chose to follow Mohammed. But that all changed in Medina. Upon moving to Medina, Mohammed gained power and raised an army to back his cause. He became a political tyrant then a brigand and a terrorist, telling the Arabs that God had sent Moses and Jesus with their miracles, yet the people did not listen to them. Now God had finally sent him, *sans* miraculous powers, to force the people to embrace his teachings or face the power of his sword. Moreover, he prohibited his disciples to enter into any arguments with respect to Islam; instead he ordered them to take up the sword, fight for it, and destroy all those who may contradict his Law.

Mohammed denied the need for miracles other than that of the Koran itself as revealed to him, an illiterate prophet. Nevertheless, his followers and those who dubbed themselves the "Disciples of Islam," attributed many fanciful miracles to him. They bragged that this self-proclaimed prophet cleaved the moon into two pieces; that trees went forward to meet him; that he fed a great company with a little food; that a camel complained to him; that a shoulder of mutton told him of being poisoned; etc., etc. etc.. They needed "miracles" to prove to the people the legitimacy of Islam. The Islamic scholars of the time recognized Solomon as being sent to proclaim the wisdom, the glory, and the majesty of God; Moses, his commandments and his mercy; and Jesus Christ to manifest the righteousness, the power and knowledge of God. Mohammed, however, was sent to the people principally to manifest the power of Allah and by **the power of the sword** convert all peoples to the faith; hence, he had no need for miracles.

From this twisted logic grew the Islamic *Doctrine of the Sword.* The religion of Islam was (and still is) to be imposed upon all infidels by the sword and all Muslims are obliged join in the fight. If they become victorious in this religious war, they will possess the women and the wealth of the conquered infidels. If they are killed, they become martyrs and are rewarded by the delights of Paradise wherein they will enjoy the company of *"chaste maidens with beautiful, big and lustrous eyes, restraining their glances, whom no man or* jinn *has touched."* (Koran, LV: 56; LVI: 22, 37–39)

"The sword" Mohammed said, "is the key to heaven and hell." On another occasion, he stated, "Paradise is under the shadow of swords."[64]

Arabs have a proverb that says, "The history of the sword is the history of humanity," and "If there were no swords, there would be no law of Mohammed." The phrase "Sword of Islam" (*saif-ul-Islam*) was a catchword of the Ottoman regime. In 1734, George Sale whose English translation of the Koran was a turning point in the re-evaluation of the Koran in the west wrote: "Mohammedanism owed its progress and establishment almost entirely to the sword."[65]

Muslim tradition has it that Ali ibn Abu Talib was sent to lead the believers but his sword, in the course of battle, suddenly broke. So Allah, from heaven, dispatched the angel Gabriel with an ornate magical two-edged sword, the *Dhu'l fagar.* Gabriel handed down this sword to Mohammed who in turn gave it to Ali. Thereafter, Ali was able to suppress any dissention or revolt against Islam. Among the companions of Mohammed, none was more qualified to wield this

---

[64] al-Muttaqi, *Kanz ul-Ummal,* II, p. 258.

[65] *al-Murtada on the Ihya,* vol. II, p. 258.

sword than Ali, whose prowess in battle was legendary. This tradition is printed to the left of a Chinese depiction of the sword.[66] He was both a cousin and a son-in-law of Mohammed, and became the fourth orthodox Caliph. Ali, the greatest hero of Islam has some verses attributed to him, which are quoted everywhere, in Arabia to celebrate his renown in battle:

> Our flowers are the sword and dagger
> Narcisiss and myrtle are naught,
> Our drink is the blood of our foemen
> Our goblet his skull when we've fought
>
> *As-Saif wa'lkhanjar rihanuna*
> *Uffan ala'l narjis wa'l as*
> *Sharabuna dam a'adauna*
> *Wa jumjumat ras al kas*[67]

Among many exegetes who have evaluated Koran, William Cantwell Smith's ideas about Koran are very enlightening. He writes:

> Muslims do not read the Koran to understand whether it is divine or not. But, they believe it to be divine, and then they read it. This makes a great deal of difference, and if secular students of the Koran wish to understand it as a religious document, they must approach it in this spirit. If an outsider picks up the book and goes through it even asking himself, "What is there here that has led Muslims to suppose this from God?" He will miss the reverberating impact. If, on the other hand, he picks up the book and asks himself, what would these sentences convey to me if I believe them to be God's word? Then he can much more effectively understand what has been happening these many centuries in the Muslim world.[68]

In Ghazali's *Book of Worship,* it is written that the preacher in the mosque rests his hand on the hilt of a sword or on a staff when he

---

[66] Samuel Zwemer, *Studies in Popular Islam* (London: The Sheldon Press, 1939), p. 37.

[67] *Ibid,* pp. 49–50.

[68] William Cantwell Smith, "Is the Koran the word of God?" in *Questions of Religious Truth* (New York: Charles Scriber's Sons, 1967), pp. 49–50.

delivers his sermon. The custom of handling a sword goes back to Mohammed himself preaching in the earliest mosque pulpit in Medina. In his historic investigation of this custom, George Sale came to the conclusion that pulpit was a judgment seat for the prophet when acting as judge and dispensing justice. The pulpit and sword go together in the history of Islam. The precepts of Islam and their enforcement by the power of the sword were welded together by its founder.[69]

There is a verse in the Koran, generally known as *Ayatu's-saif* (The Verse of the Sword). This celebrated verse, also called *Repentance* (*Sura* IX: 5), reads as follows:

> "And when the sacred months are passed, kill those who join other gods with God, whenever you shall find them; and seize them, besiege them, and lay in wait for them with every kind of ambush; but if they repent and observe the prayer, and pay the obligatory alms, then let them go their own way, for God is gracious and merciful."

It would appear that at the beginning of his career, Mohammed propagated the religion of Islam by teaching and preaching, but when he came to power in Medina, he sanctioned the use of the sword. Due to his thirst for power, the "Verse of Sword" became so important in Islamic dogma that it abrogated 124 passages of the Koran that mandate tolerance, patience, and goodwill toward unbelievers and philosophic competitors of Islam.

Mohammed Resorts to Banditry

The companions of Mohammed, who migrated to Medina, and found employment, were obliged to perform hard work to subsist. Ali, the son-in-law of Mohammed, carried water for brick making by the Jews. He received a date for each bucketful of water and he shared his tiny meals with Mohammed, who had nothing. Though it may be come as a shock to the believers in Islam, Mohammed reverted to the traditional Bedouin method of sustenance: banditry and the

---

[69] *Al-Murtada on the Ihya,* vol. III, p. 220.

plundering of the caravans that passed by Medina on their way to and from Syria.[70] With no legitimate means of support available to his converts (other than menial labor), he ordered them to begin robbing caravans. Thus, the very first converts to Islam became highway bandits.

The first attempt at banditry happened in the second year of *Hijra* (623 CE). Mohammed commanded Abu Obeida ibn al Harith to attack a Qurashi caravan defended by 60 or 80 horsemen and seize their goods. They were repulsed and the fledgling bandits returned in despair. In March of the same year, Mohammed sent his uncle Hamza (who was only four years older than he) with a party of thirty men to the Red Sea coast to try to ambush a Meccan caravan returning from Syria. The caravan was defended by 300 men under the leadership of Mohammed's old arch enemy Abu Jahl. Of course, this attempted heist also ended in failure.[71]

Seven other raids were undertaken, four headed by Mohammed himself and three by trusted followers, but all were unsuccessful. This was most disheartening to Mohammed and his companions. The reason these raids on caravans failed was due to informants among Mohammed's opponents in Medina who gave the Meccans information about his plans.[72]

The first successful robbery was took place in January 624 C.E. In order to ensure its success, Mohammed scheduled the raid in the month of *Rajab,* the very first month of the year. This month was traditionally observed by all Arabs as a sacred month of truce. During this month all wars ceased and enemies greeted each other as friends. Mohammed exploited this tradition for his own nefarious use because he knew that the Quraysh, who honored the holiness of the month, would not expect any danger and thus would not protect themselves properly. But, by the same token, he knew that his own followers might rebel against the violation of a long lasting and popular tradition.[73]

---

[70] Andrae, *Muhammed: The Man and his Faith,* p. 38.
[71] Koelle, *Mohammed and Mohammedanism,* p. 142.
[72] *Ibid.,* p. 63.
[73] Rodinson, *Mohammed,* p. 163.

To carry out this plan, Mohammed first assigned his cousin Abu Obeida to lead this raid, but he declined. He then chose Abdullah ibn Jahsh al-Asadi and, after giving him a sealed envelope, ordered him to travel eastward with a little band of eight to twelve emigrant-brigands. After two days travel, Abdullah was to open the letter and carry out the orders contained therein. By this method, no one in Medina was able to become aware of the plot and inform the Qurashi.

At the appointed time, Abdullah broke the seal of the letter and read thusly: "Go in the name and with the blessing of Allah to Nakhla (a place between Mecca and Taif)), and there set an ambush for the Qurayshite caravans. Compel none of your men to come with you; but carry out my orders only with those who follow you voluntarily."

All the members of the raiding party agreed to take part in the robbery, but two members of the party (Sa'd ibn Abi Waqqas and Otba ibn Ghazwan) deserted. When these two returned to Medina after several days, they said that their camels had gone missing and they went in search of them. It may well have been true, but their story was not believed and they were not permitted to share in the booty from the raid. The fact that Mohammed ordered Abdullah to allow his companions the option to refuse to take part in the banditry, indicates that the plan must have conflicted with Arabian standards of decency.[74] Because the operation was potentially dangerous, both physically and emotionally, all the participants must be volunteers.

Abdullah and his men reached the valley of Nakhla, found the caravan, headed by Amr ibn al-Hadrami. It was carrying raisins, leather, and other articles of trade, and guarded by only four men. To secure the trust of the guards, one of the bandits had had his head shaved, thus giving him the appearance of a pilgrim to the sacred shrine in Mecca. In this way, they were able to accompany the caravan and wait for the right opportunity to attack them. On the last day of the month of *Rajab,* the members of the gang held a council and decided that if they should further postpone the attack, the caravan would soon reach the sacred territory of Mecca, which was also taboo to such activity. So, they made a surprise attack on that last day of the sacred month; the leader of the caravan was killed,

---

[74] Tor Andrae, *Mohammed: The Man and his Faith,* p. 141.

two of his men were made prisoner; the fourth one escaped. The brigands returned to Medina with their prisoners and booty safely.[75]

The news of this blatant violation of the sacred month was received most unfavorably by the people. Mohammed realized that he had committed an egregious crime so, in order to cover up his participation, he pretended to be angry with Abdullah and insisted that he had not commanded him to shed blood or commit any violence during the sacred month of *Rajab*. To bolster this lie, he refused to take his share of the booty and kept the prisoners taken in the raid *incommunicado*. Fortunately, Mohammed's perennial rationalist, "Allah," was there to extricate him. He soon came to his messenger's aid and provided him with the following exculpatory "revelation:"

> They ask you concerning fighting in the prohibited month. Say: "Fighting therein is a great offence; but grave is it in the sight of Allah to prevent access to the path of Allah, to deny him, to prevent access to the sacred Mosque, and drive out members. Tumult and oppression are worse than slaughter. Nor will they cease fighting you until they turn you back from your faith if they can. And if any of you turn back from their faith and die in the unbelief, their works will bear no fruit in this life and in the hereafter; they will be companions of the fire and will abide therein. (Koran, II: 217)

The above passage was sufficient excuse for Mohammed to claim his share of the booty from the raid. Allah conveniently provided further divine beneficence by sending the following "revelation:"

> They ask you concerning [things taken as] spoils of war. Say, "[such] spoils are at the disposal of Allah and the messenger. So fear Allah, and keep straight the relations between yourselves. Obey Allah and his messenger, if you do believe." (Koran, VIII: 1, see also VIII: 41).

Mohammed's claim that he is in direct communication with an invisible God whose commandments are revealed to him via the angel Gabriel cannot be disproved since only he (Mohammed) can hear the celestial messenger. But isn't it remarkable how conveniently self-serving are so many verses of the Koran?

---

[75] Koelle, *Mohammed and Mohammedanism*, p. 144.

Abdullah ibn Jahsh apportioned a fifth of the booty to the puta-tive prophet and retained only four-fifths for himself and the other members of the raiding party. The relatives of the two men from the caravan captured by Abdullah sent a deputation from Mecca to re-deem them. Mohammed, who was concerned about his two com-panions, Sa'd and Otba, said, "I shall not give them up until my two companions Sa'd and Otba come back: if you kill them, we shall also kill your prisoners." Soon afterwards, Sa'd and Otba reappeared (presumably having recovered their wayward camels) so Mo-hammed accepted a ransom of forty ounces of silver for each of the Qurayshite prisoners and released them.

Arab historians have attached much importance to this criminal foray. According to Ibn Hisham, this was the first bloodshed in the history of Islam, the first booty obtained by Muslims, and the first captives seized by them.[76]

The Nakhla robbery and the "revelations" recorded in *Sura* II, verse 217 of the Koran, are blatant examples of Mohammed's men-dacity. He does not deny the sacredness of the month of *Rajab,* an important Arabic tradition and ethical principle, but he cunningly evades the criminality of Abdullah's violation of that sacred tradition. In an attempt to rationalize the violation of the sacred month of *Rajab,* he maintains that it is less outrageous than certain forms of opposition to the Islamic faith, thus laying a religious stigma upon those who criticized the criminal deed. However, the craft and se-crecy that he employed in the commission of the robbery (the sealed orders to Abdullah and his order to open tham only after two days travel) was not the work of a true Prophet, a Man of God, whose only mission was to impart the Word of God to the people.

The same passage of the Koran (II: 217), written at the end of the year 623 CE, promulgated the law of *jihad*[77] or Holy War and this has remained as one of the most despicable tenets of Islam. The sword that this passage ordered to be unsheathed has not yet been returned to its scabbard. The law promises that if the true believers conquer in battle, they may appropriate the properties of the de-feated people, even their wives (Koran XXIV: 4), and the fruits of their

---

[76] *Ibid.,* p. 145; W. Montgomery Watt, *Muhammad Prophet and Statesman* (Ox-ford: Oxford University Press, 1961), p. 109.

[77] See chapter 2.

lootings shall surpass that of any other source of earnings. If they are killed, their sins will immediately be absolved and they will be transported to paradise, there to revel in eternal pleasure in the arms of lustrous-eyed virgin houris, whom no man or *jinn* has touched (Koran, ILIV: 54 and LV: 56). Therefore, the sword is the key to heaven, if drawn in the cause of Allah. Paul Fregosi, the author of *Jihad in the West* writes, "The terrorism called *jihad* as we know it today, is linked, even if only by name, with those Muslim holy wars which began more than 1,300 years ago in Arabia and spread during the next thirteen centuries to the Middle East, Europe, Africa, and Asia and now, with the horrible massacre on September 11, 2001, to the United States."[78] It is interesting to note that before the advent of Islam, the action of one tribe against another tribe, in order to steal its possessions, was called "*razzia.*" Even if two tribes were very friendly, their friendship might cool and, in a few years, a *razzia* might occur between them. With the advent of Islam, the term "*jihad*" replaced "*razzia.*" Before Islam came into being, *jihad* was interpreted as a religious action of a sect against members of the community who did not share their faith. As the Islamic community grew, the Muslim penchant to acquire booty and women by force had to be directed ever further outwards. It was this religious character of the *jihad* which fired the minds of the Arabs so well that, in less than a century, they created a religious empire that stretched from the Atlantic and the Pyrenees in the west to the Oxus and the Pinjab in the east. It seems certain that without the religious connotation of the *jihad,* such vigorous expansion could not have succeeded.[79]

The Battle of Badr

Barely six weeks had passed and the scandal due to the violation of *Rajab* by the raid at Nakhla had not yet subsided, when Mohammed received information through his spies that a rich Meccan caravan was returning from Syria to Mecca. The merchandise carried by this large caravan of 1,000 camels was worth 50,000 dinars, and most of the

---

[78] Paul Fregosi, *Jihad in the West* (Amherst, New York: Prometheus Books, 1998), p. 15.

[79] Montgomery Watt, *Muhammad Prophet and Statesman,* p. 109.

merchants of Mecca had a share in it. About seventy guards commanded by Abu Sufyan ibn Harb, the most prominent man in Mecca and arch enemy of Mohammed, guarded this caravan. The route of the caravan passed near Medina, between a range of mountains and the sea. This presented a golden opportunity for Mohammed and his destitute followers to acquire enough booty to subsist for some time on the proceeds of its sale. As soon as he received information that the caravan was approaching, Mohammed called his followers together and told them, "There comes a caravan of the Quraysh laden with goods; march out to meet them, perhaps Allah will give them to you as prey."[80]

Not only the Muslims, but also some of the non-believers were delighted to hear this order. So eager were the infidels to participate in this banditry that several of them converted to Islam, perhaps thinking that this would ensure them a greater share when the loot was divided. This proves that the conversion of some of those who came to follow Mohammed was not necessarily religious in nature, but based on worldly avarice. As it has been said in the past, and is true today, Arabs consider Islam a license to plunder.

Mohammed set out to capture this wealthy caravan about the middle of the month of Ramazan in the second year of the Hijra. In view of its size and the force of men guarding it, Mohammed gathered up the largest force that he could muster to intercept it. His army consisted of 305 men and 70 camels. Abu Sufyan learned about Mohammed's intentions and diverted the caravan toward the sea. Mohammed's plans had also become known in Mecca. An army of about 1,000 men, 700 camels, and 100 horses was raised in that city, ostensibly to avenge the killing of Meccans at Nakhla. Unaware of this army, Mohammed and his Muslims looked forward to plundering a caravan guarded by a force smaller than theirs.[81] The raiding party of Muslims was confronted by the army from Mecca on the evening of 17th day of Ramazan in the Wadi Badr, eleven miles to the southwest of Medina. A tent was hastily erected for Mohammed and a camel was saddled in readiness for him to decamp to Medina in case of defeat. The field of battle was a plain dotted with several wells. The local people advised Mohammed to seize the best of them, which he did,

---

[80] Koelle, *Mohammed and Mohammedanism,* p. 145.
[81] Montgomery Watt, *Muhammad Prophet and Statesman,* p. 121.

and then he destroyed the remaining. This turned out to be of great advantage. The Quraysh suffered many losses in their attempts to get water. The Muslims had also the advantage of fighting on the firm soil of the *wadi,* while the Qurayshites had to advance over soft sand dunes. In addition, the prevailing wind blew sand into the faces of the oncoming Qurayshites, hampering their vision.

Many leading Meccans were killed that day, including Abu Jahl, Mohammed's bitterest opponent. There was no unity among the Meccans and this lack of central control contributed in no small measure to their defeat. To the surprise of everyone, Mohammed's small force of 300 men had defeated a much larger force of Meccans and killed many of their leaders. The list of the Meccan dead varied from forty-five to seventy and about sixty-eight prisoners were taken. The Muslims casualties were only fourteen.

The defeat of Meccans resulted in a large amount of booty for the Muslims. The ransoms of prisoners also came to a considerable sum since many of the prisoners were merchants and came from wealthy families. Much of *Sura* 8 of the Koran called "The Spoils of War," deals with God's reflections on the Battle of Badr. There was a quarrel over the division of the booty among Muslims. Those who had slain certain enemies claimed the right to possess their weapons. Others, who had guarded Mohammed and thus had no opportunity to plunder, demanded a share in the spoils. Mohammed ordered that all of the loot, including the weapons of those who were slain and the ransoms for those taken prisoner, should be collected in one place and would be divided equally among all the Muslims. Of course, one-fifth of the booty he first allocated to himself, in accordance with the Koran (VIII: verse 41).

The Arabs were basically pagans, lacking any spirituality or deep religious beliefs. They converted to Islam out of cupidity. Their only motivation for conversion to Islam was the hope of acquiring booty and the worldly comforts it could buy. Thus, many outwardly professed their belief but in fact had no inclination toward Islam and its dogma and ritual. If things went wrong, the Bedouins were ready to drop the new faith as quickly as they had adopted it.[82]

---

[82] Ibn Warraq, *Why I am not a Muslim* (Amherst, New York: Prometheus, 1995), p. 242.

CHAPTER TWO

THE KORAN
A MANUAL FOR TERRORISM

Asked if a philosopher can follow a prophetically revealed religion, Razi retorted: "How can anyone think philosophically while committed to those old wives' tales founded on contradictions, obdurate ignorance, and dogmatism?"

Structure of the Koran

The noun *Koran* is believed to be derived from the Arabic verb *qara'a,* meaning to 'read' or 'recite.' The word is spelled in different ways, such as Qur'an, which is closer to the correct sound in Arabic. But, this author uses the word Koran in this book because it is more familiar to non-Arabic readers. The Koran is the constitution of a fundamentalist Islamic state. Roughly equivalent in length to the New Testament, the Koran is a medium-sized book consisting of 114 chapters called *Sura* which in turn are composed of 6,236 verses. Some *Sura* contain more than 200 verses where as others may contain as little as three. For those readers interested in detail, the number of the words is said to be 77,934 or, according to some writers, 79,934.

The structure of the Koran is neither chronological nor thematic. Except for the first chapter, the *Suras* are roughly arranged according to length. These are further divided into 30 sections, thus enabling a devote Muslim to recite the whole book within the thirty days of the fast of Ramadan. The word *Surah* is Hebrew, meaning a row of stones in a wall. Therefore, by analogy, it is used in the Koran to indicate rows of writing. The *Suras* are divided into the Meccan and the Medinan *Suras* respectively. Mohammed claimed that 88 *Suras* of the Koran were revealed to him during his residence in Mecca and the remaining 26 after his flight to Medina. The Meccan *Suras,* written during his thirteen years residence in that city, embody the tolerant sentiments of a prophetic *Warner,* a preacher, and pacifist reformer. The Medinan *Suras* were written in the last ten years of Mohammed's life after he obtained governorship of that city.

In contrast to the relatively benign Meccan espousals, the Medinan passages recommend the merciless killing, decapitation, and maiming of non-believers and others defined as cursed people. (*Sura* XXXIII: 61) Thus, many of the Meccan "tolerant" *Suras* are later abrogated by some Medinan passages. For example, the famous verse in *Sura* IX: 5, "Slay the idolaters whenever you find them," is said to have canceled 124 verses that dictate toleration and patience.[83]

The Koran was first printed in Arabic in Rome in 1530.[84] The first translation in French was done in 1647, and from it, the first English translation was made soon after in 1657. While structured differently, the Koran draws on many of the beliefs and stories that are explained in the Bible.[85] Much of the Koran is plagiarized from scholarly Jewish writings, usually from the Talmud. These same stories have been told and retold dozens of times and contain many contradictions and a plethora of scientific and historical errors. However only Allah, as revealed by his prophet in the Koran, sanctions lying, thievery, deception, slavery, rape, torture, mass murder, and terrorism.[86] Only a person who has blindly accepted the faith of Islam (for whatever reason, be it personal gain, promise of loot, or paradise after death) can rationalize the contradictions inherent in the Meccan vs. the Medinan verses. A detached reader would be hard put to believe they were the work of a single author.

Mohammed, the arrogant author of the Koran, repeatedly and in varied emotional terminology, eulogizes the Book as a divine utterance, spelling out its merits one by one. He brags that it is a glori-

---

[83] Ibn Warraq, *Why I am not a Muslim,* p. 115.

[84] Dr. Anis A. Shorrosh, *Islam Revealed* (Nashville, Tennessee: Thomas Nelson Publishers, 198), p. 26.

[85] Toby Lester, "What is the Koran," in Ibn Warreq, ed. and trans. *What the Koran Really Says* (Amherst, New York: Prometheus Books, 2002), p. 119.

[86] Winn, *Muhammad, Prophet of Doom,* p. XVIII.

ous record (XV: 87), inscribed in the celestial Preserved Tablet (LXXXV: 22) and the Heavenly Archetype (XLIII: 4). It is strictly inimitable (XVII: 90) (II: 21) (X: 38) (XI: 15); unchangeable for all time (X: 64) (XVIII: 26) (VI: 115); free from all deception (XVIII: 1) and all inconsistency (IV: 84). It is a treasury of divine wisdom (XI: 1) (XIII: 37); of healing and of mercy (XVII: 84). It is awe-inspiring, to such an extent that its recital causes the skin of the faithful to tremble (XXXIX: 24) and if it were revealed to a mountain, the mountain would split asunder and collapse for fear of Allah (LIX: 21). The *jinn,* half human, half non-human, on hearing it recited, bowed down before its superiority (LXXII: 1). Nothing on earth or in heaven is omitted from it (XXXIV: 3) (VI: 59) (X: 61) (XI: 7) and (XXVII: 77). Contact with it is forbidden to the impure (LVI: 78).[87]

In his scholarly survey, Torrey[88] states, " . . . the Arabian Prophet himself declared Islam, as defined in the Koran, to be the true heir of the *Old* and the *New Testaments.*" Unquestionably, Mohammed copied much of the content of the Koran from the scriptures of the Jews of Hijaz. The doctrines that fill the earliest pages of the Koran: The resurrection, the judgment, heaven and hell, the heavenly book, revelation through the angel Gabriel, and the merit of certain ascetic practices were characteristically Jewish or Christian. The term *Allah,* "the God" which has always been peculiar to Islam, was already well known to the native tribesmen of Arabia. This is proven, according to Torrey, in the familiar passage in the *mu'llaqat* of the poet Zuheir (line 27f.):

> Keep not from Allah what your heart enfolds,
> Thinking 'tis hid; he knows each word and deed.
> Payment may lag, all booked and kept in store
> For the Last Day, for vengeance come with speed.

Or the line from one of an-Nabigh's poem (*Diwan,* ed. Ahlwart, line 19):

---

[87] Faruq Sheriff, *A Guide to the Contents of the Koran* (United Kingdom: Reading, 1995), pp. 60–61.

[88] Charles Cutler Torrey, *The Jewish Foundation of Islam* (New York: KTAV Publishing House, Inc., 1968), pp. 1,2, 7, 54.

"For Allah gives no man his recompense."

Discussing the preposterousness of the Koran, Nöldeke writes:

"The unbounded reverence of the Muslims for the Koran reaches its climax in the dogma (which appeared at an earlier date through the influence of the Christian doctrine of the eternal Word of God) . . . that this book . . . is consequently *eternal* and *uncreated.* Some theologians did indeed protest against it with great energy; it was in fact, too preposterous to declare that a book composed of unstable words and letters, . . . was absolutely divine. But what were the distinctions and sophisms of the theologians for, if they could not remove such contradictions, and convict their opponents of heresy?"[89]

In support of the authenticity of Nöldeke's idea, the author of this book would like to refer to Jane Dammen McAuliffe's article *Quranic Hermeneutics.*[90] She quotes Tabari, who offers the theory of *muhkamat* and *mutashabihat* for interpretation of verses of the Koran. *Muhkamat* are those verses that are characterized by clarity and detail and permit only one interpretation, such as revering God as one and respecting one's parents. *Mutashabihat,* on the other hand, are those verses that dissemble and are amenable to more than one interpretation. While the *muhkamat* are decipherable to theologians, the *mutashabihat* are comprehensible to no one but God (Allah) himself.

Tabari initiated such a sophism to cover the absurdities and contradictions in the Koran, on the sis of verse 7 of *Sura* III of the Koran which states:

"He is the one who has sent down the Book upon you. In it are verses basic or fundamental. They are foundation of the Book; others are allegorical. But those in whose hearts are perversities follow the part thereof that is allegorical, seeking discord, and searching for

---

[89] Theodore Nöldeke, "The Koran," in *The Origins of the Koran,* ed. Ibn Warren (Amherst, New York: Prometheus Books, 1998), p. 63.

[90] Jane Dammen McAuliffe, "Quranic Hermeneutics: The Views of at-Tabari and ibn Kathir," in Andrew Roppin, ed. *Approaches to the History of the Interpretation of the Qur'an* (Oxford: Claredon Press, 1988), pp. 51–52.

its hidden meanings, but no one knows its hidden meanings except Allah . . . ."

The first part of the verse which states' "He is the one who sent the book upon you," is *muhkamat,* because its meaning is quite clear and it has only one interpretation. The rest is *mutashabihat,* because the subject has different meanings and more than one interpretation.

If one were to believe such sophistry, then it follows that the true believer is faced with a "catch 22." The "God" whom Mohammed invented and whose words are recorded in the Koran, decreed certain instructions to his followers. Some of these precepts were understandable and could be followed to the letter. However, in the same Holy Book, He prescribed instructions which were indecipherable but nonetheless must be followed or face consignment to Hell. Therefore, a true believer is damned from the start. If the Muslims throughout the world were to come to their senses and realize that the entire content of the Koran is mere *mutashabihat* (euphemism for "idle talk"), then they would consign the so-called "Holy Book" to its proper place: the trash can.

However, since, the goal of this book is to expose the Koranic verses that legitimize terrorism, the author will concentrate on those portions of the Koran that contain "divine injunctions" to do so. Keep in mind the precept that a **true believer** must abide by **all** of the words of the Koran, both those that are understandable and those comprehensible **only** to Allah.

The Koran on Human Rights

One of the frightening aspects of the Koran and the religion of Islam is the absolute authority it has ascribed to its "Allah." This monster, invented by Mohammed for his own interest, is always in full control of all existence, lives beyond time and space and strikes fear in the heart of every Muslim. Though all powerful, His mind is so trivial, arrogant, and abased that He admits, in the words revealed to Mohammed: "He has created *jinns* and mankind only to worship him." (Koran, LI: 56)

Since there was no concept of personal freedom or civil rights in the tribal life of seventh-century Arabia where Islam was born, the

Koran does not decree any kind of personal freedom for Muslims such as are guaranteed in the Bill of Rights of the Constitution of the United States: Freedom of speech, freedom of religion, freedom of assembly, or freedom of the press, etc. Even freedom of choice is denied. Verse 36 of *Sura* XXXIII of the Koran states:

> "It is not fitting for a believer, man or woman when a matter has been decided by Allah and His messenger, to have any option about their decision: If anyone disobeys Allah and his Messenger, he goes indeed astray on a clearly wrong path."

The third article of the Declaration of the Rights of Man and Citizens in the French Constitution adopted in 1789 states: "The source of all sovereignty lies essentially in the Nation. No corporate body, no individual may exercise any authority that does not expressly emanate from it." But this imaginary Allah of Islam concocted by Mohammed has ordained his own absolute sovereignty in the Koran saying, " . . . does not share his government with any person whomsoever" (Koran, XVIII: 25), and therefore rejects anything suggesting inherent human rights. The French Declaration of the Rights of Man, the Bill of Rights of the Constitution of the United States as well as the Universal Declaration of Human Rights adopted by the United Nations Assembly in 1948, all reject any theocratic control over the basic rights of all mankind.

While Allah does not allow any human rights other than those written in the Koran, His "divine" edicts allow persecution, thievery, and torture, all in His name. The Koran says, " . . . Allah knows the secrets of the heaven and the earth . . . ." (Koran, XVIII: 26); Muslims cannot claim any human rights absent His knowledge and approval. The civilized peoples of the world respect certain human rights as fundamental, but Islam and the Muslim theocracies do not accept any human right as inherent or, as the Constitution of the United States terms it, "inalienable." The Islamic conference in Jeddah in 1979 composed a Draft for an Islamic Declaration of Human Rights derived from the absurd tenets of the Koran and Bedouin traditions. Therein are found even more verses in the Koran which corroborate the absolute sovereignty of Allah such as the following:

> "To the God belongs all things in the heavens and earth and he encompasses everything." (Koran, IV: 126)

"Whatever beings there are in the heavens and the earth do prostrate themselves to God, acknowledging subjection with good will . . . ."
(Koran, XIII: 15)

There are also a number of references in the Koran indicating
that everything in this world belongs to Allah *and* His Messenger
and that Muslims do not have any right whatsoever to handle their
own lives. The following are a few examples:

> Mohammed said, "I have been ordered to fight with the people till
> they say, 'None has the right to be worshipped but Allah,' and whoever
> says, 'None has the right to be worshipped but Allah, his life and prop-
> erty will be saved by me except for Islamic love and his accounts will
> be with Allah,(either to punish him or to forgive him'"[91]
> Mohammed said to the Jews, "You should know that the earth be-
> longs to Allah and his Apostle (Mohammed), and I want to expel you
> from this land [the Arabian Peninsula], so, if anyone amongst you owns
> property, he is permitted to sell it. Otherwise, you should know that the
> Earth belongs to Allah and His Apostle."[92]
> Mohammed's last words at his deathbed were, "Turn the pagans
> (non-Muslims) out of the Arabian Peninsula."[93]

It is obvious that the fundamental concepts of human rights, developed in the West with the help of John Locke (1632–1704 CE)
and other founding fathers of the Enlightenment, have not had any
impact on Islam even to this day. Hard-line Muslims have openly admitted this fact. In January 1985, Saeed Raja'i-Khorasani, the permanent delegate to the United Nations from the Islamic Republic of
Iran, declared, "The very concept of human rights is 'a Judeo-Christian invention' and inadmissible in Islam." According to Khomeini,
one of the late Shah's 'most despicable sins' was allowing Iran's in-
clusion in one of the original groups of nations that drafted and approved the Universal Declaration of Human Rights in 1948.[94]

---

[91] *Sahih al-Bukhari,* vol. 4, p. 196.

[92] *Ibid.,* 4: 393.

[93] *Ibid.,* 5: 716.

[94] Amir Taheri, *The Spirit of Allah: Khomeini and the Islamic Revolution* (London: Adler & Adler, 1986), pp. 20, 45.

The Koran and Islam relegate the "true believer" to the status of a slave, deprived of all rights, and confined in this most miserable condition by adherence to the "Word of God" as set down in the Koran. Islam demands that man have no dignity or self-respect and that the sole purpose of mankind and *jinn* on earth was to serve Allah (Koran, LI: 56) **and** His Apostle, whom even Allah and His angels salute (Koran, XXXIII: 56). Then, as a reward, he is promised a heavenly brothel to enjoy for eternity a life of debauchery with the lustrous-eyed heavenly houris whom no man or *jinn* has touched (Koran, LV: 74).

Mohammed's Own Promiscuity Sanctioned by the Koran

Twenty out of the 73 verses of *Sura* XXXIII of the Koran are devoted to the legitimizing Mohammed's marriages and his behavior toward his wives. These verses allow his marriage to the divorced wife of his adopted son; describe the categories of women with whom he may marry; admonish the wives of Mohammed to obey him; prescribe the manner in which Mohammed's wives were to wear the veil; and contain strict injunctions forbidding believers to marry Mohammed's widows after his death. The other verses of this chapter teach Mohammed's followers how to conduct themselves towards him, including the prohibition of entering his house without his permission. Verse 57 of same *Sura* warns that whosoever vexes or ill-treats him will be doomed to eternal torment. The whole of *Sura* LXVI deals with a marital crisis that arose due to his sleeping with one of his harem concubines out of turn.

In *Sura* XXXIII: 51, Allah assumes a managerial role in Mohammed's harem and gives him liberty to ignore the previously ordained order of sequence of sexual intercourse with the wives of his harem. He allows him to ignore the connubial rights of the members of his harem and allows him to bed any of his wives whenever he wishes. When this verse of the Koran allowing Mohammed to postpone the turn of any wife was revealed and when Mohammed said that Allah allowed him to marry his adopted son's wife, Ayesha, the beloved first wife of Mohammed's harem, sarcastically observed: "O Allah's Apostle! I see that your lord hurries to please you."[95]

The revelation of Ayesha's alleged sexual dalliance with a handsome young man named Safwan ibn Moattal resulted in the instructions regarding punishment for adultery that form an important part of Sura XXIV.[96]

In Sura XXXIII: 50, the God (Allah) exempts Mohammed from all the ethical values He has ordained for True Believers with respect to marital relationships and permits His Prophet to own any woman who offers herself to him, provided he is also interested in her.

More Admonitions From Above

In Sura XLIX: 1–5, Allah advises Muslims, not to raise their voices above the voice of His Apostle, nor speak loudly to him such as they might speak to each other. If they should do so, they will "lack understanding." In Sura XXIV: 62, Allah is purported to judge the degree of faith of Muslims by their politeness toward His Apostle and admonishes Muslims not to depart from his presence until they ask his permission. Here Allah is so kind to His Apostle that he adds to the Scripture, " . . . even when the Muslims ask the permission of the Apostle to depart, he has the option to give permission to those whom he wants and reject those whom he wishes." In Sura XXXIII: 53, Allah teaches the faithful believers of Islam how to enter His Prophet's home; how to praise the meal that has been prepared for them; what to do after they have finished the meal; and, finally, how to leave his home.

In verse 103 of the Sura called Tobeh, Allah addresses His Apostle directly and orders him to take alms from the wealthy Muslims, in order to purify and absolve them and in Sura LVIII: 12 Allah commands believers in Islam to pay something to Mohammed whenever they wish to consult with him privately, but the payment

---

[95] Sahih al-Bukhari, vol. 7, p. 48.
[96] Sherif, A Guide to the Contents of the Qur'an, p. 7.

should be made *before* the consultation, just as a prostitute demands money up front before providing her services. After all, Mohammed had invented Allah in order to provide himself with a convenient, non-debatable, all powerful religious entity to help him achieve his ambitious goals. However, the notion that a godly revelation would focus on the temporal and sensual desires of a satyr is beyond imagination.[97]

Mohammed Stands above God

Throughout the entirety of the Koran and other Islamic Scriptures, one very rarely finds the word "God" disassociated from "Prophet" or vice versa. This was a deliberate, cunning and subliminal technique on the part of Mohammed to usurp the authority of Allah. No one has access to God, much less to see him; therefore, the people will hear the voice of the unseen God only through His Prophet. As an example, verse 4 of *Sura Anfal* (VIII) or "the spoils of war" decrees, "and know that out of all the booty that you may acquire (in war), a fifth share is assigned to God—and to The Apostle . . . ." In addition, verse one of the same *Sura* says, "They ask you concerning [things taken as] spoils of war. Say, 'Such spoils are at the disposal of God and the Apostle . . .'"

It becomes apparent as one reads the Koran that Mohammed is not happy to be equal of Allah. He would like to be considered above him. For that reason, in *Sura* XXXIII: 56, Mohammed puts himself above Allah and on behalf of Allah he orders his followers to send blessings on him and salute him with all respect, as Allah and His Angels will do. This verse says:

> "Truly, God and his Angels salute the Prophet: O you who believe, send your blessings on him [Mohammed], and salute him with all respect too."

Who should salute whom? It is generally understood that a person of lower rank salutes one of a higher rank. Therefore, if God and

---

[97] Winn, *Muhammad, Prophet of Doom,* p. 562.

His Angels are supposed to salute Mohammed with all respect, it would appear that he is above his All-mighty God.

Allah, the Deceitful Avenger

In many verses of the Koran, Allah asserts that he is "deceitful;" in some verses he admits that his artifice is strong: (Koran, VII: 183; LXVIII: 45); in some verses, he considers himself the best contriver (VIII: 30; III: 54). In *Sura* XXXIX: 36, Allah calls himself a mighty avenger.

Quite a number of verses of the Koran confirm that Allah is treacherous; " . . . whomever he leads stray, shall have no guide and will be strayed for good." (Koran, IV: 143; VII: 186; XIII: 3 and 33; XXXIX: 23; XXXVI: 4; XXIX: 43; XXXV: 8 and LXXIV: 31)

Tabari names seven people among other companions of Mohammed, including Ibn Abbas and Ibn Masu'd, who have heard the following scripture from his own lips. This incident shows what a crafty, conniving God the Muslim worship:

> "When Allah said to Adam, "Dwell you and your spouse in paradise Eat of its plenty wherever you wish, but do not eat of the fruit of this tree, or you will be wrongdoers," Eblis wanted to go and meet them in paradise, but the keepers [of Paradise] prevented him from entering. He went to the snake that was originally blessed and walked on four feet as if it was a camel—it seemed like one of the most beautiful of animals. Eblis talked to it trying to persuade it to let him enter its mouth and take him into Adam. The snake let him do it, passed by the keepers, and entered without their knowledge, because that was Allah's planned."[98]

Goebbels, the Nazi Minister of Propaganda, has stated: "If a lie is repeated often enough, it will eventually be perceived as true." This cynicism is a perfect explanation for the acceptance of the Islamic injunctions by Muslims throughout the world. The superstitious

---

[98] Tabari, *The History of at-Tabai,* vol. 1, pp. 275–76.

principles of Islam have become truisms to the "Believers." They believe that Allah is "the One God," Ka'ba, is "the House of God," the
Koran is "the Word of God," and killing non-Muslims, plundering their
properties, abducting their women, and terrorizing them are all an
approved form of "worship."

When the contents of the Koran are read out of curiosity and not
through the eyes of faith, the words speak for themselves. The dispassionate reader cannot help but conclude that the Koran is a preposterous fabrication by an ignorant person. Mohammed, the author
of the Koran, was a licentious Arab, who married one wife after another, even after he reached the age of 50. How could such an ignoble person dictate human values to others? He was also a cruel
murderer who shed the blood of many innocent people to achieve
power and a schemer who did not hesitate to compromise the basic
tenets of his so-called "heavenly faith" to obtain worldly gain. A complete and comprehensive book could be written about the absurdities and contradictions contained in the Koran, and many authors
have already done so. The aim of this writer is to familiarize the
reader with the general nature of the book, and then show how it is
a terrorist's manual masquerading as a religious tome. Therefore, I
shall stop writing about the gross irrationalities in the Koran and go
on to the parts that focus on terrorism and terrorist activities.

Jihad (Holy War), the Excuse for Islamic Imperialism and Terrorism

The Islamic expansion beginning in the seventh century CE with the
intent to create an Islamic world has its modern counterpart in the
aims proclaimed by the early Communists who declared that their
system of government would slowly but surely spread throughout
the world, uniting all countries under the red banner. Mohammed,
for his own gains, taught the Muslims that the means to achieve an
Islamic world was by the divine precept "*Jihad.*" The word *Jihad* literally means exertion, striving; but in the pseudo-judiciary jargon of
the fundamentalist Muslim, it signifies the exertion of one's power to
the utmost in the cause of Allah and the spreading of belief in Allah
in order to make His creed supreme in the world. Death in such a

sacred endeavor is rewarded by a trip to paradise. This definition is based on the following passages of the Koran:[99]

> "O you who believe! Shall I guide you to a bargain which will save you from painful punishment? Believe in Allah and his Apostle and carry on warfare (*Jihad*) in the cause of Allah with all your possessions and your persons. That will be best for you, if you know. He will forgive your sins, and will place you in the Gardens beneath which the rivers flow, and to beautiful Mansions the Gardens of Eternity: that is indeed the supreme achievement." (*Sura* LXI: 10–13)

Therefore, a *jihad* is a **continuous** Holy War that commands the Muslims to force people to convert to Islam by the dint of the sword and, if not successful in converting them, kill or exile them from their land. *Jihad* or fighting in the cause of Allah (*Jihad fi sabil-Allah*) is a fundamental tenet of Islam, like *Kalima* (belief in the single god, Allah), praying, *Zakat* (alms giving), fasting and *hajj* (pilgrimage to Mecca).When closely examined, the eighth *Sura* of the Koran (*Anfal*), and the ninth (*Tuba*), are the truly *jihad* chapters. However, *jihad* is mandated in many other *Suras* of the Koran as well.

Some Islamic apologists maintain that *jihad* in Islam is the struggle against one's baser instincts just as a devote Christian fights his personal battle against sin (as defined by his sect), but everyone familiar with Islam knows that viewing *jihad* as such is a misleading apology. There are many references to the word *jihad* and its different derivatives in the Koran. Yusaf Ali is an apologist of Islam, but he has openly translated the word *jihad* in his Koran as "fighting."[100] Some of his translated verses are (II: 189 and VIII: 40), "Fight against them (the idolaters) until idolatry is no more and Allah's religion reigns supreme;" (II: 215), "Fighting is obligation for you and you may dislike it. But to accomplish that which you may dislike is good for you;" (IV: 84), "Fight in Allah's cause; you are accountable to none but yourself;" (IV: 35), "Fight violently for His cause so that you may triumph;" (VIII: 65), "O Apostle, rouse the believers to the fight. If

---

[99] Imam Muslim, *Sahih Muslim,* trans. Abdul Hamid Siddiqi, 4 vols. (Beirut, Lebanon: Dar al-Arabia, 2000), 3: 938.

[100] Abdullah Yusaf Ali, *The Holy Koran* (Brentwood, Maryland: Amana Corporation, 1989), p. 442, note 1270.

there are twenty amongst you, be patient and preserving, they will vanquish two hundred, a hundred true believers will vanquish a thousand of the unbelievers;" (IX: 73), "O Prophet, make war on the unbelievers and hypocrites and deal rigorously with them, [so that] their home shall be hell;" (IX: 124), "O believers, fight the infidels who dwell around you, and deal rigorously with them;" (XXII: 78), "Fight for the cause of Allah with the devotion due to Him;" (XLIX: 15), "The true believers are those . . . who fight for His cause with their wealth and their persons;" (LXI: 4), "Allah loves those who fight for His cause in ranks as firm as a mighty edifice;" (XLVII: 4), "When you meet the unbelievers, smite at their necks; at length when you have thoroughly subdued them, bind them firmly. Thereafter, it is the time either for generosity or for ransom until the war lays down its burdens."

Verse 54 of *Sura* XXV says:

> "Therefore, obey not disbelievers, **but do *jihad*** against them here with a great ***Jihad*.**"

Does the word *Jihad* in the above verses indicate, "Fighting against one's inner evils?" Even a deceitful mullah, whose secular existence in life is dependent upon his gulling the public, must admit the fallacy of such an interpretation. Verse 39 of *Sura* VIII reads:

> "Fight against them until there be no more tumult and the only worship be that of Allah."

The verb used in that verse is "*qatala*" (to kill), not "*Jahada* (striving against inner evils), so that all arguments, based on the assertion that in the Koran *qatala,* does not mean "make war or kill the others," but means "to strive earnestly for personal purity," lose any significance and do not soften the nature of the fierceness and brutality of the Koranic decrees. It means that Islam was meant to be propagated by sword. This tradition will go on until the Day of Judgment. The extent of the violence and bloodshed permitted in *Jihad* is clearly stated in the Koran. Verse 5 of *Sura* IX of the Koran leaves no doubt in this regard:

> "When the sacred months have passed away, then slay the idolaters where so ever you find them, and take them captive or besiege them, and lie in wait for them at every likely place. But if they repent

and keep up prayer, establish worship and pay the zakat, then let them go their way."

The tradition forbidding bloodshed in the sacred months (Zelqa'deh, Zilhajjeh, Moharram, and Rajab), was violated by Mohammed himself, True to form, he justified his blasphemy by a revelation from God. With this new revelation (Koran, II: 217), he abrogated the above verse and committed the first bloodshed during a sacred month by ordering his cousin, Abdullah ibn Jahsh to rob a caravan.[101]

The great expansion of Islam was largely due to the militant spirit of the new faith. Although the wording of one verse (*Sura* II: 186) implies that fighting is justified only when the enemy has attacked first, this was generally ignored. There is absolutely no substance in the argument that *Jihad* should be considered primarily as moral endeavor at self-improvement in the service of Islam.[102]

One of the *mullahs* writes about *Jihad:* "It is our opinion that whoever accepts any existing religion today other than Islam, is a nonbeliever. He should be asked to repent. If he does not, he must be killed as an apostate because he is rejecting the Koran."[103] *The Encyclopedia of Britannica,* writes, "*Jihad,* (fight or battle) a religious duty imposed on Muslims to spread Islam by waging war, has come to denote any conflict waged for principle or belief and is often translated to mean 'holy war.'"[104] One Muslim extremist of the Islamic Liberation Party reminded his companions just before the scheduled opening of the party's international rally in London in August, 1994, that "there are 123 verses in the Koran about killing and fighting." And he added, quite unnecessarily, "Ours is not a passive religion."[105]

Among voluminous literature written about *Jihad* in Islam, the above statements of a *mullah,* a Muslim extremist, and a reputable

---

[101] Please see chapter one under the title "Mohammed Resorts to Banditry."

[102] Sherif, *A Guide to the Contents of the Qur'an,* p. 167.

[103] Sheikh Muhammad as-Saleh al-Uthaimin, *The Muslim's Belief,* p. 22.

[104] *Encyclopedia Britannica,* 15th ed., s.v. "Jihad."

[105] Fregosi, *Jihad in the West, Muslim Conquests from the 7th to the 21st Centuries,* p. 18.

encyclopedia leave no doubt that *Jihad* or holy war is defined by Muslims as the killing and murdering those who do not accept the superstitious and preposterous tenets of Islam. No matter how hard Muslim scholars try, they are not able to coin an allegorical explanation or a non-violent interpretation for *Jihad.* As an example, verse 74 of *Sura* IV, says very clearly:

> "Let those fight in the way of Allah who are ready to sacrifice their lives in this world for everlasting life in the world to come. And whosoever fights in Allah's cause and attains either victory in the field or martyrdom, [Allah] soon will give him a great reward."

This verse clearly shows that there is nothing allegorical in the nature of Jihad; it is simply armed war and nothing else. This idea has been further explained in verse 77 of the same *Sura* IV:

> "Do you not see those people *who* were once in favor of fighting [in Allah's cause]? We said to them, "Hold back a while; first perform your prayers, then pay your zakat so that your spirit may be strengthened." But when the time for the battle was ripe, some of them were more afraid of fighting the enemy than they were of fighting Allah Himself. And they said, "O Lord! Why have you made fighting incumbent upon us? Why are we forced to go forward or, offering excuses for our absence, send others in our place? Why do you not postpone the battle so that we may procure more weapons and muster troops that are younger and fitter, thus sustaining fewer casualties?" Say [to them], "The pleasure of this worldly life is few; for those who fear Allah and do well, the pleasure of the hereafter are better."

The above verse clearly shows that, instead of "withdrawing one's hand," *Jihad* requires the waging of unremitting armed conflict. Obviously, Mohammed made up this verse to silence those Muslims who had been pleading against bloodshed and wanted release from the duty of engaging in murderous confrontations.[106] There is also a verse in the Koran, which clearly says that in Islam those who participate in *Jihad* and those who do not, should not be considered equal.

---

[106] Suhas Majumdar, *Jihad: The Islamic Doctrine of Permanent War* (India, New Delhi: Voice of India, 1994), p. 12

"The believers who stay at home—apart from those that suffer from a grave impediment—are not equal to those who fight for the cause of Allah with their wealth and lives. Allah has granted a grade higher to those who fight with their possessions and bodies to those who sit home. He has promised all a good reward; but far richer are the degrees of honor, forgiveness and mercy is the recompense of those who fight for Him." (Koran, IV: 95)

Sahih Muslim is quite concise and articulate in this regard. He writes:

"Believers who sit home and those who go out for *jihad* in Allah's cause are not equal."[107]

The Shiites or Twelvers (those who trace Ali's heirs through twelve direct successors) concept of *Jihad* differs from the Sunni idea in a number of significant points. Though the Shiites accept most of the ideas on *Jihad,* they also believe that it is a legitimate goal to wage holy war on non-Shiite Muslims. In fact, this *Jihad* is regarded by some Twelvers as even more meritorious than the struggle against other nonbelievers. In Shiite legal theory, failure of a Muslim to obey the Imam (Shiite term for the Caliphate) would make him liable to a *Jihad* against him[108] just the same as the failure of a non-Muslim to believe in Allah. According to the Twelvers theory, only one of the original Imams—one of the twelve acknowledged successors or someone designated by them—can proclaim and lead a *Jihad.* The Imam should appeal to the inner conscience of the believers to remind them of the religious duty "to fight in Allah's path." The Shiites believe that to wage war against other Muslims who do not accept the Imam as their Pope, as well as nonbelievers, is part of their religious obligation.[109]

Warfare was common in Arabia before Islam. Since the tribe or clan was the basic political unit, war took the form of raids, mainly for robbery or as vendetta. This state of affairs had, as observed by Ibn

---

[107] *Sahih Muslim,* trans. Abdul Hamid Siddiqi, 4 vols. (Beirut, Lebanon: Dar al Arabia, 2002), vol. 3, pp. 1051–1052.

[108] Abdullah IBM Mufti, *Shah al-Azhar,* vol. 5 (Cairo: 1358 A.D.), p. 525.

[109] Alvin Cottrell and William Olson, "Jihad: The Muslim View of War," *Middle East Insight,* 39.

Khaldun, fostered among the Arabs a spirit of self-reliance, courage and cooperation between members of a single tribe.[110] However, these very traits intensified the character of warfare and rivalry between the tribes and created a state of instability and unrest.[111]

The importance of *jihad* in Islam lay in shifting the focus of attention of the tribes away from their internecine conflicts to the outside world; Islam outlawed all kinds of war except the *jihad,* or "the war in the path of Allah." It would indeed, have been very difficult for the Islamic state to survive had it not been for the doctrine of *Jihad* which diverted that enormous energy of the Arab tribes from internal strife and united them to fight against the outside world in the name of the new faith, Islam.[112] What is called terrorism today is simply a continuation of the *Jihad* which began over a millennium ago.

This concept of *Jihad,* as revealed by Mohammed, made it the duty of every able-bodied Muslim to contribute to the spread of Islam even to the extent of sacrificing his life and his property. Thus, he introduced a precept in Islam found neither in Judaism nor in Christianity: that of a monotheistic religious state with imperialistic ambitions. Judaism is not a missionary religion, for Jews are God's "chosen people" and their "holy war" is for the defense of their religion, not for its spread. Christianity, while also a missionary religion, is a redemptive religion based on ones salvation from sin by the sacrifice of Jesus; it is a catholic or universal religion but supposedly tolerant of all religions.

Islam is radically different from both. It extols the concept of an imperialistic state ruled by a universal religion. It allows for a peaceful means for achieving that ultimate objective but also condones violence to that same end. Islam calls for a unification of all believers within the world of Islam. Its offensive nature demands a state of permanent warfare against all non-believers.[113]

The immediate goals of *jihad* were four in number: (1) the spread of Islam by war; (2) the destruction of infidels; (3) jizyah (religious tax), and

---

[110] Ibn Khaldun, *al-Muquddima,* ed. Quartermere (Paris: 1858), vol. II, pp. 220–21.

[111] Majid Khadduri, *War and Peace in the Law of Islam* (Baltimore: John Hopkins Press, 1955), p. 2.

[1112] *Ibid.,* p. 62.

[113] *Ibid.* p. 63–64.

(4) plunder. *Ghanimat* (plunder) in *jihad* is broadly interpreted to include not only forced acquisition of property but also the enslavement of the women and children of vanquished infidels.[114] According to devout Muslims, *jihad* is a form of prayer. In Islam, fighting in cause of Allah is a religious exercise of supreme merit, more important in the sight of Allah than any other form of piety. Even a noncombatant who loses his life or his substance in the holy war (*Jihad*) is thereby assured of eternal life.[115]

Jihad is a war that Muslims worldwide are obligated to wage in order to bring the whole world under the banner of Islam and destroy all nations, governments, and states that are opposed to the ideology and tenets of Islam. Therefore, it can be said that *Jihad* is a euphemism for terrorism and terrorism is divinely sanctioned. It is not a "Holy War" but merely an excuse for intolerance and imperialism masked in religious phraseology.[116] Nonetheless, to the devote Muslim it is an incumbent religious duty established by Allah for the purpose of advancing Islam.

The great expansion of the Arab Islamic Empire which, by 750 C.E. stretched from the frontiers of China to the Pyrenees in Spain was due largely to the terrorist nature of the Islamic faith. It was due to the precept of *Jihad* that the energies of a remote, poverty-stricken nation of nomads were channeled in such a way that they created an empire in less than a century. Otherwise, that expansion would not have occurred.[117]

Women's Role in *Jihad*

The Holy Koran never considered males and females as equal human beings. The following verses show how the Koran discriminates against women:

> "Men are the protectors and maintainers of women, because Allah has given men more strength than women, and because males will

---

[114] Majumdar, *Jihad: The Islamic Doctrine of Permanent War,* pp. 15–16.

[115] Alfred Guillume, *The Traditions of Islam* (Salem, New Hampshire: Ayer Company Publishers, Inc., 1987), p. 111.

[116] Ram Swarp, *Understanding the Hadith* (Amherst, New York: Prometheus Books, 2002), p. 105.

[117] W. Montgomery Watt, *Muhammad, Prophet and Statesman* (Oxford: Oxford University press, 1061), p. 109.

support women by their work. Therefore, a righteous woman should be obedient to her husband; otherwise, he has the right to beat her." (Koran, IV: 34).

Verse 228 of *Sura* II also clearly places men superior to women:

" . . . And women shall have rights similar to the rights against the. . . . But men shall have a degree of advantage over them. . . ."

Men are permitted to marry four official wives and possess and cohabit with an unlimited number of concubines (female slaves).[118] The Koranic law considers women as merely "things," the property of their owners. The latter can dispose of them as he likes, by sale, by gift, dowry, or in other ways."[119] Married women taken in war are, according to the Koran, entirely at the disposal of the Muslim conqueror (Koran, IV: 28).

In two instances, a woman is considered as half a man. The first is the rules governing inheritance. The share of a male heir is as twice that of a female inheritor (IV: 11, 176–178). A few verses of the Koran state in some detail the rules for the division of an inheritance, but by no account may a woman inherit more than the man and the portion of a kinsman is always twice that of a kinswoman. For example, if the deceased is a woman who leaves no children, but two sisters, they shall inherit two thirds of the estate (it is not clear as to what happens to the remaining third; presumably it reverts to the state or charity). If there are sisters and brothers, the share of the male shall be twice that of the female.

The other instance regards attestation in legal matters. Verse 282 of *Sura* II requires all transactions pertaining to the contraction of debt be put in writing. The signing of such documents must be witnessed by two people. The Koran rules that two male witnesses may do so but if two men cannot be found, then one man and two women will suffice. The obvious conclusion is that it takes *two* women to replace *one* man.

---

[118] Muir, *Mahomet and Islam,* p. 334.

[119] *Encyclopedia of Islam,* ed.H.A.R. Gibb *et al,* s.v. Abd., 1960.

Verse 11 of *Sura* XLII regards women as merely a necessity for procreation and a sexual toy. Addressing men He says, *"The creator of heaven and earth has made for you pairs from among yourselves and pairs among cattle in order to multiply you . . . ."* Apart from her duty as a procreator, it is obvious that the Creator had intended woman to be the ever-available partner of men in sex. Verse 223 of *Sura* II, addressing men says, *"Women are your fields; go then into your fields as you please."* Some Islamic jurists interpret the above verse as sanctioning anal sex with women, particularly during their menses. Although they do consider that an abominable practice, it is not illegal according to Islamic law.

According to Tabari, in his farewell sermon Mohammed equated women to cattle. Mohammed said:

> "Allah permits you to shut them in separate rooms and to beat them, but not severely. If they abstain from [evil], they have right to their food and clothing in accordance with their custom. Treat women well, for they are [like] domestic animals and do not possess anything for themselves."[120]

The science of psychology considers sexual intercourse as a *mutual* psychobiological interaction between males and females, but many Muslims, based upon their interpretation of the Koran, believe that females were created to be the passive sex object of males. The scholars, Abbas Mahmud al-Aqqad and Imam Ghazali, both believe that women have been granted the power to deceive and defeat men, not by force, but by cunning and intrigue. While Aqqad interprets this female power as a divine attempt to offset the weaker female physical constitution, Imam Ghazali, on the other hand, sees this power as the most destructive element in the Muslim social order and equates it with Satanic influence. The social order of Islam therefore ordains that the woman's "negative" power be subdued and its "destructive effects" neutralized.[121]

In Islam, no transaction between married couples is easier than divorce. The Koran gives absolute power to the man to repudiate his

---

[120] Tabari, *The History of at-Tabai,* vol. 9, p. 113.

[121] Fatima Mernissi, *Beyond the Veil: Male-Female Dynamic in Modern Muslim Society* (Bloomington and Indianapolis: Indiana University Press, 1987), p. 33.

wife unilaterally at his discretion and marry another woman without any formalities (Koran, IV: 20). It does not require any court, counselor, lawyer or judge. One phrase from a husband, repeated three times, is enough to break the marriage bond; "You are divorced; you are dismissed; join your folk; or you are unlawful for me."[122] Thus, mere words uttered by the husband is enough to render the wife homeless and throw her, along with any children that he doesn't want, on the public street to beg, borrow, or steal (the husband has the right to keep male offspring if he so desires).[123]

Ghazali concludes that women are a dangerous distraction and must be used by men for the specific purpose of propagating the Muslim nation. Men should quench their instinctual sexual tension and in no way make a woman an object of personal desire. Women should be considered not only outside of humanity but a threat to it as well. Therefore, many of the Muslim religious laws may be interpreted as an attack on, and a defense against, the "negative disruptive power" of female sexuality.[124]

There are also a number of *Hadith* (purported quotations by Mohammed) that corroborate the above-mentioned Koranic verses and considers women inferior to men. The following are some of them:

Osama ibn Said quoted Mohammed as saying, "After my disappearance there will be no greater source of chaos and disorder for my nation than women[125] and:

> Ask your wife's opinion, but follow your own.
> Ask your wife's opinion, but do the opposite.
> Don't ever follow your wife's suggestions."[126]

Mohammed, as reported by Abu Huraira, said, "A woman may be married for [one of] four qualifications: on account of her money;

---

[122] *Sahih al-Bukhari,* vol. 7, pp. 131, 137–38.

[123] Jones and Jones, *Women in Islam,* p. 53, quoted by Anwar Hekmat, *Women and the Koran* (Amherst, New York: Prometheus, 1997), p. 228.

[124] *Ibid.,* p. 45.

[125] Abu Abdullah Muhammad ibn Ismail al-Bukhari, *Kitab al-Jami' al-Sahih* (Leyden, Holland: 1986), p. 419.

[126] E. Westermark, *Wit and Wisdom in Morroco,* p. 329. The first two proverbs can be traced to the second Caliph, Umar ibn al-Khattab. See al-Ghazali's *Revivification,* p. 44, quoted by Mernissi, *Beyond the Veil: Male-Female Dynamic in Modern Muslim Society,* pp. 110–11.

on account of her noble pedigree; on account of her beauty; or on account of her faith; but if you do it for any other consideration, may your hands be rubbed in dirt."[127]Also, "If I had ordered anyone to prostrate to another, I would certainly have ordered a woman to prostrate before her husband."[128]

Abdullah ibn Omar narrated that Mohammed said, "A woman, a house, and a horse are bad omens."[129]

When Mohammed was informed that the Persians had made Kasra's daughter their king, he exclaimed, "A people that entrusts its affairs to a woman will never prosper."[130]

The subordinate position of women in the religious life is likewise fixed by tales of Mohammed's conversations with them. Once he went out to offer the prayer of al-Adha or al-Fitr. As he passed by some women he said, "O company of women give alms, for I have seen that many of you will be inhabitants of hell."

"Why?" said they.

He replied, "Because you curse much and deny the kindness of husbands. I have not seen—despite your deficiency in intelligence and religion—any sharper than you in captivating the mind of the resolute."

They said, "What is the defect in our religion and intelligence?"

He answered, "Is not the witness of a woman equal to half the witness of a man?" This is the defect in her intelligence. And when she is ceremonially impure, she neither prays nor fasts. This is the defect in her religion."[131]

Based on the contents of the Koran and the *Hadith* mentioned above, a psychoanalyst might label Mohammed a dedicated chauvinist. That is not quite so. There was one occasion when he might be characterized as a protector of women's rights but only insofar as their right to participate in *jihad*. According to Anas ibn Malik, on the

---

[127] *Mishkat al-Masabih,* trans. A. N. Matheus, vol., art. 171 (Culcutta, India: 1809), p. 454.

[128] Abu Isa Muhammed al-Tirmidhi, al-Jami' (The Collection), 3 vols. (Cairo: 1937).

[129] Samuel M. Zwemer, *Across the World of Islam* (London: Fleming H. Revell Company, undated), p. 104.

[130] *Sahih al-Bukhari,* trans. Dr. Muhammad Khan.

[131] Guillume, *The Traditions of Islam,* p. 126

Day of Hunain, Umm Sulaim took out a dagger she had in her possession. Abu Talha saw her and said, "Messenger of Allah, this is Umm Sulaim. She is holding a dagger."

The Messenger of Allah asked her, "Why are you holding this dagger?"

She replied, 'I took it up so that I may tear open the belly of a polytheist who comes near me.' The Messenger of Allah began to smile [at these words]."[132]

Anas ibn Malik asserts that the Messenger of Allah allowed Umm Sulaim and some other women of the Ansar to accompany him when he went to war; they would give water (to the soldiers) and would treat the wounded.[133]

Also, "On the Day of Uhod 'I saw Ayesha Bint Abu Bakr and Umm Sulaim. Both of them had tucked up their garments, so I could see the anklets on their feet. They were carrying water-skins on their backs and would pour water into the mouths of the people. They would then go back (to the well), would fill them again and would return to pour water into the mouths of the soldiers.'"[134]

However, to the disappointment of the Islamic apologists, while it is true that he allowed women to fight in *jihad* like his male soldiers, still women were not qualified to receive the same share of the booty as male soldiers. They were given only a "prize" or a "reward" from the spoils. Islamic narrators are articulate on this matter:

> "It has been narrated on the authority of Yazid ibn Hurmuz that Najda wrote to ibn Abbas inquiring of him whether the Messenger of Allah took women to participate with him in *Jihad*. And, if the answer to this question is positive, whether or not He allotted them a regular share from the booty. Ibn Abbas wrote to him, "The Messenger of Allah did take them to the battle and sometimes he fought along with them. There was nothing of the sort for them [share of booty] except that they were given a prize."[135] Another *Hadith* with a little variation in wording states,

---

[132] *Sahih Muslim,* trans. Abdul Hamid Siddiqui, 4 vols, vol. 3 (Beirut, Lebanon: Dar al Arabia, 2002), No. 4453, p. 1001.

[133] *Ibid.,* vol. 3, No. 4454, p. 1001.

[134] *Ibid.,* vol. 3, No. 4455, p. 1001.

[135] *Ibid.,* vol. 3, No. 4453, pp. 1002–1003.

"there was no fixed share for them except that they will be given some reward from the spoils of war."[136]

Merciless Persecution of all Infidels

Verses 61–62 of *Sura* XXXIII of the Koran, say:

> "If the hypocrites and those who have disease in their hearts and those who stir up sedition in the city, do not desist . . . they are cursed people, seize them whenever you find them and kill them without mercy."

The evil intention of Mohammed in including the above verse in the Koran is very clear. "*Hypocrites,*" "*those who have disease in their hearts,*" and "*those who stir up sedition in the city,*" are, in fact, those who disagree with the superstitious folderol an ambitious, power-seeking camel herder is preaching in order to suborn others to his will. These people should be seized wherever they are found and killed mercilessly. This is the justice of the God "Allah," who is called in the Koran "the Most Gracious" and "the Most Merciful" at least 114 times. This bloodthirsty and murderous God is indeed a monstrosity, invented by an ambitious mortal in order to use His tongue to further "His Prophet's" ambitions and line his pockets.

Like it or Not, Killing is Obligatory for Muslims

Verse 216 of *Sura* II of the Koran says:

> "Killing (fighting) is obligatory for you, much as you dislike it. You may hate a thing although it is good for you, and love a thing although it is bad for you. Allah knows but you do not."

In the above verse, the Allah of Arabia commits his Arab slaves to murder, terrorism and hatred regardless of any personal distaste

---

[136] *Ibid.* p. 1004.

for same. There is no mention of love, affection, fraternity, or coexistence with non-Muslims. He has prescribed these atrocities in his Holy Book and has made them obligatory. Since they are ignorant and weak, Allah's creatures may dislike these duties, but the Almighty, All knowing Allah, knows the perfidious capabilities of his creatures better than they themselves. Therefore, He feels no compunction in making it obligatory for them to commit atrocities. The obvious author and benefactor behind such devilish orders is Mohammed. All enemies of Allah's Messenger should be annihilated to pave the way for the sovereignty of the Messenger himself.

Apostates Should be Slain by the Faithful

As I shall explain in chapter five of this book, in several *hadith* Mohammed has clearly ordained the death punishment for apostates. In the Koran, also Islam condemns apostasy and assigns grievous penalty for those who apostatize. The following verses will indicate how serious a sin apostasy is in Islam:

> "Those who reject faith after they accepted it and then go on adding to their defiance of faith, never will their repentance be accepted for they are those who have deliberately gone astray." (Koran, III: 90)
> "O you who believe, if you obey the unbelievers they will drive you back on your heels, and you will turn back from faith to your own loss." (III: 149)
> "The unbelievers wish that you should reject the faith as they do and thus be on the same footing as they. But take not friends from their ranks until they flee in the way of Allah from what is forbidden [convert to Islam], and if they turn renegades [apostatize] seize them and slay them wherever you find them. And in any case take no friends or helpers from their ranks." (Koran, IV: 89)
> "Those who believe, then reject faith, then believe again, and again reject faith and go on increasing in unbelief Allah will not forgive them, nor guide them on the way." (Koran, IV: 137)
> Allah said, "I will send it down unto you: But if any of you after that resisted faith [Islam], I will punish him with a torment such as I have not inflicted of my creatures." (Koran, V: 115)

In the above verse, Allah excels even his cruel creatures in inflicting pain and punishment, terror, and savagery. And, again:

"Those who after accepting faith in Allah fall into unbelief, on them are wrath of Allah, and a dreadful penalty." (Koran, XVI: 106)

"Allah will not guide those who reject faith. They are whose hearts, ears and eyes Allah has sealed up. Without doubt in the hereafter they will Perish." (Koran, XLVII: 25)

It is no exaggeration to say that if an Islamic government based solely on precepts and laws laid down in the Koranic injunctions were established by any country, then the lives of the people in that society would be most miserable, a living hell on earth. It is true that there are certain governments in our contemporary world that call themselves "Islamic," such as the governments of Saudi Arabia, Iran, and Pakistan. However, not one of these governments has been able to foist upon its people as much as ten per cent of the precepts of the Koran and Islam.

As was mentioned above, verse 48 of *Sura* IV adjures Muslims not to take unbelievers as their friends and instructs that such people should be seized and slain by the believers. Verse 51 of *Sura* V also says, "Take not Jews and Christians as your friends and protectors and he amongst you that turns to them is of them." Is it really possible to imagine a hman society where all the people should believe in a collection of superstitious absurdities and in the event that some of them do not, those nonbelieves should be ostracized or slain by the other members of the society? If that were to become so, then every "believer" is potentially the judge and executioner of every non-believer. Naturally, such a society would not even need a jail. What a heavenly utopia indeed!

Allah Orders Decapitation of the Unbelievers and Tests Muslims by Their Terrorist Activities

In verse 4 of *Sura* XLVII of the Koran, Allah orders his Messenger to tell Muslims that He wants them to smite, wound, kill, overpower, subdue, and imprison unbelievers:

"Therefore, when you meet the unbelievers [in *jihad*] smite at their necks; At length, when you have thoroughly subdued them, bind a bond firmly on them [your captives]. Thereafter, [it is the time for] generosity [release] or ransom. Until war shall lay down its burdens, Thus: (are you commanded]. Had Allah willed, He could Himself have punished them; but he has ordained it thus that He might test you, the one by other. . . . ."

It is so interesting that in the above verse Allah says he is able to kill the opponents of His Messenger, but he does not do so. Rather, he leaves the job to his followers in order to compare the killing ability of one to another. What an All-knowing, wise, and insightful Allah he really is! Probably the reason that Allah does not kill the infidels himself and leaves them to be killed by his Muslim slaves is that he wants his faithful Prophet to receive one-fifth of the ransacked properties, the wives of the slain people and the proceeds from the selling of their children in the slave market. The Messenger who brought these commands from on high knew what he was doing!

Allah Promises Divine Aid in Battle

Verses 9, 12, 17 and 65 of *Sura* VIII of the Koran say:

Remember ye implored the assistance of your Lord. And he answered you: "I will assist you with a thousand of the angels, ranks on ranks." (VIII: 9)

Remember your Lord inspired the agents with the message, "I am with you, give courage to the believers. I shall instill terror into the hearts of the infidels. Strike off their heads and smite all their finger-tips." (VIII: 12)

"It was not you, but Allah who slaughtered them; it was not you who threw (stones at them)—it was Allah who did that." (Koran, VIII: 17)

"O Prophet, rouse the believers to the fight. If they are twenty steadfast men among you, you shall vanish two hundred; and if there are a hundred, they shall vanquish a thousand unbelievers, for these are a people without understanding." (Koran, VIII: 65)

Who is an "infidel" in the Islamic lexicon? The answer is very simple: An "infidel" is a person who does not accept the superstitions that Mohammed preached on behalf of his self-made Allah. Why should his head be smitten and his fingers cut off? Because he does not participate in the religious battles (terrorist raids) that will help to annihilate the enemies of Mohammed and, at the same time, will add twenty per cent of the spoils of wars to his wealth.

While Allah tells Mohammed that if they are twenty, they shall vanquish two hundred and if they are a hundred they shall vanquish one thousand, it is clear that in the battle of Uhod, Allah's promise was not realized. This battle proved disastrous for the Muslims and they suffered a terrible defeat. In this battle seventy-four of Mohammed's men lay dead upon the field, including several of his companions, among them the gallant Hamza (Mohammed's uncle), whose dead body was savagely mutilated by Hind (the wife of Abu Sufyan who ate his liver) and the brave standard-bearer, Musab; the enemy lost only twenty soldiers. Mohammed himself was knocked senseless by a blow to his head, badly wounded in the face and lost a tooth. The sword of Ibn Kami'a was barely warded off his head by the naked hand of Talha at the expense of his fingers. If a party of Mohammed's followers had not shielded his body, he surely would have been slain.[137]

Was Mohammed a Bloodthirsty Individual?

The following verse 67 of *Sura* VIII of the Koran sheds light on this question:

> "No Prophet has ever been allowed by Allah to take prisoners of war without first bringing under control the enemy territory and slaying all who oppose him; only then may prisoners be taken and ransomed. Your desire for material gain [in] the form of ransom for prisoners is a symbol of your desire for the perishable goods of this worldly life rather than the everlasting treasures of the Hereafter. But Allah, in His compassion, wants you to reap the rewards of the life to come. And He is the Almighty, Possessed of absolute wisdom."

---

[137] Muir, *The life of Mohammad,* p. 261.

At least, two points can be learned from the above words of Allah. The first is that Mohammed's main goal is to kill his enemies rather than to take them prisoner and hold them for ransom. That is why, through the tongue of Allah, he ratiocinates that taking control of a territory is more important than taking prisoners. The second is that this is an example of his ubiquitous duplicity. Herein, he makes Allah the author of his vicious thoughts and tries to pretend that it is not his goal to kill his opponents but it is the decision of Allah, who is commanding him. A psychologist might opine that he makes Allah his defense mechanism.

A *hadith* relates that Mohammed had captured a slave called Yaser in the battle of Muharib and he put him in charge of his milch camels to watch over them in the neighborhood of al-Jamma. Eight Bedouin of the Qays tribe of Bajila had at some time previously visited Medina, embraced Islam and chose to live in that city. The miasma of the climate "affected their spleen," so they came to Mohammed complaining of illness. Mohammed suggested that they go to the desert and ask his camel herder to give them milk and urine of the camels to drink as a treatment of their illness. They complied with this suggestion and subsequently recovered no doubt due to Nature's healing power or "tincture of time." When they recovered their health, they attempted run off with the herd of camels. Yaser, a posse of one, pursued the plunderers, but he was seized and barbarously killed by them.

When the news of this treachery reached Mohammed, he dispatched Kurz ibn Jabir,[138] who had returned from the raid of Dhu Qarad with twenty horsemen, to capture the robbers. They surrounded and seized the robbers and recovered all the camels save one, which had been slaughtered by the thieves. The captives were conducted to Mohammed who ordered their hands and feet to be

---

[138] In the summer and fall of 623 A.D., when Mohammed returned to Medina from one of his unsuccessful robbery attacks on caravans, he was informed that some of the camels and flocks of Medina were robbed by Kurz ibn Jabir a-Firi, marauding Bedouin chieftains from Fihri tribe. Mohammed gave Medina in charge of Zaid ibn Hearth and pursued him as far as valley of Safwan, a place in the neighborhood of Badr. Kurz escaped and could not be overtaken. For the same reason, this expedition is called "the first Badr." Not long afterward, Kurz ibn Jabir was converted to Islam.

cut off as punishment for their thievery.[139] Another entry reads, "In addition to the above-mentioned punishments, the Prophet ordered hot irons to be drawn across their eyes, and when they asked for water, it was not given to them and they died."[140]

Allah, the Voluntary Accomplice of Mohammed's Terrorists

On the basis of verse 14 of *Sura* IX, Allah provokes a group of His slavish followers to kill another group and promises to help them to achieve their goal:

> "Make war on them, Allah will punish them by your hands, and humble them. He will grant you victory over them and heal the wounds of the faithful." (Koran, IX: 14)

Those who live in a Western civilization are fortunate to have a criminal justice system different from the Islamic one. This is especially true of those who live under a system based on English Common Law wherein the accused is presumed innocent until proven otherwise by concrete evidence and has the right to counsel to defend him and a trial by jury. He can only be sentenced to punishment after being found guilty by 'a jury of his peers' and his punishment is governed by guidelines set down by law. Other considerations such as his past record, his motive in perpetration of the crime, and any mollifying conditions under which he committed the crime may be considered in determining the severity of the punishment. If convicted, the accused may appeal to a higher court and, if that court determines that the lower court committed a mistake in law, his conviction may be overturned. In contrast, in the Islamic justice system, the functions the jury, defense lawyer, prosecutor, and judge are all relegated into the hands of a mullah, called "the Islamic judge," whose verdict is peremptory.

---

[139] Muir, *The Life of Mohammad,* p. 350.
[140] Fregosi, *Jihad in the West,* p. 47.

No other religion enjoins its followers to commit crime. It is so interesting to note that in the Koran, Allah incites a group of His followers to murder and even promises to help them. What a just Allah he really is!

Allah Disavows Pacifists but Promises Help to Those who Fight in His Name

In verse 35 of *Sura* XLVII, Allah says:

> "Be not weary and faint-hearted, crying for peace and reconciliation, when you should be striving to gain the upper hand; for Allah is on your side and will never put you in loss, for your deeds."

Apart from the reasons already mentioned, the above verse clearly shows the bellicose and terrorist nature of Islam and Mohammed's proclivity to use warfare and plundering to consolidate his power. If he were ordained by his so-called Allah to guide the people to the path of righteousness, why did he reject peace-seekers, instead of welcoming them and coming to terms with them? If his only purpose was to convert his enemies to a new faith and not to take the lands and properties of the non-believers, why did he persist in a continual war against them? In the early years of his prophecy, he was not fighting against any foreign power but was making war against the tribes of his own poor land and he concocted many ruses and fomented many wars in order to gain power over his them.

Another point of interest in the above verse is that it reveals (through Mohammed, of course) that Allah promises to be on the side of Muslims. The miserable defeat in the battle of Uhod has been already mentioned above. However, this was not the only occasion when the forces led by Mohammed were disastrously overpowered in war. In the seventh year of Hijra, Mohammed sent an army to attack the inhabitants of Fadak. The men of the tribe of Beni Murra confronted them and cut them to pieces.[141]

---

[141] *Ibid.*, p. 392.

A year after that, Mohammed dispatched an expedition to the Bani Suleim tribe, camped some distance to the east of Medina, ostensibly to convert them to his faith. The Bani Suleim slew most of the Muslims and their wounded leader, along with a few survivors, fled back to Medina.

A month or two later Mohammed sent another party to attack a group from the tribe of Bani Leith who were camped on the road to Mecca. The Muslim soldiers surprised the encampment and plundered their camels. But the Bani Leith tribesmen pursued the marauders and recovered their camels. The thieves managed to escape to Medina.[142]

On another occasion, Mohammed dispatched a small body of fifteen men to Dhat Atlah, on the Syrian border, to attack a camp of the Bani Amir, a subdivision of the hostile Hawain tribe. The Muslims were successful and each one's share of booty amounted to fifteen camels. However, on their way home, a party of Bedouins attacked the Muslims and massacred all of them except for one man who, although badly wounded, managed to escape to Medina.

Most disastrous of all was the Muslim's defeat in Syria. Up until 629 CE, Mohammed attacked and plundered only the inhabitants of Arabia. But, in September 629 CE, he essayed his first expedition to the outside world and dispatched a raiding party to the southern part of the Roman Empire. The army was placed under the command of Mohammed's adopted son, Zaid ibn Haritha. Jaafar ibn Abu Talib, the brother of Ali, was appointed second in command and Abdullah ibn Rawaha was third in succession. Mohammed told them, on leaving Medina, that he expected to see them come back "laden with spoil," the goal of all of Mohammed's expeditions.

The first battle on Roman ground took place at Muta, at the southeast end of the Dead Sea. On sighting the enemy, the Muslims retired to a favorable position, closed lines and awaited the Roman attack which came shortly. The Muslim banner was held by Zaid who was soon killed; Jaafar then took it up but met with the same fate. Then Abdullah ibn Rawaha seized it and, despite having his both hands cut off, pressed it to his body with the stumps of his arms, until he likewise fell.

---

[142] *Ibid.*

The war ended in a disastrous defeat for the Muslims and they were put to flight. They had lost their bravest men, and would have suffered still more had not the celebrated Khalid ibn Walid taken command and organized a rear guard action that allowed an orderly withdrawal from the field of battle.[143] It seems that in all of these disastrous defeats Allah was either on vacation or simply bored. He didn't stand by his pledge to support the Muslims. He didn't send armed angels from the sky, as he did in the battle of Badr, to help them out.

In brief, the Koran defines a good Muslim as a person who leaves his home, sacrifices his wealth and life in order to fight in Allah's and His Messenger's cause. In turn, he will be rewarded by Allah with plunder and women if he survives, or with a heavenly bordello if he dies. Peace lovers are bad Muslims; Allah hates them and hell's hottest fires await them.

Infidel Parents Must Not be Loved

It comes as a shock to learn that a so-called divine book that is supposed to be based on *summum bonum,* teaches children not to love their parents if they (the parents) reject the ridiculous superstitions of Islam. Sadly, some verses in the Koran do instruct True Believers to hate their parents and other relatives and to avoid them if they disagree with their beliefs. Among such verses is verse 23 of *Sura* IX of the Koran, which shamelessly evokes that cruel precept:

> "O you who believe! Do not befriend your fathers or your brothers if they choose unbelief in preference of faith. Wrongdoers are those who befriend them." (Koran, IX: 23)

Religion should promote fraternity, honesty, integrity, respect and love of family, these being essential moral guidelines for a flourishing society regardless of whatever God or gods are worshipped. But the religion preached by Mohammed teaches Muslims to castigate their fathers, brothers, and other relatives if they do not follow

---

[143] Keller, *Mohammed and Mohammedanism,* pp. 199–200.

His self-serving, preposterous, and ambitious faith. No religion in the world has ever destroyed family ties as Mohammed has done in Islam. By including certain passages such as the above in the Koran, Mohammed told Muslims that they must love him more than they love their family. Centuries later, another tyrant used the same technique. The Hitler Youth Program taught young Germans to inform on their parents if they dissented from the Nazi party line.

Also, the above verse reminds us that Islam considers women as a "commodity" rather than a "human being." While the verse restricts the faithful from befriending certain of their non-believing relatives, it mentions only "fathers and brothers" and excludes "mothers" and "sisters" or women in general as not being worthy of mention.

Another verse in this connection is the verse 14 of *Sura* LXIV of the Koran, which says:

> "O you who believe! Truly among your wives and your children are enemies to yourselves, so be aware of them."

Verse 3 of *Sura* VI of the Koran also speaks about the separation of relatives and children on the Judgment Day and has the same implication:

> "Your ties to your relatives and to your children will not avail you on the Day of Judgment; He will part you." (Koran, LX: 3)

Non-Muslims are Unclean

Verse 27 of *Sura* IX, states:

> "O believers know that the pagans are unclean. Let them not approach the Sacred Mosque after this year is ended . . . ."

To appreciate the concept of "unclean" as used in the Koran, it is necessary to understand the meaning of this word to a Muslim. "Unclean," has an abstract meaning as well as the obvious one. The latter meaning of "unclean" is a visible phenomenon and describes

a person whose appearance looks dirty and grubby (or a menstru-
ating woman). The abstract meaning of the word "unclean," to a Muslim, describes a person who is sinful. The word "unclean" in the
above verse certainly refers to this concept. Now the question
arises: What does Islam mean by a sinful person, or what is "sin" in
Islam? It is true that "sin" in Islam is divided into two classes: great
sins and little sins, but generally and practically speaking, in Islam,
"sin" is nebulously interpreted and "sinful" ascribe any person who
is against the religious authorities or whose behavior seems dubi-
ous to them.

When Khomeini came to power in Iran, he ordered the execution of thousands of innocent people under the pretext that they
were "fighting against Allah" and "doing sedition on earth." Reading
Salman Rushdie's *Satanic Verses* was an example of "sin" according to that crazy mullah. Mohammed's reason for using the word "unclean" in the Koran was to terrorize the people, strike fear and
anxiety into their hearts, and force them to submit to his power.

Webster's Third New International Dictionary defines "*terror*" as,
"A state of intense fright or apprehension."[144] The *American Heritage Dictionary's* definition of "*terrorism*" is, "Violence committed or
threatened by a group to intimidate or coerce a population, as for
military or political purposes."[145] The *Random House Unabridged
Dictionary* defines "*terror*" as "An intense or cause of intense fear or
anxiety; quality of causing terror: *to be a terror to evildoers.*"[146]

Therefore, the word "unclean" in the above verse was one of the
tools of terror that Mohammed used to intimidate whoever challenged his authority and, as will be discussed in chapter six, often
resulted in murder. Today, Muslims attribute "uncleanliness" to non-
Muslims, particularly Jews, Christians, and Bahais and their
"cleansing" has led to acts of horror, chiefly through the use of suicide bombers. The nineteenth century philosopher Nietzsche nicely
sums up the repulsion felt by an intelligent, free-thinking person toward any evangelistic religion: "When I come into contact with a religious person, I feel I have to rinse my hands."

---

[144] *Webster's Third New International Dictionary,* 2nd ed. (1993), s. v. "Terror."
[145] *American Heritage Dictionary,* 4th ed. (2000), s.v. "Terror."
[146] *Random House Unabridged Dictionary,* 2nd ed. (1987), s.v. "Terror."

Muslims Who Befriend Infidels Can No Longer be Considered Muslims

Verse 51 of *Sura* V of the Koran orders Muslims not to take the Jews and the Christians as their friends and protectors; otherwise they will be like them.

> "O you believe! Take not the Jews and Christians for your friends and protectors: They are but friends and protectors to each other. And he amongst you that turns to them [for friendship] is of them. Verily God guided not a people unjust."

It is man's nature to interact with others of his kind. Some philosophers believe that mankind will never be free of war because "it is his nature," as the scorpion said to the turtle as they both drowned. However, peaceful interaction between humans makes life easier and more enjoyable for all.

Islam, as revealed by Mohammed in his Koran, prohibits Muslims from associating with the Jews and the Christians. Other than terming them Infidels or Non-Believers, there are no reasons given in the Koran for this injunction. However, by inserting such a xenophobic admonition in the Koran, Mohammed reveals his own bigotry and confirms Tocqueville's opinion that Islam is a racist and illogical religion, a "very false and very absurd faith."[147]

We are living in a world that is becoming smaller and smaller day by day. Human beings, regardless of religion, race, skin color, language, culture or nationality should unite and cooperate with each other to make life more enjoyble and fulfilling for all. The Koranic injunction is viewed as obscene by all who believe in a peaceful, non-racist united world. This verse of the Koran seems even more preposterous when we take into consideration that Mohammed, claiming possession of the Seal of a Prophet appointed by God to

---

[147] Alexi de Tocqueville, *Democracy in America,* 2 vols. (New York: Vantage Books, 1954), vol. 2, p. 503.

all the nations of the world for eternity, announced that it had been revealed to him by God. Therefore, Muslims who have married the followers of either of those two religions or have social, commercial, or cultural relations with them cannot consider themselves Muslims.

An ignorant and selfish camel herder in the 7th century, struggling to gain power over his fellow citizens by proclaiming a new religion and, through its God, orders people who live in the same land not to interact with each other! Do Muslims really think that if the contents of such a verse were literally applied that they would not be alienated from other nations of the world? What would happen in such a world? At the very least, the following comes to mind:

1. The United Nations and all international relief organizations would be immediately dissolved.
2. All the political legations of the Jewish and the Christian countries in Muslim lands and vice versa should be shut down.
3. All contracts between Muslim countries and the Jewish and the Christians ones should be nullified.
4. The destructive and calamitous conditions which the crusades brought about for the followers of the Semitic religions for about three hundred years from the eleventh to the fourteenth centuries might be reinstated on a modern scale.
5. The Islam nations would not have access to the intellectual works and inventions discovered by Jewish people such as Albert Einstein, Sigmund Freud, Moses Hess, Baruch Spinoza, Isaiah Berlin, Walt Elias Disney, and so on. These would be considered sinful pursuits in the Muslim countries.

The Christian and other non-Muslim contributors to the knowledge and welfare of mankind would fill a book as large as a city telephone directory. It is interesting to note that history has not recorded a single Muslim among such luminaries.

If Muslims were to strictly adhere to the Koranic injunctions against dealing with Non-Believers, they would be deprived of the benefits of all modern scientific and technologic advances and all the intellectual theories, innovations and inventions of the modern world. They would revert to the life as led by a seventh century Bedouin in the barren deserts of Arabia.

Allah Threatens to Reverse the Faces of Jews and Christians who do not Believe in Islam

It is difficult for an intelligent, rational person to picture this happening but, lo and behold, it is a revelation of Allah to Mohammed and it is found in the 47th verse of *Sura* IV of the Koran. This verse invites Jews and Christians to accept faith in the Koran, which (according to the verse), verifies and confirms the true Torah and the true Gospel, before they are actually cursed and punished just as the Sabbath-breakers were punished.[148]

> "O ye who have been given the Book! [Jews and Christians] Believe in what we have revealed, verifying what you have, before we alter the faces beyond all recognition and turn them backwards, or curse them as We cursed the Sabbath-breakers for the decision of Allah must be carried out." (Koran, IV: 47)

In the above verse, Allah clearly says that Jews or Christians should accept the Koran, obey Mohammed as a prophet and be converted to Islam or he will turn their faces to the back. Allah does not leave any shadow of doubt: If the Jews and the Christians do not comply with his demand, then he will do with them what he had already done with Sabbath-breakers. The Sabbath-breakers story will be explained in the next chapter. Most interesting of all, the above verse asserts that the command of Allah is *always* executed.

Has anyone ever seen, read, or heard of in the past 1400 years since Mohammed introduced his fictitious superstitious religion, the face of any infidel (as defined by Islam) being reversed to his back? If not, then we know two facts: (1) the Muslim's Allah is a clown, and

---

[148] Alexi de Tocqueville, *Democracy in America,* 2 vols. (New York: Vantage Books, 1954), vol. 2, p. 503.

(2) His beloved Messenger is the most outrageous liar the world has ever seen!

Opponents of Allah and His Apostle Should be Mutilated, Executed, and Crucified

The Western legal codes governing sentencing emphasize that the punishment should fit the crime and that the circumstances under which the crime was committed should be considered in deciding the punishment. But it seems that the All-knowing Allah and His messenger follow their own punitive law and procedures. If a person disagrees with the so-called Apostle, Allah orders Mohammed to execute him, crucify him, cut off a hand and a foot from opposite sides, or exile him from his land.[149] Of course, this is the light part of his punishment and not the end of it. He still has to incur the worst of it: the part in the hereafter.

> "The punishment of those who wage war against Allah and His Apostle, and commit horrendous crimes through the land is: execution, or crucifixion, or cutting off of hands and feet from opposite sides, or exile from the land: that is their disgrace in this world, and a heavy punishment is theirs in the Hereafter." (Koran, V: 36).

The above is the most barbarous verse ever issued in the name of religion. For example, if someone argues the validity of Mohammed's self-proclaimed "revelations," he or she could be imprisoned, exiled, mutilated, executed or crucified. Mere opposition to the superstitious ideas that Mohammed is preaching makes one liable to the above punishments.

As with most of the other verses of the Koran, Mohammed has plagiarized the above horrendous verse in part from Jewish Scriptures. Verses 123–124 of *Sura* VII and verse 49–50 of *Sura* XXVI of the Koran say that Pharaoh threatened his magicians with cutting off their hands and feet on opposite sides and *crucifixion* because they

---

[149] Winn, *Muhammad, Prophet of Doom,* p. 614.

thought Moses' power superior to theirs. These verses raise two interesting points: First, they show that Mohammed has copied part of the verses from Jewish Scriptures. Second, they reveal his ignorance about the history of crucifixion. According to the *Encyclopedia Britannica,*[150] crucifixion was practiced from about the sixth century before Christ, while Moses lived between 1350 to 1250 years before Christ. Therefore, this practice did not exist at a time of Moses and, as such, a reference to same in the Koran in the above context is as inaccurate as many other passages.

Mohammed fabricated a cruel, capricious and irrational god who speaks on his behalf in order to fulfill his own ambitions. In the "system of justice" ordained by Allah and Mohammed, the fate of a dissident is mutilation, execution, crucifixion, or exile from his land. What a just and merciful religion is Islam!

Plundering—the Catalyst For Conversion to Islam

The plundering of defeated people in the Islamic wars is one of the spoils of *Jihad* or, as the Koran puts it, *"ghanimat"*. The reward of a Muslim warrior—the one who participates in *Jihad*—and dies is a ticket to a Paradise in the hereafter, but for the surviving warrior his reward is the plundering and ransacking of the property of unbelievers and the taking of their women and children. The word *"ghanimat"* in Islamic parlance means "loot."[151]

After Mohammed's flight from Mecca to Medina and the wars with the Meccans, the spoils from raids on the commercial caravans of the Bedouins and Jewish tribes became an important source of income for Mohammed and his companions. Historians have stated that the prospect of taking booty could have been the sole motivation of those who took part in these expeditions. When, in 628 CE, Mohammed was preparing to go on pilgrimage to Mecca, some of his followers stayed behind because there was no prospect of plunder. Referring to this the Koran says:[152]

---

[150] *Encyclopedia Britannica,* 15th ed., s.v. "Crucifixion," p. 762.

[151] Majumdar, *Jihad, the Islamic Doctrine of Permanent War,* p. 26.

[152] Sherif, *A Guide to the Contents of the Koran,* p. 170.

"Those who lagged behind (will say), when you are free to march and take booty in war, 'Let us follow you,' intending to change Allah's words. Say, 'You shall not follow us; thus has Allah said already.' They will then say, 'No, you are jealous of us.' Rather they understand but a little." (Koran, XLVIII: 15)

The capture of property and women from non-Muslims in *Jihad,* whether by force or not, confers upon the Muslim warrior all the rights and perquisites of the original owner. Non-Muslims are deprived of their possessions as a punishment for their persistent disbelief and refusal to adopt Islam and submit to Islamic rule.[153]

The term *"ghanimat"* is applied specifically to property acquired by force from non-Muslims. It includes, however, not only property (both moveable and immoveable) but also prisoners who could be ransomed, as well as women and children.[154]

Allah makes the nature of spoils explicit in verses 26 and 27 of *Sura* XXXIII:

"And those of the people of the Book [Jews and Christians who supported the Meccans] God did take down from their strongholds, and cast terror into their hearts. Some you slew and some you took captive."

"And he made you heirs of their lands, their houses, and their goods and of a land which ye have not frequented before. . . ."

Verse 24 of *Sura* 4 of the Koran, elaborates on the rights of the Muslim warriors over captured infidel women in Jihad with brutal frankness:

"And all married women are (forbidden unto you) except those whom your right hands possess [women captured in *Jihad* who

---

[153] Majid Khadduri, *War and Peace in the Law of Islam* (Baltimore: The John Hopkins press, 1955), p. 119.

[154] Sarakhsi Muhammad ibn Ahmad, *Kitab al-Mabsut,* vol. X (Cairo: 1324 A.H.), p. 22; Shaybani, *al-Siyar al-Kabir,* with Sarakhsi's Commentary, vol. II (Hyderabad: 1335 A.H.), p. 250; Ali ibn Abi Bakr Marghinani, *The Hedaya (Guide: A Commentary on the Mussalman Law),* Trans. Charles Hamilton (Delhi, India: Islamic Book Trust, 1982), vol. 2 p. 100, all cited in Majid Kadduri, *War and Peace in the Law of Islam* (New York: AMS Press, 1979).

become slaves regardless of their marital status]. Such is the decree of Allah."

The spoils of war may either be divided in the *Dar al-Harb* (foreign territory) or carried to *Dar al-Islam* (Islamic territory). Before the Battle of Badr (624 C.E.), Mohammed directed the division of the spoils on the basis of the laws traditionally recognized by Arabs. But this led to quarrels among his followers that were resolved as usual; Allah came to his favorite Messenger's assistance and revealed the following verse to him:

"And know that when you have taken any booty, one-fifth belongs to Allah and to the Apostle, and to the near kin, and to orphans, and to the poor, and to the wayfarer . . . ." (VIII: 41)

Verse 69 of *Sura* VIII says:

"You [are] allowed to take booty for yourselves and enjoy what you take in war; it is religiously lawful and pure."

In the above verse, Allah removes any misgivings that might arise by the pricking of conscience and invites His Muslim slaves to loot the belongings of those infidels conquered in His name.

Verse 1 to 3 of *Sura* 110 of the Koran states:

"When comes the help of Allah and victory, and you see men embrace His religion in multitudes, celebrate the praise of your lord and ask His forgiveness. He is ever disposed to mercy."

But contrary to the above, upon the death of Mohammed, Islam fell apart in Arabia. Muslim historians state that most Arabs considered Islam synonymous with plundering and loot. After the death of Mohammed, Arabs thought that with Mohammed out of the picture, there would be no more lucrative raids or wars to line their pockets and satisfy their lust. Hence, many of the Arab tribes repudiated Islam and became renegades.

Abu Bakr, Mohammed's successor, turned his attention to the difficult task of suppressing the renegade tribes and consolidating the Islamic power in Arabia. On all sides, the tribes were rising in revolt. Many of the Arabian tribes had been converted by the sword and the main task of Abu Bakr and the ruling elite was to overcome the tribal opposition to Islamic domination that had arisen all over the Arabian peninsula. The revolt spread from tribe to tribe, until the newly built Islamic Empire suddenly shrank to the cities of Mecca, Medina, and Taif. It may be deduced that the prospect of the loss of the spoils of war contributed to the disenchantment with the religion of Islam.

The opposition movements that arose took one of two forms. One group challenged both the political control of Medina and the religious claims of Islam by proposing rival ideologies. The leaders of the opposition to Islam posed as prophets and political leaders, hoping to emulate Mohammed. This category included the rebellion of the Bani Asad in the Najd, led by Talha ibn Khalid, who claimed to be a new prophet; the opposition of the Bani Hanifa in Yamama, led by Maslama ibn Habib, who also considered himself a prophet; the uprising of clans of the Bani Tamin[155] and the Bani Taghlib in northeastern Arabia, led by a woman, called Sajah, who claimed to be a prophetess and ultimately joined forces with Maslama and the Bani Hanifa; and the insurrection of the Bani Ans in Yemen, led by Aswad al-Ansi, another self-proclaimed prophet.

There was, in addition, a second type of rebellion that was more political in character. It was a tax rebellion against the Islamic state, led by the Bani Fazra, branches of the Bani Asad, and some of the Bani Tamim, all in the Najd.[156]

Although, Mohammed was dead at this time, the sword of Islam was not buried with him and Abu Bakr dispatched Khalid ibn al-Walid and other Muslim commanders to different parts of Arabia to subdue the renegades and rebels. After some bloodshed, the Muslim armies succeeded in suppressing the rebellions. Muslim historians denote the "defection" of the tribes in Arabia after Mohammed's death, as the *Hurb al-Riddah* or "wars of apostasy."

The wars of apostasy again demonstrate that the spread of Islam was based above all on the lure of plunder and ransacking. As

---

[155] Led by Malik ibn Nuwayra, who advanced upon Medina.

[156] Fred McGraw Donner, *The Early Islamic Conquests* (Princeton, New Jersey: Princeton University Press, 1981), p. 8; *Mahomet and his Successors,* ed. Henry A. Pochmann and E.N. Feltskog (Madison, Milwaukee: The University of Wisconsin Press, 1970), p. 85.

it was explained in chapter one, Mohammed started his prophetic career at Medina with a raid upon a Qurashite caravan.[157]

Religion is supposed to instill ethical behavior, promote human values and culminate in social reforms and the construction of a better human society. But from the beginning, Islam was based on terrorist activities and today, after 1400 years, Westerners have finally realized the term "terrorism" describes their code of behavior. Faruq Sherif a Muslim writer states:

> "The taking of booty was a primary objective in the case of raids on caravans and tribes, and it was the result in the case if *Jihad* or holy war. The importance of booty as a means of attracting people to the new faith or maintaining their allegiance has been mentioned in the historical accounts. From the general tenor of the verses, relating to the spoils of war it may be inferred that the motive of the Arab Bedouin who took part in the wars and the raids was often the expectation of a share in a trophy (captives, land, buildings, and goods.)"[158]

Allah in verses 20 and 21 of *Sura* XLVIII, he promises his Prophet more spoils to come:

> "Allah has promised you abundant spoils, which you will acquire, and he has given you these beforehand; and he has restrained the hands of men from you . . . . And you acquire other spoils which are not within your power, but which Allah has compassed . . . ."

In summary, the Koran and Islam make the property, wealth, land, women, and children of the infidels, without exception, the lawful booty of the *Jihad* warriors. Undoubtedly, the promise of such plunder was the major force fueling the spread of Islam.

Slaves, an Islamic Commodity

In Mohammed's time, slavery was part of the social tradition of Arab tribes and Mohammed did nothing to forbid it. On the contrary in the Koran, it is recognized it as a normal part of life. The Koran makes

---

[157] Please see chapter one "Mohammed Resorts to Banditry."
[158] Sherif, *A Guide to the Contents of the Koran,* p. 170.

frequent references to slavery and describes the rights possessed by slave owners. According to the Koran (IV: 32, 28, 29, 40; XVI: 77; XXIII: 5; XXIV: 33; XXX: 27; XXXIII: 49; LII: 29), all male and female slaves taken as plunder in the Islamic wars are the lawful property of their master. The master may carnally enjoy any female slave, whether married or single. The position of a slave in Islam is help-less but, on the other hand, they should be treated with kindness, and be granted their freedom whenever they so ask and are able to pay for it.

The Imam (Muslim chieftain), according to Mohammed's teach-ings with respect to captives, has the right to slay them or, if he chooses, he may make them slaves or release them. However, it is not lawful for the Imam to release idolaters or apostates of Islam.[159]

Slave traffic is not only allowed but also legislated and sanc-tioned by Islam.[160] Slaves, male or female, are treated merely as ar-ticles of merchandize. For example, "A master is not slain for the murder of his slave," nor "if one or two partners in [the ownership of] a slave kill the slave, is retaliation incurred."[161] Here the Islamic law differs from that of Judaism. The Hebrew law in this regard says, "When a man strikes his slave, male or female, with a rod, and the slave dies under his hand, he shall be surely punished. However, if the slave survives a day or two, he is not to be punished; for the slave is his money."[162]

In Islam, the owner of a slave, but not a part owner, may cohabit with any of his female slaves who are a Muslim, a Jew, or a Christ-ian, if he has not married her to another man, but he cannot have in-tercourse with a pagan slave. Jews and Christians have the same right regarding their female slaves, except that they have to wait a certain period (generally from a month to three months) after the ac-quisition of a female slave before they can have intercourse with her.

---

[159] A *Dictionary of Islam.* 1965 ed., "Slavery."

[160] *Sahih Muslim,* vol. 1, p. 2.

[161] *Hidayah,* vol. IV, p. 282.

[162] *Exodus,* XXI: 20.

There is absolutely no limit to the number of slave-girls with whom a Muslim may cohabit.[163]
Tabari writes:

> "The Prophet sent Ibn Abi out with a party of sixteen men. They were away for fifteen nights. Their share of booty was twelve camels for each man; each camel was valued in the accounting as being twelve sheep. After the people whom they had raided fled in various directions, they took their women, including one young woman who was very beautiful. She fell to Abu Qatadah. The Prophet asked Abu Qatadah for her. He said' 'she came from the spoils.' The Messenger said, 'Give her to me.' So, Abu Qatadah gave her to him, and the prophet gave her to Mahmiyah."[164]

It can be truly said that, no commodity could be traded easier than a slave in the Islamic culture.

The Scurrilous Tongue of Allah in the Koran

Indecent language is normally the jargon of low-bred, discourteous people who are lacking in civility and good manners. We expect well-bred, educated people to be decent in their speech and behavior and hope that the same courtesy will be extended by all, regardless of birth or education. A curse or imprecation uttered by a person who desires to harm another person, but finds him or herself physically powerless to do so, appeals to a supernatural power to inflict such harm.[165] Amazingly, in the Holy Koran—a religious book sacred to over one billion people—the Almighty Allah calls his human followers "frightened asses," "ignoble," and "base-born creatures." Moreover, He casts imprecations upon them and wishes them death. The following excerpts from verses in the Koran illustrate this infamy:

---

[163] A *Dictionary of Islam,* 1965, s. v. "Slavery."

[164] Tabari, *The History of at-Tabari,* vol. VIII, p. 151.

[165] Sherif, *A Guide to the Contents of the Koran,* p. 170.

"Ignoble, besides that, base-born." (Koran, LXVIII: 13)
"As if they were frightened asses." (Koran, LXXIV: 50)
"Death to men! How ungrateful are they!" (Koran, LXXX: 17)
"Fie upon you and what you serve besides Allah; what! Do you not understand?" (Koran, XXI: 67)
"Death to the falsehood mongers!" (Koran, LI: 11)

The words of Allah as written in the Koran show His lack of courtesy. In *Sura* LXII of the Koran, Allah resorts to a very didactic analogy as the following:

> "The similitude of those who were charged with [the obligations] of Mosaic Law but who subsequently failed in those obligations is that of a donkey which carries hugh tomes but understands them not. . . . ."

It is so interesting that, in the verses 32 and 60 of *Sura* XXXIX of the Koran, Mohammed condemns lying, saying:

> "Who is more wicked than the man who invents a falsehood about Allah and denies the truth when it is declared to him?" (Koran, XXXIX: 32)
> "On the Day of Judgment, you will see those who told lies against Allah—their faces will be turned back. Is there not in Hell an abode for the haughty?"

If, as the Koran says: 'there is no one more wicked than a man who invents falsehood about Allah,' what would be the retribution of a person who invents a fictitious God, makes Him his own puppet and attributes a whole book of preposterous and, at times, contradictory ideas to Him in order to deceive the people for his own benefit? And, 'if in the Day of Judgment those who told lies against Allah, their faces will be turned black,' then the face of Mohammed should be turned into tar and his abode, according to Dante Alighieri, will be in the eighth circle of Hell with the sowers of scandal, schismatics and heretics.[166]

---

[166] Dante Alighieri, *Divine Comedy,* trans. Lawrence Grant White (New York: Pantheon Books, 1948), pp. 48–49.

Moreover, is it conceivable that a God would use such vulgar language to address his followers? The answer is that Mohammed's God Allah, is the largest of the traditional idols kept among the other 359 idols in the Ka'ba. Therefore, such vulgar words and obscene language is the cultural heritage of His Messenger, a cameleer brought up in a desert.

Allah and His Apostle Discourage Questions about Religion

Given the ambiguity and irrationality of the Koran and Islam itself, it is not surprising that Muslims are warned that if they ask questions about the Islamic faith, they will lose their faith in Islam. Despite the fact that several verses of the Koran (III: 7, XXVI: 2, XXXVI: 69, XLIII: 1, LIV: 17), assert that Allah has made the contents of the book clear and easy to understand and to remember, there are also some verses in the Koran and some *hadith* that prohibit questioning the enigmatic verses of the Koran. Those verses are:

> "O you who believe! Ask not questions about things which, if made plain to you, may cause you trouble . . . ." (Koran, V: 101)
> "Some people before you did ask such questions and on that account lost faith. . . . ." (Koran, V: 102)

In his famous commentary on the Koran, *The Meaning of the Koran,* Abul Ala' Maudoodi exhorts Muslims to stick to their blind faith and not to probe too deeply into Islam.[167] His comment on the above verse is, "The prophet forbade the people to ask questions or to pry into such things."[168]

It was not only in the Koran that Mohammed forbade Muslims to question the faith; in *hadith* also he repeats that asking questions about the faith is not permitted. Sahih al-Bukhari writes, "The

---

[167] Seyyed Abul 'Ala Maudoodi, *The Meaning of the Qur'an,* vol. 3, (Lahore: Islamic Publications, 1982), pp. 76–77.
[168] *Ibid.*

Prophet was asked about things which he did not like, and when the questioner insisted, the prophet got angry . . . ."[169]

Sahih al-Buikhari also has mentioned the following tradition in this regard:

> Narrated Ash-Sha'bi, "The clerk of al-Mughira ibn Shu'ban narrated, Mu'awiya wrote to al-Mughira ibn Shu'ban, 'Write to me something which you have heard from the prophet.' So, al-Mughira wrote, 'I heard the prophet saying,' Allah has hated those who ask many questions about religion."[170]

> Narrated Abu Musa, "The prophet was asked questions which he did not like to reply, but when the questioner insisted, the Prophet became angry."[171]

The taboo regarding questions about the Koran and Islam is due to the fact that the absurdities of the Islamic faith must be hidden; otherwise, no rational person would accept Islam and its fallacious canons. Muslims should believe in Islam and the Koran with blind fanaticism, otherwise the whole structure of the faith would be destroyed. This is the main reason that Islamic jurists and mullahs prohibit non-Arabic Muslims to recite the Koran in any other language than Arabic.

Obviously, asking questions about the Islamic religion is prohibited because there is no cogent explanation for the absurdities mentioned in the Koran. That is why many secularists believe the surest way to turn people away from Islam, is to expose the nonsensical ideas espoused in the Koran. However, Muslims (as do Christians and Jews) believe in their religion out of faith rather than rational or informed knowledge. They follow their hereditary faith and do not know the Prophet of their religion very well. They live in ignorance and follow rituals learned by rote. I am reminded of the story about the old devote Persian lady who every day "read" the Arabic Koran before saying her prayers. Her daughter gave her a copy of the Koran translated from Arabic to Farsi. A few days later, the daughter

---

[169] *Sahih al-Bukhari,* vol. 1, No. 92.

[170] *Sahih al-Bukhari,* vol. 2, p. 323; vol. 1, p. 76.

[171] *Ibid.,* vol. 1, p. 75.

noticed that the Farsi translation was on the bookshelf and her mother was "reading" from the Arabic one. She enquired of her mother why she did not use the Farsi version and her mother replied:

"When I 'read' the old book, I feel that I am praying to God. After I read the Farsi translation I understood more about Islam and didn't feel that I was praying to a Holy Being, so I went back to the Arabic book".

Suppose a Muslim asks an Imam to explain verses 92 to 98 of *Sura* XVIII and also verses 96 to 97 of *Surah* XXI of the Koran that describe the Gog and Magog, two tribes who are hidden behind a dam on the earth and will appear on the Day of Judgment to attack the people. "Where is the dam?" "How have these two tribes survived there for several thousands of years?" "Why have the scientists who have explored space and celestial bodies not been able to locate the location of these two tribes on the earth?" How could the Imam answer these questions?

Or, suppose a Muslim should ask him, "Why has no one proven the existence of the *jinn,* the creatures that the Koran speaks about in *Sura* LXXII?" There can be found tens of questions like those! The standard answer is, "No one knows the answer to such questions, except Allah," thus demonstrating that Muslims have abandoned all rational and scientific thought. Such an answer should move the questioner to exert his common sense and abandon the stupid superstitious beliefs that Mohammed fabricated to make his deceitful business flourish.

The verse 105 of *Sura* V noted above, was invented to counter such free thinking. This is precisely why Muslims protect their doctrine by attacking anyone who quotes from their Scriptures.[172] There is no doubt that if Muslims were liberated from the oppression of this religion, mankind will be saved from the scourge of Islamic terrorism.

It seems that Mohammed himself knew that the baseless rot in the Koran would incriminate him. For that reason, he ordered the Muslims not to take the Koran with them into other lands. This injunction has been explained in Sahih Muslim:

---

[172] Winn, *Muhammad, Prophet of Doom,* p. 169.

"It has been narrated on the authority of Abdullah ibn Omar that the Messenger of Allah said, "Do not take the Koran on a journey with you, for I am afraid lest it should fall into the hands of the enemy." Ayyub (one of the narrators of the chain transmitters) said, "The enemy may seize it and may quarrel with you over it."[173]

"The Koran," Zwemer writes, "may not be sold to unbelievers, and soldiers are advised not to take it with them into hostile territory for fear the unbelievers should take hold of it."[174] The Islamic manner in keeping Muslims unaware of the irrationality of Islam is in full conformity with the philosophical dictum which says, "Faith in something which we do not know anything about and we can never obtain any knowledge about, makes faith in a religion secure and steadfast."

Ibn Khaldun writes, "Historians and commentators of the Koran and eminent translators have committed frequent errors in reporting stories and events. They accepted them as they were transmitted, without regard for their value. They did not check them with the principles underlying historical events, nor did they measure them with the yardstick of philosophy, with the help of knowledge of the nature of things, nor with historical insight. Therefore, they strayed from the truth and found themselves lost in the desert of untenable assumptions and errors."[175]

It seems that the great historian, Ibn Khaldun perceived the contents of the Koran and Islamic *hadith* as rational ideas and proper teachings; philosophical writings worthy of critical evaluation. He ignores the premise that when an idea or theory is to be judged, it must undergo critical evaluation by means of scientific tests, analysis of provenance, *et cetera.* If a theory appears baseless and preposterous, it is not worthy of being tested and should be ignored. If an insane person, states that "God is holding the sky, so it won't fall over the earth," everybody will simply scoff at such an idea, without bothering to test it. When verse 65 of *Sura* XXII of the Koran, says the same thing, everybody should have the same reaction.

---

[173] *Sahih Muslim,* chapter DCCLXXVI, pp. 1040–1041.

[174] Samuel Zwemer, *Studies in Popular Islam* (London: The Sheldon Press, 1939), p. 80.

[175] Ibn Khaldun, *Mughaddima.*

Therefore, it can be said that Muslims either do not read their scripture and are unaware of the baseless contents of the Koran, or else they read the Koran with the blinded eyes of unquestioning faith, ignoring the many fallacies and contradictions therein. There is a Latin axiom *Credo quia absurdum*—I know it is absurd, still I would like to believe it. Psychologically speaking, one may unconsciously think one feels better by abandoning common sense, embracing ignorance and believing in absurdities. "The way [in order] to see by faith," says Benjamin Franklin, "one has to shut the eye of reason."

The reason that the author of this book has written several books, exposing the pitilessness of Islam and impostures of Mohammed is the emergence of several fundamentalist religious Islamic governments such as in Iran, Sudan, Saudi Arabia, and so on. The tyrannical leaders of such governments have trodden on the human rights of their people. Under the pretext of serving Allah and hiding behind scriptures and the sayings of a false and importuning Prophet, they have perpetrated shameless atrocities against the people of their nations. Such inhumanities justify the author spending his life unveiling the terrible and irrational principles enshrined in the Koran.

Islamic Scholars' Evaluation of the Koran

The average Muslim believes that the Koran is the infallible word of God as revealed to Mohammed through the angel Gabriel and whatever is written therein is eternal and copied from an Original Tablet kept in Heaven. However, many scholars believe that the Koran is terrible book, lacking any pretence of sensible organization by subject, context, or chronology. Among others, Clair Tisdall, in his brilliant work entitled The Original Sources of the Qur'an has shown with remarkable power and erudition that much of this book is related to events and people whom Mohammed knew in his daily life. If so, the Koran should be considered nothing more than a collection of the legends and traditions of the nomadic Arabs of the early seventh century. Clair Tisdall writes:

> "The morality of the Qur'an, its view of the Divine nature, its anachronisms, and its many defects make it impossible for us to doubt that it is Mohammed's own composition. When *Surahs* are arranged in

the chronological order of their composition and compared with the events in Mohammed's life, we see that there is much truth in the statement that the passages were—not, as Muslims say, *revealed,* but—composed from time to time, as occasion required, to sanction each new departure [folly or whim] made by Mohammed. The Qur'an is a faithful mirror of the life and character of its author. It breathes the air of the desert, it enables us to hear the battle cries of the Prophet's followers as they rushed to the onset, it reveals the working of Mohammed's own mind, and shows the gradual declension of his character as he passes from the earnest and sincere though visionary enthusiast into the conscious impostor and open sensualist. All this is clear to every unprejudiced reader of the book."[176]

Rana Kabbani cites two remarks by Fay Weldon and Conor Cruise O'Brien. In *Sacred Cows,* her contribution to the Rushdie debate, Weldon writes:

"The Koran is food for no thought. It is not a poem on which a society can be safely or sensibly based. It gives weapons and strength to the thought-police, the thought-police are easily set marching, and they frighten . . . I see it as a limiting text when it comes to the comprehension of what I define as God."[177]

However, Conor Cruise O'Brien, reverting to the tradition that makes any respect for Islam a cultural defection, writes:

"Muslim society looks profoundly repulsive . . . It looks repulsive because it is repulsive . . . A Westerner who claims to admire Muslim society, while still adhering to Western values, is either a hypocrite or an ignoramus or a bit of both . . . Arab society is sick, and has been sick for a long time. In the last century, the Arab thinker Jamal al-Afghani wrote, 'Every Muslim is sick, and his only remedy is the Koran.' Unfortunately, the sickness gets worse the more the remedy is taken."[178]

---

[176] W. St. Clair Tisdall, *The Original Sources of the Qur'an* (New York: E.S. Gorham, 1905), p. 27.

[177] Fay Weldon, *Sacred Cows* (London: 1989), pp. 6, 12, quoted in Karen Armstrong, *Muhammad, A Biography of the Prophet* (San Francisco, 1992), p. 43.

[178] Conor Cruise O'Brien, *The Times,* 11 May 1989, quoted in Armstrong, *Muhammad, A Biography of the Prophet,* p. 43.

The use of abrogation of previously recorded dogma also makes a mockery of the Muslim contention that the Koran is an unalterable reproduction of the original scriptures, produced and preserved in heaven. If Allah's words are uncreated, unalterable, eternal, and of universal significance how, then, can they be changed? Does abrogation of some verses of the Koran, mean that God sometimes loses his wisdom and makes mistakes? According to William Muir, some 200 verses of the Koran have been canceled by later ones. Thus we have the strange situation that not all the passages of the Koran are true and, if Mohammed were still alive, subject to modification depending upon his needs or lusts. We are told to believe that the entire Koran as recited is the word of God, and at the same time abide by the fact that many passages of the book are "untrue."[179]

Abu Bakr, the successor of Mohammed, made the first collection of the *Sura* that make up the Koran. Abu Bakr's motive in compiling the Koran was that a man named Mosailema in Yemama, hoped to achieve the same selfish ends as Mohammed by calling himself a prophet. To bolster his claims, Mosailama composed a Koran and published it for his followers. Abu Bakr thought it necessary to publish Mohammed's Koran in order to oppose the upstart impostor and propagate the True Faith of Islam to which he was devoted.

So many contradictions and absurdities were discovered in the book that Othman, the Caliphate, deemed it necessary to refine it and put it in a better form. To further this project, he ordered all copies be tendered to him under the pretext of correcting them; then he commanded them to be burned. He then compiled and published the one that is now used by Muslims. This was done in the 32nd year of the Hijra, in the year 652 CE, twenty-one years after the death of Mohammed. The book has undergone no other corrections.[180] A reader who finds in the current Koran so many solecisms, can imagine how ridiculous it must have been before Othman refined it.

Although one may be dispassionately neutral in this research, it soon becomes apparent that the Koran is saturated with all matter

---

[179] Ibn Warraq, *Why I am not a Muslim,* p. 115.

[180] Toby Lester, "What is the Koran," in Ibn Warraq, ed., and trans. *What the Koran Really Says,* p. 121.

of obscurity. The Koran claims for itself that it is "*mubeen,*" or "clear," but every fifth sentence or so simply does not make sense.
Robert Morey writes:

> "Muslims believe that Allah in heaven, before the advent of Mohammed, wrote the Koran on a stone tablet and its text is eternal and unchangeable. If so, the question remains, why then Othman took the labor to standardize common text and destroyed all the "other" manuscripts? Moreover, we know that many people recited Othman's text in favor of their own texts and Othman was compelled to use the threat of death to force the people to accept his revised text."[181]

Charles Adams says, "It must be emphasized that far from there being a single text passed down inviolate from the time of Othman's commission, literally thousands of variant readings of particular verses were known . . . ."[182]
Arthur Jeffrey also explains that Muslims try to conceal any variant version that seem to differ from Othman text. He writes:

> "[The late Professor Bergstrasser] was engaged in taking photographs for the Archive and had photographed a number of the early Kufic Codices in the Egyptian Library when I drew his attention to one in Azhar Library that possessed certain curious features. He sought permission to photograph that also, but permission was refused and the Codex withdrawn from access, as it was not consistent with orthodoxy to allow a Western scholar to have knowledge of such a text . . . With regard to such a variant as did survive there were definite efforts at suppression in the interests of orthodoxy"[183]

Many Western and Eastern writers, even Muslim authorities, have considered the Koran a misleading book that has no divine characteristics or ethical value. The content of the Koran has made even less impression upon Western scholars. Voltaire called it an in-

---

[181] Robert Morey, *The Islamic Invasion* (Eugene, Oregon: Harvest House Publishers, 1992), p. 125.

[182] Charles. E. Adams, "Quran: The Text and its History," in ER, pp. 157–76, quoted by Ibn Warraq, *Why I am not a Muslim,* p. 109.

[183] Quoted in Ibn Warraq, *Why I am not a Muslim,* p. 110.

comprehensible book that violates common sense on every page. Most European readers have found that the Koran is most boring. George Sale wrote, "It is certainly one of the most convincing proofs that Mohammedanism was nothing other than a human invention."[184] Maxim Rodinson has written, "It is evident that I do not believe that the Koran is the book of Allah."[185]

Maxim Rodinson writes that he firmly believes that the Koran is *not* the revelation of a supreme being.[186]

In 1280 also Ibn Kammuna wrote, "the people generally convert to Islam only in terror or in quest of power, or to avoid heavy taxation, or to escape humiliation, or if taken prisoner, or because of infatuation with a Muslim woman."[187] If the Koran is considered aesthetically, by no means can it be considered interesting. Ali Dashti, an Iranian Muslim scholar, vehemently denies any of the miracles ascribed to Mohammed by some proselytizing Muslim "scholars." After Dashti, reviewed the grammatical, syntactic and other aberrations of the Koran, he stated that it contained more than one hundred aberrations from the normal rules and structures of Arabic grammar.[188]

Commenting upon these errors in the Koran, Ali Dashti writes:

"The Koran contains sentences which are incomplete and not intelligible; foreign words, unfamiliar Arabic words, and words used with other than the normal meaning; adjectives and verbs inflected without observance of the concords of gender and number; illogically and ungrammatically applied pronouns which sometimes have no referent [dangling modifiers]; and predicts which in rhymed passages are often

---

[184] Norman Daniel, *Islam and the West* (Edinburgh: Edinburgh University Press, 1960), p. 300.

[185] Rodinson, *Mohammed,* pp. 217–218.

[186] *Ibid.*

[187] Ibn Kammuna, *Examination of the Three Faiths,* trans. Moshe Perlmann (Berkley and Los Angeles: 1971), quoted in Ibn Warraq, *Why I am not a Muslim,* p. 3.

[188] Ali Dashti, *Twenty-Three Years: A Study of the Career Prophetic of Mohammed* (London: 1985), pp. 48–50.

remote from the subjects . . . To sum up, more than one hundred Koranic aberrations from the normal rules and structure of Arabic have been noted."[189]

The Mu'tazilites, an Islamic sect, came into being in the second Islamic century, 1 A.H. Some researchers call them the "freethinkers of Islam," while others have called them "rationalists." They believed that the Koran was written by Mohammed himself and deny its revelation to the Prophet by God. They asserted that there is nothing miraculous in the Koran and that Arabians could have composed something not only equal, but superior to it, in eloquence, method, and purity of language.[190]

The Abbasid Caliph al-Ma'mun adopted the Mu'tazilites ideas about the Koran and ordered the chief officials in every province throughout the Islamic empire to publicly announce that the dogma in the Koran was created by Mohammed rather than Allah.

Many other Islamic enlightened figures, including Djad ibn Dirham, Ibn Abi-l-Awja, and Abul Athiya believed that the Koran did not possess any divine characteristics and was made up by Mohammed. These first two scholarly critics were executed.

The German scholar, Solomon Reinach, writes:

> "From the literary point of view, the Koran has little merit. Declamation, repetition, puerility, a lack cohesiveness and coherence strike the unprepared at every turn. It is humiliating to the human intellect to think that this mediocre literature has been the subject of innumerable commentaries and that millions of men are still wasting time in absorbing it."[191]

Craig Winn writes:

> "No one has to dig deep to find the truth. Even a cursory reading of the Koran is sufficient to prove that it is a fraud. There is no way the creator of the universe wrote a book devoid of context, without chronology or intelligent traditions. Such a creative spirit would not need to pla-

---

[189] *Ibid.,* p. 48.

[190] *Koran,* trans. George Sale (London: 1896), p. 53.

[191] Quoted in Winn, *Muhammad, Prophet of Doom,* p. 573.

giarize. He would know history and science and thus would not have made such a fool of himself. The God who created man would not deceive him or led him to hell as Allah does. Nor would he order men to terrorize, mutilate, rob, enslave, and slaughter the followers of other Scriptures he claims he revealed, wiping them out to the last. One does not need a scholastic review of the Koranic text to disprove its veracity. It destroys itself quite nicely.[192] It condones rape, incest, thievery, kidnapping for ransom, the slave trade, mass murder, and worst of all, would conquest by way of sword. In addition, it is a literary disaster with grammatical errors, missing words, and meaningless words. It is little more than a childish rant revealing the demented, decadent, and delusional nature of its author. It is unsound in every way."[193]

On another occasion Winn writes, "Personally, I share William Muir's contention that: 'The Koran is the most stubborn enemy of Civilization, Liberty, and the Truth which the world has ever known.'"[194]

All of the above quotations and references reinforce the author's contention that the Koran is a mishmash of calumny created by a man to justify his own thievery and prurience. One might mourn for and pity those poor fools who have embraced this man-made religion, the heirs of greedy, avaricious Bedouin Arabs who first followed the lure of religiously sanctioned looting and rapine.

---

[192] *Ibid.*, p. IX.

[193] *Ibid.*, p. XIX–XX.

[194] *Ibid.*, p. XXXIX.

CHAPTER THREE

ABSURDITIES OF THE KORAN

All religions, with gods, demigods, prophets, messiahs, and saints, are the product of the fancy and credulity of men who have not yet reached the full development and complete possession of their intellectual powers.

M. A. Bakunin: *Dieu et l'etat,* **1871**

To hide the irrational and vile messages of the Koran, Muslim clerics claim that it cannot be translated and should only be recited in its original language, Arabic. The truth of the matter is that they simply don't want anyone to know what Allah's book actually says. They know it is rubbish and that it preaches hate, violence, and intolerance. They know that it promotes immorality and encourages terrorism. That is not to say that the Koran is completely void of uplifting thought. About five percent of it, taken out of context and translated, can be construed as peaceful and tolerant.[195] But as a whole, the contents of the Koran are fallacious and irrational as we shall see in the following chapters.

Allah Before Creation

One of the companions of Mohammed asked him. "Where was our Lord before he created the Heavens and the earth?" Mohammed replied, "In a cloud with air above and underneath it. Then he created His Throne as the first thing upon the water and sat straight on it. . . . And all that was going to be was written on the memorial tablet before anything else was created."[196]

---

[195] Winn, *Muhammed, Prophet of Doom,* p. XXI.
[196] Tabari, *The History of al-Tabari,* vol. I, p, 204.

In explaining the location of Allah before creation, it seems that Allah's messenger was mouthing pure fantasy. The actual "location" of Allah before his creation by Mohammed was among the trees of the Arabian Peninsula. The Arabs created an idol from the wood of those trees and placed it among the other idols kept in Ka'ba. However, since the Arabs made this particular idol bigger than the other 359 idols kept in Ka'ba, they called it "Allah-o-Akbar," meaning Allah is greater than the other idols. Thus the almighty, all-knowing, all-powerful God Allah began his career as a log!

Allah Transmogrifies Transgressors

The Koran says that there was once a town located on the sea shore. Allah told the inhabitants of the town not to catch fish from the sea on the Sabbath day. Quite interestingly, on the Sabbath day, the fish swam up to the shoreline and stuck their heads out of the water, tempting the villagers to catch them. The fish did not do this on the other days of the week.

Some of the inhabitants of the town ignored the warnings of Allah and caught fish on the Sabbath day whilst others complied with His injunctions concerning Sabbatical behavior. The All-knowing, All-seeing Allah noticed that some of the villagers in their insolence disobeyed his warnings, so He turned them into monkeys, telling them, "Become monkeys! You nasty evil-doers [are] despised and rejected."

If the more skeptical readers of this book are hesitant to believe this miracle of Allah, please open the Koran to *Sura* 2 and read verse 65 and then, *Sura* 7, verses 163–166. See also Sahih al-Bukhari, vol. IV, chapter 32, p. 415. The following are the germane passages of the Koran:

> "You have surely heard of those of you that violated the Sabbath. We said to them, 'You shall be changed into detested monkeys.' We made them an example to their own generation and to those who followed them and a lesson to the righteous." (Koran, II: 65)
> "Ask them about the town which overlooked the sea and what befell its people when they broke the Sabbath. Each Sabbath, their fish used to appear before them floating on water, but on the week-days they never came near them. Thus we tempted the people because they

had done wrong. And when one group of them said, 'Why do you admonish men whom Allah had doomed to destruction or to terrible punishment?' They replied, 'We admonish them so that we may be free from blame in the sight of your Lord, and that they may guard themselves against evil.' Therefore, when they forgot the warning they had been given, we saved those who were forbidding evil, and sternly punished the wrongdoers for their misdeeds. And when they had scornfully persisted in what they had been forbidden, we said to them, 'Be miserable monkeys.'" (Koran, VII: 163–166)

In *Sura* 5 of the Koran, Allah becomes even nastier, extending his wrath to non-Jews. He states that He has transformed those who incurred His curse and His wrath into apes and swine:

> "Say, [to Christians and Jews] "Shall I point out to you something much worse than this, (as judged) by the treatment it received from Allah?. . . . .Those who incurred the curse of Allah and His wrath, those of who some he transformed into apes and swine . . . ." (Koran, V: 63)

Mankind should be indeed grateful to Allah that he had never taken greater advantage of His miraculous power over us sinful creatures to teach us an admonitory lesson. But who knows, perhaps many of the apes living in the forests and zoos, are former humans whom Allah transmogrified!

Allah and His She-Camel

Allah ordered a female camel be sent to the people of the Thamud tribe in order to try them. He ordered them to let the she-camel graze on His earth and not to hurt her in any way. Particularly, Allah emphasized that if ever they should harm the camel, they would be seized by a terrible punishment. The Apostle of Allah (Salih) also told the Thamud tribe that the camel belonged to Allah and warned them not to hinder her from drinking. But the Thamud rejected him. One of the tribesmen took a sword in his hand and, insolently defying the order of the Lord, ham-strung her then slew her. To punish the people of the Thamud tribe, Allah sent against them a mighty earthquake and they became like the dry straw used by one who beds cattle pens. The passages of the Koran describing this fable say:

"And to Thamud We sent their brother Salih. He said, "Serve Allah, my people for you have no God but Him. A clear proof has come to you from your Lord. Here is Allah's she-camel: assign for you. Leave her to graze at will in Allah's land and do not molest her, lest you incur a woeful punishment . . . ." (Koran, VII: 73)

"Those who were haughty said, 'We deny all that you believe in;' they slaughtered the she-camel and defied the commandment of their Lord, saying to Salih, 'Bring down the scourge, with which you threaten us if you truly are one of the messengers.'" (Koran, VII: 77)

"[The]Thamud, too disbelieved Our warnings. They said, 'Are we to follow a man who stands alone among us? We would surely then fall into error and madness. Did he alone among us receive this warning? He is indeed a foolish liar.'" (Koran, LIV: 23)

"To him we said, 'Tomorrow they shall know who the foolish liar is. We are sending to them a she-camel, that We may put them to the proof. Observe them closely and have patience. Tell them that the water is to be divided between (her and) them and that every share of the water should be attended.' They called their friend, who took a knife and slew her. I warned them, and then how stern was My punishment and warnings! Then We sent against them a single mighty blast and they became like the dry stubble used by one who pens cattle." (Koran, LIV: 26–31)

"Thamud people rejected their Apostle in their rebellious pride when the wicked of them broke forth. Allah's Apostle said to them, 'This is Allah's she-camel. Let her drink. They disbelieved him, and slaughtered her. So their Lord destroyed them for their sins and raised their city to the ground . . . .'" (Koran, XCI: 11–15)

Allah Turns a Persian Woman into the Planet Venus

"Believe it or not!" Verse 102 of Sura II recognizes "witchcraft" in Islam and, more importantly, so does all the interpreters of the Koran. According to the tenor of this verse, the planet Venus had once been a beautiful Persian woman whom Allah had turned into the planet Venus. This verse states:

"And they believed what the devils said about Solomon's kingdom. Not that Solomon disbelieved; but the devils did, teaching the people witchcraft and that which was revealed in Babylon to the two angels, Harut and Marut. Yet those two angels did not teach anybody without saying to him beforehand: 'We have been sent to tempt you; do not disbelieve.' From these two, they learn that by which they can create discord between husband and wife, although they can harm none with what they learn except by Allah's permission. They learn, indeed, what harms them and does not profit them; yet they know full well that any one who chose it would have no share in the life to come. Vile is that for which they have sold their souls, if they but knew it! Had they embraced the faith and kept from evil far better for them would his reward have been, if they knew it."

Most early commentators, including Ibn Mas'ud, Ibn Abbas, Abdullah ibn Omar, and Qatadah, as well as a large number of contemporary interpreters have covered this incident in their writings, but this author will draw mainly upon the comprehensive research that Dr. Mahmoud Ayoub[197] has brilliantly accomplished in his two volume book.

He has critically reviewed the observations of various authors who have commented on this verse of the Koran. According to Dr. Ayoub, interpreters of this verse agree that at the time of the Prophet Enoch (Idris), when the children of Adam had increased on earth and committed acts of disobedience, the angels of the sky, heavens, earth, and mountains appealed to Allah, in an attempt to incite His anger against mankind. They said to Allah, "Our Lord, would you not destroy these sinners from the earth?" Allah replied, "I have put lust into the hearts of the children of Adam. Had I done the same thing to you and given Satan authority over you and you were to descend to earth, you would do the same." The angels did not agree with Allah's explanation and believed in their hearts that if they were sent down to earth, they would not commit sin.

In order to prove His contention, Allah commanded the angels to choose the best among them. The angels consulted one another and, finally, chose three angels who were the strongest willed and the most critical of human beings. These three angels were called, "Uzza," "Uzaya," and "Uzryaeel." Allah then created in these angels the faculties of eating, drinking, lust, fear, and hope, just as He had in the children of Adam and commanded them thusly: "Go down to

---

[197] Dr. Mahmoud Ayoub, *The Qur'an and its, Interpreters,* vol. 1, (Albany: State University of new York, 1984) pp. 128–136.

earth, rule over the children of Adam but beware that you do not associate anything with me [do so in My name], kill the soul which I have prohibited to be slain, commit adultery, or drink wine."[198]

For a while, the angels complied with the commands of Allah; they ruled the earth and judged among men justly by day and ascended to heaven by night. One of these three angels, "Uzryaeel" was smart enough that on the very first day, feeling himself too weak to resist earthly temptations, he requested that he be taken back to heaven. The other two, named "Harut" and "Marut" remained on earth and continued to rule over human beings. They are mentioned in the Koran.[199]

This interpretation presents the basic elements of the story as accepted by the most classical commentators.[200] Some *hadith,* however, relate the story of the two angels to Allah's revelation in verse 30 of *Sura* II of the Koran, saying:

> "When your Lord said to the angels' 'I am putting a vice-regent on the earth,' they replied, 'Will you place one who will spread corruption in it and shed blood, while we sing Your praise and glorify Your sanctity?' He said, 'I know what you do not know.'"

According to this view, Allah sent down Harut and Marut to earth to demonstrate to the protesting angels man's uniqueness as a creature endowed with special faculties which even angels could not possess without also falling into sin and disobedience.[201]

A beautiful Persian woman called Zohreh (Venus) brought a dispute with her husband before the angels (Harut and Marut), and sought their help in resolving it. The angels, however, could not resist her beauty. They fell in love with her and propositioned her to separate her from her husband and sleep with them. She agreed. Then they took her to a certain place to consummate the act. She

---

[198] Ibn Kathir, vol. 1, pp. 241–242; Tabarsi, vol. 1, pp.395–96; quoted in Dr. Ayoub, *The Qur'an and its, Interpreters,* vol. 1, p. 132.

[199] Tabari, *The history of at-Tabari,* vol. II, p. 428f., quoted in Dr. Ayoub, *The Qur'an and its, Interpreters,* vol. 1, p. 131.

[200] Dr. Ayoub, *The Qur'an and its, Interpreters,* vol. 1, p. 131.

[201] Nisaburi, vol. 1, p. 242, quoted in Dr. Ayoub, *The Qur'an and its, Interpreters,* vol. 1, p. 132.

told them that she was an idolater and she would submit herself to them on the condition that they renounce their faith in Allah and adopt her creed. They answered, "We shall never deny Allah." She left them and returned later with an infant. When they again asked her to submit herself to them, she said, she would do that provided that they would kill the infant. Again they refused. She next returned with a bottle of wine and suggested they drink it. They were so sorely tempted and frustrated that they drank the wine. Then, in their drunkenness, they committed adultery with her, killed an innocent baby, and renounced Allah. When the angels awoke from their drunkenness, the woman reproached them saying, "You left nothing undone which you refused to do before drinking wine and becoming intoxicated."[202]

When the angels tried to ascend home to heaven that night, they were not permitted to do so, nor were their wings able to carry them. They begged a righteous man of the children of Adam for help. He answered, "How can the inhabitants of the earth intercede for the inhabitants of heaven?" They said, "We heard that your Allah speaks well of you in heaven." The man prayed for them and his prayers were answered.

Thus, the fallen angels were given the choice between the punishment of this world or that of the world to come. They chose the punishment of this world.[203] Whereupon Allah ordered them to be chained with heavy iron chains, hung upside down by their feet with their heads in a well in Babylonia as their punishment in this world. Part of their punishment was that water be held in front of their mouths but out of reach (Enc 273). According to some authors, Allah ordered Harut and Marut to teach humans magical practices on earth in order that they would be able to oppose those who claimed prophethood falsely.[204]

As to the fate of Venus who deceived the angels, it is said that when the angels were intoxicated, she learned from them the word

---

[202] Ibn Kathir, vol. 1, quoted in Dr. Ayoub, *The Qur'an and its, Interpreters,* vol. 1, p. 132.

[203] Tabari, *The History of at-Tabari,* quoted in Dr. Ayoub, *The Qur'an and its, Interpreters,* vol. 1, p. 131.

[204] Dr. Ayoub, *The Qur'an and its, Interpreters,* vol. 1, p. 135.

by which they were able to ascend to heaven and also the word to descend to earth. She uttered the word for ascension and flew to the sky, but Allah caused her to forget the word to descend. Allah then changed her into a radiant heavenly body and named it *Venus*.[205] It is related that whenever, Abdullah ibn Omar, one of the close companions of Mohammed who had heard the story of Venus from him, saw that planet in the night, he cursed her, saying, "She is the one who tempted Harut and Marut."[206]A. Geiger has noted that these elements are mentioned in the Jewish Midrash and the book of Jude in the Old Testament.[207]

We may now consider ourselves expert astronomers. Verse 102 of *Sura* II of the Koran brilliantly teaches us that planet Venus was a beautiful Persian lady, and because she deceived two angels of Allah, He changed her to a planet, called Venus (in Arabic *Zohreh*). The stupid tropology that inspired the invention of such inane fiction has inadvertently undermined Allah, His Prophet, and the metaphysical sources with which they intended to buttress their own beliefs. The following points are worthy of consideration in this regard:

1. Verse 102 of *Sura* II of the Koran openly recognizes witchcraft and sorcery as factual practices and Allah even assigns Harut and Marut to teach magic and witchcraft to human beings. By entitling *Sura* LXXII of the Koran "*Jinn*," Muslims seem to endorse the idea that magic and sorcery are real.
2. The Almighty Allah puts lust in the hearts of angels, thus giving them the potential to do evil, then, because they so do, he punishes them by chaining them with heavy chains and hanging them by their feet with their heads in a well in Babylonia. This is called the justice of Allah and Islam.
3. It is so interesting that although Allah himself admits that he had endowed the nature of human beings with lust and gave

---

[205] Ibn kathir, vol. 2, p. 242, quoted in Dr. Ayoub, *The Qur'an and its, Interpreters,* vol. 1, p. 135.

[206] Tabari, *The History of at-Tabari,* quoted in Dr. Ayoub, *The Qur'an and its, Interpreters,* vol. 1, p. 136.

[207] *First Encyclopedia of Islam 1913–1936,* ed. s. v. "Harut and Marut," by "A. J. Wensinck."

Satan the authority to mislead them and make them to commit sin, still He is so kind and just to his human creatures that he roasts them in Hell because of wrong-doing that He perpetrated via Satan.

4. It is amazing that in none of the historical records, even in the non-Islamic religious myths, is there any mention of the time and place wherein Harut and Marut ruled over humankind for a while, or is there any indication of the location of the angel's prison-well in Babylonia or elsewhere.

5. Why, among all nationalities of the world, was a Persian woman chosen by the fiction writers to deceive Allah's angels and, as a result, changed to a planet?

There may be two reasons behind that: first, Mohammed himself was inimical to the Persians and in verse 2 of *Sura* XXX of the Koran predicted that the Romans will defeat the Persians. Mohammed hated the Persians so much that, according to Al-Muttaqi, he has said, "May Allah curse both lots of foreigners, the Persians and the Byzantines (Rome). The ruin of the Arabs will come when the sons of the daughters of Persia grow up."[208] Secondly, the beauty of the Persian women has been known throughout the history, particularly among the Arabs. They have always wished to have a Persian woman as their wife.

Solomon Talbure in this regard is articulate:

> "Another great tragedy of rich and advanced and peaceful people with a great culture were the Persians, the Iranians. Before the Arab armies invaded and plundered that country, Iran was a center of many great scholars and thinkers who had influenced Judaism and Christianity in profound ways. When the Arabs invaded Persia they plundered it, they robbed the Persians of all their riches, they made it a point to kill most of the males because Persian women were among the most beautiful in the whole world. Persian women were so delicate and beautiful that they were the pride of the Persians, and poets throughout the world wrote of them. Men from the farthest reaches of the world

---

[208] Al-Muttaqi, *Kanz ul-Ummal,* VII, page 204, quoted in *Islam: From the Prophet Muhammad to the Capture of Constantinople,* ed. and trans. by Bernard Lewis, vol. 2 (London: The MacMillan Press Ltd., 1974), p. 196.

sought to obtain a wife from Persia for thousands of years. Once the Arabs invaded, Iran was no more; it is still there in name, but it is now a most tyrannical Islamic Arab theocracy. The pinnacle of glory Persia once had was thrust into the ground almost overnight by Allah's savages."[209]

6. It was so gracious of Allah to prohibit His angels from killing any earthly mortals, but why did he not issue the same rule for His beloved prophet Mohammed? Is the shedding of blood on earth a sin for angels, but legitimate for the Prophet? If slaying innocent people is a sin, why did Allah reveal in so many messages to His Prophet, orders to kill so many innocent individuals and commit so many atrocities on Earth?

If someone suffering from both an inferiority complex and megalomania rises to become the leader of a nation, then he will probably behave as Mohammed did in order to satisfy his irrational desires and assuage his psychological needs.[210]

Elephants are Defeated by Birds

The contents of *Sura* CV of the Koran are indeed a source of laughter and amusement. This *Sura* contains five verses, which say:

1. Seest thou not how thy Lord dealt with the Companions of the Elephant?
2. Did He not make their treacherous plan go astray?
3. And He sent against them Flights of Birds
4. Striking them with stones of baked clay.
5. Then did He make them like an empty field of stalks and straw of which the corn has been eaten up.

All the interpreters of the Koran agree that this *Sura* refers to an incident that occurred during the invasion of Mecca by Abraha, the

---

[209] Solomon Talbure, *President George W. Bush is a Moron, Islam is not Peace* (U.S.A.: Xlibris Corporation: 2002), pp. 24–25.

[210] Please look at chapter 11 of this book.

famous Abyssinian viceroy of Yemen, in the year 570 CE, almost two months before the birth of Mohammed. Abraha, riding on an elephant, was about to capture Mecca when his army was attacked by vast flights of birds dropping pebbles on the Abyssinian troops. According to tradition, this miracle occurred because Abd al-Mutallib, the grandfather of Mohammed and head of the Hashim clan charged with the guardianship of the Ka'ba prayed to the Deity to defend the Ka'ba. At the same time, a smallpox epidemic erupted amongst the invaders and caused their withdrawal. Abraha himself (according to Islamic myth) was afflicted by putrefying sores and died miserably on his return to San'a. Al-Wakidi, after describing this calamity in the fanciful style of the Koran, adds: "And that was the first beginning of smallpox."[211]

Since Abd al-Mutallib died before the rise of Islam,[212] he must have been praying to the idols in the Ka'ba if his prayers were answered by the putative miracle described in *Sura* CV, verses 1–5. These verses are talking about a miracle performed by the idols of the Ka'ba and not by Allah, the Muslim God. Logically then, when Mohammed preaches absolute belief in the words of the Koran he is, in this instance, teaching paganism. If only the believers in Islam understood the contents of their sacred book, they would abandon the fallacious faith conjured by Mohammed!

One of the Koranic scholars, whose *bona fides* are guaranteed by the Al-Azhar University, writes about the contents of the afore mentioned *Sura* as follows:

> "Sura 105 was revealed in the sixth year before the Hijra. It is meant to remind the Quraysh of what befell to Abraha, the Abyssinian ruler of the Yemen that they might fear God and accept the Islamic call. Abraha, who was acting as the viceroy for the Abyssinian king, thought that in order to divert people from pilgrimage to the Ka'ba in Mecca to his own church (Kalis), he would demolish the Ka'ba and subjugate the people of that area. He used elephants in his attack, but they were all destroyed by birds or something like birds flocking in groups, pelting them with clay-stones said to be from hell. Thus the

---

[211] Quoted by Muir, *The Life of Mohammad,* p. cxvi.

[212] Montgomery Watt, *Mohammed, Prophet and Statesman,* p. 80.

Ka'ba was saved. This year is called the Elephant's Year in which the Prophet Mohammed was born (A.D. 570 or 571)."[213]

More interesting and farcical than the above commentary, is the virtue ascribed by *Majma'-al-Bayan* to the reciting of *Sura* CV during prayer

> "On the virtue of reciting this Surah, a tradition from Imam Sadiq says, "He who recites Surah Fil (elephant) in his obligatory prayers, any level land, mountains or any clods of dirt will bear witness for him, on the Day of Judgment that he has been one of the prayerful (believers). And, on that Day, a herald calls saying, 'You are right about my servant. I accept your witness for him or against him. Let him enter Paradise without reckoning him. Verily, he is one of whom he and his action I like.'"[214]

The Oaths of Allah

Many verses of the Koran contain oaths of Allah. Seventy-four verses of the Koran consist wholly, and seven verses partly, of oaths by Allah. An oath is a sacred pledge or promise, signifying an intention to be bound in conscience to the faithful and true performance of certain acts. The oath has its origins in religious customs and has become an accepted part of some secular activities such as in legal proceedings or Boy Scout meetings. Also, when one feels distrust toward a person with whom one is dealing, one may require that person to swear an oath in order to ensure his compliance with certain promises or actions. If that person breaks his oath, presumably divine wrath will descend upon his head. A more certain punishment is inflicted upon one who breaks an oath sworn as a participant in legal procedure (perjury) which may result in fines or incarceration. A person, in the execution of an oath, should swear to sacred authorities or valued entities that stand above him or at least have a unique significance in their life.

---

[213] Dr. M. M. Katib, *The Bounteous Koran,* authorized by A-Azhar (London: McMillan Press, 1984), p. 822.

[214] *Majma'–al-Bayan,* vol. 10, p. 539.

Notwithstanding the fact that there is no sacred or supernatural being above Him, amazingly Allah swears oaths in the Koran, in seventy-four verses wholly and in seven verses partly.[215] There are also some verses in the Koran where the Almighty Allah imprecates his followers. When a person has a conflict of interest with another person and desires to harm him, but finds he is powerless to do so, he appeals to a divine power to affect such harm (e.g. God damn you!). Allah seems to be in the same position as one of His desperate creatures that has no power over his enemy and therefore resorts to cursing and imprecation. Certainly, none of the Koranic oaths or imprecations fit into the characteristics described above and they are therefore *sui generis* in their absurdity.

But, amazingly, in the Koran, the Almighty Allah swears to the following entities:

> Winds (LI: 1), clouds (LI: 2), ships (LI:3), the mountain (LII: 1), Ka'ba (LII: IV), elevated canopy (LII: 5), swollen sea (LII: 6), stars (LIII: 1), pen (LXVIII: 1), resurrection day (LXXV: 1), self reproaching soul (LXXV: 2), dawn (LXXXIX: 1), ten nights (LXXXIX: 2), even and odd (LXXXIX: 3), city (XC: 1), night as it conceals the light (XCII: 1), day (XCII: 2), glorious morning light (XCIII: 1), night (XCIII: 2), fig and the olive (XLV: 1), the Mt. Sinai (XCV: II), horses that run with panting breath (C: 1).

The following are examples of oaths by Allah as written in the Koran:

> "I swear by those who range themselves in ranks, and are strong in repelling demons, and thus proclaim the messages of Allah, verily, verily; your Allah is one, Lord of the heavens and the earth, and all between them, and word of every point at the rising of the sun." (Koran, XXXVII: 1, 5).

Neither the translators, nor the commentators can say who are those "who range themselves in ranks."

---

[215] Sherif, *A Guide to the Contents of the Koran,* pp. 30–31.

"I swear by the scattering winds dispersing and those that lift and bear heavy weights and by the runners that speed gently, and by those that divide the affair, surely, what you are promised is true." (Koran, LI: 1–11).

"By the Mount Tur, by the inscribed Book, in a scroll unfolded, and by the inhabited house, and by the uplifted canopy, and by the swollen sea, your Lord's Doom Day will surely come to pass." (LII: 1–7).

"By the fig and the olive, and the mount of Sinai, and by this safe land, we have created man in the best shape." (XCV: 1–4)

"It needs not to swear by this city and by your lodging in this city, and by the begetter and that which he begot, verily we have created man into toil and struggle." (XC: 1–4)

Translators and interpreters of the Koran have translated the word "begetter" as "Adam," the so-called father of humankind in Semitic religions. If so, it is so interesting that Allah having expelled Adam from heaven because he disobeyed Allah's command, thus committing a sin, is still one by whom Allah still swears in His scriptures.

"By the war steeds, that run with panting breadth, and by those, which strike sparking fire, and by those, which raid at break of day, and raise the dust on high, breaking through to the centers of throng, man is indeed to his lord ungrateful." (Koran, C: 1–6)

"By Nun, the pen and by what they write down, you are not by your Lord's grace, mad or possessed." (LXVIII: 1–2)

"By the star, when it goes down, your companion is neither astray nor being mislead, neither does he speak out of whim." (LIII: 1–3)

"By the night as it conceals the light, by the day as it appears in glory, by the mystery of the creation of male and female, your endeavors have indeed diverse ends." (XCII: 1–4)

In another inconsistency in the Koran, while Allah repeatedly swears to such nonsensical entities, verse 10 of *Sura* LXVIII of the Koran condemns swearing. Most commentators of the Koran, regarding the content that verse, have written, "It is only liars who swear on all occasions, small or great, because their ordinary word is not believed. The true man's word, according, to the proverb, is as good as his bond."[216] This observation becomes laughable when one reads the contents of verses 32 and 60 of *Sura* XXXIX. In those verses, Mohammed severely condemns those who attribute a lie to Allah. But, in so many verses as mentioned above, Mohammed identifies himself with Allah and shamelessly swears on behalf of Him!

A person reading the Koran to understand its contents and not on the basis of his faith, cannot help but conclude that the author is an uncultured megalomaniac, who takes advantage of every opportunity to gain power. Therefore, such preposterous oaths are indicative of the obsessive mentality of a person bent on influencing his fellow Arabic nomads and compelling them to comply with his ambitious desires. When venal commentators take pen in hand to attempt to explain such preposterous ideas, they find it impossible to interpret them in a literal sense and are therefore forced to give them a metaphysical meaning.

Gog and Magog

In several verses, the Koran talks about the Gog and Magog tribes. According to verses 91–98 of *Sura* XVIII, verses 96–97 of *Sura* XXI, and related *hadith,* Gog and Magog are two tribes descended from the children of Japheth, the son of Noah. They are human beings, not mystical creatures, and they are confined inside a dam. At the Resurrection, Allah will allow them to come out of their confinement in gaareat numbers. Corrupt and ill mannered, they will wander throughout the lands, eating and drinking everything they encounter to the extent that they will drink all the water on earth. They will harm the people around them. People will fear them and run for shelter, taking with them their animals and possessions. If such revelations from Allah to His Prophet Mohammed tax the reader's credulity, please look at the following verses of the Koran:

---

[216] *The Holy Koran* (Saudi Arabia: Undated), p. 1794; Abdullah Yusuf Ali, *The Holy Koran,* vol. 2 (New York: Hafner Publishing Company, 1946), p. 1586.

Then he (Zul-Qarnain)[217] followed another road, until he came between the two mountains and found beneath them a people who could barely understand a word. "Zul-Qarnain," they said, "Gog and Magog are ravaging this land. Build us barrier against them and we will pay you tribute." He replied, "The power, which my Lord has given me, is better than any tribute. Lend me a force of laborers, and I will raise a barrier between you and them. Come, bring me blocks of irons." At length, when he dammed up the valley between the two mountains, he said, "Blow with your blows." And when he made the iron blocks red with heat, he said, "Bring me molten brass to pour on them." Thus they (Gog and Magog) could not scale it, nor could they dig their way through it. He said, "This is a mercy from my Lord. However, when my Lord's promise has been fulfilled, he will level it to dust. The promise of my Lord is true." (Koran, XVIII: 91–98)

"When Gog and Magog are let loose and, they swiftly swarm from everywhere rushing headlong down every hill; when the true promise nears its fulfillment; the eyes of the unbelievers will fixedly stare (and they will say), "Woe to us! Of this, we have been heedless. We have done wrong." (Koran, XXI: 96–97)

In this regard, Mohammed himself says:

"Some of them pass by the river, and drink all what passes, leaving it dry. And those who come after them and pass by that river say, 'There was water here.' The leaders of the Gog and Magog say,

---

[217] In 16 verses of chapter 18, the Koran tells the story of Zul-Qarnain. Allah, addresses Mohammed and says, "They ask you about Zul-Qarnain. Say, 'I will rehearse to you something of his story. Verily, we established his power on earth, and we gave him the ways and means to all ends.'"

In his Koran, Yusuf Ali writes' "Zul-Qarnain, literally means, 'the two horned one,' the king with the two horns, or the Lord of two Epochs. Who was he? In what age, and where did he live? The Koran gives us no material on which we can base a positive answer. Nor is it necessary to find an answer, as the story is treated as a Parable. Popular opinion identifies Zul-Qarnain with Alexander the Great. An alternative suggestion is an ancient Persian King, or a pre-historic Hymyarite King.'" (Abdullah Yusuf Ali, *The holy Qur'an* (USA, Brentwood, Maryland: 1992), p. 753.

'These are the people of the land. We are through with them. What are left are those in the sky.'"[218]

In addition, he adds:

"One of them takes a spear and throws it in the sky. The spear comes back to him full of blood. This will bring about disaster and chaos. While they are doing this, Allah will send down worms to the Gog and Magog's necks. Then they will die. Nobody will hear a sound from them."[219]

There is also a very amusing *hadith* about Gog and Magog which shows what a great entertainer and how imaginative the Messenger of Allah was:

"Narrated Zainab bint Jahsh that one day Allah's Apostle entered upon her in a state of fear and said, 'None has the right to be worshipped but Allah! Woe to the Arabs from the Great evil that has approached (them). Today a hole has been opened in the dam [Alexander's iron barrier between the mountains] of Gog and Magag like this.' The Prophet made a circle with his index finger and thumb. Zainab added, 'I said, 'O Allah's Apostle! Shall we be destroyed though there will be righteous people among us?' The Prophet said, 'Yes, if the (number of) evil (persons) increases.'"[220]

Some Koranic commentators identify Zul-Qarnain with Alexander the Great, and yet history says that Alexander was a great Greek general who led a life of debauchery and drunkenness and died at the age of 33. He was an idolater, actually claiming to be the son of the Egyptian sun god Amun. A temple drawing depicting Alexander worshipping Amun is still on display in Egypt. There is no evidence that Alexander built a wall of iron and brass between the two mountains, a feat which would have proven him to be one of the greatest construction engineers in history.[221] It amazing that history has not given Mohammed the epithet, Great Deceiver!

---

[218] *Ibid.,* p. 58.

[219] *Ibid.*

[220] *Sahih al-Bukhari,* vol. IX, no. 249, p. 187.

[221] Winn, *Muhammad, Prophet of Doom,* p. XLVI.

Jinn, Those Invisible Creatures

In all societies and among all races, individuals can be found who, because of their mendacity, egotism or need for popular acclaim, pretend that they have contact with the supernatural world, the world of gods and spirits. The Koran includes twenty-eight examples of this chicanery. This absurdity is illustrated in *Sura* LXXII which talks about the invisible creatures, called *jinn.*

> "When the Apostle of Allah stands for to invoke Him, (the jinns) crowded upon him to listen." (Koran, LXXII: 19)

However, the interesting point is that no one can see these invisible creatures except the impostor Apostle. Allah commands Mohammed in the Koran again and again to tell the people that he is a human being who is but a *Warner.* He is only a Messenger, whose knowledge does not extend to the unseen; He is not an angel, has no access to Allah's treasures, and possesses no unusual power. (Koran, VI: 50, VII, 188). In verse 6 of *Sura* XLI, Allah commands the Apostle to say to the people that he is but a man like them. Still it seems that Mohammed will forget all of these verses and will pretend to have supernatural powers and able to see some creatures (such as *jinns*) that no one else can see.

The Beast with Four Mile Horns

The verse 82 of *Sura* XXVII is so preposterous that no fiction writer could ever have imagined it. This verse says, when the Word is fulfilled against infidels, Allah will produce from the earth a beast to face them. The beast, called "Dabbat-al-Ard," upon emerging, will possess the ring of Solomon, son of David, and the rod of Moses, son of Amran. The beast will make the face of the believer shine brighter with the rod of Moses. It will stamp the nose of the unbeliever with the ring of Solomon until the people of one land will gather together, each one saying, "You are a believer." Of the others, they will say, "You are an unbeliever."

The Prophet described the beast as a huge, furry creature with a tail and long legs.[222] The distance between his horns is six kilometers (about four miles); his head is similar to a cow, his neck to an ostrich, and his chest to a lion.[223] The beast will appear three times after the sun rises from the West. The first time the beast will come from the land of the nomads, but no one from Mecca will know about it. The beast will then disappear. It will come out again, but this time the nomads will know about it. This news about the beast's arrival will spread throughout Mecca. The third time the beast appears, the people in the Great mosque in Mecca will see it coming between the corner of the Ka'ba and the Station of Abraham. When the beast shakes his head, dirt will come off. Everyone, except the believers, will run away from it.[224]

Can Muslims really believe in such nonsense? The ignorant, superstitious Bedouin would have no problem accepting this fantasy answer as Holt Writ and thus one can understand how the charlatan Mohammed was able to bilk them into accepting his new "religion."

The Theory of Abrogation

The Islamic jurists invented the doctrine of abrogation to deal with the contradictions in the Koran. This dogma is justified by two verses of the Koran as follows:

> "We do not abrogate any verse or cause it to be forgotten unless we substitute for it something better or similar; do you not know that Allah has power over everything?" (Koran, II: 106)
> "When we change a verse in the place of another verse—and Allah knows best what he sends down. They say, 'you are but a forger.' But most of them understand not." (Koran, XVI: 101)

---

[222] Abdullah Muhammad Khoje, *The End of the Journey* (Wasington, D.C.: The Islamic Center, 1987), pp. 48–49.

[223] Mehdi Elahi Ghomshei, *Koran al-Karim* (Ghom: Osweh Publications, 1991), p. 384.

[224] Abdullah Muhammad Khoje, *The End of the Journey,* pp. 48–49.

No one denies that there are cases of abrogation in the Koran, but the authorities differ widely as to the number of the abrogated verses, some limiting the number to as few as five, others point to as many as 225.

The Koran in verse 26 of *Sura* XVIII says, " . . . Allah knows clearly the secrets of the heavens and the earth and he sees and hears everything . . . . ," and in the verse 64 of *Sura* X says, " . . . no change can there be in the words of Allah . . . ." But by abrogating verses, Allah first reveals a wrong or improper injunction to His so-called Prophet and then He corrects himself. One may wonder that if Allah is really omniscient and omnipotent and his word un-changeable, why did he not revealed the right verses to his prophet from the beginning. The answer is that this is Mohammed's way of twisting the so-called Words of Allah to his own ends. If an ordinary human being (with the possible exception of a politician) makes an improper decision, he loses his credibility. It would appear that Allah, the Clown of Islam, and Mohammed are immune from such judgment.

The most verses later abrogated are those produced by Mohammed when he was residing in Mecca at the beginning of his career. He had not yet acquired power and pretended to be but a *Warner,* a preacher, supposedly bringing verses that Allah had revealed to him to pass on to the people. He was patient with the unbelievers, leaving the punishment of the recalcitrant to Allah. The abrogating verses sanctioning the use of the sword were revealed in Medina after he had gained power. These verses command Mohammed and his followers to fight, terrorize, and kill. Below are a few examples of verses of both kinds: the original and its abrogation:

The original verses: "Say, 'O my people! Do whatever you can. I will do my part. Soon will you know who it is whose end will be (best) in the hereafter. . . . ' (VI: 135) 'But if you turn away, I have not asked you for any wage, for my wage falls only on Allah. . . . ' (X: 72) 'But warn them of the day of distress. . . . ' (IX: 39) 'So, make no haste against them. . . . ' (IX: 84) 'Therefore be patient with what they say. . . . ' (XX: 130, XXXVIII: 17) Say, 'Each one (of us) is waiting, so you too wait. . . . ' (XX: 135). Say, 'O men! I am (sent) to you only to give you clear warning.' (XXII: 49) 'If they do wrangle with you, say, 'Allah knows best, what you are doing,' (XXII: 68) 'But leave them, in their confused ignorance for a time.' (XXIII: 54) 'Repeal evil with that which is best . . . . ' (XXIII: 96) 'And have patience with what they say, and leave them with dignity.'" (LXXIII: 10)[225]

The abrogating verses: 'And slay them whenever you catch them . . . ." (II: 191) "And fight them on, until there is no more tumult of oppression, and there prevail the faith in Allah . . . ." (II: 193) "Fighting is prescribed upon you, and you dislike it . . . ." (II: 216) " . . . Seize them and slay them whenever you find them . . . ." (IV: 89) "And slay the pagans whenever you find them . . . ." (IX: 5) "Fight those who believe not in Allah, not the Last Day . . . ." (IX: 29) " . . . Fight the unbelievers whom you find round about you . . . ." (IX: 123) " . . . Whenever they are found, they shall be seized and slain without mercy." (XXXIII: 61)[226]

Islamic theology allots such importance to the doctrine of abrogation that the Muslim jurists have made it a specialized field of study in Islamic jurisprudence. One commentator (*Kashf al-Asrar*) on *Sura* 2 verse CVI says, "The orthodox view is that abrogation applies both to the Koran and to tradition (*Hadith*)." In this way, the Koran abrogates itself, *Hadith* abrogates the Koran, *Hadith* abrogates itself, and the Koran abrogates *Hadith.* All of these contradictions are firmly established and recognized by Islamic jurisprudence.[227]

The preposterous and superstitious fables which enshroud all Islamic tenets have corrupted the minds of Muslims. It is no wonder that the Islamic nations, even though endowed by geological whimsy with a great part of the natural wealth of the world, are among the most backward nations of the world. Abiding by the definition of scientific thought as defined by William Whewell in the 1800's—"Fundamental Ideas are supplied by the mind itself, they are not merely received from our observations of the world."— Michael Moravesik gives the following approximate figures for the

---

[225] Sherif, *A Guide to the Contents of the Koran,* p. 59.

[226] *Ibid.*

[227] *Ibid.,* p. 60.

number of scientific papers worldwide and in the third world countries in 1976:

World Wide	352,000
Third World Countries	19,000
Muslim Countries	3,100
Israel	6,100

It is interesting to note that he gives the scientific authorship in India in 1976 as 2.260% and in Pakistan 0.055%. India and Pakistan were both a single nation in the subcontinent of India until 1947. In that year, when the sub-continent was partitioned due to violence between Hindus and Muslims, the two predominantly Muslim regions in the northwestern and northeastern part of India formed the separate state of Pakistan and the rest of the predominantly Hindu part of the sub-continent became the new India. Since then, we have seen a great difference between the numbers of scientific works originating in Muslim Pakistan compared to that of India. Another study in 1988 enumerates the publications in science in India (population 700 million) as ninety, compared with that of Pakistan (population 90 million), only four.[228]

A Muslim has no Right to Think; Only Allah and his Messenger Think and Decide

According to the Koran, when Allah and His Apostle have decided a matter, the believer does not have any choice but to obey.

"It is not fitting for a believer, man or woman, when a matter has been decided by God and His Apostle, to have any opinion about

---

[228] Data on trade and technology in Muslim countries has been collected in useful form in the *International Conference on Science in Islamic Polity,* vol. 1(Islamabad: Ministry of Science and Technology), pp. 350–54, quoted by Pervez Hoodbhoy, *Islam and Science* (New Jersey: Zed Books, 1991), pp. 33–34.

their decision: if anyone disobeys God and His Apostle, he is indeed on a clearly wrong path." (Koran, XXXIII: 36)

Interestingly, *The Holy Qur'an* of Yusuf Ali, interprets the above verse as: "We must not put our wisdom in competition with Allah's wisdom . . . We must accept it loyally, and do the best we can to help in our own way to carry it out. We must make our will constant to the Universal Will."[229] And *The Bounteous Koran* by Katib comments on the same verse: "This verse was revealed concerning Zainab bint Jahsh, the Prophet's cousin, when she and her brother refused the Prophet's proposal to wed her to Zaid ibn Harith, his adopted son and freed bondsman. Despite her resentment, she was given to Zaid in marriage, but later was divorced at his request and was married to the Prophet . . . ."[230]

The above verse shows beyond any shadow of doubt that Islam is based on predestination and fatalism. In Islam, everything is predestined by Allah's Providence and Muslims are completely deprived of freedom of choice. They should ignore their common sense and other intellectual faculties and plod patiently in the path that Allah has predestined for them. These concepts of predestination and fatalism make Muslims believe that they are controlled by an inscrutable and inexorable power. Free will is denied to them.

The commentary by Katib is even more interesting because according to him, this Koranic verse makes a poor woman first the victim of a manipulator (Mohammed) and then the object of the sensual lust of the same person, sanctioned on both occasions by the wishes of an unseen Allah, as revealed by His so-called Prophet. On the first occasion the victim is compelled to submit to an unwanted marriage against her will and in the second one to divorce her husband toward whom she may have developed a sentimental attachment. This cruel treatment of women, sanctioned by the Koran as revealed by Mohammed, is one of the foundations of the Islamic creed. Furthermore, it confirms that fatalism and predestination are

---

[229] Abdullah Yusuf Ali, *The Holy Qur'an,* vol. 2 (New York: Hafner Publishing Company, 1946), Commentary 2731, p. 1117.

[230] Dr. M. M. Katib, *The Bounteous Koran* (London: MacMillan Press, 1984), Commentary 34, p. 555.

inherent in the Islamic religion and clearly shows that a Muslim has no free will since a believer's thoughts and ideas are determined by Allah and His Messenger.

The Scribe Who Discovered Mohammed's Imposture and Lost his Faith in Islam

One of the best proofs of the fabrication of the Koran by Mohammed is the story of Abdullah ibn Saad Abi Sarh, one of the scribes of the Koran. When the illiterate Mohammed was residing in Medina, Abdullah was one of five scribes employed by Mohammed to write down his "revelations." On a number of occasions he (Abdullah) had inserted a few words of his own into a so-called revelation, pointing out that it sounded better. Mohammed was pleased to accept the changes without any correction. Upon seeing how easily he could manipulate the so-called "divine revelations," Abdullah lost his faith in Islam and the divinity of the Koran and deemed Mohammed a charlatan. He returned to Mecca and joined the Quraysh.[231]

Mohammed ordered that certain men should be assassinated even if they had found refuge behind the curtains of the Ka'ba. Among them was Abdullah ibn Saad Abi Sarh. At the time of the conquest of Mecca, Othman, the foster-brother of Abdullah and the son-in-law of Mohammed gave him [Abdullah] shelter and asked Mohammed for clemency. Mohammed did not respond, remaining silent for a long time. Mohammed explained, "By Allah, I kept silent so that one of you might go up to him and cut off his head!" One of the Ansar said, "Why didn't you give me a sign?" Allah's Apostle replied, "A Prophet does not kill by making signs."[232] Mohammed finally reluctantly pardoned him.

Mohammed was right in saying that "a Prophet does not kill by making signs," because in all of his terrorist atrocities, as will be mentioned in chapter six, he clearly *ordered* his opponents to be assassinated.

---

[231] Ibn Warraq, *Why I am not a Muslim*, p. 115.
[232] Tabari, *The History of at-Tabari*, vol. VIII, pp. 178–79; *Ibn Ishaq*, p. 550.

Koranic Superstitions Stand Above Morals

In theology there is a doctrine called "antinomianism." This doctrine states that faith is superior to moral laws and regulations and that salvation is dependent upon faith alone and not moral law. This precept is exploited to the extreme in Islam. Islam is a religion where theology is supreme and morality succumbs to faith. A Believer is required by faith alone to believe that he is already one of God's elect or damned long before he is even born. Mohammed anticipated Luther and Calvin by a thousand years by preaching the doctrine of predestination: "None amongst you would attain salvation purely because of his deeds,"[233] Mohammed says, "Observe moderation in your doings" he advises," but if you fail, try to do as much as you can do and be happy, for none would be able to get into paradise because of his deeds alone."[234]

Immanuel Kant, the 18th-century German philosopher and probably the best known exponent of deontological ethics, believed that the moral rightness or wrongness of an action depends on its intrinsic qualities and not, as a teleologist holds, entirely on its consequences. "Deontology" was used initially to refer (in a broad sense) to the "science of duty."

In deontological ethics an action is considered morally good or not depending upon the characteristics of the action itself and not the result of the action. Deontology is an ethic that regards an act right if it conforms to moral principle. As an example, if a person does a favor for his friend or his neighbor, this action could not *per se* be as evaluated good, because he has done it for the sake of friendship or neighborliness and, probably, in anticipation of some future repayment, not because of any intrinsic good in the action. It should also be noted that deontology is not the same as "absolutism," according to which certain acts are wrong, whatever their consequences might be. So, according to deontologists, most actions are morally obligatory regardless of their consequences. This philosophy finds expression in such slogans as "duty for duty's sake," "virtue is its own reward," and "let justice be done though the

---

[233] *Sahih Muslim,* vol. IV, pp. 1472–1473.
[234] *Ibid.,* p. 1473.

heavens fall." By the same token, deontological ethics hold that some acts are morally wrong *per* se regardless of their consequences, e.g. lying, breaking a promise, punishing the innocent and murder.

By contrast, teleological ethics hold that the basic nature of morality is the value of what an action brings into being. Consequentialism is perhaps the clearest example of a purely impersonal moral theory which emphasizes: "Always strive to bring about the best consequences." All things considered, Kant put ethics and human values above metaphysics.

As it has been said before, since Mohammed bragged that he had the Seal of all Prophets and was appointed for all the nations for all time, reformative movements never appeared in Islam. The only exception was the short-lived Mu'tazila, a religious movement that was born in Basra. The proponents of this theological school adopted an "intermediate" stance between belief and skepticism. They proposed that although the commission of sin caused immediate apostasy, for Believers that particular sin had no impact upon their belief. Like the school of scholasticism, Mu'tazila tried to graft Greek philosophy onto the superstitious principles of Islam; this was a complete failure. The reason for its failure was that Islam is a dogmatic system, set in stone, which does not permit any variation or amelioration to its principles. Any innovative idea in Islam is labeled "apostasy" and its author is subject to immediate death.

Christianity is not as dogmatic and inflexible as Islam because its followers historically did not live under regimes controlled by despotic theocrats as did the Muslims. Therefore, many divergent theological movements appeared in Christianity, one of which came into being after Second World War against "antinomianism" and was in full bloom by the 1960s. It was strongly influenced by French existentialism and, to a lesser extent, postwar German nihilism. This school of thought was called "situation ethics," an understanding of morality which argues that the goodness or badness of an act is determined not by the kind of act itself, but by the context and circumstances in which the act is performed and by the intention of the agent.

In general, "situation ethics" does not reject the universal norms and principles of static ethics, but calls attention to their limits and relies on the individual conscience and responsibility in making decisions. More moderate forms of situation ethics tried to discern their relationship to the equally important factors of circumstances, context and situation. The responsible moral agent is not a person who unthinkingly follows laws and rules, but one who apprises a situation carefully, weighs the values at stake, his own intentions, the consequences of the action, whether the particular action serves or hinders human well-being, and then decides prudently.

In 1952, Pope Pius XII condemned situation ethics as contrary to Catholic moral teaching. He charged it with encouraging moral relativism, subjectivism, and individualism. But when we consider that the Islamic rules and "principles of ethics" were the product of the fantastic, self-serving, lustful brain of a bandit camel herder totally immersed in visions of plundering and sexual cacoëthes, we can understand the lack of intelligible philosophy such as that described above. His dogmatic creed left no room for the followers of his religion to focus on such cognitive niceties. Therefore, he simply relegated ethics–the most constructive element of human personality–to the following childish utterance:

> "The outcome of deeds depends upon the intentions, and the desire to get reward from Allah. And every person will have the reward according to what he is intended. And this includes faith, ablution, prayer, zakat, hajj, fasting and all the orders of Allah . . . And the Prophet said, 'Jihad and intention.' (fight for Allah's cause). When there is no call for it one should have no intention to do Jihad)"[235]

In the above statement, Mohammed openly relegates the principles and ethics of Islam to obedience to a set of injunctions easily carried out by ignorant and superstitious people: ablution, *zakat, hajj, jihad* (in particular) and so on. As I have shown in chapter two and I will discuss more in chapter five, *Jihad* in Islam is equivalent to murder and terrorist activities. In other words, whereas in non-Islamic cultures human behavior is evaluated according to ethical principles, in Islam ethics simply means a bunch of ludicrous exercises fabricated by Mohammed's cunning mind to promote his devilish goals.

---

[235] *Sahih al-Bukhari,* Chapter 42, pp. 46–47.

Moses Hess, who converted Engels to communism and even had some influence on Carl Marx, expressed, in an esoteric way, the conflict between religion and morality. The religious outlook, he contended, was essentially one of acceptance, an acceptance of the order of universe—called indifferently God, Nature, Reason, or Spirit—of which human beings were a part, and whose mysterious and purposive ways could only be dimly apprehended by faith and intelligence. The standpoint of morality on the other hand, was one of assertion—an assertion of what ought to be and what are not, an imposition of a new order and not merely the recognition of an old. The root of religion was man's feelings; the source of morality was the practical necessities of life. So long as human beings strive after ideals of perfection, there can be no completely irreligious men; so long as they live in society, they cannot be completely immoral. Irreligion is simply a word for other people's religion; immorality, a term for behavior different from our own. The essence of religion is worship; the essence of morality is consciousness.[236]

Writers and philosophers have endeavored to free humanity from superstitious beliefs and reject evil corruption. The humanitarian thinkers have attempted to make him anthropocentric instead of theo-centric and have encouraged him to devote his mental and physical energies to making his life as fruitful and prosperous as possible. They have endeavored to liberate the human mind from believing in unseen imaginary entities in the sky and tried to focus its attention on the earthly living environment. But the bearded merchant of ignorance and corruption who called himself the Prophet of Allah cunningly deceived his fellow men, leading them to belief in a fabricated divinity to the furtherance of his own ends.

Rich People Should Not Help the Poor

One of the many detractions of the Islamic religion is that there is no mention of "*humanism*" in the Koran or in any other Islamic literature.

---

[236] Sidney Hook, *From Hegel to Marx* (Michigan: The University of Michigan Press, 1966), PP. 195–196.

It seems that Allah has created the universe to make all creatures his toys and torture them throughout their life. No other school of thought is so bereft of feeling. There are so many passages in the Koran that talk about slaves and how to handle them. Though the Koran has dealt with women as commodities and described them as mere objects for men's pleasure, the conditions of slaves are even worse. Verse 71 of *Sura* XVI of the Koran says:

> "Allah has favored some of you with more worldly provisions than others. Then those who are more favored do not give their slaves equal share in their possession; where they to do so, they would be denying Allah's goodness."[237]

Like other tropologists who struggle to give the absurdities of the Koran a human face, in interpreting the above verse, Sayyid Abul Ala' Maududi writes: "The fact of the matter is that the context in which this verse occurs renders any discussion of economic questions quite out of place. The discourse is in fact devoted to emphasizing God's unity and refuting polytheism"[238] But, it is quite obvious that the intent of the passage does not have anything to do with monotheism or polytheism and Mawdudi has tried to do his mendacious best to lead people from the true tenor of the passage. The Arabic word used in the Koran is "*rezgh,*" meaning "*subsistence*" or "*food*". Now, one should ask this mullah, which dictionary in the world has defined the word "*rezgh,*" as "monotheism" or "polytheism." The answer is none: These people trying to save the face of Allah and the superstitious creed of Islam in order to keep their own religious business running profitably.

In verse 28 of *Sura Rom*, Allah uses a parable to show his favor to those on whom he has bestowed more than on others:

> "Here is comparison drawn from your own lives: do your slaves share in equal terms with you the riches that We have given you? Do you fear them as you fear one another?"

---

237 Sherif, *A Guide to the Contents of the Koran*, pp. 135–36.
238 Sayyid Abul Ala' Mawdudi, *Towards Understanding the Qur'an*, Engilsh version of *Tafhim al-Qura'n* (United Kingdom: The Islamic Foundation, 1993), p. 345.

Another example is given in verse 75 of *Sura* XVI shows the contrast between the power of Allah and the helplessness of man:

> "On the one hand there is a helpless slave, the property of his master. On the other a man on whom we have bestowed Our bounty so that he gives of it both in private and in public. Are the two alike? Allah forbids."

Once again verse 76 of *Sura* XVI Allah asks a question which shows he has created mankind differently and that some should be above others:

> "Is there equality between on the one hand a dumb and helpless man, a burden on his master, and who returns from every errand with empty hands, and on the other hand one who enjoins justice and follows the right path?"

Basically the Koran sees no injustice that some should be slaves to others; on the contrary it recognizes that this is the very order established by Allah. Verse 31 of *Sura* XLIII, referring to the manner in which Allah, in His wisdom, portions out the goods of this life to His creatures, says that He exalts some over others, so that the one may take the other into his service.[239]

Verse 25 of *Sura* IV, advises believers that if they cannot afford to marry a free woman, they should marry a Muslim slave woman. Verse 6 of *Sura* XXIII and verse 30 of *Sura* LXX, forbid married men from having extra-marital relations, other than those with slave women. Verse 52 of *Sura* XXXIII prohibits Mohammed from cohabitation with certain categories of women. Again, slave women are omitted from this list. Verse 31 of *Sura* XXIV lays down a rule that women, other than slaves, should conceal their private parts and their finery from men other than those specified within certain degrees of relationship.[240]

Marxism, (though its chief proponent, Communist Russia, is a bankrupt entity at the present time) from the standpoint of human-

---

[239] *Ibid.*, p. 136.
[240] *Ibid.*

ism, is not compatible with Islam and, in theory, stands much above it. This conclusion is based on the theoretical timetable given in the writings of Karl Marx in which he describes the order by which communism will spread throughout the world. According to Marx, after the revolution of the proletariat, the first phase called "crude communism" or socialism begins. In this stage the state and law begin to wither away, resulting in the disappearance of the bureaucracy, the police, and the armed services. At the end of this transitional period the second phase, "full communism," will bloom. Socialism or "crude communism" would be democratic, far more democratic than capitalism; but "full communism" would be a democracy so perfect, so all-embracing, that it would enable every difference of opinion to be settled without rancor.[241]

In the "crude communism" or socialistic phase, a person works according to his ability and will be paid for his labor according to his productivity but under "full communism;" a person will work on the basis of his ability and will be paid "according to his needs." Since one man's needs differ from those of another (a married man with four children, for instance, will clearly need more then a bachelor), rewards too will be different. Since under communism one receives reward based solely on need regardless of how hard or skillfully he works, there is little or no incentive to improve the quality or quantity of work.[242] The Koran and Islam make short shrift of any sharing of the wealth. According to (XVI: 71), mentioned above, "rich people do not give their slaves [this includes any one of inferior means] an equal share in their possessions, were they to do so, they be denying Allah's goodness."

Fictitious Muslims

At present time Muslims number a little more than one billion or about one sixth of the population of the world. Most of the Muslims of the world who are non-Arabic are "hereditary" Muslims: they

---

[241] P. H. Vigor, *A Guide to Marxism* (New York: Humanities Press, 1966), p.104.
[242] *Ibid,* p. 162.

inherited their faith from their fathers have never read the Koran, nor do they understand the Islamic precepts. These Muslims normally rely on whatever they have learned from their parents regarding the Koran and are fed a fictitious picture of their so-called Prophet and Allah that generally is inconsistent with the scriptures. Moreover, they are always under the influence of their own particular cleric's interpretation of the scriptures.

Naturally, no one can expect the clerics to be honest and give the followers of the faith genuine information because, in order to make a living, they have chosen a parasitic profession that deceives the people. If Islam were to suddenly disappear, Muslim clerics and dictators would lose their power and wealth. About a million of these Islamic parasites would instantly be out of work.[243]

Even if Muslims of the non-Arabic world were able to read the Koran and agree that Mohammed was indeed a real Messenger sent to the people by a genuine existing God, the contents of the Koran show that Islam has not been prescribed for them and they are not obliged to follow the Word of Allah. These Muslims do not know that they are pseudo-Muslims."

The reason behind the above rationale is that several passages in the Koran clearly state that Mohammed has been sent as a Messenger to warn *exclusively* the inhabitants of the Mother City (Mecca) and its environs of the so-called the Day of Judgment in their own language. The following verses substantiate the above reasoning:

> "Every nation has its Messenger; and when their Messenger comes, justice is done among them; they are not wronged." (Koran, X: 47)
>
> "We have sent no Apostle **except in the language of his own people,** so that he might make plain to them (his message)." (Koran, XIV: 4)
>
> "Thus We have revealed to you an **Arabic Koran,** that you may warn the Mother City (Mecca) and all around it; that you may threaten them of the Day of Gathering which is sure to come: when some will be in paradise, and some in Hell." (XLII: 7)

---

[243] Winn, *Muhammad, Prophet of Doom.*

"Your Lord is truly the Almighty, the Merciful. Verily this is revealed by the Lord of Creation. The Faithful spirit brought it down into your heart, **that you might warn the people in plain Arabic tongue."** (Koran, XXVI: 192–196)

"And this is a book which we have sent down, bringing blessings, and confirming (the revelations) which came before it: that you may warn the Mother of the Cities and all around it . . . ." (VI: 92)

Furthermore, some verses in the Koran state that it is the book only for Arabs (*Suras* XIV: 4, XLIII: 3, XLVI: 12), while others imply it is a revelation for all mankind (*Suras* XXXIV: 28, XXXIII: 40). The former *Suras* were invented when Mohammed was still in Mecca only dreaming of power. The latter ones were made in Medina, when Mohammed had gained power in that city, had called himself the Seal of Prophets, and was dreaming of invading other nations and converting them to his superstitious faith. However, from whichever aspect we approach Islam, we find it baseless, nonsensical, and preposterous.

If we allow that Mohammed was the Messenger of a true God, then the above verses leave no doubt that Islam was decreed exclusively for the inhabitants of Arabia and no other land or nation. Therefore, the non-Arab Muslims of the world are indeed "pseudo-Muslims."

Chapter Four

Astronomy of the Koran

Religion is the dream of the human mind. But even in dreams we do not find ourselves in emptiness or in heaven, but on earth, in the realm of reality; we only see real things in the entrancing splendor of imagination and caprice, instead of in the simple daylight of reality and necessity.

Ludwig Feuerbach, *Preface to 1843 edition of The Essential of Christianity (1841).*

How Allah Created the Earth

The big bang theory states that at the beginning of time, all matter and energy in the universe was concentrated in a very dense state, from which it erupted with the resulting expansion continuing into and beyond the present time. This big bang happened between 10 to 20 billion years ago. In the initial stage, the universe was very hot, but the temperature rapidly decreased, falling from 10^{13} degrees Kelvin after the first microsecond to about one billion degrees after three minutes. As it cooled, nuclear reactions took place producing the chemical elements of the universe. After many millions of years the expanding universe, at first a very hot gas, thinned and cooled enough to condense into individual galaxies and then stars. The strong evidence for the big bang theory is the feeble radio background radiation, discovered in the 1960s, that is received from every part of the sky. The expanding theory was proposed by Edwin Hubble in 1929; the term big bang was coined by George Gamow in 1946 and now is generally accepted.

But, when we consider Semitic ideas about creation, particularly Islam, the matter becomes quite amusing! Modern scholars have criticized the Bible for its claim that Earth was created in six days.

This was actually a myth contrived by early man to explain how the world was created. The Koran makes the same mistake regarding the amount of the time needed to create the universe as seen in the following verse:

> "And verily we created the heavens and the earth, and all that is between them, in six days, and naught of weariness touched us." (Koran, L: 38)

Furthermore, Mohammed says in the Koran:

> "When Allah wanted to create creation, he brought forth smoke from the water. The smoke rose above the water and hovered loftily over it. He therefore, called it 'Heaven.' Then he dried out the water, and thus made it one earth. He split it and made it into seven earths on Sunday and Monday. He created the earth upon a big fish (*hut*), that being the fish (*nun*) mentioned by Allah in the Koran (*Nun,* by the pen, Koran, LXVIII: 1). The fish was in the water. The water was upon the back of a small rock. The rock was upon the back of an angel. The angel was upon a big rock. The big rock (mentioned by Luqman: Koran, XXXI: 16) was in the wind, neither in heaven nor on earth). The fished moved and became agitated. As a result the earth quaked, whereupon he firmly, anchored the mountains on it, and it was stable. This is stated in Allah's word that he made for the earth 'firmly anchored mountains, let it shakes you up.'" (Koran XVI:15)[244]

It is a known fact that Mohammed had contact with Jews and Christians and much of the Koran is borrowed from the Old and New Testaments. The only minor difference is that the Old Testament claims that "on the seventh day God rested" (Genesis II: 2), but the Koran proclaimed that "naught of weariness touched Him," after creation. Throughout the Koran Mohammed has always applied this tactic to pretend that his mission is the sequel of the previous Semitic prophets, but his revelations are more perfect, because he is the so-called "Seal of Prophets."

Muslims, in trying to prove that the Koran is compatible with modern science, point out that the Koran says that a day for Allah and the angels is equal to 50,000 years as we reckon time (Koran,

---

[244] Tabari, *The History of at-Tabari,* vol. 1, p. 220.

LXX: 4), therefore the six day creation was completed in 300,000 years. Such rationalization only subjects the Koran to more criticism because it is a well-known scientific fact that it took billions of years for the universe to reach its present state.

Furthermore, such an absurd claim contradicts other version of the Koran. The verse that says a day equals 50,000 years (Koran, LXX: 4), states:

> "The angels ascend to Him in a day, the measure of which is fifty thousand years."

This verse seems to be discussing the speed of travel for angels saying that angels can travel in a day the distance it would take humans 50,000 years to cover. In other words, a Muslim ecclesiastical day equals 50,000 human years. This fantasy contradicts other parts of the Koran. Verse 47 of *Sura* XXII and also verse 5 of *Sura* XXXII of the Koran each claim the divine day to be equal to 1,000 human years. Irrespective of such preposterous contradictions, the creation of the universe was accomplished in a most simplistic fashion, insofar as Muslim belief is concerned: Verse 117 of *Sura* II says that at the time of creation, Allah said, "'Be!' and it was."[245]

No doubt, of all the other idols of the Ka'ba, Allah indeed deserves the title of the "greatest," because he brilliantly accomplished an incredible feat: the Creation. Alas, the scientists have ignored these "authentic" documents about creation in the Koran and are propounding such theories as the Big Bang and Evolution. Who knows better, the All Knowing Allah who has created heaven and earth in six days and His beloved Messenger, or a bunch of infidel Jews and Christians, such as: Charles Darwin, Galileo, Nicolas Copernicus, Albert Einstein, Edward Hubble, George Gamow, and so on?

Does the Koran Tell Us How Many Days Allah Took to Create the Heavens and the Earth(s)?

The Koranic wisdom about the duration of the creation is also very instructive and interesting! Different verses of the Koran vary about the

---

[245]http://www.infidels.org/library/modern/denis_giron/*islamsci*.html

number of the days that it took Allah to create the heavens and earth. The Koran states in 43 different verses that Allah created the heavens and earth. But the number of the days that it took Allah to complete the creation of heaven and earth varies from two to six days.

In four verses of the Koran (VII: 54, XI: 7, XXV: 59, and XXXII: 4), Allah says that he has created the heavens and earth in six days. In one verse (LXI: 10), Allah affirms that he created the heavens and earth in four days; and in two verses (XLI: 9 and 12), he talks about creating the heavens and earth in two days. It is so interesting that verses 9 and 10 of *Sura* 41 come one after the other but still differ in the number of days (two and four, respectively) it took to complete the Creation. How many days then, according to the Koran, did Allah labor to create the so-called "heavens" and the earth? The answer is that both Allah and his impostor Prophet are confused!

The wisdom of the Koran teaches us that in the beginning, the heavens and earth were joined together as one unit, but our Allah, the most compassionate and most merciful, separated them. He was also extremely compassionate to His creatures, creating on the earth immovable mountains to stabilize mankind during the separation:

> "Do not the unbelievers see that the heavens and the earth were joined together as one Unit of Creation before we clove them asunder? . . . ." (Koran, XXI: 30)
>
> "And we set up in the earth immovable mountains lest it should shake with them. . . ." (Koran, XXI: 31)

Turning aside from all the nonsense about creation of the heavens and earth, how many earths, according to the Koran, do exist in the solar system? In the verses below and also other passages of the Koran, Allah and his Messenger speak about seven heavens and one earth, but in the verse 12 of *Sura* LXV of the Koran, we read that there are as many earths as there are heavens:

> "Allah is He Who created seven heavens and of the earth a similar number, through the midst of them (all) descends His command: that you may know that Allah has power over all things, and that Allah. . . . comprehends all things in His knowledge." (Koran, LXV: XII)

If there are seven earths in the Islamic solar system, then where are the other six? Was this an incomplete divine anticipation of the solar system that we recognize today? Hardly! The probable answer is that the other six earths are restricted to *jinns.* Because as we cannot see *jinns,* we are not able to see the location of their residence as well! The All-knowing Allah and His impostor Apostle know things that even the most brilliant scientists do not know and they see what normal humans are unable to see.

What a pity scientists have wasted their lives and millions of dollars trying to unravel the mysteries of the universe when all of the heavenly facts were revealed to the Prophet of Islam by All-knowing Allah!

How Many "East" and "West" Exist in the World?

Sura II, verse 258; *Sura* LXX, verse 40; and *Sura* LXXIII, verse 9 all indicate that there is but one "east" and one "west" in the world. *Sura* LV, verse 17 states that there are two "easts" and two "wests" in our world. And the *Sura* XXXVII, verse 5 argues that there are many "easts" and "wests" in the world.

Then, how many "easts" and "wests" do really exist in this world? Probably the many easts and wests that Allah has alluded to and of which we human beings are unaware, are in the **jinn** world. Perhaps Allah, who several times in the Koran characterizes Himself as "deceitful," knows many things of which neither ordinary humans nor our scientists are aware. It may be that Allah is telling us so many preposterous ideas in order to test our faith. If we were to believe such nonsensical absurdities, we would be considered "faithful believers" and our eventual abode will be in paradise; if not we will be unbelievers consigned to the blazing fires of hell.

Allah Created Two Suns and Moons and Gave Them Garments

Abu Dhar Ghaffari quotes the prophet in the following conversation: "I walked hand in hand with the prophet around evening when the sun was about to set. We did not stop looking at it until it had set. I asked the Messenger of God: 'Where does it set?' He replied: 'It sets in the [lowest] heaven and then is raised from heaven to heaven until it is raised to the highest seventh heaven. Eventually, when it is underneath the Throne, it falls down and prostrates itself, and the angels who are in charge of it prostrate themselves together with it. The sun then says: 'My Lord, whence do you command me to rise, from where I set or from where I rise?' Then it runs to a place where it is to reside at night—where it is held underneath the Throne.

Gabriel brings the sun a garment of luminosity from the light of the Throne, according to the measure of the hours of the day. It is longer in the summer and shorter in the winter and of intermediate length in autumn and spring. The sun puts on that garment, and it is set free to roam in the air of heaven until it rises whence it does." Mohammed continues, "The same course is followed by the moon in its rising, its running on the horizon of the heaven, its setting, its rising to the highest seventh heaven, its being held underneath the Throne, its prostration, and its asking for permission. But Gabriel brings it a garment from the light of the Footstool. He made the sun luminosity and the moon a light."[246]

Mohammed added, "Allah then created for the sun a chariot with 360 handholds from the luminosity of the light of the Throne and entrusted to 360 of the angels inhabiting the lower heaven with the sun and its chariot, each of them gripping one of those handholds. Allah also entrusted 360 angels with the moon."[247]

The above quotations speak for themselves. Their total and complete absurdity is blatantly apparent to anyone who can read. Alexandra Pushkin, the Russian poet, who is generally considered by critics to be the most important Russian writer of all time, equivalent to Shakespeare in England or Dante Alighieri of Italy says, "The Koran! How preposterous is the book in astronomy, but great in poetry."

The Sun Sets in a Puddle of Murky Water

If one is unaware of the rotation of the earth and seeks an explanation of what happens to the sun when it sinks below the western hori-

---

[246] Tabari, *The History of al-Tabari*, pp. 231–32.
[247] *Ibid.*, p. 234.

zon, one can easily find the answer to this question by consulting the Koran and reading verse 86 of *Sura* XVIII:

> They will ask you about Dhul-Qarnain (Alexander the Great).[248] Say, "I will give you something of his story. We made him mighty in the land and gave him ways and means to (achieve) all things. He journeyed on a certain road until he reaches the West and saw the sun setting in a pool of black mud. Near it he found a certain people. We said, 'O Dhul-Qarnain,' you have the authority either to punish them, or to treat them with kindness."

The brilliant wisdom of Allah, the All-mighty (one of whose ninety-nine names is "the All-Knowing"), reveals to His Messenger that the sun sets in a puddle of black mud! It seems that on the day of that revelation, either the All-Knowing Allah was in a teasing mood or he forgot that when he created the sun, he placed it 93,000,000 miles from the earth. But we must remember that the mighty Allah's apparent sense of humor originated in the ignorant, twisted, avaricious mind of His illiterate Prophet.

The Sun Prostrates to Allah and may Rise from the West

Abu Dhar Ghaffari, on another occasion, recalled a conversation with Mohammed regarding the sun: "The prophet asked me at sunset, 'do you know where the sun goes (at the time of sunset)?' I replied, 'Allah and His apostle know better.' He said, 'It goes (i. e., travels) till it prostrates itself underneath the Throne of Allah and asks permission to rise again, and it is permitted and then (a time will come when) it will be about to prostrate itself but its prostration will not be accepted, and it will ask permission to go on its course, but it will not be permitted, but it will be ordered to return whence it

---

[248] Most of the commentators of the Koran believe Dhul-Qarnain to be Alexander the Great. Majid Fakhri, trans. *An Interpretation of the Quoran* (New York: New York University Press, 1994), p. 299n; Abdullah Yusuf Ali, *The Meaning of the Holy Quoran* (Brentwood, Maryland: Amana Corporation, 1991), p. 731.

has come and so it will rise in the west."[249] And that is the interpretation of the statement of Allah in the Koran, which says:

> "And the sun runs its fixed course for a period determined for him: that is the decree of Allah." (Koran XXXVI: 38)

Verse 37 of the same *Sura* corroborates this masterpiece of Allah:

> "A sign for them is the night. We withdraw from the day, and behold they plunged into darkness." (Koran, XXXVI: 37)

Verse 39 of *Sura* XXXVI has a brilliant divine analogy for the moon and its traverse:

> "And the Moon, We have measured for her Mansions (to traverse) till she returns. . . . It is not permitted to the Sun to catch up the Moon, nor can the night outstrip the Day . . . ."

Mohammed was an ambitious seventh-century Bedouin Arab who was brought up in the Arabian deserts and his lack of knowledge is reflected in the ridiculous absurdities inserted in the Koran. But what is really perplexing is that in the third millennium over one billion of the world's population has faith in such blatant absurdities! A Latin axiom says, "*Credo ut intelligam,*" i. e., "I believe first to understand it later." The writer of this book believes that Muslims first believe in Islam to understand it later, but they never really understand it, otherwise they could never remain a Muslim.

What Causes the Eclipse of the Sun

Allah has taught His messenger the causes and mechanism of the partial and total solar eclipse and Tabari has explained these teachings in the first volume of his history book. The author will quote him:

> "When God wishes to test the sun and the moon, showing His servants a sign and thereby asking them to stop disobeying him and to start to obey, the sun tumbles from the chariot and falls into the deep of that ocean, which is the sphere. When God wants to increase the significance of the sign and frighten His servants severely, all of the sun

---

[249] *Sahih al-Bukhari,* vol. 4, No. 421, p. 283.

falls, and nothing of it remains upon the chariot. That is the total eclipse of the sun, when the day darkens and the stars come out. When God wants to make a partial sign, half or a third or two-thirds of it fall into the water, while the rest remains upon the chariot, this being a partial eclipse . . . . It frightens His servants and constitutes a request from the lord (for them to repent). However this may be, the angels entrusted with the chariot of the sun divide into two groups, one that goes to the sun and pulls it toward the chariot, and another that goes to the chariot and pulls it toward the sun, while at the same time they keep it steady in the sphere, praising and sanctifying God with prayer, according to the extent of the hours of the day or the hours of night, be it night or day, summer or winter, autumn or spring between summer and winter, lest the length of night and day be increased in any way. God has given them knowledge of that by inspiration and also the power for it."

A person who peruses the contents of so many books of traditions (*hadith*) may say that the Koran is different from *hadith,* because the contents of the Koran are the direct revelations or the words of Allah, but the written contents of *hadith* may not be genuine. If so, such a person is in what psychologists call denial. In other words, such a person is fooling himself in order to retain his faith in the absurdities to which he has been conditioned. In fact, the absurdities of the Koran discussed in previous chapters and the contents of *hadith* are both products of the same disturbed mentality. The former are manifested in a book that is labeled the Koran and the latter are contained in a book entitled *hadith.* The contents of the Koran are as absurd as the fables of *hadith.* The Koran says the sun sets in a pool of murky water and *hadith* says the sun takes its luminosity from the Throne of Allah and prostrates in front of him. If there is anything in the world for which we should pray, it is to pray for Homo sapiens to become truly sapient.

The Phases of the Moon as an Indicator of Pilgrimage

Nothing is more blatantly absurd and ridiculous in the Koran as when it talks about astronomy. For example, in verse 189 of *Sura* II, Allah reveals to the apostle:

> "They ask thee Concerning the New Moons [crescent]. Say: they are but signs to mark fixed periods of time in the affairs of men, and for Pilgramage . . ."

This silly idea of Mohammed about the moon is derived from Jewish literature. *Talmud Yerushalmi,* indicates that the moon is an indication of the time for holidays and pilgrimages. Similarly, in *Midrash* we read that the moon serves as an indicator for pilgrimages and festivals.[250]

The science of astronomy tells us that like all other satellites and all planets, the moon shines primarily by light received from the sun. Ordinarily, only that portion of the moon illuminated by the sun's rays can be seen. An exception occurs near the crescent phase, when the earthshine reflected from the earth faintly illuminates the moon, causing the "old moon in the new moon's arms." The various phases of the moon have been a source of superstitious prophecy by mankind from time immemorial. Among certain peoples, they govern the time for the planting and sowing of crops, the slaughter of farm animals, etc. Therefore, it is not surprising that Mohammed should superstitiously use a certain phase of the moon as an indicator of pilgrimage. The phases of the moon do have an effect on the height of the ocean's tide but that can be explained by the law of gravity

Entry by the Backdoor is Irreligious in Islam

To the amazement of the reader, the same verse immediately continues:

> "It is no virtue if you enter your houses from the back. It is virtue if you fear Allah. Enter houses through the proper door and fear Allah. That you may prosper."

The writer of this book was perplexed of the tenor of the above-mentioned verse, particularly the relationship between "crescent moons" and "entering the houses from their proper doors." To find out about this conundrum, I consulted several commentaries and as usual, to my disappointment, I found the commentaries not only contradictory, but also even more bewildering than the verse itself.

---

[250] *Gen.* 1:14; *ps.* 104:19.

In the *Qur'an, the Fundamental Law of Human Life,* Seyyed Anwar Ali writes:

"The Arabs were very superstitious, and when anyone of them used to set before himself an important subject, and was unable to attain it, he would not go into his house by the front door but used to enter it from the backdoor and kept doing so for a year. Similarly, it was their practice that whenever they were in the state of *Ehraam* (performing Hajj,) they did not enter their houses from the front door but come from the back doors, and they used to think it righteousness."[251]

Yusuf Ali, in his Holy Qur'an writes:

"Much might be written about the manifold meanings of this Muslim proverb, a few may be noted here. (1) If you enter a society, respect its manners and customs. (2) If you want to achieve an object honorably, go about it openly and not "by a backdoor." (3) Do not beat about the bush. (4) If you wish success in an undertaking, provide all the necessary instruments for it."[252]

Another commentator called Dr. Katib writes:

"This verse was metaphorically used to reprove certain people who used to ask the prophet Mohammed things that were of no concern to them. The verse says that this resembled the entering of houses from the back, a matter considered a foul habit. However, the majority of commentators have said that this part of the verse was meant to reprove the Arabs for this foul habit and urged them to enter houses through doors, not from the back."[253]

If entering the houses from the backdoors has been considered a "foul habit," why (1) did Allah not tell Arabs clearly in a separate verse to abandon this habit? (2) How could the illiterate Arabs perceive that this verse is a metaphor *if* it were intended as such? (3) Why did Allah not explain to the Arabs the disadvantages of this

---

[251] Seyyed Anwar Ali, *Qura'n, the Fundamental Law of Human Life,* vol. 3, (Karachi, Pakistan: Hamdard Foundation press, 1984), p. 98.

[252] Yusuf Ali, *The Holy Qur'an,* p. 75.

[253] Dr. Katib, *The Bounteous Koran,* p. 37.

"foul habit" instead of enshrouding it in such an ambiguous manner? (4) If entering the house from the backdoor was a "foul habit," why didn't Allah ordain Arabs not to make a backdoor for their houses? (5) Is there an eschatological reference in the interrelationship between "crescent of moons" and "backdoor of the houses?"

When one considers the lustful, amoral propensities of the Messenger who dictated the words of Allah, an affirmative answer to the last of the above questions seems more and more likely.

Allah Keeps the Sky from Falling on the Earth

Believe it or not, in verse 654 of *Sura* XXII, the Koran says:

> "Have you not seen that Allah has subjected to you all that is in the earth, and the vessels that run upon the sea by his behest? And that He holds back the heaven lest it should fall on the earth, save by His leave? Truly, Allah is to mankind propitious and merciful."

Indeed Allah is very kind and gracious to His creatures, otherwise he would abolish the heavens and then the sinners would see what would happen to them! Let us thank Allah for having transformed some of the Jews into monkeys (Koran, II: 65 and VII: 163–166),[254] and some into rats and pigs,[255] and destroying the Thamud by an earthquake because they had not taken care of His she-camel (Koran, VII: 73, VII: 77, LIX: 23, 27, 29–31, XCI: 11,13,14). Fortunately, he has not yet let the sky fall upon the earth!

Devils Court Missiles

Allah says in the Koran that He has adorned the lowest heaven with lamps, and He has made such lamps as missiles to drive away the evil ones and has prepared for them the penalty of the blazing fire.

---

[254] *Sahih al-Bukhari,* vol. 4, p. 415.

[255] *Ibid.,* vol. 4, p. 333.

Quite interestingly, in verses 8 and 9 of *Sura* LXXII, the Koran says that they (*jinns* or spirits) pried into the secrets of heaven; but they found it filled with stern guards and meteors. It continues on to say that *jinn* used to sit in hidden places to eavesdrop; but now whoever listens will find a meteor-missile waiting to ambush him.

The Holy Koran and the *hadith* both tell us that the Almighty Allah, despite his visionary power, is not safe in the sky because there are some devils (*jinns*) that haunt the throne of Allah in order to spy upon celestial activities. Therefore, Allah assigns a group of angels to shoot them and stave off their presence in his heaven. The *hadith* also corroborates the passages of the Koran in this regard.

The absurdities of the Koran go beyond imagination. Mankind has been able to land human beings on the moon and, by robots, explore distant planets. But the contents of the Koran teach us that sending a man to the moon or other space exploration is just a waste of time and money. To attempt to understand this irrational, but amusing, revelation one has only to read the following passages and *hadith* from the Koran:

> "We have indeed adorned the lower sky with the ornaments of the planets, to guard against every rebellious devil. They do not listen to the Higher Assembly and are pelted from every side; expelled, and theirs is a lasting punishment. Except for him who eavesdropped once; and so a shooting star followed him." (Koran, XXXVII: 6–10)
>
> "We have adorned the lowest heaven with lamps, missiles for pelting devils. We have prepared a scourge of flames for those, and the scourge of hell for unbelievers: an evil fate." (Koran, LXVII: 5)
>
> "The jinns also said, 'We made our way to high heaven and found it filled with mighty guards and flaming stars. And that we used to sit in some of the sitting places eavesdropping, but eavesdroppers find flaming darts in wait for them.'" (Koran, LXXII: 8–9)
>
> Abu Qatada mentioning Allah's statement said, "The creation of these stars is for three purposes, i. e., as decoration in the sky, as missiles to hit the devils, and as signs to guide travelers. So, if anybody tries to find a different interpretation, he is mistaken and just wastes his efforts, and troubles himself with what is beyond his limited knowledge (e.g. to send a man over the stars or moon etc. is just wasting of money and energy)."[256]

---

[256] *Ibid.,* p. 282.

See also (Koran, XV: 16–18, LV: 33–35, LXXXVI: 2–3).

Fairy tales are amusing, but the Koranic fables and Allah's injunctions are funny in a pitiful way. If all the Koranic "knowledge" were to be accepted by our scientists, we would not have the beautiful, detailed pictures of our neighboring planets or the knowledge sent back by our deep space probes. Allah and His Messenger are purveyors of pure quackery. Why don't the Muslims of the world realize this when they see actual photographs of Mars, Jupiter and other planets?

The Earth is Stationary

The Koran states that the earth is stationary and does not move. Another mystery that Koranic astronomy has unearthed for mankind is that the All-knowing Allah has created heavens without visible pillars; that he has spread the earth like a bed and has put unmovable mountains in there like pegs lest it should move away with you.

> "He created heavens without visible pillars, and put immovable mountains upon the earth lest it should shake with you, and he dispersed upon it animals of every kind; and We send down waters from the sky, then caused to grow therein (vegetation) of every noble kind." (Koran, XXXI: 10)
> "And He set firm mountains upon the earth lest it should move away with you; and rivers and roads that you may be rightly guided." (Koran, XVI: 15)
> "Did we not spread the earth like a bed and raise the mountains like pegs?" (Koran, LXXVIII: 607)

This depiction of the compassion of the Almighty Allah in providing "pegs" made of mountains to prevent movement of the earth makes a lovely and poetic myth. However, the Messenger of Allah must have been a superb salesman to have been able to sell belief in this fantasy to pragmatic Bedouin Arabs who were eye witnesses to the earthquakes prevalent in that region of the world!

The All-Knowable Allah

The epistemology of Allah as recorded in the Koran is also very interesting and informative. In the last verse of *Sura* XXXI, the

Almighty, Omniscient, and Cognizant Allah brags that he is the only one who knows these five things: (1) The Hour (time of resurrection), (2) When it shall rain, (3) The gender of the foetus in the womb of a pregnant woman, (4) What a person will earn on the next day, and (5) The land wherein one shall die.

> "Verily Allah alone has knowledge of the Hour and when he sends rain, and knowledge of what is in the wombs. No one knows what he will earn tomorrow; no one knows in what land he will die. Surely Allah is Knowing, and Aware." (Koran, XXXI: 38)

An exegete (especially if Arabic) may be ultra generous and give the benefit of doubt to Allah on three occasions of the five above-mentioned points, but attributing two of them to Allah is indeed ridiculous. One is the knowledge of the gender of a foetus in the womb of a pregnant woman and the second, weather forecasting. Probably, the Allah who revealed the Koran to Mohammed about 1400 years ago was quite different from the Muslim's Allah of today. Today, with better than fair accuracy, meteorologists are able to forecast weather conditions about four days in advance. By means of a sonogram or amniocentesis, we can determine the sex of a foetus seven months prior to delivery,

Although science and technology have developed tremendously in our era, the beliefs of Muslims have remained set in stone for 1400 years. Even in those seventh century days of scientific ignorance, there were people who rejected the mendacities of the religious impostures. It is a pity that in the space age of today and 300 years after the inception of the Enlightenment, some *homo sapiens* [alleged] are still victimized by such charlatanism.

The Ocean in the Air

Mohammed said:

> "Allah created an ocean 18 kilometers removed from the heaven. Waves contained (Koran, XXI: 33), it stands in the air by the command of God. No drop of it is spilled. All the oceans are motionless, but that ocean flows at the rate of the speed of an arrow. It is set to move in the

air evenly, as if were a rope stretched out in the area between east and west. The sun, the moon, and the retrograde stars (Koran, LXXXI: 15). run in its deep swell . . . Each swims in a sphere. The sphere is the circulation of the chariot in the deep swell of the ocean. By Him who holds the soul of Mohammed in His hand If the sun were to emerge from the ocean, it would burn everything on earth, including even rocks and stones, and if the moon were to emerge from it, it would afflict (by its heat) the inhabitants of the earth to such an extent that they would worship gods other than Allah. The exception would be those of Allah's friends whom he would want to keep free from sin . . . All of the other stars are suspended from heaven as lamps are from mosques, and circulate together with heaven praising and sanctifying Allah with prayer." The prophet then said, "If you wish to have this made clear, look to the circulation of the sphere alternately here and there."[257]

Who is a Muslim? A Muslim (and not necessarily a good one), believes in the teachings of Allah, His Messenger, the Koran, and *hadith.* If so, the more than one billion Muslims of the world should believe what has been written above, or they are not Muslims. If they are really Muslims, they must believe in the fantasies conjured up by a cameleer about 1400 years ago. If they exercise their innate common sense and reject such witless absurdities, they are not Muslims. Those who have faith in such irrationalities make themselves the victim of a self-seeking, blood thirsty, philandering Bedouin.

---

[257] Tabari, *The History of at-Tabari,* vol. 1, pp. 235–236.

CHAPTER FIVE

HADITH, THE TERRORIST MANIFESTO OF ISLAM

Mohammed: "I have been victorious with terror and while I was sleeping, the keys of the treasures of the world were brought to me and put in my hand."

Sahih al-Bukhai, vol. 4, p. 140.

What is the *Hadith*?

Islam deals not only with theology, it governs all political, military, social, penal, commercial, ritualistic, and ceremonial matters. It enters into every aspect of human life, even into such private areas as one's dress, mating and marriage, and even behavior in the toilet. The non-Muslim world is not familiar with the importance of *sonna* or *hadith*[258] in Islamic theology. The Koran is the theological constitution of Islam and, as such, is its most sacred scripture. The *hadith* is the major source of Islamic laws, precepts, and practices and is just as important as the Koran. The *hadith* is sometimes called the "second inspiration" with the Koran being the "first inspiration."[259]

The Koran and *hadith* are the two foundations upon which is raised the structure of Islam; the former being the word of God, and the latter being its elucidation. It stands to reason that just as the Islamic religious

---

[258] In the religious literature of Islam *Sonna* and *hadith* are used synonymously. There is, however, a slight difference in them. The word *sonna* means precedent and custom. In the technical sense it implies the doings and practices of Mohammed only. *Hadith* originally means a piece of news, a tale, a story or a report relating to a present or past event. In the technical sense it stands for the report of the words and deeds, approval or disapproval of Mohammed. It contains two parts: the chain of transmission and the text.

[259] Ludwig W. Adamee, *The A to Z of Islam* (Scarecrow Press, Inc., 2002), p. 106.

scholars would not like the absurdities of the Koran to be exposed to non-Muslims; they would not like the details of their religious "legal system" scrutinized by unsympathetic infidels. In this regard, Muir writes: "As to the *hadith,* I altogether fail to understand how any translator can justify rendering into English much that is contained in the sections, on marriage, purification, divorce, and female slavery."[260]

The word *hadith* is a noun formed from the verb *hadatha,* which means "to be new." In the Hebrew *hadash* has the same meaning and the noun *hodesh* means "new moon." The sources of Islam are actually two: the Koran and the *Sonna* or *hadith,* both products of the self-serving, self-called Prophet, Mohammed. Indeed the Koran minus *hadith* remains unintelligible in many cases in the work-a-day life of Muslims.[261] The Koran provides the text, the *hadith* the context. As an example, according to the Islamic jurists, the Koran says, "keep up prayer and pay zakat." This has been repeated many times, but yet it did not specify the manner of prayer or particulars re zakat. It was the *hadith* or practices of Mohammed that gave both a specific shape and form. Thus in Islam, every point, however remote, was illustrated and explained by Mohammed himself in his precepts and examples.

A good Muslim therefore needs both a copy of the Koran and a copy of the *hadith* to guide his feet along the path of Allah.[262] In fact, the Koran cannot be understood without the aid of the *hadith,* because every verse of the Koran has a context which can only be understood by reading the *hadith.* The *hadith* gives flesh and blood to the Koranic so-called revelations and reveals their earthly application.[263] The *hadith* is the total sum of words and deeds attributed to Mohammed by his contemporaries. As used by Muslim theologians, it also includes his tacit approval of words attributed to his wives, relatives, and companions. The word *hadith* means "communication, sayings or traditions." This is the Talmud of Islam and is as authoritative to the followers of Mohammed as the Koran itself.

---

[260] Muir, *The life of Mohammed,* p. 334.

[261] Alhaj Maulana Fazlul Karim, *Mishkat-ul-Masabih,* trans. Alhaj Maulana Fazlul Karim, book 1 (Calcutta, India: Mohammadi press, 1938), p. 3.

[262] *Ibid.* vol. 1, p. 2.

[263] Ram Swarup, *Understanding the Hadith* (Prometheus Books, 2002), p.7.

Mohammed said:

> "He who loves not my *Hadith* is not my follower. He who in distress holds fast to the *Hadith* will receive the reward of a hundred martyrs."[264]

While Mohammed was alive he was the sole guide in all matters, whether spiritual or secular. *Hadith,* or tradition in the technical sense, may be said to have started at his death. The extraordinary influence of his personality on his companions and associates created from the beginning a need for believers to learn what the so-called prophet had done and taught in various circumstances in order that the life of the Muslim community might be modeled on him.[265] The Shi'a community adds the traditions of the Twelve Imams, who they deem to be as infallible as the Prophet, to Islamic *hadith.*

The *hadith* forms a voluminous literature in Islam. It consists of details of Mohammed's life, some most trivial, which became not only a model but led to imperatives for Muslims to follow. Though Allah commands Mohammed in the Koran to tell the people that he is just a human being no different from them (Koran, XLI: 6), Mohammed assigned many "divine" attributes to himself and these have been incorporated in the Muslim conception of him as the perfect role model. Thousands of *hadith* have been collected and used as a source of Islamic law. Muslims try to imitate every aspect of his life. What Mohammed did and did not do is taken to be binding even in such matters as marrying, diet, how to eat, hair-styling, mating, using a brush to clean one's teeth, and even toilet rules (such as which hand to use when cleansing after evacuation). In situations in which guidance is lacking, the Muslims will find themselves at loss as to what to do. It is said that Imam Ibn Hanbal, the leader of the Hanbali sect never ate watermelons, even though he knew that Mohammed had done so, because he did not know his [Mohammed's] manner of eating them. The same story is related by Bayazid Bastami,

---

[264] J. Murdoch, *Arabia and its Prophet* (Madras, India: The Christian Literature Society for India, 1922), p. 29.

[265] Guillaume, *The Traditions of Islam,* p. 13.

a great Sufi, whose mystical teachings went against orthodox Koranic theology.[266]

The believers in Islam are conditioned to look at the whole religious system through the eyes of faith and ignore their own common
sense. A non-Muslim, when looking at Mohammed's life, finds it sensual, cruel and inhumane. Morality, as defined by non-Muslim values, did not govern Mohammed's actions, but his actions determine
and define morality to the True Believer. Mohammed's behavior was
not considered that of an ordinary human, but rather Allah's own
acts. By such absurd logic, Mohammed's opinions became the sacred dogma of the religion of Islam and his personal habits and idio-
syncrasies became moral imperatives to True Believers.[267]

Hadith and the Koran

Hadith has been used in the Koran twenty-three times. Next to the
Koran, it is the most important part of the Islamic law; its teachings
are just as binding. As evidenced by the official Islamic introduction
to the Koran, Islamic scholars contend: "The Koran is one leg of two
which form the basis of Islam. The second leg is the *Sonna* of Mohammed. What makes the Koran different from the *Sonna* is its form.
Unlike the *Sonna,* the Koran is quite literally the so-called Word of
Allah, whereas the *Sonna* was inspired by Allah but the wording and
actions belong to Mohammed. Muslims believe that no human
words are used in the Koran. Its wordings are letter for letter fixed by
Allah."[268] It is amusing, as noted in the second chapter of this book,
that some parts of the Koran are written in such a scurrilous manner that no courteous, decent person would ever use that filthy language, much less a man of letters.

Mohammed had said, "I have bequeathed to you two things; if
you hold fast to them, you will never go stray. They are the Koran and

---

[266] Swarup, *Understanding the Hadith,* p. 4.

[267] *Ibid.* p.11.

[268] Winn, *Muhammad, Prophet of Doom,* p. v.

Sonna."[269] Therefore, *hadith* is so important in Islamic theology that it is regarded as on a par with the Koran. The Koran says:

"And (the apostle) does not say of (his own) desire. It is no less than inspiration sent down to him." (Koran LIII: 3 and 4)

". . . . And whatsoever the apostle gives you take it; and whatsoever he forbids avoid it . . . ." (Koran, LIX: 7)

". . . . We have sent to you the message so that you may explain to the people what has been sent to you." (Koran, XVI: 44)

"He who obeys the apostle, obeys Allah . . . ." (Koran, IV:80)

"You have indeed in the apostle of Allah a beautiful example (of conduct)." (Koran, XXXIII: 21)."

An Arab author says that all the sayings, and the actions of Mohammed were divinely inspired. He states:

"The *Sonna* and *a hadith* are not to be taken as the wise sayings of sages and philosophers or the verdicts of rulers and leaders. One should believe with full conviction that the words and actions of the Prophet represent the will of Allah, and thus one has to follow and obey them in each and every circumstance of life."[270]

The above passages clearly indicate that the sayings and the conduct of Mohammed as the Apostle of Allah is equivalent to the Koranic verses. More than that, *hadith* may explain certain statements in the Koran[271] where an explanation is needed to complement the Koran. Muslim theologians make no distinction between the Koran and the *hadith.* To them both are the works of revelation or inspiration. They believe the *hadith* is the Koran in action, in the sense that in the Koran, Allah speaks through His so-called Apostle; in the *hadith,* He acts through him.

The Koran by itself is difficult to follow; it leaves readers confused as it jumps from story to story, with little background narration or explanation. In some instances the *hadith* prevails over the Koran. For

---

[269] Mohammed Abdul Rauf, *Al-Hadith* (Washington, D.C.: The Islamic Center, 1974), p. 11.

[270] Dr. Mazhar U. Kazi, *A Treasury of a Hadith,* Introduction.

[271] *Ibid.*

example, the Koran refers to three daily prayers (*Suras* XI: 114, XVII: 78, XXX: 17). The *hadith* demands five. Muslims prostrate themselves in accordance with Mohammed's *Sonna* orders rather than Allah's Koranic command.[272]

In one sense, the significance of *hadith* literature in Islam is even greater than that of the Koran. A Koranic text might imply different meanings according to various interpreters. But a *hadith,* since it is allegedly a true recording of Mohammed's practices, is a unique truth for all time to come and need not be interpreted.[273]

The Shi'ah, specifically the *Twelvers,* also rely on *hadith* as a major source of authority. The Shi'ah share many *hadith* with the Sunni Muslims, yet among the former, the authority of a *hadith* is much more certain when it depends on the word of the Imams rather than the line of transmitters. Many Shi'ah *hadith* are not accepted by the Sunnis, because they represent the teachings of the Imams.[274]

Allah Made Plundering Lawful to Mohammed

Mohammed recognized the legitimacy of Judaism and Christianity and the apostleship of Moses and Jesus, but he claimed to have superiority over them in five respects, including the legality of war booty. *Hadith* 1: 1062 of Sahih Muslim and 1: 199–200; 7: 1. 331 of Sahih al-Buchari in this regard say:

> Narrated Jabir Ibn Abdullah: The Prophet said, "I have been given five things which were not given to any one else before me."
>
> "Allah made me victorious by awe, (by His frightening my enemies) for a distance of one month's journey."
>
> "The earth has been made for me (and for my followers) a place for praying and a thing to perform Tayammum, therefore anyone of my followers can pray wherever the time of a prayer is due."
>
> ***Booty has been made lawful for me yet it was not lawful for anyone else before me.***

---

272 Winn, *Muhammad, Prophet of Doom,* p. v.

273 Majumdar, *Jihad, The Islamic Doctrine of permanent War,* p. 10.

274 *The Encyclopedia of Religion,* 1987 ed., "Hadith," by "L. T. Librande."

Every Prophet used to be sent to his nation only but I have been sent to all humankind.[275]

I have been given the right of intercession (on the Day of Resurrection).[276]

"Spoils of war" or "war booty" is a euphemism for plundering and ransacking. Its importance in the Islamic lexicon is such that the Koran and *hadith* have covered it on many occasions. Booty obtained by war was categorized in two forms: *al-ghanima* and *fai'*. The first form includes spoils which will be distributed among the Muslim combatants after the conflict is over and the properties of the defeated people have been plundered; the second one is the properties of the people who surrendered without offering resistance.

In the second chapter it was mentioned that according to the Koran (VIII: 41), One-fifth of the spoils of war is assigned to the so-called prophet (Mohammed). Keeping the plunder for oneself and not giving the commander his cut or misappropriation of the spoils is a great sin. In this regard, Mohammed says:

"Fight against those who disbelieve in Allah. Make a holy war; do not embezzle the spoils."[277]

The sanction against embezzlement or "skimming" of the spoils is in addition to the injunctions in the Koran about plunder. Plundering is an inevitable and natural sequel to a savage Bedouin victory in battle. When the victors go on a plundering spree, it is only the iron discipline imposed by their leader that prevents them from fighting amongst themselves for a larger share of the gain.

Now, if Allah were to invoke divine sanction and rules governing plundering, He must make similar provision against misappropriation of the fruits of battle. The two things hang together, and what the

---

[275] This statement of Muhammed is a blatant contradiction to the verse 7 of the chapter 42 and the verse 4 of the chapter 14 of the Koran. The former states, "We have revealed to you this Arabic Koran, that you may warn the Mother City (Mecca) and all around it of the Day of Assembly , of which there is no doubt. . . . And the latter verse says, "We have sent no apostle but in the language of his own people, so that he might make plain to them (his message). . . . ."

[276] *Sahih Muslim,* vol. 1, pp. 265–266; *Sahih al-Bukhari,* 1: 199–200.

[277] *Sahih Muslim,* No. 4294, p. 943.

Hadith has added to the Koran is only a legitimate extension of it.[278] In the second chapter it was mentioned that according to the Koran (IV: 24), Muslims have the right to have sexual intercourse with women captured in wars, even if they are married women. The following *Hadith* brings this out very clearly:

> "Abu Sa'id Khaduri reported that at the Battle of Hunain Allah's Messenger sent an army to Autas . . . Having overcome (the infidels) and taken them captives, the Companions of Allah's Messenger seemed to refrain from having intercourse with the captive women because of their husbands being polytheists. Then, Allah's Most High, sent down regarding that: 'Forbidden unto you are the woman already married except those whom your right hand possesses." (Koran, IV: 24) (i. e. they were lawful for them when their Idda period [three menstrual cycles] comes to an end).[279]

A far more significant extension made by the *hadith* to the doctrine of spoils is the proprietorship of the whole earth which belongs completely to Allah and His Apostle. The Koran (48: 21) speaks of the "other gain which the Muslims have not yet been able to achieve." But the following *hadith* touches the issue of Islamizing the whole of humanity. The *Sahih Muslim* narrates of the authority of Abu Hurairah:

> "We were sitting in the mosque when the Messenger of Allah came out and said, 'Let us go to the Jews. We went out with him until we came to them. The Messenger of Allah stood up and called out to them: O you assembly of Jews, accept Islam and you will be safe." (No. 4363).

In other words, the whole earth is the goal of Mujahid's eventual conquest. The *hadith* has not minced matters, but divulged the supreme mission of the Islam with absolute frankness.[280]

The injunction of *Fai'* is even more interesting than "war booty." The booty derived from a war not actively fought against non-Muslims entirely falls to the lot of the Prophet. The verse 7 of *Sura* 59 says:

---

278 Majumdar, Jihad, *The Islamic Doctrine of Permanent War*, p. 31.

279 *Sahih Muslim*, No. 3432, p. 743.

280 Majumdar, *Jihad, The Islamic Doctrine of Permanent War*, p. 32.

"What Allah has bestowed on His Messenger (and taken away) from them—for this you made no expedition with either cavalry or camelry: and they thought that their fortresses would defend them from Allah! But the (Wrath of Allah) came to them from quarters from which they little expected (it), and cast terror into their hearts, so that they destroyed their dwellings by their own hands and the hand of the believers. . . . ."

The *hadith* also will back the injunction of the Koran and says:

"It has been narrated on the authority of Abu Huraira that the Messenger of Allah said: 'If you come to a township which has surrendered without a formal war and stay therein, you have a share that will be in the form of an award in the properties obtained from it. If a township disobeys Allah and his Messenger and actually fights against the Muslims one-fifth of the booty seized therefrom is for Allah and his apostle and the rest is for you'"[281] Omar, also has said: 'The properties abandoned by Bani Nadhir were the ones which Allah bestowed upon his apostle for which no expedition was undertaken either with cavalry or camelry. These properties were completely assigned to the prophet.'"[282]

One plot of land from the confiscated properties known as "the summer garden of Mary," Mohammed donated to his Coptic slave-concubine. He also had seven other gardens in Medina which, according to some, were bestowed on him by a Jew named Mukhayriq, but according to others were a portion of the confiscated estates of Bani Nadhir. Similarly he had properties at Khaibar, part of the spoils that accrued to him when that Jewish community was defeated.[283]

In short, the *hadith* perpetuate Mohammed's mission and atrocities, so that he and his aggressive behavior remain a living example for each generation of Muslims of the world. Mohammed keeps Allah as close to himself as his skin and since no one can see Allah and talk to him except His Messenger, common sense indicates that

---

[281] *Ibid,* No. 4346, pp. 953–54.

[282] *Ibid,* No. 4347, p. 954.

[283] Swarup, *Understanding the Hadith,* p. 113.

the words "Allah," "Mohammed's near relatives", "orphans," "the needy" and so on, are a *nom de plume* for the Messenger himself. Mohammed knows how to talk with the tongue of Allah on behalf of himself to make his wishes seem divinely inspired and thus secure the obedience of his fellow-citizens.

But who really is this Allah, who is so intertwined with His Apostle? This unseen entity was resident in the Ka'ba, before Mohammed thought of making himself a candidate for apostleship. Allah was the largest of the wooden idols of Ka'ba. Mohammed shrewdly took advantage of the worshippers of this idol and used its name for the God for whom he considered himself the Apostle. This Allah was larger than the other idols, particularly the *banatollah* (his three daughters) and that is why every day more than one billion Muslims throughout the world constantly recite "*Allaho Akbar,*" meaning "Allah is greater," not that "Allah is the greatest." To satisfy the rules of English grammar, consider Allah as one entity and all of the remaining 359 idols as a *single* separate entity.

In light of the above-mentioned injunctions of Allah in the Koran and Mohammed's sayings as written in the *hadith,* one can agree that "*terrorism*" was, by Mohammed's way of thinking, a useful tool to employ to achieve his goals. This explains why he perpetrated so many atrocities while pursuing his ambitions. When he talks about "spoils being made lawful to him," he is creating another "revelation" from his own puppet-God to justify his own greedy and lustful actions.

An axiom says that it is better to tell the truth than to lie since one can remember the truth but may easily forget a lie. Not only in the above *hadith,* but also in the verse 158 of the *Sura* VII, Mohammed boasts of being the prophet of all mankind and even *jinns* and also the Seal of all the Prophets. In claiming that Allah has made him a prophet to all mankind and the line of prophets ends with him, Mohammed forgot that when he was in Mecca, only a few people of his own household gathered around him. In verse 4 of *Sura* XIV of the Koran he said:

> We sent not an apostle except (to teach) in language of his (own) people, in order to make (things) clear to them . . . ."

Also in verse 47 of *Sura* X, he said:

"To every people (was sent) an apostle: when their apostle comes (before them), the matter will be judged between them with justice, and they will not be wronged."

And in verse 7 of *Sura* XLII, he said:

"We sent to thee an Arabic Koran: that thou mayest warn the mother of cities and all around her, and (warn) them of the day of assembly, of which there is no doubt: (when) some will be in the garden, and some in the blazing fire."

These contradictions clearly show that Mohammed was a power hungry man who used prevarication and fraud to obtain dominion over the people of Arabia. The preposterous norms presented in the form of *hadith* and the Koranic verses, are aimed at mesmerizing ignorant Arabs, negating their common sense and enslaving them to his absurd ideas.

Paradise is Under the Shadow of Swords

The above saying is ascribed to Mohammed.[284] The sword, Mohammed also said, "is the key to Heaven and Hell."[285] Abdullah Ibn Abi Aufa wrote that Mohammed declared, "You have to know that Paradise is under the shade of swords."[286] Arabs have a proverb that says, "The history of the sword is the history of humanity," and "If there were no sword there would be no law of Mohammed." *Saif-ul-Islam* (Sword of Islam) was the catch word of the Ottoman Empire (Turkish regime). The Muslims of the Ottoman Empire were taught, the following axiom:

"The needs of life are three, my water, food, and the *Jihad*."[287]

---

[284] Bernard Lewis, ed. and trans., *Islam from the Prophet Muhammad to the Capture of Constantinople,* 2 Vols., vol. 1 (United Kingdom: Macmillan Press, 1975), p. 210.

[285] Al-Muttaqi, *Kanzal al-Ummal,* p. 258.

[286] *Sahih al-Bukhari,* vol. 4, p. 55.

[287] Ameen Rihani, *Arabian Peak and Desert* (London: Constable & Co. Ltd, 1930), p. 109.

The *hadith* below shows that Mohammed wanted his self-made religion to be spread primarily by the sword. It is filled with injunctions to make war upon non-Muslims and force them to embrace Islam. Anas Ibn Malik narrated that,

> Allah's Apostle offered the Fajr prayer when it was still dark, then he rode and said, "Allaho Akbar! (God is great) Khaibar is ruined. When we entered the arena of nation, the most unfortunate is the morning of those who have been warned." The people came out into the streets saying, "Mohammed and his army." Allah's Apostle vanquished them by force and their warriors were killed; the children and women were taken as captives. Safiyyah was taken by Dahya al-Kalbi and later she belonged to Allah's Apostle who married her and her *Mahr* (marriage settlement) was her manumission.[288]

In his commentary, *Book of Worship,* al-Ghazali stated that the preacher in the mosque occupies his hands with the hilt of a sword or staff when he delivers his sermon. The custom of holding a sword in hand apparently started with Mohammed himself in the pulpit of the earliest mosque in Medina. In his scholarly investigation of this custom, Edward William Lane came to the conclusion that the pulpit was the judge's bench for Mohammed when he dispensed Islamic justice. The pulpit and sword are inseparable throughout Islamic history. The preaching of Islam and the power of its warlike propaganda were welded together by its founder.[289]

The German Orientalist, C. H. Becker, in his monograph on the pulpit in early Islam, corroborates Lane's idea about the usage of sword in Islam. He writes, "The preacher ascends the pulpit with a staff or sword or lance or bow in his right hand."[290]

Valentine Chirol writes:

> "Islam alone of all the great religions of the human race was born sword in hand. Islam has always relied on the sword, and for thirteen

---

[288] *Sahih al-Bukhari,* vol. 2. No. 68, p. 35.

[289] Edward William Sale, *Manners and Customs of the Modern Egyptians* (London: Darf Publishers Ltd, 1986).

[290] C. H. Becker, *Die Kanzel im Kultus des alten Islam* ("Islam Studien," Leipzig, 1924), pp. 451, 456, 469, quoted by Zwemer, *Studies in Popular Islam,* p. 35.

hundred years the mullah who reads the Friday prayers in the mosque wears a sword, even if only made of wood, as a symbol of his creed."[291]

William Muir also writes, " . . . the sword is the inevitable penalty for the denial of Islam. . . . ." and continues, "The sword of Mohammed and the Koran are the most fatal enemies of civilization, liberty and truth, which the world has still to know [*sic*]."[292]

In 1734, George Sale, whose English translation of the Koran was a turning point in the re-evaluation of the Koran in the West, wrote: "It is certainly one of the most convincing proofs that Mohammedanism was no other than a human invention, that it owed its progress and establishment almost entirely to the sword."[293]

Islam and Peace are Incompatible

In the second chapter it was said that on the basis of verse 35 of *Sura* XLVII of the Koran, Allah hates peace-seekers. There are also some *hadith* which indicate that Islam is not a religion of peace and that Allah advocates bellicosity. The Koran defines good and bad Muslims. It says a good Muslim is the one who has the passion to fight, to terrorize, and to kill. He is a man who leaves his home, sacrificing his wealth and life, to fight in Allah's cause. Allah says he will be rewarded with the plundered belongings of the victims of his savagery if he survives, or with a heavenly bordello if he dies in battle. On the other hand, Allah characterizes a bad Muslim as one who is a lover of peace and as such is despised by Allah. He even says that peaceful Muslims are "the vilest of creatures" and that hell's hottest fires await them.[294]

Mishkat al-Masabih has quoted a *hadith* which clearly shows that peace and Islam are indeed wholly incompatible. The following

---

[291] William Chirol, *Foreign Affairs,* vol. I, No. 3.

[292] Muir, *The Life of Mohammad,* p. 522.

[293] Norman Daniel, *Islam and the West,* p. 300.

[294] Winn, *Muhammed, Prophet of Doom,* p. v.

shows how contemptuous Mohammed was of religions that advocate peace. Abu Umana related:

> "On certain occasions we went out with the Prophet on a campaign. One man among us was passing by a well standing by the side of a field studded with green vegetation. The spot roused in his mind a strange longing (for a life of seclusion, and he thought): 'How glorious would it be if I could renounce the vanities of the world and reside in this spot (for the rest of my days).' He sought the permission of Allah's Messenger. Said His Highness: '(Listen to me, O man of little understanding): I was not sent down (by Allah) to preach the religion of Jews and Christians. To keep oneself busy in the way of Allah for a single morning or afternoon is better than the whole earth and whatever (wealth) it possesses. And to get imprisoned in the field of battle is better than being engaged in surplus prayers for as many as 60 whole years.'"[295]

The above *hadith* indicates that even the partial pacifism of Judaism and Christianity was not acceptable to Mohammed and his Islam.[296]

Allah Becomes Angry with Those Murdered by His Holy Prophet

Hammam Ibn Munabbih narrated a number of *hadith* from Mohammed as told to him by Abu Huraira. One of these was that the Messenger of Allah said, "Great is the wrath of Allah upon a person who has been killed by the Messenger of Allah."

This *hadith* means that not only is Mohammed, the so-called Beloved Messenger of Allah, authorized to murder whomever he wishes, but his victim will also be subject to the wrath of Allah.[297]

---

[295]*Mishkat al-Masabih,* No. 4489, quoted by Majumdar, *Jihad, the Islamic Doctrine of* Permanent *War,* p. 22.

[296] *Ibid.* p. 23.

[297] *Ibid.,* p. 986.

The Punishment for Giving up Islam (Apostasy) is Death

A person may embrace the religion of Islam voluntarily, but when he becomes a Muslim, if he decides to give up Islam, he becomes an apostate and the punishment for the sin of apostasy is death. *Hadith* (numbers from 4130 to 4132) of Sahih Muslim say:

"Anas Ibn Malik reported that eight people belonging to the tribe of Uraina came to Allah's Messenger at Medina and swore allegiance to him on Islam, but the climate of Medina did not suit them and they became sick. Then they complained to Mohammed and he allowed them to go to the fold of his camels and drink their milk and urine to get recovered.[298] They did so and drank the camel's milk and urine and regained their health. They then fell upon the shepherds and killed them and turned away from Islam and drew away the camels. When the news reached Mohammed, he sent twenty of his followers after them to track their footprints. They were caught and brought back to him. He commanded their hands and feet to be cut off, their eyes to be put out, and be thrown on the stony ground in the sun, until they died. When they were dying, they asked for water but they were not given that."

Sahih al-Bukhari also states that:

"Narrated Abu Musa: A man embraced Islam and then reverted back to Judaism. Mu'adh Ibn Jabal came and saw the man with Abu Musa. Mu'adh asked: 'What is wrong with this (man)?' Abu Musa replied: 'He embraced Islam and then he reverted back to Judaism.' Mu'adh said: 'I will not sit down unless you kill him (as it is) the verdict of Allah and his Messenger.'"[299]

Another *hadith* of Sahih al-Bukhari says:

---

[298] In the footnote number 2120, Sahih Muslim elaborates the word "urine" in the Arab culture as, "The urine of camel was used to cure certain diseases."

[299] *Sahih al-Bukhari,* vol. 9, p. 201.

" . . . Ibn Abbas narrates that the Prophet said, "If somebody (a Muslim) discard his religion, kill him."[300]

More interesting than the above-mentioned *hadiths* about apostasy in Islam is the following one:

Narrated Ikrima, "Some pagans were brought to Ali (son-in-law of Mohammed) and he burnt them. The news of this event, reached Ibn Abbas who said, 'If I had been in his place, I would not have burnt them, as Allah's Apostle forbade it, saying, Do not punish anybody with Allah's punishment (fire). I would have killed them according to the statement of Allah's Apostle. Whoever changed his Islamic religion, then kill him.'"[301]

There is also a *hadith,* mentioned by Sahih al-Bukhari which clearly confirms that if a person discards his religion, he should be killed:

Narrated Krama that the Propher said, "I heard Mohammed said, If somebody discards his religion, kill him."[302]

Among the many contradictions in the Koran are the various stances taken on religious choice. The verse 256 of *Sura* II of the Koran says, "There is no compulsion in religion—the right way is indeed clearly distinct from error." This verse clearly indicates that belief in any religion is a personal concern and that one is given the choice of adopting one way or another as one wishes. However, to the amazement of the reader of the Koran, verse 85 of *Sura* V contradicts the above verse and says, "And whoever seeks a religion other than Islam, it will not be accepted from him, and in the hereafter he will be one of the losers." In addition, even more perplexing is the verse 33 of the same *Sura* saying, "The only punishment of those who wage war against Allah and his Messenger and strive to make mischief in the land is that they should be murdered or cruci-

---

[300] *Ibid.* vol 4, No. 260, p. 161.

[301] *Ibid.,* vol. 9:57, p. 45.

[302] *Sahih al-Bukhari,* vol. 4, pp. 161–162.

fied, or their hands and their feet should be cut off on opposite sides, or they should be imprisoned."

Sahih al-Bukhati also writes in *hadith* number 271:

> Narrated Abu Musa: A man embraced Islam and then reverted back to Judaism. Mu'adh Ibn Jabal came and saw the man with Abu Musa. Mu'adh asked, "What is wrong with this (man)?" Abu Musa replied, "He embraced Islam and then reverted back to Judaism." Mu'adh said, "I will not sit down unless you kill him (as it is) the verdict of Allah and His Messenger."[303]

The justification and rationale of the death penalty for apostasy in Islam is indeed very interesting. The *hadith* writer tells us that the death penalty for apostasy in Islam should not be considered barbarous. His rationale is that the precepts of the Kingdom of Heaven are found in the hearts of True Believers and should be externalized in every aspect of society, i.e., in politics, in economics, in law, in manners and in international relations. In such circumstances it is quite obvious that when a person rebels against the Kingdom of Heaven within his heart, he commits high treason against the Kingdom of Heaven on earth. His sin is exactly like the person who rebels against a political order and who is punished by the legitimate government. In Islam, religion is not a matter of private relationship between man and God, but it is intertwined with government and an integral part thereof. Therefore, when a Muslim abandons Islam, he in fact revolts against the authority of the Islamic state and society and, as a traitor to his country; he should be punished by death.[304]

In western culture religion is considered a matter of private and individual choice and the state is the arbiter of societal life. The rationale behind this theory is that religion deals with the ethical values of human beings and their relationship with an unseen God or other metaphysical authority whereas the political government defines by law the secular activities of the people. In this way, the government leaves its governed completely free to choose their own religion as they wish and change it as they please. The theories of

---

[303] *Ibid.,* vol 9, p. 201.

[304] *Sahih Muslim,* Nos. 4152–4156, pp. 899–90.

secularism and laicism indicate that the state should be completely separate from religion and neither of these two entities should interfere with the affairs of the other. Moreover, the constitutions of most non-Muslim countries consider religious discrimination a violation of human rights and liable to litigation and punishment.

But in Islam and Islamic countries, the case is quite different. State and religious faith are two sides of the same coin. In western culture, God is restricted to the church but in Islam, Allah and His Prophet are omnipresent in every aspect of human life; in the legislative assembly, in the administrative policies of the government and in economic activities. Islam even prescribes the manner in which personal chores are to be carried out in toilet, in bed, in hair cutting, in eating, and other private matters.

In democratic countries, if the government chosen by the people does not carry out its functions properly or does not comply with the wishes of the people, they have the right to air their dissatisfaction and change their government. But, in Islamic societies, the governmental authorities consider themselves the representative of the unseen God and finding fault with the government is considered a religious sin and equivalent to apostasy. As we mentioned before, the punishment for apostasy is death. Individuals or groups who disagree with the Islamic government are, by Islamic law, rebelling against Allah's injunctions and polity, and therefore subject to a traitor's punishment by execution. Khomeini put to death 12,000[305] of his opponents in the name of Allah in 1988. Amnesty International recorded the names of 2,500 political prisoners reportedly executed during mid-1988 and describes the vast majority of the victims as "prisoners of conscience" as they had not been charged with actual deeds or plans of deeds against the state.[306] The barbarous religious mullahs consider blasphemy equivalent to treason against the state and the political order, punishable by death.

An example of the horror of Islamic "justice" is the case of the Afghani Abdol Rahman who, in 1991, converted to Christianity. His conversion did not become known until 2006. He was immediately

---

[305] N. Mohajer, "The Mass Killings in Iran," *Aresh* 57 (August 1996): 7.

[306] Amnesty International, *Iran: Violations of Human Rights, 1987–1990* (London: 1991), 12.

sentenced to death by the Islamic court but managed to escape the country and found asylum in Italy. But how long will he continue to live since, by decree of the Islamic clerics, he is still under sentence of death?

What a just, Almighty, All-Knowing and Merciful God and Prophet governs the lives of the Muslims of this world! By His decree, they must obey the contradicting injunctions written in His sacred Book and then, because it is impossible to do so, they are consigned for eternity to the fires of Hell. A good Muslim is damned if he does and damned if he doesn't!

The Punishment of Adultery and Murder is Death

Hadith number 4152 of Sahih Muslim says:

> "Abdullah Ibn Mas'ud reported Mohammed as saying: It is not permissible to take the life of a Muslim who bears testimony (to the fact that) there is no God but Allah, and I am the Messenger of Allah, but in one of three cases: the married adulterer, a life for life, and the deserter of Islam, abandoning the community."

The punishment of fornication is one hundred lashes both for the man and the woman (Koran: XXIV: 3); for adultery, it is stoning[307] to death of the parties involved. The same *hadith* confirms that there is almost a consensus of opinion amongst the jurists that apostasy from Islam (*ertedad*) must be punished with death.

A Muslim Must Not be Killed if He Kills a Non-Muslim

If a disbeliever (Kafir) is killed by a Muslim, the latter should not be punished, because it is the right of a Muslim to kill a person who does not believe in Islam.

---

[307] Article 119 of the Islamic Penal Code of Iran (*Hodoud* and *Qesas*) states, "In the punishment of stoning to death, the stones should not be too large so that the person dies on being hit by one or two of them; they should not be so small either that they could not be defined as stones."

Narrated Abu Juhaifa, "I asked Ali, 'Do you have anything Divine literature besides what is in the Koran?' Or, as Uyaina once said, 'Apart from what the people have?' Ali said, 'By him who made the grain split [germinate] and created the soul, we have nothing except what is in the Koran and the ability [gift] of understanding Allah's Book which He may endow a man with and what is written in this sheet of paper.' I asked, 'What is on the paper?' He replied, 'The legal regulations of Diya (Blood Money) and the (ransom for) releasing of the captives, and the judgment that no Muslim should be killed in Qisas [equality in punishment] for killing a Kafir (disbeliever).'"[308]

The Muslim's duty is to go on a murder spree and wreak destruction and death upon all people who refuse to convert to Islam[309] or who are against Islam.

William Montgomery Watt of Edinburgh University has stated:

It should be emphasized that the Arabs did not regard killing a person as in itself wrong. It was wrong if the person was a member of your kin-group or an allied group; and in Islam this meant the killing of any believer. Out of fear of retaliation, one did not kill a member of a strong tribe. In other cases, however, there was no reason for not killing.[310]

It is Permissible to Hurt or Steal from non-Muslims

The Washington Post, one of the most reliable newspapers in the United States, interviewed the students of the Islamic Saudi Academy in Virginia. The paper reads, "School officials would not allow reporters to attend classes. But a number of students described the classroom instruction and provided copies of the textbooks. Ali al-Ahmad, whose Virginia-based Saudi Institute promotes religious tolerance in Saudi Arabia, has reviewed numerous textbooks used at

---

[308] *Sahih al Bukhari,* vol. 9, pp. 37–38.

[309] Dr. Solomon Talbure, *Islam Exposed* (Coral Springs, Florida: Metier Books, 2002) p. 139.

[310] Montgomery Watt, *Mohammed's Mecca,* pp. 18–19.

the academy and said many passages promote hatred of non-Muslims and Shi'te Muslims.

The 11th grade textbooks, for example, say one sign of the Day of Judgment will be that Muslims will fight and kill Jews, who will hide behind trees that say: 'Oh Muslim, Oh servant of Allah, here is a Jew hiding behind me. Come here and kill him.' Several students of different ages, all of whom asked not to be identified, said that in Islamic studies, they are taught that it is better to shun and even to dislike Christians, Jews, and Shi'ite Muslims. Some teachers 'focus more on hatred,' said one teenager, who recited by memory the signs of the coming of the Day of Judgment. 'They teach students that whoever is *Kaffir* [non-Muslim], it is okay for you to hurt or steal from that person.'"[311]

The Eyes of a Voyeur Should be Poked

Sahih al-Bukhari writes,

> "Narrated Sahl ibn Sa'd As-sadi that a man peeped through a hole in the door of Allah's Messenger's house when Allah's Messenger was rubbing his head with an iron bar. When Allah's Messenger saw him, He said, "If I had been sure that you were looking at me through the door, I would have poked your eye with this sharp iron bar." Allah's Apostle added, "The asking for permission to enter has been enjoined so that one may not look at what there is in the house without the permission of the people."[312]

Likewise, Abu Huraira narrated that Mohammed said,

> "If any person peeps at you without your permission and you poke him with a stick and injure his eye, you will not be blamed."[313]

---

[311]Valerie Strauss and Emily Wax, "Where Two Worlds Collide," *Washington Post,* Monday February 25, 2002, sec. A1, p. 1.

[312] *Sahih al-Bukhari,* vol. 9, pp. 30–31.

[313]*Ibid.,* p. 31.

Jihad, the Inhumanity of Islam

In the second chapter it was explained that Holy War (*Jihad*) is a euphemism for Islamic imperialism and terrorism. In this chapter, we shall concentrate on that group of *hadith,* that advocate terrorism or "sacred bloodshed." *Jihad* is an integral, ever present part of Islam. Mohammed has said, "*Jihad* will last until the Day of Judgment."[314] An author has written that the objective of *Jihad* is to aggressively conquer all non-Islamic countries and establish therein the theocratic Islamic system of government.[315]

The following *hadith* quoted by Sahih al-Bukhari, confirms that the most sacred action a Muslim can perform is to "fight." If so, then it can truly be said that **Islam is indeed the religion of terrorists:**

> Narrated Abu Huraira' "A Man came to Allah's Apostle and said, "Instruct me as to such a deed as equals jihad (in reward)," He replied I do not find such a deed." Then he added, "Can you, while the Muslim fighter is in the battlefield, enter your mosque to perform prayers without cease and fast and never break your fast?" The man said, "But who can do that?"[316]

Another *hadith* quoted by the same writer says:

> Narrated Ana Ibn Malik, "The Prophet said, 'A single endeavor (of fighting) in Allah's cause in the forenoon or in the afternoon is better than the world and whatever is in it."[317]

The tenor of the above tradition confirms that *jihad* is superior to all five pillars of Islam combined. *Hadith* number 35 of volume 1 of Sahih Al-Bukhari also states:

> Narrated Abu Huraira that the Prophet said, "The person who participates in (Holy Battles) in Allah's cause and nothing compels

---

314 *Ibid.,* p. 31.

315 A. Ghosh, *The Koran and the Kafir (Islam and the Infidel),* (Houston, Texas, 1983), p. 88.

316 *Sahih al-Bukhari,* vol. 4, p. 36.

317 *Ibid.,* vol. 4, p. 41.

him to do so except the belief in Allah and His Apostle, will be recompensed by Allah either with a reward, or booty (if he survives) or will be admitted to Paradise (if he is killed in the battle as a martyr). Had I not found it difficult for my followers, then I would not remain behind any expedition going for jihad and I would have loved to be martyred in Allah's cause and then made alive, and then martyred and then made alive, and then again martyred in His cause."

The above tradition has been narrated by Abu Bakr, Othman, Ali, Mu'adh ibn Jabal, Abu Musa Ashari, Abdullah Ibn Abbas, Khalid ibn Walid and a number of other companions of Mohammed and is found in all the authentic *hadith* collections.[318] Was Mohammed really serious in uttering such words? The Islamic clerics of today do not tell us whether Mohammed was honest or dishonest in the above *hadith*. However, no one has ever seen an Islamic cleric or one of his relatives strapping on a bomb and detonating it to receive the divine reward of a trip to paradise, yet they enjoin others to do so. Mohammed was not renowned for his bravery in battle but rather, is remembered as a gatherer of spent arrows during one battle as noted in a previous chapter.

During the eight year war between Iran and Iraq (1980–1988), Iranian Islamic clerics would tie plastic keys (made in Communist China) to the neck of children ten years of age or younger and send them over Iraqi minefields. They would tell them that those were the keys to heaven and then, after martyrdom, they could open the door of heaven with the keys and step inside. There were about one million casualties in that war, but not a single cleric or member of their families was lost. It is amazing that no suicide bomber has ever asked a bloodthirsty cleric who enjoins others to blow themselves up along with innocent bystanders, "If it is such a great divine act rewarded by immediate admission to paradise, why are you not doing it yourself?"

There is another *hadith* related to Mohammed that states:

In no way it is permitted to shed the blood of Muslims who testifies that "there is no god except God" and "I am the Apostle of God"

---

[318] Robert A. Morey, *Winning the War Against Radical Islam* (Las Vegas, Nevada: Christian Scholars Press, 2002), p. 92

except for three crimes: (1) He has killed someone [fellow Muslim] and his act merits retaliation. (2) He is married and commits adultery. (3) He abandons his religion and is separated from the community.[319]

The fact that *jihad* is the supreme duty of a Muslim is described in the *hadith* very clearly, without ambiguity or room for doubt. In the course of ten years' stay in Medina, till his death, Mohammed himself engaged in as many as 82 *jihads*, 26 of which he led. He apparently acquired some semblance of courage in battle and "made his bones," as the *Mafiosi* put it, for these 26 *jihads* are called *ghazwas* indicating that he became a *ghazi* or (*warrior*) by slaying his opponents, i.e., those whom he called infidels.[320] Mishkat al-Masabih has quoted a tradition which clearly shows that peace and Islam are indeed wholly incompatible. The following *hadith* shows how Mohammed was contemptuous of religions that advocate peace. Abu Umama, related:
According to Imam Sahih Muslim:

> It has been narrated on the authority of Abu Hurairah that the Messenger of Allah said, "One who dies but did not fight in the way of Allah nor did express any desire (or determination) for *jihad* died the death of a hypocrite."[321]

To understand the tenor of the above *hadith*, first we have to know what the word "hypocrite" (*monafiq* in Arabic) means in the Koran. The word "*monafiq*" in the Koran refers to those people of Medina who, having given shelter to Mohammed and his followers, had gradually grown disenchanted with them because of their violent character, but did not dare to rise in open rebellion against them. The leader of this disaffected faction of Medina was Abdullah Ibn Ubay. The Koran has cursed these so-called hypocrites with words of the harshest denunciation and scorn. Allah has called these people "hypocrites" because they are unwilling to fight. He even says

---

[319] *Ibid.*

[320] Majumdar, *Jihad, The Islamic Doctrine of Permanent War,* p. 20.

[321] *Sahih Muslim,* No. 4696. p. 1057.

that peaceful Muslims are "the vilest of creatures" and that hell's hottest fires await them. Allah hates those who are peace-loving Muslims.[322]

The *hadith* also announced that the reward of all hypocrites is the lower layer of hell–a whole layer below the one allotted for idolaters.[323] Therefore, the foregoing *hadith* is even more uncompromising than the Koran itself in that it indicates that a pacifist Muslim—the one who does not participate in *jihad* or killing non-Muslim—is not a Muslim at all, and his terrible fate in the hereafter, is hell.[324]

The following *hadith,* excerpted from Kanz al-'Ummal,[325] are related to Mohammed, and clearly imply that the martyr's merit exceeds that of all others.

> Where the believer's heart shakes on the path of God, his sins fall off from him as the fruit falls off a date palm.
>
> If anyone shoots an arrow at the enemy on the path of Allah and his arrow reaches his enemy, whether it hits him or misses, it is accounted equal in merit to liberating a slave.
>
> A day and a night of fighting on the frontier are better than a month of fasting and prayer.
>
> The best thing a Muslim can earn is an arrow in the path of Allah. Swords are the keys of paradise.
>
> Every prophet has his monasticism, and the monasticism of this community is the Holy War in the path of Allah.
>
> If a campaigner by sea is seasick, he has the reward of a martyr; if drowned of two martyrs. Warfare is deception.
>
> Expel the Jews and the Christians from the Arabian Peninsula.
>
> The bite of an ant is more painful to the martyr than the thrust of a weapon, which is more desirable to him than sweet, cold water on a hot summer day.

Al-Tirmidhi and ibn Maja report that Mohammed has said, "The martyr has six privileges with Allah: (1) his sins are pardoned when

---

[322] Winn, *Muhammed, Prophet of Doom,* p. v.

[323] Majumdar, *Jihad, the Islamic Doctrine of permanent War,* p. 20.

[324] *Ibid.,* p. 21.

[325]Quoted by Lewis, *Islam, from the Prophet Muhammad ton the Capture of Constantinople,* pp. 210–121.

the first drop of blood falls; (2) he is shown his seat in paradise; (3) he is safe from the punishment of the grave and secure from the great terror (i.e. hell); (4) a crown of dignity is placed on his head, one jewel of which is worth more than the world and all that is therein; (5) he is married to seventy-two dark-eyed virgins, (6) and he makes successful intercession for seventy of his relatives.[326]

Scholar Ahmad Hassan Az-Zayat wrote in al-Azhar, the most popular Egyptian magazine:

> "Holy war (*Jihad*) is an Arabic virtue, and a divine obligation: the Muslim is always mindful that his religion is a Koran and a sword . . . the Muslim then forever is a warrior."[327]

Sheikh Saleh Al-Fawzan, the chief author of the Saudi religious books currently used to teach five million Saudi students, both within Saudi Arabia and in the Saudi schools abroad (including those in the Washington, D.C. metro area), has expressed his unequivocal support for the legalization of slavery and has said, "Slavery is a part of Islam, a part of *Jihad* and will remain as long there is Islam."[328]

Al-Fawzan is an authority on Islamic government, a member of the Council of Clerics (Saudi Arabia's highest religious body), a member of the Council of Religious Edicts and Research, the Imam of Prince Mitaeb Mosque in Riyadh, and a professor at Imam Mohammed Bin Saudi Islamic University, the main Wahhabi center of learning in the country. This prominent Islamic scholar has also refuted the mainstream Muslim pretension that Islam worked to abolish slavery by introducing equality between the races. He advocates inequality between the races and says, "Those who express such opinions, they are ignorant, not scholars, they are merely writers. Whoever says such things is an infidel."[329]

Al-Fawzan's most famous book, *Al-Tawheed–Monotheism,* is a text for Saudi high school students. In it, he says that most non-Mus-

---

[326] Guillaume, *The Traditions of Islam,* p. 112.

[327] Ahmad Hassan az-Zayat, *al-Azhar,* August, 1959.

[328] 2004–Saudi Information Agency, quoted from the website: www.arabiannews.org/English/article.cfm?qid=132&sid=2 by Ali Al-Ahmed.

[329] *Ibid.*

lims are polytheists, and their blood and money are therefore free for the taking by "true Muslims."[330] In his other book *Al-Mulkhas Al-Fiqhee* (*Digest of Law*), Al-Fawzan issued a *fatwa* (decree) forbidding the watching of TV. He also claimed that elections and demonstrations are imitations of western culture.[331]

The *Dictionary of Islam* states, "One of the most urgent duties enjoined by Mohammed upon the Muslim true-believer is found in verse 244 of *Sura* II, the *"Jihad fi sabili 'llah,"* (literally, 'killing in the road of Allah'), i.e. the promulgation of Islam by warfare (*jihad*) against infidels, both within and without Arabia. Thus, the whole world was regarded as being divided into two great portions, the Daru al-Harb and Daru al-Islam—the Territories of War and the Territories of Peace.[332]

Tabari writes that on one occasion Mohammed ordered Thabit ibn Qays, one of his close companions to respond to the speech of a man who had challenged Mohammed. Thabit got up and, among other things, he said:

> "Arabs are the noblest people in lineage, the most prominent, and the best in deeds. The first of creation to answer and respond to Allah, when the Messenger of Allah summoned them, were we. We are the helpers of Allah and the viziers of his Messenger, and we fight people until they believe in Allah. He who believes in Allah and his Messenger have protected his life and possessions from us; as for one who disbelieves, we will fight him forever in the cause of Allah and *killing him is a small matter for us.*"[333] (Italics by the writer).

As an Arab who had traveled much among the desert people, Mohammed was aware that the tribesman would embrace a faith more readily if they knew that it countenanced warfare for profit.[334] If some should ask, "In case we fail in *jihad*, what will be our reward?"

---

[330] *Ibid.*

[331] *Ibid.*

[332] A *Dictionary of Islam,* 1965 ed. s. v. "Zimmi."

[333] Tabari, *The History of al-Tabari,* vol. ix, p. 69.

[334] R. V. C. Bodley, *The Messenger: The Life of Mohammed* (New York: Doubleday & Company, Inc., 1946), p. 151.

Unhesitatingly Mohammed would reply: "Paradise! You will be considered a martyr and a drop of blood shed in the cause of Allah, a night spent in arms (fighting), is of more avail than two months of fasting and prayer. Whoever falls in battle, his sins shall be forgiven. On the Day of Judgment, his wounds shall be resplendent in vermilion and odoriferous as musk, and the loss of his limbs shall be supplied by the wings of angels and cherubim."[335]

This delusive exhortation opened a whole new vista to the thinking of the ignorant Bedouin converts to Islam and recruits to Mohammed's army. It did more to promote heroism and instill a disregard for discomfort, for fatigue, even for life itself, than any order of the day, intensive training, or any earthly reward could do. It set an ideal in the minds of Arabs that they have held dear ever since. Instead of fearing death, they look forward to it as the deliverance from earthly pain and grief. This ancient superstitious maxim still functions as the inspiration for the Muslim suicidal terrorists who shed the blood of innocent people throughout the world.[336] In a word, this *hadith* declares even more uncompromisingly than the Koran itself that a pacifist Muslim is not a Muslim at all.[337]

According to the injunctions of the Koran and *Hadith,* it can be said that *Jihad* has no less than five objectives: (1) Forcible spreading of Islam. (2) Destruction of infidels. (3) Imposition of Islam on the defeated infidels. (4) The acquisition of war booty in the form of material property. (5) The enslavement of the women and children of the vanquished enemy.[338]

Non-Muslims Have Three Choices: Conversion, Paying Tax, or Decapitation

When an infidel's land is conquered by a Muslim ruler, its surviving inhabitants are offered three choices: (1) The acceptance of the faith

---

[335] *Ibid.,* p. 157.

[336] *Ibid.*

[337] Majumdar, *Jihad, The Islamic Doctrine of Permanent War,* p. 21.

[338] *Ibid.,* p. 34.

of Islam, (2) The payment of a tax (*Jizyah*), (3) Death, to those who will do neither.

The institution of *Jizyah* is ordained in the Koran. Verse 29 of *Sura* IX says:

> "Fight those who believe not in Allah nor the Last Day, nor hold that forbidden which had been forbidden by Allah and his messenger, nor acknowledge the religion of truth, from among the people of the book, until they pay the tribute (*jizya*) with willing submission and feel themselves subdued."

All non-Muslims of the world are considered infidels. However, the infidels are divided into two groups: people of the faith and *zimmis*. The word *zimmi*, from the root *zamm*, means to blame. Like Muslims, the Jews and Christians are considered people of the faith, but followers of the rest of the religions, such as the Zoroastrians, the Sabeans, the Buddhists, the Hindus, the Jains, the Sikhs and so on, are called infidels. The latter group are worse than the former and do not have the right to exist in this world unless they convert to Islam unconditionally. Free non-Muslim subjects of a Muslim government, i.e. Jews and Christians, are allowed to pay a capitation or poll tax, called *Jizya*, to be secure and enjoy personal freedom and religious toleration in an Islamic state. This is akin to the "protection racket" as practiced by modern criminals.

The *zimmi* is obliged to pay the payment personally and not by an agent. The *zimmi* must come on foot and make the payment standing, while the Muslim receiver should be seated and after placing his hand above that of the *zimmi* should take the money and cry out, :Oh, *zimmi!* Pay the commutation money."[339] This humility is inflicted upon the *zimmi*, to honor the latter part of verse 29 of *Sura* IX of the Koran, mentioned above which says, "Until they pay the *Jizyah* with willing submission and feel themselves subdued."

Many writers consider Islam synonymous with plundering and ransacking. Bertrand Russell, a renowned philosopher of the twentieth century writes:

---

[339] Ghosh, *Islam and the Infidel*, p. 85.

The Arabs, although they conquered a great part of the world in the name of the new religion, were not a very religious race; the motives of their conquests were plunder and wealth rather than religion. It was only in virtue of their lack of fanaticism that a handful of warriors were able to govern, without much difficulty, vast populations of higher civilization and alien religion. The Persians, on the contrary, have been, from the earliest times, deeply religious and highly speculative. After their conversion, they made out of Islam something much more interesting, more religious, and more philosophical, than had been imagined by the Prophet and his kinsmen.[340]

An Arab historian called Motaval writes that for Arab Bedouins plundering the property of the defeated nations was more important than Islam and *Jihad*.[341] Another writer also maintains that although Arabs would give three choices to their defeated foes, *i.e.,* (1) acceptance of Islam, (2) paying a poll tax, or (3) death, they would prefer that their victims reject Islam and pay the tax. He continues that though Iranian farmers converted to Islam, still Hajjaj ibn Yusuf Thaghafi, the incumbent governor, forced them to pay the same amount of poll tax that they were paying before their conversion to Islam. This resulted in a rebellion.[342] Still another Arab writer points out that the main motive of the Islamic wars was to achieve political supremacy, not religious conversion. He believes the Arabs were trying to build up an Arabic Empire under the guise of Islam.[343]

Arabs also would extort the poll tax from *zimmis* not only under humiliating conditions, but also by torture. The Arab agents in the northeast of Iran (Khorasan), whipped the inhabitants and shod their hands with horseshoes to extort *Jizyah* from them.[344] On another occasion, the inhabitants of one of the other provinces of Iran (Isfa-

---

[340] Bertrand Russell, *A History of Western Philosophy* (New York: Simon and Schuster, 1945), p. 421.

[341] Motavval, *Tarikh al-'Arab,* vol. 1, p. 195.

[342] Ibn Khordad Beh, *Almasalik valmamalik,* ed., M. J. De Goege (1889), pp. 14–15.

[343] Abdolaziz al-Dowry, *Moghaddamah fi Tarikh Sadre Islam* (Beirut: Catholic Press, 1960), pp. 44–46.

[344] Dr. Mohammed Malayeri, *The History and Culture of Iran,* vol. 3 (Tehran: Tus Publications, 1379), p. 231.

han) refrained from paying their poll tax. Hajjaj Ibn Yusuf Thaghafi, the governor of Kufeh, commissioned an Arab to go to Isfahan to extort the delinquent taxes. Upon his arrival, he took two dignitaries of the city as hostages and gave the people a two month grace period to pay their taxes. At the termination of the grace period, he summoned the people and demanded the money.

They said that since it was the month of fasting (Ramadan), they had been unable to work as hard as usual and were unable to pay their tax on time but, since they considered themselves law-abiding citizens, they would soon pay it. The agent swore that if by the end of the day they did not pay the tax, they [the hostages] would be beheaded. Since the people of the city were unable to pay their taxes before sunset, the Arab agent summoned the hostages and ordered them beheaded, one after the other. Then he put the head of each of them in a bag, wrote the name of the person on the bag and sealed it. When the inhabitants of the city saw such barbaric atrocity, they asked the agent to halt any further slaughter and paid him the money.[345]

A Raid Does Not Need Warning

According to *hadith* number 4292 of Sahih Muslim, it is not necessary to warn the non-Muslims, before raiding them. Abdollah ibn Omar, the son of the second Khalif, who was among the raiding troops, and Juwairiya, a beautiful married woman of the Jewish Bani Mustaliq tribe captured in the raid and sent to Mohammed's harem, both attested that Mohammed made a raid upon the Bani Mustaliq while they were innocently watering their cattle. In this preemptive raid, Mohammed killed those who fought against him and imprisoned others.

Ibn 'Aun reported: I wrote to Nafi inquiring from him whether it was necessary to extend (to the disbelievers) an invitation to accept (Islam) before engaging them in fight. He wrote (in reply) to me that it

---

[345] *Ibid.,* pp. 220–221.

was necessary in the early days of Islam. The Messenger of Allah made a raid upon Bani Mustaliq while they were unaware and their cattle were having a drink at the water. He killed those who fought and imprisoned others. On that very day, he captured Juwairiya bint al-Harith. Nafi said that this tradition was related to him by 'Abdullah Ibn Omar who (himself) was among the raiding troops.[346]

It is narrated on the authority of Jabir and Abu Huraira that Mohammed has clearly said, "War is a stratagem." (Sahih Muslim, Hadith number 4311).

Permissibility of Killing Women and Children in the Night Raids

Sa'b ibn Jaththama has asked Mohammed, whether it is permissible to kill women and children during raids. Mohammed, the founder of the religion of terror responded, "They are from them."[347]

This *hadith* is actually complementary to the previous one. Because according to the previous *hadith,* Mohammed had permitted the raid on non-Muslims without warning them and in this *hadith* he permits the killing women and children of those raided. How can a religion be considered a "Divine Revelation" whilst allowing such atrocious barbarism?

Attacking innocent people and seizing their properties without warning is the *modus operandi* of professional robbers, not that of a holy "prophet." Legally, *robbery* is considered more serious than *theft* because *theft* is defined as the taking of another's property without their knowledge or consent, but *robbery,* in its precise legal usage, is the act of taking a victim's property by means of violence and/or intimidation. Naturally, since the Prophet of Allah performs every move with His consent, he therefore has Allah's permission to attack and imprison people and deprive them of their belongings violently rather than performing such a crime stealthily and without their knowledge.

---

[346] *Sahih Muslim,* No. 4292, p. 942.
[347] *Ibid.,* Nos. 4319–4324, pp. 946–947.

Since Allah names himself in the Koran as: the best plotter (III: 54, VII: 99, VIII: 30, X: 21, XIII: 42, XXVII: 50); omnipotent (VI: 18); death giver (VII: 28); predominant (XII: 21); dominant (XIII: 42), compeller (LIX: 23); then His Messenger should consider these characteristics to be his by his own revelation!

The Property of the Murdered Belongs to His Murderer

Abu Qatada reported that in the Battle of Hunain, he killed one of the polytheists and the battle ended in a victory for the Muslims. Then, when Mohammed sat down to distribute the spoils of war he said, "One who has killed an enemy and can bring evidence to prove it will get his belongings."

Abu Qatada says, "At this point one of the people attested to my claim but explained that he had the belongings of the enemy I killed and wanted me to forgo my right. Abu Bakr and Mohammed disagreed with the person and required him to give the belongings to me. So, he gave them to me. I sold the armor that was a part of my share of the booty and with the proceeds, bought a garden in the street of Bani Salama. This was the first property I acquired after embracing Islam."[348]

Abd al-Rahman ibn Awf also narrated, "While I was standing in battle array on the Day of Badr, two boys from the Ansar, quite young in age, told me that if they could recognize Abu Jahl, they would battle with him and would not leave him until he was killed. When I showed him to them, they dashed toward him, struck him with their swords until he was dead. Then they returned to Mohammed and informed him of their deed. Mohammed examined their swords and since blood was still dripping from them, he ordered the belongings of Abu Jahl to be handed over to them. These two young men were called, Mu'adh ibn Amr ibn al-Jamuh and Mu'adh ibn Afra."[349]

---

[348] *Ibid.,* No. 4340, pp. 950–951.
[349] *Ibid.,* No. 4341, pp. 951–952.

Salama ibn al-Akwa narrated: "We were fighting in the Battle of Hawazin along with Mohammed. One day, when we were having our breakfast with Mohammed, along came a man riding a red camel. He made it kneel down, extracted a strip of leather from its girth and tethered the camel with it. Then he began to take food with us and was looking nervously around. We were in a poor condition as some of us were on foot, having no riding animal. All of a sudden, he left us hurriedly, went to his camel, unfettered it, made it kneel, mounted and urged the beast to run off with him. I followed him on foot and ran until I was near the thigh of the she-camel. I advanced still further until I caught hold of the nose ring of the camel. I made it kneel down. As soon as it placed its knee on the ground, I drew my sword and struck at the head of the rider who fell down. I brought the camel, leading it along with the man's baggage and weapons. The Messenger of Allah came forward to meet me with his followers. When Mohammed understood that the man was killed by me, he ordered everything of the man to be handed over to me."[350]

In the above mentioned *hadith,* the Messenger of God pontificates to his faithful Muslims that by shedding someone's blood, one becomes the owner of that person's belongings. Do professional robbers commit this crime differently? The answer is probably "Yes." Professional robbers after they have committed the crime do not routinely murder their victims nor do they usually rape their wives. But Muslims are not hindered by any ethical rules; Allah in verse 24 of *Sura* IV of the Koran permits sexual intercourse with women married to defeated infidels. In other words, the men of faith are encouraged to kill non-Muslims to "lawfully" obtain their property, including their women and children, and allowed to rape the women.

Jihad of the Prophet's Wives

The favorite member of Mohammed's harem, Ayesha, (called Mother of the Faithful) narrated, "On one occasion, Mohammed's wives re-

---

[350] *Ibid.,* No. 4344, pp. 952–953.

quested the prophet to permit them to participate in *Jihad*." He replied, 'Your Jihad is the performance of Hajj."[351]

Could anybody expect any other response from the canny Holy Prophet of Allah? Allah was smart enough to select His Messenger from among the horniest of the lascivious Arabs. The holy Prophet of Allah was not inclined to permit his wives to go for *Jihad* and leave him alone and lonely in bed. All the promises of Paradise that he has ascribed to martyrs, apply to faithful believers **other** than his wives. What if Ayesha, Maria, or Zeinab were wounded in battle or captured by Mohammed's enemies and they (the enemy) were to apply the tenor of verse 24 of *Sura* IV of the Koran to them? Then who would bathe him and sleep with him?

Certainly, when he told his wives, "Your *Jihad* is the performance of Hajj," he was trying to be diplomatic, otherwise he would have simply and candidly answered them, "Your *Jihad* is to satisfy the holy Prophet of Allah with all your heart in bed."

Irrespective of what we have said with regard to *Jihad,* one wonders why such an Almighty, Omniscient, All-Knowing, etc., etc. Allah needs his servants to fight and kill on his behalf in order to eliminate his enemies? Couldn't this almighty Allah, described in the Koran as oppressor, avenger, and deceiver do away with his enemies without any mortal help?

The Merits of Martyrdom in *Jihad*

According to a tale told by Abu Huraira, the Messenger of Allah said: "Every wound received by a Muslim in *Jihad* will appear on the Day of Judgment in the same condition as it was when it was inflicted, and will be bleeding profusely. The color of its discharge will be the color of blood, but its smell will be that of musk. I would not lag behind any expedition undertaken for *Jihad*, but I do not possess abundant means to provide my soldiers with riding animals, nor do all of them have abundant means to provide themselves with all the means of *Jihad* to follow me, nor would it please their hearts to stay

---

[351] *Sahih al-Bukhari,* vol. 4, pp. 83–84.

behind. By the being in Whose Hand is my life, I love that I should be killed in the way [service] of Allah; then I should be brought back to life and be killed again in his way . . . ."[352]

Anas Ibn Malik is credited with quoting the Messenger of Allah as follows: "Nobody who enters Paradise will ever like to return to this world even if he were offered everything on the surface of the earth as an inducement except the martyr who will desire to return to this world and be killed ten times for the sake of the great honor that He has been bestowed upon him."[353]

Abu Huraira narrated that the Messenger of Allah was asked, "What deed could equal *Jihad* in the way of Allah?" He answered: "You do not have the strength to do that deed." When Mohammed was asked the same question thrice, he said, "One who goes out for *Jihad* is like a person who keeps fasts, stands in prayer constantly, obeying Allah's behests contained in the verses of the Koran, and does not exhibit any lassitude in fasting and prayer until the warrior returns from *Jihad*."[354]

It has been told that, according to Anas Ibn Malik, Sahl Ibn Sa'd as-Sa'di, and Abu Huraira, the Messenger of Allah said, "A journey undertaken in the morning or evening for *Jihad* in the way of Allah will merit a reward better than the world and all that is in it."[355]

Is Mohammed being truthful when he states that he would 'love to be killed in the way of Allah, then be brought back to life and be killed again in this way. . . . ?' When his life was jeopardized by the inhabitants of Mecca he fled, in September 622 CE, to Medina with Abu Bekr, his new father-in-law. This action answers the question beyond all doubt. He was never willing to be killed in the service of Allah.

Also, in the battle of Uhod, he would have been easily slain by the Quraysh if a party of his devoted followers (seven Ansars and seven refugees) had not rallied around him and shielded him. Despite such protection, a missile wounded his lower lip and broke one of his teeth. Another blow drove the rings of his helmet deep into his cheek, and made a gash in his forehead. His head was barely saved

---

[352] *Ibid,* No. 4630, pp. 1043–1044.

[353] *Ibid,* No. 4635, p. 1045.

[354] *Ibid,* No. 4636, p. 1045.

[355] *Ibid,* No. 4641, p. 1046.

from the sword of ibn Kami'a by the naked hand of Talha, son of Obeidullah, who sacrificed his fingers to save The Messenger. Mohammed fell to the ground and ibn Kami'a returned to his comrades, claiming that he had killed him. The cry was taken up all around and resounded from the rocks of Uhod. It spread consternation among His followers, "Where is," they cried, "the promise of Allah now?"[356]

Undoubtedly, the Prophet was readily able to fabricate another "revelation" to explain away any doubts voiced by His followers!

One of the Rituals of Pilgrimage is Running Seven Times between Two Mountains

According to verse 97 of *Sura* III of the Koran, every adult Muslim of both sexes, has to perform Hajj at least once in the course of their life, provided they are able to do so. Arab lexicographers generally give the meaning of *Hajj,* which is considered the fifth of the five pillars of Islam, as "to betake oneself to."[357] Every year; on the eighth, ninth, and tenth days of the last month of the Islamic lunar calendar (Zul-Hijjaj), about two million Muslims go to Mecca in Saudi Arabia to accomplish this pilgrimage and obtain the religious title of "*Hajji,*". One of the obligatory rituals of the pilgrimage is running seven times between the mountains of Safa on the south and Marwah on the north, a distance of about ¼ mile. The Muslim tradition offers two legendary explanations for the practice, one "pagan" and one "Abrahamic," each one more preposterous than the other.

The latter is derived from the Bible,[358] historians,[359] and Tabari.[360] When Abraham was 85 and his wife Sara 76 years of age, they were childless and had no hope of having a child at that advanced age. One night God told Abraham, "You will be blessed by

---

[356] Muir, *The life of Mohammad,* pp. 261–62.

[357] *The Encyclopedia of Islam,* 1971 ed. s. v. A. J. Wensinck, "Hadjdj".

[358] *Genesis,* 15: 5, 16: 10–11, 17: 20–21, 21: 8–21.

[359] Karen Armstrong, *Muhammad* (London: Victor Gollancz Ltd., 1991), p. 161; F. E. Peters, *The Hajj* (Princeton, New Jersey: Princeton University Press, 1994), III, p. 31.

[360] Tabari, *The History of al-Tabari,* vol 2, pp. 72–74.

me and have children." Then, Sara gave him her Egyptian maid-servant, Hagar, to take as a concubine. So, Abraham had intercourse with Hagar and she gave birth to Ishmael. Then Abraham had intercourse with Sara and, miraculously, she became pregnant and bore him a son they named Isaac. But after Sara gave birth to Isaac, she became jealous of Hagar and Ishmael and insisted that Abraham expel them. So, Abraham brought Hagar and their son to the valley of Mecca and abandoned them there.

Ishmael became very thirsty so his mother went looking for water for him, but could not find any. She listened for the sound of running water and thought she heard it near Safa (the southern mountain) and went there to look for it but found nothing. Then she heard a similar sound from the north, the mountain called Marwah. She ran there, looked around, and saw nothing. Then she heard sounds like beasts stamping in the valley where she had left Ishmael. She ran to him and saw that the angel Gabriel was teaching him to strike his foot on the ground from whence a spring gushed forth. Allah had taken care of them! This spring became the sacred well known as Zamzam. It is said that this very well brought Mecca into being. The ritual of running seven times between Safa and Marwah commemorates the running back and forth of Hagar in search of water. The Arabian Jews believe that Ishmael became the ancestor of the Arabs and Isaac the ancestor of the Jews.

The second legend behind the ritual of running seven times between Safa and Marwah is explained by Ibn Ishaq,[361] Ibn Kathir[362] and many other writers and traditionalists. According to Ibn Ishaq, before the advent of Mohammed and Islam, a man named Isaf ibn Omar and a woman named Na'ila bint Wai'l, both from Juhrum tribe, met in Ka'ba wherein they fornicated. By doing so, they profaned the sacred place of Ka'ba, so the gods turned them into two stones. Ibn Ishaq quotes Ayasha (Mohammed's favorite wife) as saying, "We always heard that Isaf and Na'ila were a man and a woman of Juhrum

---

[361] *Ibn Ishaq,* 1955:3.

[362] Ibn Kathir, *The Life of the Prophet Muhammad,* trans. Prof. Trevor Le Gassick, vol. 1 (United Kingdom: Garnet Publishing Limited, 2000), pp. 39, 47.

who fornicated in the Ka'ba, so Allah, Almighty and Glorious, turned them both into stones."[363]

As a warning to others, the people of Quraysh put the stone statue of Isaf on top of Safa Mountain and the stone statue of Na'ila on top of Marwah Mountain. Since then, every faithful Muslim making *Hajj* is required to commemorate the blasphemy of Isaf and Na'ila by running seven times between the stone statues of the two fornicators on Safa and Marwah. Ibn Ishaq further states, "After a great deal of time had passed, these two stones became an object of worship, aside from Allah, during the period of Khuza'."[364]
There are at least five questions concerning the latter explanation that no Islamic scholar can answer:

1. Since no one has seen any trace of them, where are the two stone statues now?
2. Why should pious Muslims worship the statues of two sinners who have committed fornication in the so-called "Sacred House of Allah?"
3. What is the divine rationale behind running *seven* times be tween stone statues of two fornicators?
4. Why, instead of ordering the stone statues of sinners put in Hell, did the all-Knowing Allah decided to keep them near His own home?
5. Would it not be more rational if Almighty Allah had ordered the statues of Adam and Eve to be put at the top of Safa and Marewah instead of two fornicators damned by His word?

No Muslim scholar can answer these questions and the ordinary ignorant Moslem dare not ask them!

Lying and Deceit are Permitted in Islam

Mohammed, a person who pretended to be the Prophet of Allah, clearly admits, "War is deceit," and, moreover, lying and deception

---

[363] *Ibid.,* p. 39.
[364] *Ibid.,* p. 47.

are encouraged in the Holy Book. It is no wonder that in Shi'sm, "dissimulation" is one of the precepts of that sect. Sahih Al-Bukhari and Sahih Muslim, both explain in *hadith* that, according to them, Mohammed permitted lying, deceiving and duplicity in human relations. Machiavelli said something of the same kind nine centuries later, Napoleon two hundred years after that, and the Japanese in the mid-twentieth century.[365] But, none of these people associated these amoral precepts with the word of any God. Mohammed stands alone in this respect. Sahih al-Bukhari, writes:

> "Narrated Abu Huraira, the Prophet said, 'Khosrow will be ruined, and there will be no Khosrow after him, and Caesar after him and you will spend their treasures in Allah's Cause.' He called war deceit."[366]

In the next two *hadith* Sahih al-Bukhari repeats, Mohammed, Prophet of Allah, said, "War is deceit." There is an incident [factual] in Mohammed's life which will authenticate the above-mentioned *hadith* recorded by Arab historians. When Medina was surrounded by the confederation of tribes against Mohammed, he sought the service of a recent convert to Islam, Nuaim ibn Masood of the Ghatafan tribe, who was known for his deceit, as a go between. Mohammed employed him to sow distrust amongst the enemy by lies and false reports, 'For,' said Mohammed, 'what else is War but a game of Deception?' On Mohammed's order, Nuaim went to the Bani Khoreiza and, representing himself as a friend, artfully insinuated that the interests of the allied tribes were not necessarily theirs and before they irretrievably committed themselves by joining in the renewed attack on Medina, they ought to demand from Quraysh hostages as a guarantee against being deserted and left to face Mohammed's forces alone. Suspecting no harm, they agreed to act on his advice.

Then, he went to the Quraysh chieftains and warned them that the Bani Khoreiza had taken sides with Mohammed and intended to ask for hostages in order to give them up to Mohammed as a means of making their peace with him. This insidious plot worked and distrust was sown between Quraysh and Bani Khoreiza. Ibn Ishaq al-

---

[365] Bodley, *The Messenger, The Life of Mohammed,* pp. 154–55.

[366] *Sahih Al-Bukhari,* vol. iv, No. 267, pp. 166–167; *Sahih Muslim,* vol iii, p. 945.

leges that it was Mohammed who thought of this plan and sent Nuaim to execute it.[367]

In another *hadith,* Sahih Al-Bukhari, states:

> "Narrated Jabir, the Prophet said, 'Who is ready to kill Ka'b Ibn Ashraf (i.e. a Jew).' Mohammed ibn Maslama replied, 'Do you like me to kill him?' The Prophet replied in the affirmative. Mohammed Ibn Maslama said, 'Then allow me to lie so that I will be able to deceive him.' The prophet replied, 'I do (You may do so)'"[368]

Ibn Ishaq illustrates an incident which adds to the unscrupulous character of Mohammed. He states that as soon as Khaibar was conquered, Hajjaj Ibn Ilat, one of his followers, asked permission of Mohammed to leave the army and go to Mecca, in order to collect some debts that were owed to him. "Hajjaj said to the Apostle," writes Ibn Ishaq, "I have money scattered among the Meccan merchants, so give me permission to go and get it. After getting Mohammed's permission, he said, 'I must tell lies.' The Apostle said, 'Tell them.'"[369]

Having obtained permission to act unethically, Hajjaj departed to Mecca and told the first party of Meccans he met that he had joyous news for them. Mohammed had been completely defeated and his companions had been slain! Mohammed himself had been taken prisoner by the Jews. They did not intend to kill him because they wanted this to be done in Mecca, whither they were now bringing him, so that the Meccans might avenge their brethren whom he had slain. This good news was at once proclaimed throughout the city. Then Hajjaj requested the people of Mecca to assist him in collecting his debts, so that he might hasten back to Khaibar and buy the booty taken from Mohammed and his companions before the arrival of other merchants.

The Meccan believed Hajjaj and brought great pressure on his debtors to pay their debts to him. Having speedily collected his

---

[367] Muir, *The Life of Mohammad,* p. 313; John Bagot Glubb, *The Life and Times of Muhammad* (New York: Stein and Day, 1970), p. 247.

[368] *Sahih Al-Bukhari,* vol. iv, Nos. 270 and 271.

[369] *Ibn Ishaq,* p. 519

debts, he went to Abbas, Mohammed's uncle, and exacting a promise from Abbas that he would not announce before the end of three days (at which time he hoped to be beyond the reach of any pursuit) what he was about to confide to him, made this startling announcement: "By Allah! When I left your nephew, he about to marry the daughter of the chief (he meant Safiyyah); he has conquered Khaibar and taken as spoil all it contained, so that it now belongs to him and his companions."[370]

Legitimization of "lying" in Islam shows that either Mohammed was unaware of the *Ten Commandments* or his morality was so low that he simply ignored them.

The ninth commandment says: "You shall not bear false witness against your neighbor" (*Exodus 20: 16*). This commandment is also repeated in the same form in *Deuteronomy 5: 20.* For the Psalmist the bitterest thing of all is that false malicious witnesses rise up against him (Psalm 27: 12; 35: 11). This sin is repeatedly condemned in Proverbs. One of the six things that God abhors is 'a false witness who breathes out lies.' (*Proverb 6: 19*). The man 'who speaks the truth gives honest evidence, but a false witness utters deceit (*Proverb 12: 17*). Not only is a liar condemned, 'he will not go unpunished.' In the New Testament, "false witness is one of the sins which come out of the evil heart of man." (*Matthew 15: 19*).

But Mohammed and the Allah whom he created to serve his purposes are so deficient in morality that lying is considered legitimate in Islam. It is true that Mohammed did his best to pretend that he was chosen by the same God who gave missions to Moses and Jesus but, with regard to lying and deceit, he stuck to his tribal culture.

The Bodies of Green Birds Contain the Souls of Martyrs

Abdullah ibn Omar on one occasion was asked about the meaning of the verse 169 of *Sura* III of the Koran which says:

---

[370] S. W. Koelle, *Mohammed and Mohammedanism,* 1972), pp. 184–185.

"Think not of those who are slain in the Allah's way as dead. Nay, they are alive, finding their sustenance in the presence of their Lord."

He replied, "We asked the meaning of the verse from Mohammed who answered: 'The souls of the martyrs live in the bodies of green birds that have their nests in chandeliers hung from the throne of the Almighty. They eat the fruits of Paradise from wherever they like and then nestle in these chandeliers. Once their Lord cast a glance at them and said, 'Do you want anything?' They answered, 'What more shall we desire? We eat the fruits of paradise from wherever we like.' Their Lord asked them the same question thrice. When they saw that they will continue to be asked and not left without answering the question, they said, 'O Lord, we wish that thou mayest return our souls to our bodies so that we may be slain in Thy way once again.' When Allah saw that they had no need, they were left to their joy in heaven.'[371]

Islamic Justice Does not Permit Giving Water to Dying People

A group of eight Bedouin Arabs of 'Ukl tribe came to Medina and embraced Islam. They stayed in Medina and lived with the people of As-Suffa. But the unpleasant climate of the city did not suit them; it 'affected their spleen,' so they went to Mohammed to seek help. Mohammed recommended that they go to the desert in the neighborhood of al-Jammu' and drink the milk and urine of his (Mohammed's) milch-camels as medicine. The Bedouins recovered their health despite following this repulsive advice. Then, true to their Bedouin nature, they stole the herd and attempted to escape. The herdsman, called Yasir, pursued the plunderers, but they killed him and took the camels away.

When the news of this outrage reached Medina, Mohammed dispatched Kurz Ibn Jabir[372] with twenty horsemen to capture Yasir's

---

[371] *Sahih Muslim,* No. 4651, pp. 1047–1048.

[372] In the second year of Hijrah (623), Kurz Ibn Jabir, a marauding Bedouin chieftain of the Fihri tribe raided the flocks of Medina which were pastured in al-Jamma', a few miles of the city and had carried them away. Mohammed pursued him and reached a valley called Safawan in the region of Badr, but failed to overtake him. This was the first expedition of Badr. Later on, Kurz Ibn Jabir converted to Islam.

killers. They captured the robbers and recovered all the camels save one that had been slaughtered. The captives, who justly deserved the death penalty according to Arab tradition, were brought to Mohammed. The brutal punishment that he inflicted upon them could only have been concocted by a dedicated sadist, not by a person who represented himself as a religious leader and the Messenger of God. Mohammed ordered their arms and legs to be cut off and their eyes to be gouged out. Then, their mutilated sightless trunks were impaled upon the plain of Al-Ghaba (where Mohammed chanced to camped), until they died. Even more sinister and inhuman, according to Sahih al-Bukhari whose credibility is well regarded, when the mutilated and sightless dying captives asked for water, they were not given any and they died thirsty.[373]

In a separate *hadith,* Sahih al-Bukhari states, "The Prophet did not give water to those who turned renegades and fought against Allah and his Apostle, until they died."[374]

Following the above-mentioned masterpiece of savagery the Messenger of Allah authored verse 38 of *Sura* V of the Koran:

> "Those that make war against Allah and His Apostle and spread disorders in the land shall be put to death, crucified, or have their hands and feet cut off the opposite sides, or be banished from the land. They shall be held in shame in this world and sternly punished in the next: except those that repent before you reduce them. For you must know that Allah is Forgiving and Merciful."

After explaining this incident, Muir states, "Such is the cruel law throughout Islam to the present day, so sanctioned by the above verse of the Koran."[375]

---

[373] *Ibn Hisham,* p. 998f.; at-Tabari, 1:1559; Muhammad ibn Umar al-Waqidi, *Kitab al-Maghazi,* 1966, p. 240f.; *Ibn Sa'd,* p. 67f. quoted in William Muir, *The Life of Mohammad,* p. 350; *Sahih al-Bukhari,* 3: 519–522.

[374] *Sahih al-Bukhari,* viii: 520–521.

[375] Muir, *The Life of Mohammad,* p. 350.

Allah Permitted Mohammed to Commit any Crime against his Opponents

Bedouin Arabs were polytheists from time immemorial. By tradition, they would never commit bloodshed during certain four months of the year and they would never kill anybody within the Ka'ba. But Mohammed, calling himself a Prophet and claiming that he had been sent to propagate the monotheism of Allah, violated both of these traditional rules. He sanctioned killing in those four forbidden months in verse 5 of *Sura* IX of the Koran. Moreover, he ordered a number of his opponents to be killed even if they were found behind the curtains of the Ka'ba.[376] As Ibn Ishaq writes, Mohammed said:

> "It was not lawful for anyone to shed blood in Mecca. It was not lawful to anyone before me and it will not be lawful after me. If anyone should say, 'The apostle killed men in Mecca,' say, 'Allah permitted His apostle to do so but He does not permit you.'"[377]

When Mohammed obtained power in Medina, he became so arrogant and selfish that he openly claimed "Allah has permitted me to kill anybody I wish." Moreover, committing any kind of atrocious crime was not the only privilege that Allah granted to His beloved Messenger; he permitted His favorite Apostle to be free to call to his bed any woman who offered herself to him provided, of course, that he would want her (Koran: XXXIII: 5). This verse emphasizes, "This is exclusively for you and not any other believer."

---

[376] Please, see chapter two.
[377] *Ibn Ishaq*, p. 555

CHAPTER SIX

MOHAMMED ORDERS DEATH TO HIS OPPONENTS

Those who are against killing have no place in Islam. Our Prophet killed with his own blessed hands. Our Imam Ali killed more than seven hundred on a single day. If the survival of the faith requires the shedding of blood, we are there to perform our duty.

**Sheikh Sadegh Khalkhali,
Islamic Judge (Amir Taheri, *Holy Terror*, p. 36)**

The astounding success of the Battle of Badr (February, 624 CE) was a turning point in the history of Islam, the world and the life of Mohammed. It was as important as Constantine's victory over Maxentius at Milvian Bridge or of Attila's defeat at Chalons. Mohammed, an ambitious caravan thief, now could achieve his long cherished goal and don the mantle prophethood. This victory considerably strengthened Mohammed's position in Medina and it was also a vindication of the faith that had sustained Mohammed and his companions through adverse times. The Badr triumph encouraged him to consolidate his power. Muslims regarded the Battle of Badr as a miracle, the work of Allah, as the Koran asserted (VIII: 17):

> "You did not kill them, but Allah killed them, and when you did throw, it was not you but Allah, who threw, so that He might generously reward the believers."

After the Battle of Badr Mohammed's power kept on increasing and fortune continued favorably for him. Partly by conquest and partly by treaty, the lands between Medina and Mecca westward towards the coast had been won by Mohammed and his followers. A prophet, who also specialized in camel thievery, probably appeared to be a most worthy character to the desert Bedouins.[378]

Mohammed expected the Jews of Medina to adopt his new faith, but when he noticed that only a small number were they willing to do so and hail him as a prophet, he broke with them. As a result, the great majority of the Jews not only rejected Islam, but became increasingly hostile. Being illiterate and thus incapable of replying to the slurring satires and puns the Jewish poets composed against him, he resorted to terrorist activities and barbarously eliminated them one by one.

Assassination of Asma bint Marwan

As noted above, the victory of the Battle of Badr was a turning point in the advancement of Mohammed's ambitions and had strengthened immeasurably his authority in Medina. Although he was successfully consolidating his power, Mohammed was still afraid of being exposed as a fraud. He ruthlessly annihilated those who still ventured to raise their voices against him and deny his revelations.

In an illiterate society, poets, by song and verse, are the disseminators of news to the masses. Asma Bint Marwan was a poetess whose family had not abandoned their ancestral faith and was a member of the disaffected Bani Aws tribe. They disliked Islam and were against Mohammed. As a poetess, she composed uncomplimentary verses, insulting Islam and castigating those who put their faith in a murderer who warred against the people. Semitic people learn poetry easily, and in a short time the poems of Asma were being repeated throughout Medina making Mohammed and his followers very angry.

Asma Bint Marwan's verses were more forceful than other satirists:

> Fucked men of Malik and Nabit, and of Awf
> Fucked men of Khazraj [clans and tribes of Medina]:
> You obey a stranger, who does not belong among you,

---

[378] Margoliouth, *Mohammed and the Rise of Islam,* pp. 288–89.

Who is not of Murad, nor of Madh'hij [Yemenite tribes]:
Do you, when your own chiefs have been murdered,
put your hope in him
Like men greedy for meal soup when it is cooking?
Is there no man of honor who will take advantage of an unguarded
moment and cut off the Gulls' hopes?[379]

The poems were the press and TV of that era and strongly influenced the people. They quickly spread from mouth to mouth and Mohammed began to fear for his recently won power. Therefore, according to Professor William Muir, quoting Ibn Hisham, Mohammed said publicly:

"Who will rid me of this woman?"[380]

Umayr ibn Adi, a blind member of the same tribe and a former husband of the poetess, volunteered to carry out Mohammed's vicious wishes. This was only a few days after the return of Mohammed from Badr (the 2nd year of *hijrah*). In the dead of night, Umayr entered Asma's house. Asma was asleep, surrounded by her little ones, the youngest sucking from her breast. The blind man groped for her, removed her suckling babe and with heartless cruelty plunged his sword with such a force into her breast that it passed through her back.

The next morning, while at prayer in the Mosque, Mohammed, asked Umayr, "Have you slain the daughter of Marwan?"

"Yes," Umayr answered and then added, "But tell me now, have I committed anything sinful?"[381]

"None whatever," said Mohammed, "O Umayr! You have done a service to Allah and His Messenger; two goats will not knock their heads together for it."[382]

Then turning to the people gathered in the Mosque, he said, "If you desire to see a man who has assisted Allah and His prophet, look at this man."[383]

---

[379] Ibn Hisham, ed. Cit. 292f., quoted in Rodinson, *Muhammad*, pp. 157–58.

[380] William Muir, *The life of Mohammed,* 4 vols., (Osnabruck, Biblio Verlag: 1988), vol. 3, p. 131, Rodinson, *Muhammad*, p. 171.

[381] Muir, *The Life of Mohammad*, p. 239.

[382] *Ibid.*

[383] Bodley, *The Messenger: The Life of Mohammad*, p. 170.

"What!" cried Omar ibn Khattab, "the blind Umayr?"

"Call him not blind," said Mohammed, "rather call him *Umayr, the seeing.*"[384]

As the blind murderer was returning to his home in upper Medina, he came across the sons of Asma burying their mother. They suspected him of the murder and one of them, with a voice that sounded both sad and angry, asked Umayr whether he had assassinated her. Without feeling any compunction, the blind thug avowed his guilt and added, "You may fight me if you wish. By Him Who dominates my soul, if you should deny that she composed her abusive poetry, I would fight you until either you or I fall." This fierce threat had the desired effect and caused the tribe to return to Islam. Some of them had already converted to Islam but, fearing persecution at the hand of their fellow tribesmen, had denied Mohammed. Now, cowed by the terrorism of Mohammed and his followers, the whole tribe reluctantly embraced the false faith proselytized by the brigand prophet. The assassination of Asma, mother of five sons, was the first blood shed in Medina by order of Mohammed.[385]

The Murder of Abu Afak, Age 100

About a month after the ruthless assassination of Asma Bint Marwan, while Mohammed and his followers were still savoring their victory in the Battle of Badr, another brutal murder was committed on the express command of Mohammed.[386]

A Jewish tribesman, named Abu Afak, from the Bani ibn Awf clan of the tribe Bani Ubaid, lived in the suburbs of Medina. He was a tough old man, over one hundred years of age, and a poet who actively opposed Mohammed and his new religion. Abu Afak composed verses disparaging Mohammed and his followers and inciting

---

[384] *Ibid.,* pp. 239–40.

[385] Muir, *The life of Mohammed,* 1923), p. 239.

[386] *Ibn Hisham,* p. 994 f.; *Al-Waqidi,* p. 91; *Ibn Saad,* p. 19, quoted in William Muir, *The life of Mohammed,* p. 240.

his own tribe to rise against him. Thus, he became a target of Mohammed's murderous wrath. Abu Afak was so determined to undermine Mohammed and the Muslims that, even after the Battle of Badr, he still composed abusive poetry against Mohammed's cause. He taunted Muslims with allowing a stranger, who only followed his own self-interest and thirst for power, to control their lives. He maintained that if the people of Medina wished to be ruled by force and tyranny, they would be better off under the despotic old kings of Yemen.

Rodinson describes satirical poets who composed poetries against Mohammed and Muslims, as "the journalists of the time."[387] These poets accused the Muslims of Medina of dishonoring themselves by submitting to a refugee. Abu Afak showed his disaffection, when Mohammed killed al-Harith ibn Suwayd ibn Samid and taunted the children of Qaylah (the Aws and the Khazraj):

> I have lived a long time, but I have never seen
> Either a house or gathering of people
> More loyal and faithful to
> Its allies, when they call on it
> Than that of the children of Qaylah
> (The Aws and Khazraj) as a whole
> The mountains will crumble before they submit
> Yet there is rider come among them who had divided them.
> (He says), "This is permitted, this is forbidden"
> To all kinds of things. But if you have believed in power
> And in might, why did you not follow a *Tubba*[388] [a South Arabian ruler]

Abu Afak in effect asked, "The *Tubba* was after all a South Arabian king of great reputation, but you resisted him; now what has happened to you that you have accepted the claims of a Meccan refugee?"

---

[387] Rodinson, *Muhammad*, p. 194f.; "A tribal poet among the Bedouins," as Loel Carmichael puts it, "was no mere versifier, but a kindle of battle," his poems were "thought of as a serious beginning of a real warfare." (*The Shaping of the Arabs, A Study in Ethnic Identity*, New York: 1967, p. 38).

[388] *Ibn Hisham,* ed. Cit., 292f., quoted in Rodinson, *Muhammad*, p. 157.

Mohammed was deeply annoyed by Abu Afak's stinging verses and signified his wish for his assassination by saying to his followers, "Who will rid me of this pestilent fellow?"[389]

One Abu Afak's fellow tribesmen who had recently converted to Islam, Samir ibn Umayr, took it upon himself to carry out Mohammed's malevolent order. He attacked the poor aged man as he slept in his own courtyard and, in the same way as Asma was murdered, dispatched him with one blow of his sword.

The sounds of the inhuman murder of Abu Afak drew the neighbors to the spot, but though they vowed vengeance against the murderer, he escaped unharmed.[390] No one dared to molest the murderers of Asma or Abu Afak: it was no secret that the foul deeds had been approved by Mohammed, and that he treated the perpetrators with marked favor.[391]

An old Persian saying states, "A sleeping person is immune to any harm and even a snake does not bite a person who is asleep." But it would appear that under the rule of Allah and His messenger, this benevolent axiom regarding slumber is not valid. Since the ethics of His prophet are divinely determined by Allah, they supersede the mores of those who live on earth. It therefore follows that the killing the innocent people in their sleep is ethical and lawful.

The Killing of Ka'b Ibn al-Ashraf

Through lies and deceit, Mohammed ordered the murder of one of his opponents, Ka'b ibn al-Ashraf, the son of an Arab who belonged to a distant tribe, the Tayyi'. Since his mother was a Jewish woman of the Bani Nadhir, he behaved as if he belonged to his mother's clan of an-Nadhir. He was a rich and learned man; a rabbi and highly esteemed poet who wrote in Arabic. He followed Mohammed so long as he favored Judaism, but when he changed the Muslim's *qibla,* or direction of prayer from Jerusalem to Mecca, Ka'b ibn Ashraf dis-

---

[389] Bodley, *The Messenger: The Life of Mohammad,* p. 171.

[390] Muir, *The Life of Mohammad,* p. 240.

[391] Koelle, *Mohammed and Mohammedanism,* p. 169.

avowed him. When he learned of the victory of Mohammed in the Battle of Badr, he became violently enraged and cried out, "By God! If Mohammed has actually defeated the Quraysh and has slain those fine men, then the belly of earth is a better place for us than its surface."[392]

Being a friend of the Quraysh tribe, he composed verses about the slain heroes of Badr and then went to Mecca to recite his poems to extol them and incite the Quraysh to avenge their death at the well of Badr. To this end he wrote many biting satires.

> O that the earth when they were killed
> Had split asunder and engulfed its people,
> That he who spread the report had been thrust through
> Or lived cowering, blind and deaf.[393]

Ka'b's verses made it very clear to the Quraysh that many people, particularly Jewish tribes, were against Mohammed. Poetry had a great impact on the social and political life of the Arabs and Ka'b's songs renewed the courage of the depressed Qurayshi and incited them to rise against Mohammed.

Most of the leaders of Quraysh had been killed and Abu Sufyan had become one of the most important figures in Mecca after their defeat. Therefore, it became incumbent upon Ka'b to direct a new war against Mohammed and revenge the Badr defeat. He also openly joined hands with the enemies of Mohammed, at Medina. In an elegy to those who fell at Badr he sang of their nobility and cried out for vengeance:

> Badr's mill ground out the blood of its people
> At events like Badr you should weep and cry.
> The best of the people were slain round their cisterns.
> Don't think it strange that the princes were left lying
> How many noble handsome men,
> The refuge of the homeless were slain
> Liberals when the stars gave no rain

---

[392] Tabari, *The History of at-Tabari,* vol. VII, p. 94; Maudoodi, Syed Abul Ala' *Al-Jihad Fil Islam,* p. 258.

[393] Guillume, *The Life of Muhammad,* p.365.

Who bore other's burdens, ruling and taking their due forth
I was told that al-Harith ibn Hisham
Is doing well and gathering troops
To visit Yathrib with armies
For only the noble, handsome man protects the loftiest reputation.[394]

In another cry for vengeance, Ka'b wrote:

Drive off that fool of yours that you may be safe
From talks that have no sense!
Do you taunt me because I shed tears
For people who loved me sincerely?
As long as I live I shall weep and remember
The merits of people whose glory is in Mecca's houses.
By my life Murayd used to be far from hostile
But now they are become as jackles.
They ought to have their noses cut off
For insulting the two clans of Lu'ayy ibn Ghalib
I give my share in Murayd to Ja'dar
In truth, by God's house, between Mecca's mountains.[395]

Mohammed had ways of learning what was going on in Mecca. After being informed of Ka'b's incitements against him, he sent his court poet Hassan ibn Thabit to Mecca to satirize al-Mutallib ibn Abu Wada'a, Ka'b's host in Mecca. This resulted in Ka'b's return to Medina, where he continued to cajole the people into rebellion against Mohammed. While Asma was putting Aws and Khazraj tribes to shame, Ka'b ibn Ashraf was singing erotic propositions to Mohammed's wives,[396] and composing insulting verses about the Muslim women.[397] To this end, he wrote many erotic verses of an insulting nature, attacking Muslim women's honor and chastity, a curious and favorite mode of annoyance amongst the Arabs:

---

[394] *Ibid.*

[395] *Ibid.,* p. 366.

[396] Muhammad ibn Sallam al-Jumahi, *Tabaqat al-Shura,* ed. Joseph Hell (Leiden: 1916), p. 71.

[397] *Ibn Hisham,* p. 550.

Are you leaving without stopping in a valley,
and abandoning Umm al-Fadl in the Harem?
Pale-skinned she is, and scented with saffron; if she
were squeezed, she would exude scent, henna and hair-dye
Where she makes to rise, but then does not, what
lies between her ankles and her elbows quivers.
Like Umm Kakim when she was close to us,
the bonds that link us are firm and unreserved
One of the Bani amir by who my heart is driven
to madness; but if she wished, she could cure Ka'b of his sickness.
The chief of women; and her father is the chief of
his tribe, a people of high repute, who live up to their obligations.
Never before her have I seen a sun rising at
night, appearing to us when there is no moon.[398]

Mohammed feared that the open hostility of Ka'b would sap his authority in Medina. He aired his animosity against Ka'b, praying loudly, *"Oh Lord, deliver me from the son of Ka'b, in whatsoever way it seemeth good unto thee, because of his open sedition and his verses."*[399]

But instead of choosing an honorable way to confront Ka'b, he decided to assassinate him. So he said to his followers,

"Who is ready to kill Ka'b ibn al-Ashraf, the son of Ka'b, this pestilent fellow, this Jew who has really hurt Allah and His Apostle? Thereupon Mohammed ibn Maslamah, one of the Ansaris, came forward and replied,

"I will rid you of him. I will kill him."

"Do it then," Mohammed said, "if you can."[400]

Mohammed ibn Maslamah, left Mohammed and for three days refrained from eating or drinking, except for that which would keep him alive. When he was informed of Moslamah's fast, Mohammed summoned him and asked him why he abstained from food and drink. Mohammed ibn Maslamah, replied,

---

[398]Guillume, A Translation of Ibn Ishaq's *Sirt Rasul Allah, The life of Muhammad,* pp. 366–67.

[399] Muir, *The Life of Mohammad,* p. 246.

[400] *Ibn Ishaq,* p. 365.

"I have promised you something that I am not sure I am able to fulfill."

"All you have to do is try it," Mohammed replied.

"But, to accomplish this plan, we have to tell lies and false things in order to deceive him," said Moslamah.

"Say what you like," Mohammed replied. "You are free and absolved in this matter."[401] To further allay Maslamah's trepidations, Mohammed advised him to consult with the chief of his tribe, Sa'd ibn Moadz.

Since Ka'b ibn Ashraf lived on the outskirts of Medina in a strong castle that was difficult to penetrate, Sa'd ibn Moadz, advised Mohammed ibn Moslamah to resort to trickery. Mohammed ibn Moslamah collected four other Muslims from the Bani Aws tribe, including Ka'b's foster-brother, Abu Nai'la, and one of the Bani Abd al-Ashhal tribe, named Silkan ibn Salama.

To pave the way for the perpetration of the heinous crime that the Messenger of Allah had ordered Mohammed ibn Maslamah and his accomplices to accomplish, Abu Nai'la called on the Jewish poet one moonlit evening and spoke to him for a whole hour of many things, including a loan. He complained to Ka'b of the calamities and poverty that the advent of Mohammed had brought upon them. He further added,

"The tribes have become our enemies and fight against us; our caravan routes are impassable; our families divided; our souls troubled and our lives exhausted."

Ka'b answered, "I kept telling you, Abu Nai'la; I warned you that these things would happen." However, with guile and flattery, Abu Nai'la obtained Ka'b's confidence and asked him to lend him some money for himself and his friends. Ka'b demanded collateral and Abu Nai'la offered to pledge their valuable armor as such. Ka'b, however, demanded their sons as surety.

Abu Nai'la said, "That is insulting to us." Ka'b then agreed to Abu Nai'la's original proposal and they decided to meet late one night at Ka'b's home where the conspirators were to leave their arms, as pawn for payment of the loan. Thereupon Abu Nai'la returned to his

---

[401] Tabari, *The History of at-Tabari,* vol. III, p. 95.

companions, told them what had happened, and ordered them to bring their arms.

Then, towards the evening of the appointed night, Mohammed ibn Maslamah took his five accomplices to The Prophet's home and gained his final approval to carry out the crime. It was a bright moonlight night, and Mohammed accompanied them to the outskirts of Medina. As they were departing, he said to them,

"Go in Allah's name; O Allah, help them assassinate the outspoken Jew! May Allah aid you!"[402] Having thus obtained Mohammed's confirmation to assassinate Ka'b ibn Ashraf, the conspirators set out on the Messenger of Allah's bloody mission.

Walking two or three miles northward from the outskirts of Medina, they reached Ka'b's stronghold. Ka'b had retired to bed with his bride, a charming young lady whom he had only recently married, when Abu Nai'la arrived and called to him. He jumped out of bed, clutching a bed sheet round him. His bride caught him by it and begged him not to go, pointing out that he was a warrior with enemies and anyone calling him out at that time of night was up to no good.

Ka'b said, "But it is Abu Nai'la, who is like a brother to me, calling. Do you not hear his voice? Had he found me sleeping he would not have woken me."

She answered, "By Allah, I can feel evil in his voice."

Ka'b said, "What shall I fear from him?" So he pulled away from her and, while dressing, added, "Shall a warrior challenged not respond? A man has to respond to a call at night. Even if the call were to result in a stabbing, a brave man must answer it."[403]

So, Ka'b left his wife and joined the group of assassins, believing that they had come to deliver their arms as a pledge for the promised loan. Together, they walked and talked for a whole hour, enumerating and complaining about the misfortunes that Medina had to suffer under Mohammed's regime, particularly the lack of food. Thus, they lulled Ka'b into a sense of security. They wandered along, till they reached a waterfall.[404]

---

[402] Emile Dermenghem, *The Life of Mahomet* (Great Britain: StephenAustin and Sons, Ltd., 1930), p. 214; Tabari, *The History of at-Tabari*, vol. VII, p. 95.

[403] *Sahih al-Bukari*, vol. 5, p. 369.

[404] Al-Waqidi, calls it Shaj al ajuz and Tabari calls it Shab al-ajuz.

On the banks of the waterfall, they stopped to enjoy the beauty of the moonlit night. Abu Nai'la t, from time to time, had thrown his arm around his soon-to-be victim, touching Ka'b's hair and exclaiming, "Truly, I have never smelt anything so fragrant in my life." Ka'b said it was probably scent from his bride. Then, after gaining Ka'b's complete trust, Abu Nai'la seized him by the hair, and dragged him to the ground, shouting,

"Kill the enemy of Allah with all your might!" All the Muslim conspirators drew their swords and fell upon their victim. In the darkness, one of their own comrades was wounded. The betrayed Ka'b fought valiantly but, in spite of his rigorous resistance, he was doomed to die. Mohammed ibn Moslamah stabbed him in the heart with his dagger. He said later, "When I saw that our swords were of no avail, I remembered a long, thin dagger that I had in my scabbard, and took hold of it. I plunged the dagger into his breast and pressed upon it so heavily that it reached his pubic region, and the enemy of Allah fell."[405]

As Ka'b received the fatal wound, he uttered a fearful scream that awakened people and lights were seen shining through the windows of the terrified neighborhood.

Probably, verse 61 of *Sura* XXXIII of the Koran was quoted:

> "They shall have a Curse on them wherever they are found; they shall be seized and murdered mercilessly."

The murderers severed the head of Ka'b and fled in haste. But one of the criminals (al-Harith ibn Aws), had received two deep sword cuts intended for Ka'b and was unable to keep up with the others. Trying not to be seen, they tried to pass through the territory of several Jewish and Arab tribes. The wounded criminal (al-Harith), weakened by loss of blood, had lagged behind, so they waited for him for some time until, following their tracks, he rejoined them. Finally, the other murderers decided to carry their wounded comrade in their arms and so brought him to the gate of the mosque, where Mohammed was waiting for them.

---

[405] Tabari, *The History of at-Tabari,* vol. III, p. 97.

As the murderers entered the gate of the mosque, Mohammed came out to meet them.

"Welcome!" He exclaimed; "for I see that your faces beam with victory."

"And you too," they exclaimed, as they threw before him the ghastly head of their victim. Mohammed received it and enthusiastically congratulated them.[406] The murderers told Mohammed of their victory and the slaying of the enemy of Allah. When Mohammed, noticed the wounded murderer, he spat upon his wounds.[407]

The following day Mohammed made it known that he would always justify a Muslim killing a Jew. He declared, "Kill every Jew in the country." The edict was acclaimed by the people of the Mosque, and the Jews no longer dared to venture out of their doors after sunset.[408]

This criminal decree greatly perturbed the Jews and they entreated Mohammed to enter into a treaty with them.[409] There was not a Jew who was not fearful for his life.

The ruthless murder of Ka'b is one of the most flagrant examples of the terrorist roots of Islam and the immoral behavior of Mohammed. The lack of righteousness in Mohammed's character and his barbarous nature is expressed throughout the Koranic verses, endowing the Islam religion with principles of inhumanity and terrorism. Every detail in the foregoing barbaric incident is in accordance with Koranic principles that serve the self-interests of Mohammed, interpreted at the expense of truth and with the direct approval of his Deity.

In the above incident when Mohammed was trying to convince his followers to murder Ka'b, he said,

"Who is ready to kill Ka'b Ibn Ashraf, the Jew who has really hurt Allah and His Apostle?" In this statement, Mohammed openly says that "Ka'b is harming Allah," but there are at least four passages in two *Sura* of the Koran which say that "no one can harm Allah in any way." These verses are as the following:

---

[406] Bodley, *The Messenger: The Life of Mohammad*, p. 173.

[407] Guillume, *The Life of Mohammad*, p. 368.

[408] Bodley, *The Messenger: The Life of Mohammad*, p. 173.

[409] Montgomery Watt, *Muhammad at Medina*, p. 210.

" . . . If any did turn back on his heels, not the least harm will he do to Allah . . . ." (Koran, III: CXLIV)

"Let not those grieve you who rush headlong into unbelief: not the least harm will they do to Allah . . . ." (Koran, III: CLXXVI)

"Those who purchase unbelief at the price of faith, not the least harm will they do to Allah . . . ." (Koran, III: CLXXVII)

"This, because they said to those who hate what Allah has revealed, 'We will obey you in part of (this) matter,' but Allah knows their (inner) secrets.'" (Koran, XLVII: XXVI)

The above passages clearly state that no one can ever do the least harm to Allah, but Mohammed said that Ka'b was harming Allah and his prophet and for that very reason he ordered his followers to slay Ka'b so savagely. Who is fabricating falsehoods; Allah, the Koran or Mohammed? The answer, of course, is all three.

Allah and the Koran are both fantasies of a hypocritical Bedouin who decided to call himself "Prophet of God" and created them to beguile his fellow citizens. Through his imaginary "Allah," he conspired to power and riches. Since he ascribes the absurdities he is preaching to his imaginary friend in the sky (Allah), earthly creatures are not wise enough to comprehend them fully, but no one should dare to criticize or evaluate them. Unfortunately, after hundreds of years of brain washing, the lies, inconsistencies and absurdities have become religious dogma in the minds of millions of people resulting in the poor quality of life led by masses of Muslims as well as the degradation and humiliation of their women. Modern scientific and technological advances are unknown to the average Muslim and those countries ruled by the fundamentalist Muslim theocracy no longer produce much in the way of scholarly achievement.

In all probability, the earliest religion started when one member of a clan of prehistoric cave men who was a little better developed mentally and lazier than his fellow clansmen, decided that he could explain the origin of natural phenomena by ascribing them to a god or gods with whom he was in communication. In exchange for this "knowledge," he would be happy to receive gifts and tribute and, therefore, was able to subsist on the work of others.

Thus was born the first of a long line of prophets and priests: witness our present day TV evangelists begging for contributions as evidence of their victim's faith. After writing was invented, the sayings and myths surrounding these priests and prophets became sacred tomes to enable future generations of parasites to prey upon the gullible. Mohammed cunningly bypassed all previous religious dogma (except for an occasional acknowledgement of historical figures), invented his own "God" and dictated his own "Bible." By this clever maneuver, he was able to divinely justify what ever atrocity he committed in pursuit of his lust for power, riches and women!

Assassination of Abu Sunayneh

The morning after the murder of Ka'b ibn Ashraf, Mohammed gave sweeping permission to his followers to do away with all Jews: "whoever of the Jews falls into your hands, kill him."[410] After hearing this, Muhayyisah ibn Mas'ud happened to run into Ibn Sunayneh, a Jewish merchant and a member of his tribe with whom he had close personal and business relationships: He killed him.[411]

Huwayyisah ibn Mas'ud (the elder brother of Muhayyisah), who had not accepted Islam at that time, was angered by his brother's murder of Ibn Sunayneh and beat him saying, "O enemy of God, why did you kill this innocent man? The food he gave you from his wealth is still in your belly."

Muhayyisah replied, "By Allah, if he who ordered me to kill Ibn Sunayneh, had commanded me to kill you, I would have cut off your head."

On hearing this, Huwayyisah exclaimed, "What! Do you hear what you are saying? You would slay your own brother at Mohammed's command? Has the new faith reached to this?"

Muhayyisah replied, "Yes, by God, if Mohammed had ordered me to kill you, I would have done it."

Huwayyisah's reaction was a surprise. "By God, a faith that has brought you to this is indeed a marvel." Upon uttering these words, Huwayyisah was converted to Islam that very moment.[412]

Muhayyisah composed the following verses describing their conversation:

---

[410] *Ibn Hisham,* 553f.; Tabari, *The History of at-Tabari,* vol. VII, p. 97.

[411] *Ibn Hisham,* 553f.; Tabari, *The History of at-Tabari,* vol. VII, p. 97;

[412] Waqidi, p. 191; Guillume, *The Life of Mohammad,* p. 369.

> My brother blames me because if I were ordered
> to kill him
> I would smite his nape with a sharp sword,
> A blade white as salt from polishing.
> Whose stroke never misses its mark.
> It would not please me to kill you voluntarily
> Though we owned Arabia from North to South.[413]

The assassination of Abu Suneyneh, states Muir, "is alluded to by the biographers rather for the purpose of explaining the sudden conversion of the assassin's brother Huwayyisah, than to record the murder of a petty Jewish trader."[414] What was written by Muir, brings up the question of the psychological mechanism impelling conversion to Islam.

Rarely can a book be found about Islam that does not state that Islam was imposed on conquered people by trickery and use of the sword. The Syrians, Egyptians, Persians, Indians, and the Berbers accepted Islam to save their lives. The Arab conquerors gave the defeated nations three options: believe, pay religious tax, or perish. So, the first generation of "converts" chose conversion to survive rather than pay the "freedom of religion" tax. Taking the new faith lightly, they pretended to become a Muslim to escape persecution. To save their children from the punishments of the barbarian conquerors, not only did the first conquered generation pretend to be submissive to the new faith, they also taught their children to comply with the principles of the new religion. While the second generation was brought up to believe in Moslem dogma, they also were subject to residual pagan influence retained by their parents and still entertained some thoughts of rebellion. Succeeding generations, however, became completely Islamized.

The Killing of Abu Rafi'

Some of the Bani an-Nadhir, after their exile, found refuge among other Jews in Khaibar. A well-known and wealthy Jew named Abu

---

[413] Guillume, *The Life of Mohammad,* p. 369.
[414] Muir, *The life of Mohammad,* p. 249.

Rafia' Sallam ibn Abu'l-Huqayq (a.k.a. Abu Rafi) was the chief of a subdivision of the tribe Bani an-Nadhir'. After being expelled from Medina, he had settled in a castle near Khaibar and proceeded to continue the work of Ka'b ibn Ashraf against Mohammed. He was also suspected of inciting the Bani Fezara, and other Bedouin tribes against Mohammed and Muslims. The expulsion of the Jewish tribe of Bani an-Nadhir and the assassinations of Asma bint Marwan, Ka'b ibn Ashraf, and Abu Sunayneh were only the beginning of a purge Mohammed felt he should mount to ensure his power.

Ali, Mohammed's son-in-law, with a hundred Muslims, had mounted an expedition against Bani Sa'd ibn Bakr, who had plotted with the Jews of Khaibar against Mohammed. While this foray resulted in a rich booty of camels and flocks, it produced no other effect.[415]

However, there were two tribes in Medina who competed to further the cause of Mohammed. These were the Aws and Khazraj tribes, both from Ansar. Five people of Aws tribe had already carried out Mohammed's order to assassinate Ka'b ibn Ashraf, and now the Bani Khazraj, emulous of the honor that the Bani Aws had gained, declared their readiness to perform a similar favor for Mohammed. Therefore, when Mohammed said,[416] "Who will deal with this rascal for me?,"[417] four friends of Bani Salima Khazraj, Abdullah ibn Atik; Mas'ud ibn Sinan; Abdullah ibn Oneis; Abu Qatada al-Harith ibn Rib'i; and Khuza'l ibn Aswad, and an ally from Aslam, volunteered to assassinate Abu Rafi. Mohammed appointed Abdullah ibn Atik, who had a Jewish foster-mother, spoke their language fluently, and was familiar with the Bani Nadhir and the town of Khaibar, as leader of the team of assassins.

The would-be murderers left Mohammed and set out for Khaibar. By the time they drew close to it, the sun was setting, and the people were bringing their flocks back from pasture. The gate-keeper thought they were residents and said, "You there, if you want to come in, go ahead, since I want to shut the gate." Abdullah ibn Atik and his team entered and hid in a barn while the residents of

---

[415] Muir, *Mohomet and Islam,* p. 348; Guillume, *The Life of Mohammad,* p. 369.

[416] Dermenghem, *The Life of Mahomet,* p. 216.

[417] Guillume, *The Life of Mohammad,* p. 675.

the castle dined. Certain that everybody had come in, the gate-keeper shut and locked the door and hung the key on a wooden peg.

When everyone had gone to bed, Abdullah took the key of the entrance gate from the wooden peg, so as to be able to get out. Abu Rafi' was in an upper room reached by a spiral stairway. The assassins mounted the stairway, went to the Abu Rafi's door and knocked softly. His wife came to the door and asked who they were. They told her that they were Arabs in search of grain. She told them that her man was there and that they could come in. Afraid that a patrol might catch them at their bloody work, they shut the door behind them after entering. The wife went to apprise Abu Rafi of his uninvited business guests, but the murderers rushed upon him with their swords before he had a chance to get out of bed. The darkness prevented the murderers from performing a swift job. The only thing that guided them in the blackness was his pallor which shone like a piece of Egyptian cotton.

Seeing the flash of swords, Abu Rafi's wife shrieked, but one of the murderers quickly raised his sword and slashed her neck, stilling her voice. After they had fruitlessly hacked him with their swords, Abdullah ibn Oneis finally thrust his sword into Abu Rafi's stomach so hard that it went right through him, while he was shouting, *Qanti, qanti,* (enough, enough).[418] Satisfied that they had successfully completed their bloody assignment, they left their victim and the crime scene. Abdullah ibn Atik, had poor night vision and fell off the stairway, severely spraining his ankle, so the other four murderers lifted him up and took him to one of the water conduits, where they all hid until the furor died down.

Abu Rafi's servants lit lamps and searched for the murderers in all directions, but finally gave up hope and went back to their master, gathering round him as he was dieing.

Tabari,[419] quotes the murderer Abdullah ibn Atik as follows:

> "When I reached him, he was in a dark room along with his family. As I did not know where he was in the room, I said, 'Abu Rafi'!' and he said, 'Who is that?' I rushed toward the sound and gave him a blow with

---

[418] Tabari, *The History of at-Tabari,* vol. VII, p. 101; Ibn Ishaq, p. 483.

[419] *Ibid.,* vol. VII, pp. 100–101.

my sword, but I was in a state of confusion and did not achieve any-thing. He gave a shout, and I left the room but remained close at hand. I then went in again and said, 'What was that noise, Abu Rafi'?' 'God damn it,' he said, 'there is a man in the house who has just struck me with his sword.' Then I hit him and covered him with wounds, but I could not kill him, so I thrust the point of my sword into his stomach until it came out through his back. At that, I knew that I had killed him, and I opened the doors one by one until I reached a flight of stairs. Thinking that I had reached the ground, I put my foot out but fell into a moonlit night and broke my leg. I bound it up with my turban and move on. Fi-nally, finding myself sitting by the door, I said to myself, 'By Allah, I will not leave tonight until I know whether I have killed him or not.' When the cock crowed, the announcer of his death stood upon the wall and said, 'I announce the death of Abu Rafi', the profit-maker of the people of Hijaz.' I went to my companions and said, 'Deliverance! Allah has killed Abu Rafi'.'"

The murderers were still not sure whether their victim was dead. So one of them volunteered to go back and confirm whether or not he was. He mingled with the crowd and on his return, he reported that Jews and his wife were crowded around him so he could not get a good look but he did hear Abu Rafi's wife say,

"By God, I recognized the voice of Abdullah ibn Atik, and then I decided I must be wrong and thought, 'How could Abdullah ibn Atik be in this country?'" With a lamp in her hand, she looked into Abu Rafi's face and said, "By the God of the Jews, he is dead."

When the murderous team was assured of the accomplishment of their crime, they picked up their injured companion and returned to Medina, to report to their terrorist leader, Mohammed, that his order had been carried out successfully. When Mohammed saw them approaching, he exclaimed,

"Success attends you."

"And you too," replied the murderers. They recounted to him all that had happened, each of them taking personal credit for the infa-mous deed. Mohammed examined their weapons and announced,

"It is the sword of Abdullah ibn Oneis that killed him; I can see the marks left by bones on it."[420]

---

[420] Tabari, *The History of at-Tabari,* vol. VII, p. 103.

When the faithful Muslims became aware of the terrible atrocities sanctioned by their Prophet, they faced two options: either they could dismiss them as propaganda disseminated by infidels or they could fall back on their faith and believe that since the crimes, no matter how horrible, had been committed by the True Prophet, the acts must be considered as sacred duties imposed on the Prophet by the Almighty Allah. It is interesting that when we read such of such atrocities we regard the perpetrators as depraved criminals. But when we regard the acts as divine injunctions, they become not only socially acceptable, but sacred acts and we condone the malefactors.

Assassination of Oseir ibn Razim and a Number of Jews

The assassination of Abu Rafi' and other Jews still did not relieve Mohammed of his apprehensions concerning the Jews of Medina, the city that he intended to govern as a prophet-king. Oseir ibn Razim, a prominent Jew of Khaibar, was collecting *Ghatafanin* in Khaibar to attack Mohammed. Mohammed deputized Abdullah ibn Rawaha, a leader of the Khazraj, along with three other Muslims, to conduct a feasibility study of a raid on Oseir ibn Razim. They found the Jews exceedingly security conscious, so the assassination of Oseir appeared almost impossible.

Abdullah ibn Rawaha returned to Medina and reported the situation to Mohammed. In keeping with his crafty nature, Mohammed resorted to treachery. He ordered Ibn Rawaha to go back to Oseir with a group of thirty Muslims mounted on camels and tell him that if he would visit Mohammed, The Prophet would make him ruler of Khaibar and treat him with great honor. They gave Oseir a solemn guarantee of safety if he did so. After considerable urging, and despite warnings from his friends, Oseir finally accepted the offer and accompanied by a number of his fellow tribesmen, set out with the thirty Jews. Each Muslim took one Jew with him on his camel to ride back to Medina.[421] Abdullah ibn Oneis mounted the unfortunate

---

[421] Muir, *Mohammad and Islam,* p. 349; Rodinson, *Muhammad,* p. 249; Ibn Saad, p. 66f.

chief, Oseir ibn Razim, on his camel and rode behind him. When they reached al-Qarqarqa, about six miles from Khaibar, Osier changed his mind about going to visit Mohammed.[422]

Abdullah ibn Oneis became suspicious of Osier whom he caught, once or twice, reaching out his hand toward his sword. He dismounted and rushed at Oseir, striking him with a deadly blow that cut off his leg. As Osier fell mortally wounded from the camel, he hit Oneis with a crook that he had in his hand, wounding his head. When they saw the fight between Oneis and Osier, each of the Muslims turned upon his Jewish companion and murdered him except for one man, who escaped the massacre on foot.

Following the slaughter of the Jews, the followers of the so-called Messenger of God continued their journey back to Medina. When Abdullah ibn Oneis came to Mohammed, he spat on his wound and said,

"Verily, Allah has delivered you from an unrighteous people."[423]

The Murder of Sufyan ibn Khalid

The defeat of Mohammed at Uhod, encouraged his opponents to rally their forces against him. Among these was Sufyan ibn Khalid, the chief of Lihyan, a branch of the Hudheil, and other neighboring tribes that occupied a territory two days east of Mecca. Sufyan ibn Khalid began collecting warriors at Orana (Nakhla) an oasis between Mecca and at-Taif.[424]

When Mohammed heard of Sufyan ibn Khalid's threatening activities, he decided to do away with him. He contacted Abdullah ibn Oneis and told him that he had heard that Sufyan ibn Khalid was assembling an army to attack him and he wanted Sufyan assassinated. Oneis asked Mohammed to describe him, in order that he should recognize him. Mohammed told him,

---

[422] Tabari, *The History of at-Tabari,* vol. XL, p. 120.

[423] Muir, *Mohammad and Islam,* p. 349.

[424] *Ibn Hisham,* p. 975; Tabari, *The History of at-Tabari,* vol. I, p. 1759; Al-Waqidi, p. 151f.; *Ibn Saad,* p. 35f.

"A sure sign of him is that if you see him, you will be so horrified that you think you are facing Satan."[425] After receiving proper instructions from Mohammed, the assassin girded his sword and set out on his bloody mission.

A few days later, Oneis reached Orana and found Sufyan who was looking for lodging accommodations for a number of women who were traveling with him in a howdah. Oneis advanced toward Sufyan, bowed to him, and told him that he was an Arab who had heard that Sufyan was gathering a force against Mohammed and that he wanted to join his army as a volunteer. Sufyan welcomed him and Oneis started walking with him, conversing and gaining his trust. As soon as they were alone, Oneis attacked Sufyan and cut off his head. He carried it off, leaving the women to weep over the headless corpse.

Having accomplished his bloody job successfully, Oneis rushed to Medina and safety and presented himself before Mohammed in the mosque. Mohammed welcomed him, and asked about his adventure. Abdullah replied by displaying the head of his victim. Upon seeing proof of the successful assassination of Sufyan, Mohammed rejoiced and took Abdullah into his house. In token of his gratitude he gave him a piece of a stick, telling him to keep it by himself. The assassin took it and thanked him, but he was perplexed as to its use. When his friends asked him about the stick, he said the Apostle just gave it to him and told him to keep it. They advised Abdullah to go back to the Apostle and ask him how he should use it. He returned and, after asking, Mohammed told him,

"This is a sign between you and me on the day of resurrection. Verily, few men on that day will carry sticks tied to their waist."[426] Abdullah ibn Oneis, fastened the stick to his sword and wore it by his side till his death, then it was fastened to his body with the shroud and buried with him. Presumably, he is still carrying it in Paradise, or perhaps it was used to kindle the fires of Hell.

Abdullah ibn Oneis has described his horrible mission:

> I left Ibn Thaur like a young camel
> Surrounded by mourning women cutting their shirts into strips.

---

[425] Guillume, *The Life of Mohammad,* p. 666.

[426] *Ibn Hisham,* vol. 2, pp. 395–96.

When the women were behind me and behind him
I fetched him a stroke with a sharp Indian sword
Which could bite into the heads of armored men
As a flame burns up the tinder.
I said to him as the sword bit into his head
I am Ibn Oneis, no mean horseman;
I am the son of one who never removed his cooking-pot,
No niggard he-wide was the space before his door.
I said to him, "Take that with the blow of a noble man
Who turns to the religion of the prophet Mohammed."
Whenever the prophet gave thought to an unbeliever
I got to him first with tongue and hand.[427]

The murder of Sufyan ibn Khalid dispersed the forces against Mohammed at Orana (Nakhla) and did not significantly affect his reputation; the Arabs already knew him to be a murderer. However, shortly afterwards several of his followers were killed by an armed band of Beni Lihyan at Ar-Raji', who thirsted to avenge the assassination of their chief.[428]

The Murder of Rifa'a ibn Qas al-Jushami

According to Tabari,[429] al-Waqidi,[430] and Ibn Hisham,[431] and other historians,[432] in the year 630 CE, Abdullah ibn Abi Hadrad al-Aslami went to Mohammed and said,

"I married a woman from my tribe, promising her a nuptial gift (dowry) but I was unable to pay it and consummate my marriage."

Mohammed asked me about the amount of nuptial gift and when I answered 'two hundred dirhams,' he said, 'By Allah, he had nothing with which to help me.' I waited for some days. Then a man named Rifa'a ibn Qays arrived and encamped at al-Ghabah with a

---

[427] Gillume, *The Life of Mohammad*, p. 789.

[428] Muir, *The Life of Mohammad*, p. 277.

[429] Tabari, *The History of at-Tabari*, vol. VIII, pp. 149–50.

[430] *Al-Waqidi*, vol. 2, pp. 777–80.

[431] *Ibn Hisham*, vol. 4, pp. 629–31.

[432] Guillume, *The Life of Mohammad*, pp. 671–72.

large group of men from Jusham. He had a high reputation among Jusham and, with his tribesmen and companions, intended to join with the tribe of Qays to make war on Mohammed. Mohammed summoned me and two other Muslims and said,

"Go out to this man and either bring him [his head] to us or bring us a report and information about him." To accomplish this job, Mohammed provided us with an emaciated old camel and mounted one of us on it.

Then he said, "Make do with her, and ride her in turn."

We set out, armed with arrows and swords. We arrived near the settlement in the evening as the sun was setting. I hid myself in one place and commanded my two companions to hide themselves somewhere else near the men's encampment. I told them,

"If you hear me shout, 'Allah is Great!' and see me attack the encampment, shout 'Allah is great!' and attack with me."

When the nightfall came, one of their herdsmen who had gone out in the morning was late coming back and they were worried about him. Their leader, Rifa'a ibn Qays, stood up took his sword, and said,

"By Allah, I am going to follow the tracks of this herdsman of ours. Some harm must have befallen him." Some of his companions begged him not to go without their protection, but he insisted on going alone. He set out and passed by me. When he came within range, I shot him in the heart with an arrow, and he died without uttering a word. I leaped at him and cut off his head. Then I rushed toward the encampment and shouted, 'Allah is greater!' My two companies rushed and shouted, 'Allah is greater!' In no time at all, we took all that we could—wives, children, and any property light enough to carry. We drove away a great herd of camels and many sheep and goats and brought them to Mohammed, the Messenger of Allah. I brought him Rifa'a's head, which I had carried with me. Mohammed gave me thirteen camels from that herd to help me pay my nuptial gift, so I was able to consummate my marriage."

According to Tabari,[433] the account of the noted historian, al-Waqidi regarding this incident is as follows, "The Prophet sent Ibn Abi Hadrad to this expedition with Abu Qatada. The party consisted of sixteen men, and they were away fifteen nights. Their shares [of

---

[433] Tabari, *The History of at-Tabari,* vol. VIII, p. 150.

booty] were twelve camels [for each man], each camel being accounted equal to ten sheep or goats. When people fled in different directions, they took four women, including one young woman who was very beautiful."

Assassination of Abdullah ibn Khatal

According to Tabari,[434] quoting Ibn Ishaq, Ibn Humayd, and Salamah, when Mohammed conquered Mecca, he ordered his commanders to kill a group of people, even if they had hid behind the curtains of the Ka'ba. Among them was Abdullah ibn Khatal, a member of Banu Taym ibn Ghalib. The reason for his assassination was that, being a Muslim, Mohammed had sent him along with one of the Ansar tribesmen to collect *zakat.* Abdullah ibn Khatal had taken along a Muslim slave. When he halted at a resting place, he commanded his slave to slaughter him a goat and make him a meal; then he went to sleep. When he woke up, he found that his slave had done nothing; so he attacked him and killed him. Rather than be tried as a murderer under Islamic law, he rejected Islam and reverted to polytheism. He had two singing girls; called Fartana and Sara. These two used to sing satires about Mohammed and his faith, so Mohammed commanded that all three be killed.

Two Muslims, Saeed ibn Hurayth al-Makhzumi and his relative Abu Barzah al-Aslami, executed Mohammed's order and killed Abdullah ibn Khatal. As for Ibn Khatal's two singing girls, Fartana was killed and Sara fled. Mohammed was later asked to grant her mercy, and he did so. She lived until someone's horse trampled and killed her at al-Abtah.

Assassination of al Huwayrith ibn Nuqaydh

Another person whom Mohammed ordered assassinated, even if he were found behind the curtains of the Ka'ba, was al-Huwayrith

---

[434] *Ibid.,* pp. 178–79.

ibn Nuqaydh. He was one of those who had opposed Mohammed at Mecca. This person was killed by one of Mohammed's favorite executioners, his son-in-law Ali ibn Abitalib, who later became the fourth Kaliph.[435]

The Killing of Miqyas ibn Subabah

Another of the Prophet's victims was Miqyas ibn Subabah. Mohammed commissioned his assassination because he had killed a member of the Ansar tribe who had killed Miqyas' brother by mistake. Miqyas then returned to the Quoraysh as a renegade.[436] Numaylah ibn Abdullah, a man of his own clan, carried out the assassination order. The sister of Myqyas said:

> By my life, Numaylah ashamed his clan
> And distressed winter guests by [killing] Miqyas.
> How excellent it was for one to see a man like Miqyas
> In times when no food was prepared even for
> woman in childbirth![437]

The Mission to Assassinate Abu Sufyan ibn Harb

According to Tabari,[438] in the year 625 CE, Mohammed ordered Amr ibn Omeiya al-Darmi and one of the Ansar to go to Mecca and kill his archenemy, Abu Sufyan ibn Harb. Amr ibn Omayyah's account of this mission is as follows:

"When Mohammed ordered me to kill Abu Sufyan, I had a camel, but my Ansari companion did not and he had a weakness in his foot, so I carried him on my camel until we reached the valley of Ya'jaj. I

---

[435] *Ibid.,* pp. 179, 181.

[436] *Ibid.,* pp. 179–80.

[437] *Ibid.,* pp. 179–80.

[438] Tabari, *The History of at-Tabari,* vol. VII, pp. 147–50.

had with me a dagger which I had ready to kill anybody who laid hold of me. My companion insisted that we first go and circumambulate Ka'ba seven times and pray there. So we did.

When we came out we passed a group of men sitting together. When they saw us one of them shouted, 'That is Amr ibn Omayyah, by Allah; I am sure he has not come here for any good purpose!' (Amr had been a cutthroat and a desperado before accepting Islam.) They set out in pursuit of me and my companion, and I said to him, 'Let us get out of here! This is just what I was afraid of! We will never reach Abu Sufyan now; save your own skin.' We left at full speed and hid in a cave. I concealed the entrance with stones. When in the cave, I noticed Othman ibn Obay Dullah come up, riding proudly on his horse. I said to my companion, 'This is Ibn Malik. If he sees us, he will tell everyone in Mecca about us.' So, I went out and stabbed him below the breast with my dagger. He gave a shout which all the Meccans heard, and they came up to him while I went back to my hiding place. The Meccans hastily followed the shout, and found him on the point of death. They asked him who had wounded him. 'Amr ibn Omeiya,' he replied and died.

They could not find anything to show them where we were, and merely said, 'By Allah, we knew that they came for no good purpose.' The death of their companion slowed their search for us because they took time to carry him away.

We remained in the cave for two days until the pursuit had died down and then went out to al-Tan'im, where the Khubayb ibn Abi's body was kept. Khubayb was among six Muslims that Mohammed had sent to teach Islam to Adal and al-Qarah, but was slain by them. I was planning to carry his corpse to Medina, but when I was carrying him on my back, they spotted me. I threw the body down and took the path to al-Safa and they went back. Meanwhile, my companion made his way to our camel, mounted it, rode to the Prophet and told him what had happened to us.

I proceeded on foot until I was overlooking Ghalib Dajnan. There I went into a cave with my bow and arrows. While there, a tall one-eyed man came in driving some sheep. Then, after some chatting, he lay down next to me, and raised his voice in song:

I will not be a Muslim as long as I live,
and will not believe in the faith of Muslims.

I said, "You will soon see." Before long the Bedouin went to sleep and started snoring. I went to him and killed him in the most dreadful way that anyone ever killed anybody. I leant over him, stuck the end of my bow into his good eye, and thrust it down until it came out of the back of his neck. After that I rushed out like a wild beast and took to the highway like an eagle, fleeing for my life. On my way to Medina, at al-Naqi, there were two Meccans whom the Quraysh had sent to spy on the Messenger of Allah. I recognized them and called them to surrender. They resisted, so I shot an arrow at one of them and killed him, and then called upon the other to surrender. He did so and I tied him up and took him to the Messenger of Allah.

I showed him my prisoner, whose thumbs I had tied together with my bowstring, and the Messenger of Allah looked at him and laughed so that his back teeth could be seen. Then he questioned me and I told him what had happened.

'Well done!' he said, and prayed for me to be blessed. Verily, how compassionate is Allah! How humanitarian is His Messenger and how benevolent a religion is Islam!"

The Old Woman who was Split into Two Parts

According to Tabari,[439] Waqidi,[440] and Ibn Hisham,[441] in the month of Ramazan in 627 CE, Mohammed sent a party led by Zaid ibn Harith to Wadi al-Qura, where they encountered the Bani Fazarah. Some of his companions were killed there, and Zaid himself was carried away wounded. One of those killed by the Bani Fazarah was Ward ibn Amr.

While Zaid was recovering from his wounds, he vowed to abstain from sexual relations until he had raided the Bani Fazarah. So, after he recovered, the Messenger of Allah sent him with an army against the Bani Fazarah. Zaid met with them in Wadi al-Qura and inflicted casualties on them. Qays ibn Musahhar killed Mas'dah ibn Hakamah

[439] *Ibid.,* vol. VIII, pp. 96–96.
[440] *Al-Waqidi.,* 2, pp. 564–65.
[441] Ibn Hisham., IV, pp. 617–18.

and took Fatima Bint Rabi'h prisoner. He also took one of Fatima's daughters and Abdullah ibn Mas'dah prisoner.

Zaid ibn Harith ordered Qays to kill Fatima, who was a very old woman, and he killed her cruelly. With a rope, he tied each of her legs to a camel and drove them apart until they split her in two. Then they brought Fatima's daughter and Abdullah ibn Mas'dah to Mohammed. Fatima's daughter was from a distinguished family but she now belonged to Qays ibn Musahhar, who had taken her. The messenger of Allah asked for her, and Qays gave her to him. Mohammed then gave her to his maternal uncle, Hazn ibn Abi Wahb, and she bore him Abd al-Rahman ibn Hazn.

The above barbarous assassinations are only a sampling of the murders Mohammed personally ordered for his own aggrandizement. Six more men and four more women were to be assassinated.[442] According to prominent Arab historians and reliable sources the total dead, due to Mohammed's raids against Arabs and non-Arabs and the massacres he presided over during his governorship in Medina, amounted to eighty-one. On the basis of reliable sources, Montgomery Watt has listed in his book all the raids against innocent tribes, the number of men killed and women and children kidnapped, including dates, number of participants in the raids, etc.[443]

---

[442] *Ibid.*, p. 181.

[443] *Ibn Hisham,* vol. IV, pp. 178–89; Montgomery Watt, *Muhammad at Medina,* pp. 339–43.

CHAPTER SEVEN

WERE MOHAMMED'S INSPIRATIONS GENUINE?

Knowledge and history are the enemies of religion.
Napoleon 1, *Maxims* (1804–15)

Religio peperit scelerosa atque impia facta. (Too often religion has been the mother of impious acts and criminals).
Lucretius De Derum Natura, 1, 76.

Various "forensic scholars" have attempted to dissect Mohammed's psyche. Koelle considers the aforementioned account of the event in Mohammed's childhood when he was five years old of great importance in understanding his claim to be the Messenger of God. According to Koelle, the hysterical paroxysms to which he attributed his call to prophecy did not result from the visit of an angel bringing him Divine revelations, as Muslims have been led to believe, but were probably the result of a congenital physical disorder. Just as in maturity he claimed that he remembered the "revelations" given to him during his cataleptic fits, so, as related by his Bedouin wet-nurse, Halima, he was also able to describe the imaginary event that occurred in his childhood fit as if it had been a reality.[444]

The disorder from which he suffered has been termed *hysterical muscularis* by his medical biographer Sprenger. Although its attacks closely resembled common epileptic fits, they also differed from them, inasmuch as the victim retains a recollection of imagined

---

[444] Koelle, *Mohammed and Mohammedanism,* pp. 41–42.

events occurring during a paroxysm, which is not the case in ordinary epilepsy. Mohammed's hysterical sensations and visionary fantasies obviously were involuntary, and yet proceeded from within his own psyche, just as our ordinary dreams come involuntarily, but are nevertheless originated by ourselves. The nature of both phenomena is purely subjective.[445] The assertion that the "attacks" were involuntary is subject to some skepticism in view of the obvious use of the "revelations" by Mohammed to achieve power and satisfy his satyriasis.

Muir states that the attacks which alarmed Halima were "fits of a nervous nature in the constitution of Mohammed. . . . .the normal marks of those exited states and ecstatic swoons which perhaps suggested to his own mind the idea of inspiration."[446]

Palmer maintained that Mohammed's revelations were due to a psychic disorder. He writes, "From youth upwards he had suffered from a nervous disorder which tradition calls epilepsy, but the symptoms of which closely resembled certain hysterical phenomenon . . . and which are almost always accompanied with hallucinations."[447] Another author, Rodwell, believed that the visions with which Mohammed's prophecy began "may actually have occurred during the hallucinations of one of the epileptic fits from which Mohammed from early youth appears to have suffered."[448] This idea completely dovetails with Sprenger's diagnosis of Mohammed's psychological pathology. That is, there was causal connection between Mohammed's physical and psychic state and his revelations.[449]

Noldeke held that during a revelation, Mohammed would fall into an epileptic seizure which could be interpreted as a disease of mind and body. "The signs of these severe paroxysms were foaming of the mouth, head drooping, face blanching or reddening, crying like a

---

[445] *Ibid.*

[446] *Ibid.*

[447] *The Qur'an,* Introduction, XX-XXII, XLVI, quoted by John Clark Archer, *Mystical Elements in Mohammed* (New Haven: Yale University press, 1980), p. 16.

[448] J. A. Rodwell, *Koran* (London: J. M. Dent & Sons Ltd., 1953), p. 21, note 1.

[449] Sprenger, *Das Leben und die Lehre des Mohammad* (Berlin, 1869).

camel colt, and profuse perspiring even in winter time."[450] He states that Al-Waqidi called such paroxysms "fever," but others, following Byzantines [thought], have called "epilepsy."[451]

Margoliouth tends to relate Mohammed's revelations as symptoms that were artificially reproduced.[452] He believes that only in two instances, "the fits were not subject to Mohammed's own control; once when he fainted during the intense excitement of the Battle of Badr and once when he had himself bled after fasting."[453] Evaluating Mohammed's contention of divine revelation, Archer states, "We may infer from Margoliout's argument that Mohammed possessed some form of mental power superior to any physiological ailment, and some power of discernment not impaired by any 'fit' of the moment."[454]

Many of the scholars who have researched the life of Mohammed, including Torrey,[455] Otto Stoll,[456] and John Archer[457] have come to the conclusion that whenever Mohammed was pretending to receive revelations, he was hypnotizing himself.

John Clark Archer maintains that Mohammed was a practicing mystic and that he employed certain methods of self-hypnosis that induced trance-like conditions. These techniques were commonly practiced by the mystics of the highly civilized lands adjoining Arabia, and among certain dwellers in Arabia itself. Repetition of such self-induced trances resulted in his belief that the "ecstasy" that came upon him was of Divine origin."[458]

---

[450] Noldeke, *Geschichte des Korans* (Gottingen, 1860), p. 26.

[451] *Ibid.*

[452] David S. Margoliouth, *Mohammed and the Rise of Islam* (New York: New World Book Manufacturing Co., Inc., 1972), p. 46.

[453] *Ibid.*

[454] John Clark Archer, *Mystical Elements in Mohammed* (dissertation), (New Haven: Yale University press, 1924), pp. 71–74, 87.

[455] Charles Cutler Torrey, *The Jewish Foundation of Islam* (New York: Ktav Publishing House, Inc.), p. 59.

[456] Otto Stoll, *Suggestion und Hypnotismus* in der völkerpsychologie. 2 umgearb und verm aufl (Leipzig: Veit & comp., 1904), pp. 256–58.

[457] Archer, *Mystical Elements in Mohammed,* pp. 18–19.

[458] *Ibid.*

Evaluation of Scholars' Theories about Mohammed's Pretended Revelations

This author believes that Mr. Archer and other writer's evaluation of Mohammed's revelations could be termed naïve. A short but attentive look at some of the cruel and irrational actions of Mohammed is sufficient to prove this contention:

When Mohammed, among other atrocities, cruelly ordered the date palms of the Jewish Bani Nadhir tribe, their chief source of revenue, cut down (Koran, LIX: 5), was he really under the influence of self-hypnotism and receiving a Divine revelation?

Sometimes Mohammed held private meetings with Dahya ibn Khalifh Al-Kalbi, one of the most attractive young men in Arabia. He ordered that on those occasions no one was permitted to intrude upon their privacy.[459] He also claimed that the angel Gabriel on occasion appeared to him in the form of Dahya.[460] Now, someone should ask Mr. Archer: When Mohammed claimed Gabriel was personified as Dahya and he met privately with Dahya, was he really receiving Divine revelations or were they perhaps engaged in more worldly and personal pursuits?

We also know that Mohammed raided the Jews of Khaibar, the richest village in the Hijaz, in an attempt to reinvigorate his followers after their defeat at Hudaibiyah. Kinana ibn Rabi', the chief of Khaibar, and his cousin were captured and interrogated as to where they had concealed their treasure and gold vessels. Kinana yielded some treasure to Mohammed, maintaining that it was all the money he possessed. Upon hearing this, Mohammed ordered his torturers to work on him until he gave up the rest of his wealth. Kinana was subjected to cruel torture (burning coals were placed upon his breast until he almost expired) until he revealed where the remainder of his wealth was concealed. Mohammed then ordered the chief and his cousin decapitated[461] following which, he took the latter's beautiful

---

[459] Mulla Mohammed Bagher Majlesi, *Bahar el-Anwar fi Akhbar el-Aemmatel Athar* (Persian text), vol. 8 (Tehran: 1110 AH), pp. 2, 326.

[460] Margoliouth, *Mohammed and the Rise of Islam,* p. 366.

[461] Muir, *The Life of Mohammad,* p. 37

17 year old bride to bed. Did he really commit all of these shameless atrocities by the command of God as revealed to him by Gabriel?

On another occasion, Mohammed agreed to the massacre of all of the seven hundred males of the Jewish tribe Bani Quraiza, along with the confiscation of their property and the enslavement of their women and children. In order to justify this barbarous, bloody act, Mohammed "revealed" verses from 9 to 27 of *Sura* XXXIII of the Koran. Was he really carrying out a Divine commandment when he committed all these inhumane atrocities? It is interesting to note that when Mohammed ordered his followers to murder Asma bint Marwan, whilst her babies slept beside her or suckled her breast, and when he ordered the murder of Abu Afak and Ka'b ibn Ashraf, he did not claim that Allah had sent a revelation allowing those atrocities.[462]

In light of the above examples, this author believes that with regard to Mohammed's pretension of receiving revelations, "self-hypnosis" should be differentiated from "Divine revelation." Mohammed may have been hypnotizing himself as an independent variable in order to invest whatever he had in mind with a Divine origin, and his physical symptoms while in a fit were not the result of a Divine dependent variable. According to the social scientist, Archer, Mohammed was using "self-hypnosis" as a "dependent variable" and "Divine revelation" as an "independent variable," whereas the reverse is probably the case.

Dependent variable in social sciences is thought to be the result of some other factors (independent variable). The independent variable is not considered as determined by anything in particular. Independent variable is also called predictor of the dependent variable and is said to predict or explain the dependent variable. Put it in a very simple way the dependent variable is an effect, and an independent variable is the cause—or at least a suspected cause.

On the basis of these theories, it can be said that Mohammed's pretension of revelation was a dependent and self-hypnosis was an independent variable. In other words, Mohammed was not manifesting physical symptoms because of awe-inspiring presence of the angel Gabriel, but rather he knew what he wanted to accomplish

---

[462] See chapter six for details.

and, to that end, he hypnotized himself into fits and seizures and pretended that they were the psychological and physical ramifications of Divine revelation.

"As for the fits, or seizures, resembling epilepsy, out of which he brought forth some of the 'messages' received in times of most urgent need," Torrey also writes, "I have long believed that they were obtained through self-hypnotism. Before Mohammed made his public claim to prophecy, he had acquired the technique of this abnormal mental condition in the same way in which countless others have gained it, namely through protracted fasting, vigils, and meditation . . . . The well known phenomenon of self-hypnotism agrees strikingly with the description of Mohammed's 'fits' given by his biographers."[463]

The author of this book has been involved in the science and practice of hypnosis and hypnotherapy for more than twenty years and is the recipient of two awards for innovations in the field, one from the national Guild of Hypnotists in 1991 and the second from the Eastern Institute of Hypnotherapy in 1995. Furthermore, one of his books on hypnosis, *Modern Hypnosis: Theory and Practice,* has been selected as a text book by more than ten colleges and universities in the United States. He has authored several publications on smoking cessation, alcoholism, weight control and treatment of sexual deviations and sexual dysfunctions by hypnosis and hypnotherapy for use by professional hypnotherapists and physicians. He has also written tens of articles about hypnosis and hypnotherapy that have been published in magazines.

Although "*hypnosis*" had not yet been scientifically described at the time of Mohammed, the author tends to agree with those scholars who believe that when Mohammed pretended the angel Gabriel was bringing him revelations from so-called Allah, he was somehow hypnotizing himself, as said above, as an independent variable.

It should be taken into consideration that in addition to self-hypnosis, there are other relaxation techniques (such as the Silva technique, autogenic training, etc.) by which the conscious mind can be so intensely focused that external and internal stimuli may be suppressed or intensified. Events relegated to the unconscious mind

---

[463] Torrey, *The Jewish Foundation of Islam,* pp. 59–60.

can be recalled and habits changed. For example smoking, which is a habit governed by both the conscious and the unconscious mind, can be rendered repulsive and thus broken.

The perception of pain is a function of the autonomic nervous system which is controlled by the subconscious mind. By means of hypnosis, analgesia of part or all of the body may be accomplished and surgery performed without using conventional anesthetics.

When the author of this book was studying in the University of London, he helped relieve the labor pains of birthing ladies in the London University Hospital. If such good anesthesia can be obtained through hypnosis, certainly, with diligent practice, self-hypnosis may be used to induce the states into which Mohammed fell at the time he was pretending that a heavenly angel was bringing him revelations.

In an effort to explain the psycho-pathology of Mohammed's attacks, Macdonald maintains that whether or not the fits were self-induced, they were a device to lend legitimacy to his alleged revelations. Macdonald believes that there is not a definitely proven causal relationship between the epilepsy and the revelation as mentioned by others. Mohammed's epileptic experiences at the time of so-called revelations could be considered a mixture of "diseased personality" and "his genius."[464]

Certain Byzantine and Western writers, even in recent times, have thought Mohammed was epileptic, relying on his wife Ayesha's statement: "At the time of revelation, Allah's Apostle was attacked by fever and even on a very cold day, beads of perspiration rolled from his face." If, as is sometimes still argued, all types of semi-conscious and trance-like states, including occasional loss of consciousness, and similar conditions, are all to be called epileptic attacks, then it can be said that Mohammed was an epileptic. Elaborating on this subject, Andrae comes to the conclusion that Mohammed's pretension to a call to prophecy psychologically has no other basis than an exaggerated conception of the power and significance of his own personality.[465]

---

[464] Duncan Black Macdonald, *Aspects of Islam* (Freeport, New York: Books for Libraries Press, 1943).

[465] Tor Andrae, *Mohammed: The Man and his Faith,* pp. 50–52

Having explored impartially, all these scholarly ideas about Mohammed, how should we judge him? Was he an "impostor" as believed by the old European biographers, or on the basis of the surveys of the modern ones, was there a pathological causation behind his "epileptic" or "hysterical" fits? Where were those paroxysmal symptoms, such as the drooped head, foaming of the mouth, reddening or pallor of the face and perspiration at the moments of revelation, coming from? Were they induced voluntarily and consciously from within to legitimize them as the effects of a supernatural inspiration, or were they really the ramifications of the stimuli inflicted from above?

A New Look at the Mechanism of Mohammed's State of Revelation

Scholars who understand the art of theatrical performance can offer an explanation of the mystical behavior of Mohammed at the time of his so-called revelations. Konstantin Stanislavski, the celebrated Russian actor, who has had a major influence in the training of actors for western theater, introduced a system which became known as "the Stanislavski method." A brief description of this method may help us understand the psycho-biology of Mohammed's performances at the time of so-called revelations. The "Stanislavski method" teaches an actor to produce realistic dramatic performances by intertwining his own past emotions and experiences with the role he is portraying on the stage.

The actor must first arouse certain emotions that he felt in past experiences and then graft them onto his portrayal of a character. This requires the actor to achieve absolute relaxation and to be totally detached from the audience. He should also concentrate deeply in order to attain complete identification—intellectually, emotionally, and spiritually—with the character he is playing while there is a flow of psychic energy from his unconscious mind.[466] The more

---

466 *Collier's Encyclopedia,* 1994 ed., s.v. "Stanislavsky's Method," by Rodolph Goodman.

the actor can use his unconscious forces, the more he will be able to "fit his own human qualities to the life of his role persona, and pour into it all of his soul."[467] Stanislavski describes ideal acting on the stage as the following:

"The actor's contribution consists of an *inner characterization* and its *outer form.* To create the outer form–the way the character looks, moves, gestures, and speaks–the actor draws from pictures, engravings, drawing books, stories, novels, or from some simple incident—it makes no difference."[468]

Another writer in the field writes:

"The first level of characterization, unconscious role playing refers to the way in which characters in plays, like people in daily life, relate to one another in recognizable, unself-conscious social relationship. The unconscious role-playing relationships are those without any manipulation or self-awareness about the nature of the relationship as a role being played. Such roles are performed effortlessly in life. Unconscious role-playing includes mother-child relationships–all relationships that are naturally assumed and performed in life without the participant being consciously aware that a relationship is being enacted by social beings."[469]

Still another writer explains the same theory under "the law of motor response." He believes that every stimulus impressed upon the human organism, leads to a direct motor response, the nature of which depends upon two factors: (1) The nature of the stimulus, and (2) the nature of the past experience of the organism.

A "*stimulus*" is an impression received through one of the senses and conveyed to the brain, by the sensory nerves; but a remembered or imagined stimulus is also capable of inducing a motor response. A motor response is an impulse carried to the muscles of

---

[467] Konstantin Stanislavsky, *An Actor Prepares,* trans. Elizabeth Raynolds Hapgood (London: Methuens, 1984), p. 5.

[468] Konstantin Stanislavsky, *Building A Character* (New York: Theatre Arts Books, 1949), p.7

[469] Ramon Delgado, *Acting With Both Sides of the Brain* (New York: Holt, Rinehart and Winston, 1986), p. 137.

the body through the motor nerves. If the impulse is strong enough and is not inhibited or suppressed in any way, it results in a clearly defined muscular action. Every time we see, hear, touch, taste, or smell something, we experience almost instantly a corresponding motor response, imperceptible to the eye.[470]

An analysis of the interaction of mind and body with respect to the psychobiology of the workings of the autonomic nervous system will reveal the *modus operandi* of Mohammed's so-called revelations. If an actor is able to summon unconscious memories to generate certain emotional symptoms, Mohammed being an adept role player could have done the same. Whenever he was pretending to receive a revelation from the sky, he taught himself to sweat, turn red, and to loll his head by mobilizing his subconscious imagery.

A person may be affected by the magnetic personality of another person on the first few encounters after which his personality will appear quite mundane and normal. We are also aware of the fact that repetitive stimuli lose any surprise effect over time. Normally, we will be surprised by material which does not exist in the storehouse of our memories. Only information of which we are not already aware, may surprise us, produce emotions and change our psychological make up.

Therefore, it is not logical to believe that *whenever* Mohammed met with Gabriel, his awe would overwhelm him and make him develop strange psychobiological symptoms. If he were to go through any psychological change while pretending he was receiving a revelation, he would have induced those states in himself by summoning his subconscious memories as the masters of dramatic arts have explained. For example, when Mohammed fell in love with Zainab, the wife of his foster-son, and pretended that a verse (*Sura* XXXIII: 37) was revealed to him from the sky legitimizing his marriage with her, he knew what he had in mind and was aware of what he was doing. Therefore, if he had produced any psychobiological symptom at the time of putative revelation, he was inducing that state in himself by activating his unconscious mental energies rather

---

[470] John Dolman Jr. and Richard K. Knaub, *The Art of Playing Production* (New York: Harper & Row Publishers, Inc., 1973), pp. 12–13.

than being affected by his awe of the angel Gabriel. The tenor of the passage would already have been fabricated in his mind.

Another point demonstrating the fallacy of his claims as to how he received the "revelations," is Mohammed's tale of visionary travel to the skies. In his recounting of the events of these so-called 'trips to seven skies,' nowhere can we find any statement that he was awe-struck by the previous prophets whom he brags to have visited in different skies nor by facing Allah himself. Is the angel Gabriel more awe-inspiring than visiting legendary prophets in the grandeur of the seven skies and talking with Allah? Moreover, according to his own canting, we have to bear in mind that it was his first visit with Allah and the prophets but he had had regular coversations with Gabriel. Not only did none of these supernatural visits have any awe-inspiring effect on him; on one trip he becomes so audacious that five times he goes back and forth from the sixth sky to the seventh sky to bargain with Allah over the number of prayers required of Muslims.

Another author succinctly sums up our discussion of Mohammed and his revelations by the following cogent observation: "But the most troubling part about our absolute reliance on Mohammed's testimony that he and his Koran were divinely inspired is that the prophet's character was as deficient, and his life was as despicable, as anyone who has ever lived.[471]

History's Judgment of Mohammed

No religion in the world has been as harshly criticized as Islam. Attacks pointing out the irrationality of Islam started from Mohammed's day and they are still continuing. Throughout this book, I have frequently exposed the contradictions of Islam and the Koran and I have quoted many Eastern as well as Western scholars who have ridiculed the faith of Mohammed. However, at this point, I would just like to chronicle some statements made about Mohammed's bragging.

---

[471] Winn, *Muhammad, Prophet of Doom*, p. XXVI.

After he explained his night journey to heaven to his cousin Umm Hani, when he was leaving her, she clung to his garments and begged him not to tell the tale to others, because she knew that the Arabs would scoff at this crazy fantasy. Mohammed did not listen to her and when he told the story to the Meccans, the disbelievers ridiculed his vision and, with howls of laughter and derision, said, "Do we need any better proof of your madness?" All but his faithful close companions bowed their heads in shame and were ready to leave Islam because never had anyone ever heard such fantasy.[472]

Arab historical writings show that the pagan Arabs did not accept the fables recounted by Mohammed and scoffed at the notion of the resurrection of the body. Pagan Arabs converted to Islam because of their cupidity; Mohammed's promise of worldly gain. Thus, many outwardly confessed their belief but in fact had no inclination toward Islam and its dogma and ritual. It is not strange therefore that the early heroes of Islam such as Saad ibn Waghghas, the conqueror of Iran; Khalid ibn Walid, the victor in many wars including some in Byzantine territories and Iran; Amr ibn Alas, who conquered Egypt; and Othman ibn Talha, the hereditary custodian of the keys of the Ka'ba, all of whom amassed fortunes from their conquests were, in fact, not so much interested in religion as they were infatuated with riches.

Although the drinking of alcoholic beverages is prohibited in Islam, Yazid ibn Muawiya, the second Umayyads Caliph (682–686 CE), was always inebriated. He dispatched ibn-Uqba to lead an army to suppress the rebellion of Abdullah ibn Zubayr who had proclaimed himself the Commander of the Faithful in Medina. Ibn-Uqba defeated Abdullah ibn–Zubayr and turned the mosque of Mohammed into a stable. Abdullah fled to Mecca and took sanctuary in the Ka'ba which, by tradition, was held sacred and inviolate. But ibn-Uqba burned the Ka'ba to the ground, and split the black stone into three pieces.[473] Marwan ibn-Hakam, the old Caliph of another branch of the same dynasty, went to the mosque to lead prayer but he was so drunk that in the midst of praying, he vomited on the altar.

---

[472] Essad Bay, *Mohammed* (London: Cobden–Sanderson, 1972), p. 126.

[473] Robert Payne, *The History of Islam* (New York: Dorset Press, 1987), p. 127.

In an attempt to make amends he said, "If you let me to pray in this state, I will do it as much as you wish."[474]

Later on, Abdul-Malik, the son of Marwan, while reading the Koran heard the news about his father's death and his own elevation to the caliphate. He immediately closed the book and said, "This is the last time we meet [referring to the Koran], I will not have anything to do with you while I am alive," and went to the palace for his inauguration. Later on, he ordered all copies of the Koran burned. One day he announced from his throne, "I am weary of being told to fear Allah. I shall smite the neck of the person who warns me against the Allah's punishment of Caliphs."[475]

His chief lieutenant, Hajjaj ibn Yusuf, a blood thirsty man who was a pure nihilist, a man who believed in nothing, trampled the Koran. He used to tell his master that the Caliphate was superior to prophetship and the Caliph stood above the prophet. Hajjaj ibn Yusuf finally succeeded in killing Abdullah ibn Zubayr. When Abdullah had taken refuge in the Ka'ba, Hajjaj's soldiers refused to kill in the Ka'ba because of its sanctity. However, Hajjaj promised his soldiers that if they razed the Ka'ba, they would be compensated by Abdul-Malik's gifts. Hearing this, the soldiers destroyed the Ka'ba.[476]

When Mecca was in the hands of Abdullah ibn Zubayr, the Muslims who went to Mecca for pilgrimage were required to pledge loyalty to him as the Muslim's Caliph. This was bothersome to Abdul-Malik so, to neutralize Abdullah's advantage, he decided to employ a political trick that was against all the Islamic tenets. He claimed to have found a *hadith* ascribed to Mohammed that indicated the Mosque of Jerusalem had the same sanctity as the Mosque of Ka'ba and the stone upon which Mohammed had stepped to start his heavenly journey, was as sacred as the black stone of Ka'ba which Mohammed had touched. Then, he built a shrine-temple over the rock with walkways around it, so that pilgrims could perform circumambulation (*tawaf*). When the Dome of the

---

[474] Hossein Emadzadeh Esfahani, *A Detailed History of Islam,* Farsi edition (Tehran: Islam Publications, 1991), p. 274.

[475] *Ibid.,* p. 284; Payne, *The History of Islam,* p. 127.

[476] Emadzadeh Esfahani, *A Detailed History of Islam,* Farsi edition, pp. 284, 327.

Rock was built, the rock itself was enclosed by a lattice of ebony wood and curtains of brocade. By use of such device, Abdul-Malik succeeded in replacing Mecca with Jerusalem and turning the center of veneration of Muslims from the Ka'ba to the Dome of the Rock, for about sixty two years (from 692 to 754 CE).

One day, Walid ibn Yazid (690–718 CE), was reading the Koran, when he came upon verse 14 of *Sura* XIV, referring to the punishments to be inflicted upon the stubborn [non-believers] and demanding complete submission to the will of Allah by all. Walid, enraged at this verse, threw the Koran to the other side of the room and said, "You hurl threats against the stubborn opponents; I am a stubborn opponent myself. When you appear before Allah at the day of resurrection just say, "My Lord al-Walid has torn me up." Then, he stuck the Koran onto a lance and shot arrow after arrow at it, until the pages were reduced to tatters. Being an accomplished poet, probably among the best of his time, he wrote the following verses:

> *Dare you threaten me in my proud rebellion?*
> *I am Walid–the most rebellious of men!*
> *O Koran, when you appear at the judgment Seat,*
> *Tell Allah who it was who tore you to shreds.*[477]

It has been said that on one occasion he woke before the time for morning prayer. Still drunk from the night before, he coupled with one of his slaves, then forced her to don his clothes and ordered her to go to the mosque to lead the faithful in prayer, even though she was also drunk.[478] Walid is said to have made a pond full of wine that he would plunged into and drink so much that breathing would become a challenge for him.[479]

Some high authorities, such as those mentioned above, were immune from prosecution because of their power and thus were able to express their feelings about the irrationality of Islam. The ordinary non-powerful intellectuals of the Islamic countries were never

---

[477] Payne, *The History of Islam,* p. 145; Ibn Warraq, *Why I am not A Muslim,* p. 243.

[478] Emadzadeh Esfahani, *A Detailed History of Islam,* p. 303.

[479] *Ibid.* p. 302.

permitted to criticize it. Those who were courageous enough to challenge the fallacies of the Koran and Islam barely survived the barbaric judgment of the Islamic authorities. A few of these legendary figures are discussed below.

The Mu'tazilites seriously criticized Islamic superstitions such as the theory of creation, revelations of the Prophet, resurrection, and ascension. They believed that the Koran was created and not eternal. Goldziher comes to the conclusion that the Mu'tazilites "set a free man over against a relatively unfree god."[480] One of the preeminent Mu'tazilites, called al-Nazzam believed that God himself should be subject to the principles of rationality and justice and that he had no power over evil.[481] Ahmed ibn Habit, a pupil of al-Nazzam, went far beyond his master's teachings, practically into disbelief, and criticized Mohammed for his many wives, and found others more virtuous than Mohammed.[482]

The Abbasid Caliph, al-Ma'mun was impressed by the Mu'tazilite's claim that the Koran was a man-made book and decreed this concept official state dogma throughout the Islamic empire. Chief officials in every province had to publicly propound the dogma that the Koran was created by Mohammed himself and was not a divine book. Al-Ma'mun even ordered an authority set up to ensure that every person acknowledge that the Koran was created by man. This organization was called "Mihna" and was actually the Muslim version of the Inquisition. Caliph Al-Wathik, nephew and the second successor of al-Ma'mun, beheaded with his own hands one of the theologians who believed in the divinity of the Koran,

Ibn Rawandi, one of the intellectuals of early ninth century, went beyond Mu'tazilite rationalism and completely refuted the central orthodox dogma of creation ex nihilo and of a divine creator. Many philosophers of the time believed in Ibn Rawandi ideas. Al-Haitham, in particular, was one of his most vociferous followers. In his book, *Kitab al-Zumurrudh,* Ibn Rawandi denies the idea of prophecy in

---

[480] Ignaz Goldziher, *Introduction to Islamic Theology and Law,* trans. Andras and Ruth Hamori (Princeton: 1981), p. 91.

[481] Montgomery Watt, *Free will and Predestination in Early Islam,* p. 73.

[482] Ibn Warraq, *Why I am not A Muslim,* p. 247.

general and of the prophecy of Mohammed in particular. He maintains that reason is superior to revelation. Either what the so-called prophets say is in accordance with reason, in which case prophets are futile and needless, since ordinary human beings are equally endowed with reason, or it does not conform to reason, in which case it must be rejected. According to Ibn-Rawandi, all religious dogmas are against reason and therefore, must be refuted. As for the Koran, far from being a miracle and immutable, it is an inferior work from a literary standpoint, because it is neither clear nor comprehensive and it is certainly not a revealed book.[483]

Some of the other rationalists who challenged the preposterous tenets of the Koran and the Islamic norms and, as a result, were brutally executed by Islamic authorities are the following:

Djad ibn Dirham believed that the Koran was a created book and that God did not talk to Moses. Dirham's followers also believed that Mohammed was a liar. Umayyad Caliph Hisham ordered Dirham to be put to death in 742 CE.

Al-Mansur, Abbasid Caliph, put many intellectuals of his time to death; the most famous being Ibn al-Moqaffa. Ibn al-Moqaffa attacked the religion of Islam, its prophet, its theology and theocracy, and its concept of God. For that reason, Al-Mansur had Ibn al-Moqaffa executed in a most barbaric way: while still alive, his limbs were cut off one by one and put into a blazing fire.

Another victim of Al-Mansur's inquisition of rationalists was Ibn Abi-l-Awja who was executed in 772 CE. Ibn Abi-l-Awja believed in the eternity of the world and rejected the existence of a creator. He did not believe that the Koran was divine and he refuted the justice of some of the punishments mentioned in the Koran. According to Al-Biruni, Ibn-abi-l-Awja was apt to shake the faith of the ordinary people with captious questions about Divine justice.[484]

Bashshar ibn Burd was a blind poet from a noble Persian family who had a low opinion of Arabs and glorified in the memories of ancient Persia. Bashshar anathematized the entire Muslim community, denied the divinity of the Koran, the resurrection, and the institution

---

[483] *Ibid.,* p. 260.
[484] *Ibid.,* p. 253.

of pilgrimage. He ridiculed the call to prayer by parodying it while he was drunk. According to Goldziher, in a congregate of free thinkers at Basra, Bashshar, referring to certain poems submitted to the assembly, said, "They are better than the verses of the Koran." On another occasion when a girl singer was reading his own poems in Baghdad, he said, "They are better than the verses of the Sura al-Hashr." One of the heretics sneered at a parable in verse 63 of the al-Safat which likens the bitter fruits of the tree Zakkum in hell to the heads of devils. He said, "In this verse of the Koran a visible is compared to an unknown. No one has ever seen the heads of devils. So, what kind of simile is this?"[485] Bashshar ibn Burd, was finally arrested, beaten to the death, and thrown in a swamp.

Salih ibn Abdul-Quddus was another poet who was executed by Caliph Al-Mahdi in 783 CE. There is no evidence that he had challenged Islam in any way, therefore Nicholson believes that he was executed because he had a speculative and philosophic mind which, in Islam, is tantamount to disbelief.[486]

Hammad Arjad was a member of a circle of free thinkers in Basra. He was accused of not praying in an orthodox manner and also of putting his own poems above the verses of the Koran. He was executed by the governor of Basra.

Abu Tamman was a writer of eulogies at the court of the Caliph al-Mutasim. Although, none of his religious doubts are expressed in his poetical works, he was put to death because he was *shown* doubting poems about Muslim religious observances while he was visiting one of his provincial followers in Fars.

In his book, *Why I am not a Muslim,* Ibn Warraq a brilliant theological writer has listed a large number of Islamic rationalists, free thinkers and *zindiqs* (heretics) who detected the absurd nature of Islam, turned away from it, were jailed, and barbarously put to death.

Western writers whose mentalities were not handicapped by suppressive Islamic theocracies were quite articulate with respect

---

[485] Ignaz Goldziher, *Muslim Studies,* 2 vols., trans. C. R. Barber and S. M. Stern (London: 1967–71), pp. 363–64.

[486] Raynold A. Nicholson, *A Literary History of the Arabs* (Cambridge: University of Cambridge, 1941), p. 374.

to divulging the lack of provenance of the Koran and preposterousness of the Islamic tenets as well as the perversions of Mohammed's character. They considered Mohammed an epileptic whose sexual life was characterized with every perversion known to man and was said to have attracted people into his religion by encouraging them to indulge their basest instincts. There was nothing genuine in Mohammed's claims: he was a cold-blooded impostor who led nearly all of his own people astray. Those of his followers who had seen through his preposterous ideas had kept quiet because of their own ignoble ideas.[487]

In his *Divine Comedy,* Dante Alighieri, places Mohammed and his accomplice Ali in the eighth Circle of Hell, with schismatics. He suffers a particularly disgusting punishment in the hell:

> A cask, when its midboard or its cant has been removed, is not so open as one I saw whose body was split right from the chin to the fart hole.
> Down between his legs his raw entrails spilled out, with his vitals visible and the sorry sack where what goes through the mawis turned to shit. I was looking at him, full of awe and wonder, when he saw me stare and spread his breast open, saying, "What me pull, see mangled Mohammed tear himself!"
> And there walking before me and weeping is Ali with his face split from his chin right to his hair.
> And since all of those other sinners that you see sowed scandal and schism in their lives, now they are ripped apart in reciprocity.
> Back there a devil waits to hack and flay each one of us with the sharp edge of his blade, cleaving anew, each time we pass his way, every member of this miserable parade, for by the time we have circled twice we are healed of the cuts he has already made.[488]

In the Encyclopedia of Islam,[489] under the heading "Mahomet," D'Herbelot, using Arabic, Turkish, and Persian sources, writes:

---

[487] Karen Armstrong, *Muhammad, A Western Attempt to Understand Islam* (London: Victor Gollanz Ltd., 1991) pp. 26–27.

[488] Dante Alighieri, *Inferno,* trans. Michael Palma (New York: W.W. Norton & Company, 2002), pp. 311–12.

[489] Edward W. Said, *Orientalism* (New York: Pantheon books, 1994), p. 66.

"This is the famous impostor Mahomet, author and founder of a heresy, which has taken on the name of religion, which we call Mohammadan.

The interpreters and the Alcoran and other Doctors of Muslim or Mohammadan Law have applied to this false prophet all the praises which the Arians, Paulicians, or Paulianists, and other heretics have attributed to Jesus Christ, while stripping him of his divinity . . . ."

English Orientalist and man of reason, Humphrey Prideaux, in his book entitled *Mahomet: The True nature of Impostor,* argued that Islam was a mere imitation of Christianity. He wrote of Mohammed:

"For the first part of his life he held a very wicked and licentious course, much delighting in rapine, plunder, and blood-shed, according to the usage of the Arabs, who mostly followed this kind of life, being almost continually in arms of one tribe against another, to plunder and take from each other all they could . . . .

His two predominant passions were ambition and lust. The course which he took to gain empire abundantly shows the former; and the multitude of women which he had to do with, proves the latter. And indeed these two run through the whole frame of his religion, there being scarce a chapter in his alcoran, which does not lay down some law of war and blood-shed for the promoting of one; or else give some liberty for the use of women here, or some promise for the enjoyment of them hereafter, to the gratifying of the other."[490]

Simon Ockley described Mohammad as "a very subtle and crafty man, who put on the appearance only of those good qualities, while the principles of his souls were ambition and lust."[491]

George Sale opined that, "It is certainly one of the most convincing proofs that Mohammadanism was no other than human invention, that it owes its progress and establishment almost entirely to the sword . . . and that he was a great lover of women."[492]

---

[490] Humphrey Prideaux, *Mahomet: The True Nature of Impostor* (London: 1708), p. 80.

[491] Norman Daniel, *Islam and the West: The Making of An Image* (Edinburgh: The University Press, 1960), p. 257.

[492] *Ibid.,* p. 300.

In 1742, in the preface of his tragedy, *Mahomet or Fanaticism,* Voltaire attacks Mohammed as a camel-driver, who stirs up rebellion, claims to have conversed with Gabriel, and to have received a nonsense book, called *Koran* in which "every page does violence to sober reason, and murders men and abducts women in order to force them to believe in his book." Such conduct can be defended by no man "unless he is born a Turk, or unless superstition has choked all of the light of nature in him," Voltaire considers Mohammed as an example of all the charlatans who have enslaved their people to religion by means of trickery and lies. In a later work, *Essai sur les moeurs,* Voltaire passed a somewhat milder judgment upon Mohammed, acknowledging his greatness and his abilities, but censuring his cruelty and brutality, and asserting that there is nothing new in his religion except the statement that Mohammed is the Apostle of Allah.[493]

Chateaubriand argued that of all religions, Christianity was the one "most favorable to freedom, but Islam was a cult enemy to civilization, systematically favorable to ignorance, to despotism, and to slavery . . . of liberty, Muslims knew nothing; of propriety, they have none: force is their God."[494] In his best seller *Journey from Paris to Jerusalem and from Jerusalem to Paris* (1810–11), Chateaubriand wrote, the Arabs "have the air of soldiers without a leader, citizens without legislators, and a family without a father." They are an example of "civilized man fallen again into a savage state."[495]

Thomas Carlyle considered Mohammed a genuinely religious person, though he condemned the Koran as the most boring and baseless book in the world. He writes, "I must say, it is as toilsome reading as I ever undertook. A wearisome confused jumble, crude, incondite; endless iterations, long-windedness, entanglement, most crude, incondite, insupportable stupidity, in short!"[496]

---

[493] Daniel, *Islam and the West: The Making of An Image,* pp. 288–91; Andrae, *Mohammed: The Man and his Faith,* pp. 174–75; Armstrong, *Muhammad, A Western Attempt to Understand Islam,* p. 37.

[494] Quoted in Said, *Orientalism,* p. 172.

[495] Quoted in Armstrong, *Muhammad, A Western Attempt to Understand Islam,* p. 39.

[496] Thomas Carlyle, *On Heroes, Hero-Worship and the Heroic in History* (Lincoln: University of Nebraska Press, 1966) pp. 64–65.

Diderot somehow demonized Mohammed's personality. He believed that Mohammed was the greatest friend [lecher] of women and the greatest enemy of sober reason who ever lived.[497]

William Muir characterizes Mohammed as a crafty and dishonest person who believed ends justify the means and he applied this behavior on numerous occasions. Muir maintains that in his prophetical career, political and personal ends were frequently compassed by *divine revelation,* which, whatever more, was certainly the direct reflection of his own wishes. Worst of all, the dastardly assassinations of political and religious opponents countenanced, if not in some cases directed, by Mohammed himself, leaves a painful reflection upon his character.[498]

Maxime Rodinson, credits Mohammed as being a sensible, remarkably able diplomat, and capable of reasoning with clarity, logic and lucidity. He adds, "Yet, beneath this surface, was a temperament which was nervous, passionate, restless, feverish—filled with an impatient yearning which burned for the impossible. This was so intense as to lead to nervous crises of a definitely pathological kind.[499]

Dagobert Runnes writes: After Mohammed settled in Medina, in true Bedouin fashion, he raided caravans and attacked villages, either massacring the inhabitants or carrying them off into captivity. Runaways were left in the desert with amputated hands and blinded eyes, and it was forbidden even to give them a drink as they perished under the sizzling desert sun. The stories of his brutal conduct are endless. Runnes quotes Ibn Hisham, "Drive all the unfaithful out of Arabia," Mohammed ordered, "and slaughter every Jew who comes into your hands." A disorderly mob, of which the old writers say "clutched their rugs about them to hide their nakedness," rallied beneath his banner to fight for the self-proclaimed prophet of Allah.[500]

William Cash maintains that anyone who reads C.M. Doughty's *Travels in Arabia Deserts* will find his accounts of traditional Arab raids exactly the same as Mohammed's raids on various tribes as given in the writings of Al-Bukhari and Al-Halabi. Muslim authorities

---

[497] Andrae, *Mohammed: The Man and his Faith,* pp. 175.

[498] Muir, *The Life of Mohammad,* p. 514.

[499] Rodinson, *Mohammed,* trans. Anne Carter, p. 57.

[500] Dagobert Runnes, *Philosophy for Everyman* (New York: Philosophical Library, Inc., 1968), p. 67.

give case after case where Mohammed aggressively attacked tribes. Assassinations were carried out, much as they are today, but then they were at the instigation of Mohammed himself, and were an easy way of removing suspected people. In inter-tribal wars the Arabs, by general agreement, always spared date palms, but Mohammed in his attacks of the Bani Nadhir had their date palms burned or cut down. The authority for this, according to Cash, is Ibn Ishaq, the oldest biographer of Mohammed and a Muslim. Mohammed treated the women in warfare very barbarously. He laid down the rule that the capture of women in battle did *ipso facto* dissolve previous heathen marriages.[501]

Craig Winn's evaluation of Mohammed is more insulting to Islam and Muslims than any writer has so far written about him. He writes:

> "Religions are supposed to be good. Most religious prophets are fine fellows, not terrorists, so all of this is a little hard to swallow. But one was a terrorist. Mohammed financed his religion entirely through piracy and the slave trade. This prophet was a genocidal maniac. Worse still, his 'God' condoned terrorism, piracy plunder, racism, genocide, deception, and assassination . . . The evidence screams out from the pages of the Koran and hadith collections of al-Tabari, Ibn Ishaq, al-Bukhari, and Muslim Salih . . . In the Koran, Allah commands Muslims to 'wipe the infidels out to the last.' In the hadith, Mohammed says, 'Kill any Jew who falls under your control. Kill them, for he who kills them will get reward." Today's terrorists are simply following their religion as it was originally convinced. The truth is obvious: the terrorists haven't corrupted their religion. Islam has corrupted them. The murderers are following their prophet's example . . . The five oldest and most trusted Islamic sources don't portray Mohammed as a great and godly man. They reveal that he was a thief, a liar, an assassin, a pedophile, a womanizer, a rapist, a mass murderer, a pirate, a warmonger, and a scheming and ruthless politician."[502]

---

[501] William Wilson Cash, *The Expansion of Islam* (London: Edinburgh House Press, 1928), pp. 18–19.

[502] Winn, *Muhammad, The Prophet of Doom,* pp. XIII–XIV.

CHAPTER EIGHT

THE MENDACIOUS STRATEGIES OF MOHAMMED'S PROPHETHOOD

What excellent fools, religion makes of men.

Ben Jonson, v, 1603

After the people of Taif expelled Mohammed from their city by stoning him and his foster son, he set out to Medina. Half-way to Medina he halted in the valley of Nakhla. That night he was aroused from sleep, perhaps woken by a call of nature or by a nightmare, and his vivid imagination conjured up the ridiculous story of the supernatural visitation of *jinns* who listened to him reciting the Koran (Koran, XLVI: 28 ff., LXXII: 1 ff.). This farce was soon followed by an even more absurd tale, the famous fantasy of Mohammed's heavenly journey. The anniversary of this celestial nocturnal safari is celebrated on 27th Rajab each year throughout Islam. It was on this fanciful trip that Mohammed received the precept of the five daily prayers. True believers are awed by this tale of Divine visitation whereas non-Muslims view it as a source of ridicule and proof of the invalidity of Mohammed's claims to prophethood. One night he stayed in the house of his cousin, Umm Hani, the sister of Ali, who lived near the Ka'ba. In the middle of the night, he woke up and went there to recite the Koran. The gist of the visionary legend according to the *Sahih al-Bukhari*[503] is as follows:

"Narrated Anas ibn Malik from Malik ibn Sa'sa'a that Allah's Apostle described to them his journey as saying, 'While I was laying in Al-Hatima or Al-Hijr, suddenly someone came to me and cut my body open from my throat to my pubic area . . . He then took out my heart. Then a gold tray full of wisdom and faith was brought to me

---

[503] *Sahih al-Bukhari*, vol. 1, pp. 211–214, vol. 4, pp. 139–149.

249

and my heart was washed with the water of Zamzam spring and was filled with wisdom and faith and then returned to its place and then closed it.'"

Then a white animal called Buraq, which was smaller than a mule and bigger than a donkey, was brought to me. The animal's step was so wide that it reached the farthest point within the reach of the animal's sight. The Buraq flew miraculously beyond Medina and Khaibar through the night until we reached Jerusalem (which the Koran calls al-Masjid-al-Aqsa). I was carried on it, and Gabriel set out with me till we reached the nearest heaven. When he asked for the gate to be opened, somebody asked, 'who is it?' Gabriel answered, 'Gabriel.' It was asked, 'Who is accompanying you?' Gabriel replied, 'Mohammed.' It was asked, 'Has Mohammed been called?' Gabriel replied in the affirmative. Then it was said, 'He is welcome. What an excellent visit he has paid!' The gate was opened, and when I went over the first heaven, I saw Adam sitting with people on his right and left. When he looked right, he laughed and when he looked left he wept. Gabriel said to me, 'This is your father, Adam; pay him your greetings.' So, I greeted him and he returned the greeting to me and said, 'You are welcome as a pious son and a pious Prophet.' I asked Gabriel about the people who were sitting to the right and left of Adam. He replied, 'Those are the souls of his offspring. Those on his right are the people of paradise and those on his left are the people of Hell. When he looks right he laughs and when he looks left, he weeps.'"

According to Sahih a-Bukhari, Gabriel took Mohammed to second, third, fourth, fifth, sixth, and seventh heavens with the same ceremonies. In the second heaven Mohammed visits Yahya (John the Baptist) and Jesus who were cousins of each other. In the third heaven he visits Joseph, in the fourth Idris, in the fifth Harun (Aaron), and in the sixth heaven, Moses. In this heaven something new happens. Mohammed explains this event as, "When I left Moses, he wept. Someone asked him, 'What makes you weep?' Moses said, 'I weep because after me there has been sent (as Prophet) a young man whose followers will enter paradise in greater number than my followers.'"

Then Mohammed continues, "Then Gabriel ascended with me to the seventh heaven with the same ceremonies. When I went (over the seventh heaven), there I saw Abraham. After greeting him, I was taken to a very high place where I heard the sound (scratching) of pens. Then, I was made to ascend to Sidrat-ul-Muntaha (i. e. the Lot Tree of the farthest limit), which was covered with various colors and I did not know what those colors were. 'Behold! Its fruits were like the jars of Hijr [a place near Medina] and its leaves were as big as the ears of elephants.' Gabriel said, 'This is the Lot Tree of the farthest limit. Behold! There run four rivers, two hidden and two visible. The two hidden rivers are in paradise and the visible rivers are the Nile and the Euphrates.' Then Al-Beit-ul-Ma'mur (i. e. the Allah's house) was shown to me and a vessel full of wine and another full of milk and the third one full of honey were brought to me. I took the milk. Gabriel remarked, 'This is the Islamic religion which you and your followers are following.'

Then the prayers were enjoined on me: They were fifty prayers a day. When I returned, I passed by Moses who asked (me), 'What have you been ordered to do?' I replied, 'I have been ordered to offer fifty prayers a day.' Moses said, 'Your followers cannot bear fifty prayers a day, and by Allah, I have tested people before you, and I have tried my level best with Bani Israel [in vain]. Go back to your lord and ask for reducing your followers' burden.' So I went back, and Allah reduced ten prayers for me. Then again I came to Moses, but he repeated the same as he had said before. Then I was admitted into Paradise, where there were strings of pearls and its soil was of musk. Then again I went back to Allah and reduced ten more prayers. When I came back to Moses he said the same, I went back to Allah and He ordered me to observe ten prayers a day. When I came back to Moses, he repeated the same advice, so I went back to Allah and was ordered to observe five prayers a day. When I came back to Moses, he said, 'What have you been ordered?' I replied, 'I have been ordered to observe five prayers a day.' He said, 'Your followers cannot bear five prayers a day, and no doubt, I have got an experience of the people before you, and I have tried my level best with Bani Israel, so go back to your Lord and ask for reducing your followers' burden.' I said, 'I have requested so much of my Lord that I feel ashamed, but I am satisfied now and surrender to Allah's Order.'"

Then, Mohammed and the Gabriel descended to the Rock at Jerusalem, and returned to Mecca the way they had come. It was still night when they reached the Ka'ba. From there Mohammed went again to his cousin's house and told Umm Hani his vision of ascending to seven heavens. When he was about to leave her home, she grabbed his mantle, and begged him not to tell this story to the people, because they would call him a liar and insult him. Mohammed rejected her proposal and went directly to the mosque and told his followers about the heavenly night journey. This made his enemies very happy, because now it would be obvious to all that Mohammed was insane.

In present-day Jerusalem one is shown Mohammed's footprint, the actual spot from which he vaulted upon his winged heavenly beast. Suratu 'l-Mi'raj is the title of *Sura* XVII of the Koran, in the first verse of which there is the only reference to the night journey of Mohammed. It is called also *Sura* Bani Isra'il, or chapter of the Children of Israel.

Those who are familiar with the contents of the Koran will wonder whether Allah and/or His beloved Messenger, is suffering from amnesia. The reason being that in verse 50 of *Sura* LIV, Allah says:

> "And We command but a single time and our will should be carried out like the twinkling of an eye."

But it seems that when Allah is entertaining His beloved Prophet in the sky, he forgets his injunction in the Koran that such a book is a glorious record (Koran, XV: 87) inscribed in the celestial preserved tablet (Koran LXXXV: 22) and the heavenly Archetype. For that reason, Allah breaks His injunction in the Koran—which is inscribed in the celestial preserved tablet—and shows incredible tolerance to His beloved Messenger to allow him to return five times to the seventh heaven and bargain over the number of prayers for his followers.

Another ridiculous point about "the story of the night journey of Mohammed to the skies" is the contents of verse 1 of *Sura* XVII of the Koran which claims that Mohammed went to the "farthest mosque" during his night's journey:

> "Most glorious is the One who did take His servant (Mohammed) for a journey by night from the sacred mosque (of Mecca) to the farthest mosque whose precincts We did Bless, in order that we might show him some of Our signs. He is indeed the all-Hearing, the all-Seeing." (Koran, XVII: 1)

According to the commentators of the Koran and *hadith,* the "farthest mosque" refers either to the Jewish Temple or the Dome of the

Rock, in Jerusalem, but neither existed in the time of Mohammed (620 CE). The Jewish temple (the Temple of Solomon) was destroyed the last time by Emperor Titus in 70 CE, and the dome of the rock (Masjidol Aqsa) was not built until 691CE by Amir Abdul-Malik, 59 years after Mohammed's death.[504]

Satanic Verses

The incident of Satanic Verses is such a shameful stigma on the forehead of Mohammedanism that no Islamic apologist so far has been able to interpret or defend it logically. It probably occurred when Mohammed was living in Arkam's house. At this time, Mohammed was trying desperately to attract the Meccans to his faith, but they were recalcitrant. Therefore, Mohammed invented a very strange and surprising way to achieve his goal in the sense that the prophet of the most uncompromising monotheistic religion turned immediately to his past polytheistic faith and brought forth three verses which authorize the worship of three traditional idols (goddesses). These verses say:

> "Did you consider al-Lat and al-Uzza and al-Manat, the third the other? Those are the swans exalted, their intercession is expected, their likes are not neglected."

According to Muslim lore, when the Quraysh heard these verses, they were highly delighted.[505] When those who were in the mosque heard Mohammed mention their deities, they prostrated themselves, Mohammed included. Then being criticized by his close companions for praising the traditional idols of polytheists, later on Mohammed pretended to receive another revelation canceling those three verses and substituting others for them:

> "For you the male sex and for him the female? That would be unfair sharing. They are but names you and your fathers named; . . . God

---

[504] *The Holy Quran,* Revised and edited by the Presidency of the Islamic Researchers, IFTA (Medina, Saudi Arabia: undated), p. 774.

[505] Al-Tabari, *The History of al-Tabari,* vol.6, p. 108.

revealed no authority for them; they follow only opinion and their souls' fancies. . . . .though from their lord there has come to guidance." (Koran, LIII: 19–23)

Both the first and the second version were proclaimed publicly, and Mohammed apologized for allowing Satan to slip in the false verses of the first version without his noticing it. Fortunately, Allah, the most gracious, benignant and merciful came to the assistance of his last beloved apostle and sent him a reassuring revelation— prophets before him had also been tempted by Satan:

> "We never sent a Prophet or Messenger before you but, when he desired something, Satan tampered with that desire. But Allah will cancel anything Satan interjected, and will confirm his signs. For Allah is full of knowledge and wisdom." (Koran, XXII: 52).

There are two points in the above verse that plainly show how irrational and preposterous is the contents of the Koran. First, while the Koran has attributed ninety nine laudatory names to Allah (among others, omnipotent and omniscient), this poor entity is so inadequate and powerless that he is not able to control a restive angel called Satan whom he had expelled from the heavens. This malevolent Satan apparently has enough power over Allah that he is able to intervene in Allah's revelations to his so-called prophet and distort them. The second point is related to verses 39 and 40 of *Sura* XV of the Koran. According to these two verses, Allah permits Satan to deceive and mislead *only* those of his servants who are not sincere and purified. Therefore, if Satan were able to deceive Mohammed and distort the revelations of Allah, it follows that Mohammed could not have been a sincere and purified servant of Allah.

The Quraysh's display of tolerance to Mohammed's proselytizing was only temporary. Soon some became even more violently hostile to Mohammed and the Meccans were once more divided. Moreover, the satanic verses incident provided a clear indication that Mohammed's new faith was in no way revolutionary because it honored the traditional goddesses of the city, respected their shrines and recognized their legitimacy. If the old Arabian divinities could intercede on behalf of sinners and save them from eternal damnation, why fear the Last Judgment of the new faith? Jews and Christians gleefully pointed out that Mohammed was reverting to his traditional ancestral idolatry.

Was Mohammed Illiterate?

Tradition has always insisted that Mohammed was illiterate, unable either to read or write, so he could not possibly have borrowed the contents of the Koran from other sources. The issue of Mohammed's alleged illiteracy has been the subject of controversy for centuries. But investigations of scholars have shown more light on Mohammed's life and character and it is now generally believed that Mohammed *pretended* to be illiterate in order to promote the "revelation" of the Koran into a miracle. He always called himself "Unlettered Prophet," and therefore attributed the eloquence of his Koran to a miracle and proof of his prophetic mission. Most Muslims still maintain that their prophet could not read or write in order to fortify their own belief in the miraculous character of the Koran.

There is much evidence showing that writing was not uncommon in Mecca about Mohammed's time[506] and we know that he was a member of the Quraysh, the noble tribe of Mecca. Ali copied out certain precepts of Mohammed and in order to have them constantly at hand, tied the rolled scripture round the handle of his sword.[507] It is also known that among Mohammed's wives, at least Ayesha and Hafza were lettered and even if he didn't have the opportunity to learn reading and writing in his childhood, he might have learned from those two wives. Moreover, Mohammed was the mercantile agent of his first wife Khadija for a long time and could not have managed such a great responsibility without knowing how to read and write and understand some basic arithmetic. The rise of Islam no doubt helped to spread the knowledge of writing.[508]

---

[506] Zwemer, *Studies in Popular Islam,* p. 101.

[507] William Muir, *The Mohammedan Controversy,* p. 114, quoted by zwemer, *Popular Studies in Islam,* p. 102.

[508] Zwemer, *Studies in Popular Islam,* p. 102.

Many Muslim writers have taken the word *ummi,* used six times in the Koran, as meaning *illiterate.* Al-Ghazali, for example writes, "The prophet was *ummi;* he did not read, cipher, nor write, and was brought up in an ignorant country in the wild desert without father or mother; but Allah himself taught him all the virtues of character and all the knowledge of the ancient and the modern world."[509] But, most scholars have asserted that the word *ummi* means "a gentile," as distinguished from an Israelite.[510] "The word was in fact misunderstood and was later thought to mean that he could not read and write."[511]

In verse 157 of *Sura* VII of the Koran, the words *al-nabi al-ummi* (the *ummi* prophet) are interpreted as "the illiterate prophet." The word "*ummi*" means either one who cannot read and write *or,* in the Arab Community of Mohammed's time, a person who was neither a Jew nor a Christian.[512] Verse 19 of *Sura* III uses the term "*ummi*" distinctly in the sense of one who does not belong to the people of the Book, i. e., Jews or Christians. It says, "Say to the people of the Book and *ummis* . . . ." This does not mean illiterate, because if it did, it would follow by implication that all Jews and Christians are illiterate which, of course, is not so.

There is still another argument on which the opinion that he was an illiterate person is based. Verse 48 of *Sura* XXIX says, "Never have you read a book before this, nor have you ever transcribed one with your writing hand. Had you done these the unbelievers might have justly doubted."[513] Modern scholarship has shown convincingly that this argument is completely false. First and formost, we know that the whole content of the Koran was fabricated by Mohammed to achieve his ambitious goals. The usage of the word *ummi* elsewhere in the Koran indicates that the word refers to those peoples who have not been given a scripture or converted, rather

---

509 Imam Al-Ghazali, *Ihya,* vol. LI, p. 250.

510 Fakhr er-Razi, vol. 1, p. 309; Rodinson, *Mohammed,* p. 240.

511 Rodinson, *Mohammed,* trans. Anne Carter, p. 240.

512 Sherif, *A Guide to the Contents of the Qur'an,* p. 25.

513 *Ibid.,* pp. 33–34.

than to illiteracy. The sophistry of Mohammed's illiteracy has been employed to buttress the divine origin of the Koran and deflect the Prophet's role as the sole author of it.[514]

Noldeke shows that the word *ummi* is used everywhere in the Koran in apposition to *Ahl ul-kitab,* which is the people of the Heavenly Books and that the myth of Mohammed's illiteracy was made up for political purposes. He also believes that on the basis of The *Hyat-ul-Kuloob,*[515] the Sunni deny his ability to read and write, while the Shia's affirm it.[516] There are many other reasons and evidence proving Mohammed was literate and that he could both read and write.

First, Imam Jafar Sadeq contends that Mohammed was able to read and write, pointing out that when Abu Sufyan marched for Uhod, Abbas sent a letter to Mohammed to inform him of the fact. He opened up the letter and after reading it, he informed his companions about the incident.[517]

Second, an egregious example of Mohammed's literacy is the celebrated incident with respect to the treaty of Hudaibiya, so named for a place three miles north of Mecca. This treaty was made in the sixth year of the Hijra between Mohammed and the Quraysh. Mohammed chose Ali as his representative to sign the treaty and the Quraysh assigned Sohail ibn Amr as theirs. Mohammed ordered Ali to write, "A treaty between Mohammed the Prophet of Allah and Solail ibn Amr," but the latter rejected the term "Prophet of Allah" and instead suggested the treaty be written, "A treaty between Mohammed

---

[514] Mircea Eliade, ed., *The Encyclopedia of Religion,* vol. 12 (New York: MacMillan Publishing Company, 1987), p. 157; See also Samuel M. Zwemer, *Across the World of Islam* (New York: Fleming H. Revell Company, 1972), chapter III.

[515] Muhammad Baghir al-Majlisi, *The Life and Religion of Muhammad,* Hyat-ul-Kuloob, trans. James L. Merrick (San Antonio, Texas: The Zahra Trust, 1982), vol. 2, pp. 86–87.

[516] Zwemer, *Studies in Popular Islam,* p. 109.

[517] al-Majlisi, Mullah Muhammad Baqir, *The Life and Religion of Muhammad, Hyat-ul-Kuloob,* trans. James L. Merrick (San Antonio, Texas: The Zahra Trust), 1982, pp. 86–87.

and Sohail ibn Amr." Ali objected harshly to this and swore on his life that he would never let it happen. Sohail cried, "If we thought you were Allah's Messenger we would never have raised arms against you." To solve this crisis, Mohammed gave in, took the pen, crossed out "Prophet of Allah," and wrote instead, "Mohammed son of Abdullah."[518] More interestingly, According to Muir, Mohammed even added a footnote to the treaty, "The same shall be incumbent upon you toward us, as is incumbent upon us toward you."[519]

Third, another occasion showing his literacy occurred when he was on his death bed. Realizing that he was dying, Mohammed asked for writing materials and said, "Bring me ink and paper, that I may record for you a writing which shall prevent your going stray for ever."[520] But he was too weak to perform the task.[521]

Fourth, in verses 1–5 of *Sura* XCVI, Gabriel, the so-called angel of inspiration, commands Mohammed to read and he complies. If Mohammed were illiterate, the All-Knowing Allah would never have commanded His Messenger Gabriel to tell Mohammed to read. Moreover, in verse 4 of the same *Sura,* Allah refers to Mohammed as the one who is taught by pen. If Mohammed could not write why does Allah say that he was taught by pen?

In view of the above evidence, it can be argued that to consider Mohammed an illiterate person is to bolster the claim that the Koran is a miracle and thus confirm the legitimacy of Mohammed as a Prophet. This would be as absurd and irrational as believing the story of his ascension to the seven heavens and communicating with Allah in the seventh, or believing that he had an audience of *jinns* while reciting the Koran in the desert. An axiom says, in part "Absolute power corrupts. . . ." It is also true that many power seekers gain power by means of corruption. After all, as I have already said, Mohammed believed that "The ends justify the means."

---

[518] Caetani, *Annali dell' Islam,* vol. 1, pp. 716–17; *Sahih al-Bukhari,* vol. 1V, p. 273; Ibn Hisham, *Sirat Rasulallah,* vol. II, p. 175.

[519] Muir, *The Life of Mohammad,* vol. IV, p. 490.

[520] *Ibid.,* p. 482.

[521] Dr. Anis A. Shorrosh, *Islam Revealed* (Nashville: Thomas Nelson Publishers, 1988), p. 52.

The Prophet of Allah Sponsors a Professional Terrorist

The Case of Abu Basir

After Mohammed returned from Hudaibiyah,[522] Abu Basir ibn Usaid, a young man whose family belonged to the Bani Thaqif and had settled in Mecca as a sept of the Qurayshite clan of Banu Zuhrah, converted to Islam and was imprisoned for his Muslim sympathies. Abu Basir managed to escape from the prison and make his way to Medina on foot. He was soon followed by two Meccans bearing a letter to Mohammed asking for his return under the Hudaibiyah agreement. Mohammed complied with the request of the Quraysh and when Abu Basir protested, Mohammed told him that he was bound by the treaty to deliver him into the hands of the envoys, adding that Allah would come to his aid and would not allow him to be forced to abandon Islam.

It is interesting to note that in the above case, Mohammed, the Prophet of Allah, tries to behave more morally than Allah himself. Because Allah in verse 2 of *Sura* LXVI says:

> "Allah had already ordained you, the dissolution of your oaths and Allah is your protector, and He is full of knowledge and wisdom."

Probably the reason that Mohammed ascribed *full of knowledge and wisdom* to Allah is to justify the decree allowing the dissolution

---

[522] A valley on the road from Juddah to Mecca where Mohammed concluded a treaty with the Quraysh in June 628. Mohammed moved from Medina to Mecca, accompanied by a force of 1,400 of his followers. He halted at Hudaibiya and stated that he wanted to perform the pilgrimage to Ka'ba. After some negotiations, Mohammed agreed to give up the pilgrimage, in return for being allowed to perform a minor pilgrimage (*umra*) the following year. He also agreed to return subjects of the Quraysh who had accepted Islam, lacking the sanction of his/her guardian, although Muslims who defected were not to be extradited.

This non-aggression pact, was supposed to remain in force for ten years, but in the following year, the Muslims performed their pilgrimage and, when circumstances precipitated Mohammed's conquest of Mecca, it was rendered moot in august 630.

of oaths by his servants. But, in this case it seems that His Prophet is surpassing Him in morality as well as in knowledge and wisdom. The reason being that although Allah has permitted His servants to dissolve their oaths, His Prophet is determined to stick to the rules of morality and respect the treaty he has already signed with the Quraysh, though in reality he did not.

Despite his youth, Abu Basir was a resourceful person and at the first halt, when he and his two captors were resting in Dhu al-Hulayfa, about eight miles south of Medina, he asked one of them,

"Is this sword of yours sharp?"

"Yes," he replied.

"May I look at it?" Abu Basir asked.

"If you wish," was the reply. Thereupon, Abu Basir got hold of the sword and killed him. The other captor, a freedman called Kawthar, ran back in terror to Medina, pursued by Abu Basir burnishing the naked sword reeking with blood. Both soon reached the presence of Mohammed; the freedman to complain of the murder, Abu Basir to plead for his freedom.

As Abu Basir had been handed over to the Quraysh, technically he was no longer a Muslim; therefore, Mohammed was not guilty of abetting the envoy's murder. Abu Basir pointed out to Mohammed that he (Mohammed) had honored the letter of the treaty by delivering him up once; therefore, he was not obligated to do so again. Mohammed gave no direct reply. His answer was enigmatic in the sense that he first uttered an exclamation of his bravery, 'Alas for his mother!'[523] Then he added, "What a kindler of war, if he had but with him a body of adherents!"[524]

Being encouraged by the words of Mohammed, Abu Basir, suggested that the arms and the armor of the dead man, together with the camels, should be treated as booty and divided according to the

---

[523] An often used ellipsis, meaning, "The man is such a hothead that his mother will soon have to mourn his death."

[524] Ibn Hisham, p. 751f.; Tabari, *The History of al-Tabari,* vol. 1, 1551f.; Al-Waqidi, p. 261f, quoted in Muir, *The Life of Mohammad,* p. 364; Ibn Ishaq, *Sira* 751, in Guillume, trans. and ed., p. 752.

law with one-fifth assigned to Mohammed. Ostensibly still under the obligations of the terms of the treaty, Mohammed rejected Abu Basir's suggestion and turning toward the horrified survivor, told him that the plunder should be his and commanded him to take Abu Basir back to Mecca. Kawthar was terrified and, hastily refusing to take responsibility for such a dangerous prisoner, fled for his life. At this point, having twice delivered up Abu Basir to the envoys of the Qurayshite, Mohammed felt himself free of the terms of the treaty and hinted to Abu Basir that he was free to go wherever he wished.

It did not take Abu Basir many minutes to realize that he was free to go. He had a short conference with five of his friends who were in Medina and together with them, fled out into the desert. In a few days, they were established on the Wadi al-Aisal-Isa, a place near the Red Sea, where Meccan caravans passed by on their way to and from Syria.

Mohammed's comments on Abu Basir's war-like abilities soon spread throughout Mecca, and the adventurous youths of the Quraysh, one after another, joined Abu Basir. He was soon surrounded by seventy followers as rapacious as he. They recognized him as their leader and became highwaymen, attacking every Meccan caravan that passed along the trade route to Syria and killing any man who came into their hands. They tore every caravan to pieces and took the goods. In no length of time, it became more dangerous for Meccan caravans to take that road than it was in the old days when Mohammed raided and plundered. Many of the young men who joined Abu Basir's gang were new converts to Islam so he became their religious leader as well, leading them in prayer and advised them on questions concerning the rites and other aspects of Islam.

Since Abu Basir's gangsters were not officially members of Mohammed's community, he did not bear responsibility for their actions and could not be accused of breaking the treaty. However, they were, in fact, Mohammed's puppets and he closed his eyes on their depredations. The Quraysh, on the other hand, after their defeat by the Muslims, had deteriorated so much that they were now too weak to bring any force against Abu Basir.

Finally, things got so bad that the Quraysh wrote a letter to Mohammed, begging him to stop the brigand's atrocities. Mohammed demurred, declaring that they were not under his control.[525] Eventually, the Quraysh begged Mohammed to take the highwaymen into his community, promising that they would not press for their extradition. In this way, they would at least be safe from the atrocities of the brigandage and would know whom to blame if the raids recurred. Mohammed acceded to their request, and wrote Abu Basir a letter, ordered him to stop robbing the Meccan caravans and murdering the merchants. He also added that he and his fellow brigands could now come to Medina.

Meantime, Abu Basir, the young leader of the marauders had fallen seriously ill and when the letter arrived, he was on his deathbed. The intrepid young highwayman had been wounded during one of the raids and probably developed septicemia. Before he died, however, he heard Mohammed's commendations for the services that he had rendered to the Muslim cause and the Prophet's assurance that a martyr's reward (including a group of houris) awaited him in Paradise.[526] After Abu Basir died, his companions prayed over him and made a mosque at his grave; then they went to join the supreme marauder, the impostor Prophet Mohammed, in Medina. Abu Basir, the freebooter, was countenanced by the Prophet in a manner scarcely consistent with the letter, and certainly opposed to the spirit, of the truce of Hudaibiya.[527] Nor did Mohammed's support of Abu Basir, a professional thug, conform with the tenets of a divine religion or with the rules of ethics.

Dar al-Harb and Dar al-Islam

On the basis of the theory of *Jihad,* mankind is divided into two groups: Muslims and non-Muslims. The Muslims are members of the

---

[525] Bodley, *The Life of Mohammed,* p. 260; Rodinson, *Mohammad,* p. 257.

[526] Bodley, *The Life of Mohammed,* p. 260.

[527] al-Waqidi, *Kitab al-Maghazi,* pp. 624–29, Muhammad ibn Isma'il al-Bukhari, LIV, ibn Ishaq, *Sirat Rasullalah,* 751–53, quoted in Martin lings, *Muhammad, His Life Based on the Earliest Sources* (New York: Inner Traditions International, Ltd., 1983), p. 258.

Province of Islam, *Dar al-Islam,* and non-Muslims are the members of the Province of War, *Dar al-Harb.* The Province of Islam is any country under Islamic control and governed on the basis of Islamic law, even if the majority of the population is not Muslim. In addition, at least one Muslim custom must be observed. The Province of War is any region not subject to Islam.

On the assumption that the ultimate goal of Islam is worldwide domination, the *dar al-islam* is always, in theory, at war with the *dar al-harb.* Muslims are required to proselyte Islam by the sword, and the Caliph is obliged to offer conversion to Islam as an alternative to paying the poll tax or fighting. Failure by non-Muslims to accept Islam or pay the poll tax makes it incumbent upon the Muslim state to declare *jihad* upon recalcitrant individuals and communities. Thus, *jihad* functions as an instrument for the Islamic state to convert the *dar al-harb* into the *dar-al-islam. Dar al-islam* will fight against *dar al-harb* forever.

Tabari wrote about one of the followers of Mohammed who quoted him as saying: "He who believes in Allah and his Messenger has protected his life and possessions from us. As for those who disbelieve, we will fight them forever in the case of Allah. Killing them is a small matter to us."[528] The universalism of Islam, in its all-embracing creed, is imposed on peoples by a continuous process of warfare, psychological and political as well as military.[529] History, as seen by the fundamentalists, consists of a series of wars between Islam and 'the rest, which is not Islam.'[530] All that was good was Islamic, and all those who were good and close to God were Muslims even before the advent of Islam.[531] According to Dr. Aziz Pasha, President of the Union of Islamic Associations in Britain and Eire, even 'Adam, Moses and Jesus' were Muslims. For Islam means 'surrender to the wishes of Allah.'

Muslims believe that between this *dar al-harb* (area of warfare) and the Muslim dominated part of the world, there can be no peace.

---

[528] Muir,. *The Life of Mohammad,* p. 514.

[529] Al-Tabari, *The History of al-Tabari,* vol. 9, p. 69.

[530] Majid Khadduri, *War and Peace in the Law of Islam* (Baltimore: The John Hopkins Press, 1955), p. 64.

[531] The theme is developed by Qutb, Khomeini, and Faraj, quoted in Amir Taheri, *Holy Terror* (London: Sphere books Limited, 1987), pp. 191, 287.

All acts of war are permitted in the *dar al-harb.* The Muslims are in a state of perpetual war with the people of the Province of War, until the whole world is converted into Islam. Practical considerations may induce the Muslim leaders to conclude an armistice, but the obligation to conquer and, if possible, convert never lapses. Nor can a territory once under Muslim rule be lawfully yielded to the unbeliever. Muslims must strive, fight, and kill in the name of Allah. The theory of Islamic imperialism was thus proclaimed, like the later-day theory of communist imperialism that Lenin labeled the 'international proletariat revolution.' Mohammed has reported to have declared that until the last infidel has been slain or converted to Islam, the *jihad,* in one way or another will remain as a permanent obligation upon the entire Muslim community. Muslims have to continue to terrorize the world until there are no more non-Muslims.[532] A saying attributed to Mohammed also declares that "war is permanently established until the Day of Judgment."[533]

According to Steven Runciman, after the fall of *dar al-harb:*

> "The conquering army is allowed three days of unrestricted pillage; and the formal places of worship, with every other building, become the property of the conquering leader; he may dispose of them as he pleases. Sultan Mehmet [after the fall of Constantinople in 1453] allowed his soldiers the three days of pillage to which they were entitled. They poured into the city . . . They slew everyone that they met in the streets, men, women and children without discrimination. The blood ran in rivers down the steep streets . . . But soon the lust for slaughter was assuaged. The soldiers realized that captives and precious objects would bring them greater profits."[534]

During *jihad* in a Province of War, it is legal to kill the males (except for the very old), children and women. The male population, other than *zimmi* (those non-Muslims who had accepted to pay tax, instead of conversion to Islam), can either be put to death or taken

---

[532] Dr. Aziz Pasha, in an interview with BBC Radio 4, 20 July 1986, quoted by Taheri, *Holy Terror,* p. 191.

[533] William Wilson Cash, *Christendom and Islam* (New York and London: Harper & Brothers Publishers, 1937), p. 22.

[534] Suleiman Abu Davud, *Sunan,* 4 vols., vol. III (Cairo: 1935), p. 4.

into captivity, as spoils of the war. As a general rule, all moveable properties seized in *jihad* are considered spoils, but land is transferred to the Islamic state. Therefore, spoils include cattle, horses, and valuables of every description, money, gold, silver, clothing and prisoners of both sexes. It is a grave sin for a Muslim to evade the battle against the unbelievers, those who do so roast in hell (Koran, VIII: 15–16, IX: 39 and IV: 74)

The summary of an article in "Al-urwata al-wuthqah" from the *Tarikh* of Mohammed Abdoh reads: "It is the duty incumbent upon all Muslims to aid in maintaining the authority of Islam and Islamic rule over all lands and once they become Muslim; they are not permitted under any circumstances to be preached to or conciliatory towards any who contend the mastery with them, until they obtain complete authority without sharing it with anyone else.[535]

The theory of "predestination," was propounded to buttress the "*jihad*" and "*martyrdom*" doctrines. According to this theory, the fate and deeds of human beings are already predestined, and nothing can change it. No one will die sooner or later than his predestined hour, and when this time arrives, whether he is in the quiet of his bed, or amid the storm of battle, the angel of death will take his life. (Koran, LIV: 49; III: 139; LXXXVII: 2; III: XVII; IX: 51; XIII: 30; XIV: 4; XVIII: 101)

---

[535] Steven Runciman, *The Fall of Constantinople 1453* (Cambridge: 1990), p. 145.

CHAPTER NINE

EXILE AND MASSACRE
OF THE JEWS FROM MEDINA

Take the news to the Jews: the army of Mohammed is on its way to Jerusalem to pour their blood in the Galleon Sea.
Muhammad Abdul Salaam Faraj[536]

From time immemorial the Jews have been expelled from countries which they themselves originally took by force. To name only a few of their conquerers, there was Nebuchadnezzar in 586 BCE, Pompey in 63 BCE, Titus in 70 CE, and the definitive expulsion by Hadrian in 135 CE.[537] Records show that Jews fleeing from persecution established colonies in the interior of the Arabian Peninsula. After Titus's sack of Jerusalem, three Jewish tribes—the Bani Nadhir, the Bani Quraiza, and the Bani Kainakaa—settled in a fertile area around Yathrib (Medina). Of these three main tribes, the Bani Nadhir and the Bani Quraiza were accomplished agriculturists and, having some of the richest land around the oasis, planted date palms, fruit trees, and some grains.[538]

The Bani Kainukaa possessed no agricultural land but had a compact settlement where they conducted a market and practiced such crafts as goldsmithry. In addition to the three main tribes, there were also about a dozen clans, such as the Bani Hadl and the Tha'labah. Collectively, the Jews of Medina occupied a prominent position in the city. Here, as in several other spots in western Arabia

---

[536] Muhammed Abdul-Salaam, was the mastermind behind President's Sadat assassination and also the author of a pamphlet entitled *Al-Faridhaat al-Ghaybah (The Occulted Duty),* of the most popular texts of *Holy Terror.*

[537] Bodley, *The Messenger: The Life of Mohammed,* p. 164.

[538] Heinrich Graetz, *History of the Jews,* vol. 3 (Philadelphia: The Jewish Publication of Society of America, 1894), pp. 54–55.

such as Khaibar, the Jews appear to have been agricultural pioneers.[539] The Bedouin Arabs who roamed the Arabian Peninsula had only thirteen strongholds compared to fifty-nine possessed by the Jews. Being followers of the Scripture, the Jewish people also enjoyed a kind of social respect among the idol-worshiping Arabs of the peninsula.

By the beginning of the first century CE, the Jews had established themselves by their industry and agriculture. When the Arab tribes Bani Aws and Bani Khazraj came to Medina from the south, they were allowed to settle, presumably on lands not under cultivation, and were under the protection of some of the Jewish tribes.[540] As time went on, the Arab tribes became stronger and they began to fight among themselves,[541] becoming strong combatants. Then strife broke out between the Jews and indigenous Arabs and this has continued to this day. Thus, Jews and Arabs were at loggerheads even before the advent of Islam.

During the years immediately preceding Mohammed's flight to Medina and his attaining power in that city, a battle occurred between the Jews and the Arabs at a place called Boath. After truce was declared, the warring factions decided to come to terms with each other and agree upon a leader to run the city. The man nominated for this office was an Arab who was friendly toward the Jews, called Abdullah ibn Ubey. But, before his appointment was confirmed, Mohammed entered Medina with his poverty stricken followers and changed everything. Abdullah ibn Ubey, influenced by the Jews, did not accept Mohammed and his religion. On one occasion he told him that it might be a good idea if Mohammed remained in one part of the oasis and minded his own business.

Mohammed at this point had not yet consolidated his power in Medina and did not wish to antagonize the Jews. He signed a covenant with them whereby, among other things, it was stipulated that Jews and Muslims were to support each other in all matters regarding the government of the city of Medina and be allies against all common enemies. The main principle of the covenant runs as follows:

---

[539] Watt, *Muhammad at Medina,* p. 193.
[540] *Ibid.*
[541] *Ibid.,* pp. 193–174.

"The Jews who attach themselves to our commonwealth shall have an equal right with our own people to our assistance and good offices. The Jews of the various branches domiciled in Yathrib shall form with the Muslims one composite nation. They shall practice their own religion as freely as the Muslims. The clients and allies of the Jews shall enjoy the same security and freedom."[542]

As Mohammed gained power, he violated this treaty and annihilated the Jewish tribes of Medina, one by one. For Mohammed the victory at the Badr was much more important than the number of Quraysh killed, the loot taken, and the death of arch enemies, such as Abu Jahl. This victory strengthened Mohammed's authority at Medina although all opposition still was not dead. He needed more successful battles to consolidate his power throughout the whole city. The only people who would not submit to his power and scoffed at his claims of revelation were the Jews.

They tested his claim to prophethood by perplexing him with knotty questions and demanding supernatural signs as the Qurayshites in Mecca had done previously. They challenged the authenticity of what he claimed to be revelations and what he had put into the Koran. They declared that some of the verses he had put in the Koran as revelations contradicted the ancient scriptures in their hands and therefore must be false. They could not be revelations and Mohammed could not be a prophet. They wrote satires about him and his followers. Some of the younger Jews even threw stones at him and there were plots to assassinate him. The Jews were a formidable economic force in Medina since they controlled the city's agriculture and industry and Mohammed could not afford their opposition. They were a powerful political entity on the Arabian Peninsula.

In the beginning of his mission, Mohammed decided to base his new faith on the Jewish religion, because at first he thought that he could not introduce an entirely new faith. He had studied the beliefs, customs, and stories of the Old Testament, and thereby conceived the idea of a universal religion of which he was the final Prophet.[543]

---

[542] Bodley, *The Messenger: The life of Mohammed,* pp. 167–168.

[543] William Wilson Cash, *Expansion of Islam* (London: Edinburgh, Hoiuse press, 1928), p. 169.

Throughout his preaching in Mecca, Mohammed was confident that the Jews and Christians, the "People of the Book," would welcome and accept his faith and become Muslims. For this reason, as it was mentioned before, he chose Jerusalem as the "*Qiblah*" (direction of Muslim prayer) and decreed that Muslims fast on the Jewish Day of Atonement, the Fast of Ashura. That is why the Koran at first speaks favorably of the "People of the Book."

> "Those who believe, Jews, Christians, and Sabians, whoever believes in God and the last day, and does what is right, will have a reward from their Lord, and on them shall be no fear, nor shall they grieve." (Koran, V: 69).

But, when Mohammed's hopes were dashed only seventeen months after his arrival in Medina, he decided to change the *Qiblah* from Jerusalem to the temple of Mecca (Koran, II: 124–150). On a November morning of 623 CE, in the middle prayer and after he had made two prostrations toward Jerusalem, he abruptly pretended that he had received a revelation and turned south toward Mecca. The congregation also turned round and faced Mecca with him.[544] A little later, he changed the fasting day from the Jewish Day of Atonement to the month of Ramadan (Koran, II: 185–187). Thus, he purposely widened the breach between himself and the Jews. Then, a new and hostile revelation from Allah abrogated the previous favorable one:

> "The Jews call Uzair a son of God, and the Christians call Christ the son of God. That is saying from their mouth. They but imitate what the unbelievers of old used to say. God's curse be on them: how they are deluded away from the truth." (Koran, IX: 30)

Thus, in accordance with the principle of *jihad,* the Jews by rejecting Mohammed's pretensions to prophethood became his enemy. The enmity of the Jews toward Islam and vice versa grew day by day and the Constitution of Medina that had been signed by Mohammed and the Jews of Medina became null and void. As

---

544 Koelle, *Mohammed and Mohammedanism,* p. 327.

usual, a couple of false revelations from an idle God who deserted the rest of the universe in order to take care of the ambitions of a power hungry Arab, gave Mohammed enough pretext to expel the Jews from Medina. These were the verses 58 and 61 of the eighth *Sura* of the Koran. The first Jewish tribe to be victimized was the Bani Kainakaa.

Verse 58 says:

"If you fear treachery from any of your allies, throw back their treaty to them in like manner. Allah does not like the treacherous."

And verse 61 says:

"But if the enemy inclines toward peace, you also do incline toward peace, and trust in Allah, because he is the one who hears and knows all things."

In the previous discussion some of the ninety-nine names of Allah were enumerated. Although among his other names, Allah has never called himself "jealous," it seems that He was unconsciously jealous as well. Why does he call himself deceitful, avenger, abettor, harmful, and so on, but at the very same time he confirms that "he does not like the treacherous," which seems to be a much milder characteristic than some others describing him. The reason is that he is jealous, and he wants to reserve the attribute of "treacherous" for himself and not apply it to others. Although there are dozens of examples to prove this contention, probably two will be sufficient:

1. We know that Allah or God, or whatever appellation one chooses to denote a Supreme Being, first appointed two prophets, Moses and Jesus—the latter purportedly being his own son—with appropriate Sacred Books to teach His servants to worship him. In those Divine Scriptures, Allah also ordered His servants to obey His Apostles and carry out the precepts written in the Scriptures. Then, after several hundred years, Allah appointed another Prophet with a different Scripture which abrogated all others. He did not call this prophet His own son and He ordered the new prophet to slay whoever does not obey him and submit to his new Scripture. *Isn't such a God treacherous?*

2. When Mohammed was appointed by Allah as an Apostle and the people of Mecca ridiculed him saying, "this poor cameleer has lost his head," Allah sent him verse 14 of *Sura* XIV, verse 110 of *Sura* XVIII and verse 5 of *Sura* XLI of the Koran and ordered the cameleer-prophet to tell them, "I am a human like yourself, however, it has been revealed to me to tell you Allah is one." But when he fled from Mecca to Medina and gained control of the government there, Allah apparently forgot his previous idea about him and sent him verse 50 of *Sura* XXXIII of the Koran saying, "We have made lawful for you, your wives, whose dowry you have paid, what your right hand owns out of the spoils of war that Allah gave you, the daughters of your parental uncles, the daughters of your parental aunts, the daughters of your maternal uncles, the daughters of your maternal aunts who emigrated with you, and any believing woman who gives herself freely to the Prophet, if the Prophet desires to marry her, ***granted exclusively to you,*** but not the believers . . . so that you may not be blamed . . . ." Isn't such an Allah (God) treacherous?

Exile of the Bani Kainakaa from Medina and the Plundering of their Properties

The first Jewish victim of Mohammed's avarice and cruelty was the tribe of Bani Kainakaa. They were chosen because the other two Jewish tribes of Medina, the Bani Nadhir and the Bani Qurayza, had long been the allied with the powerful Arab tribe, Aws. But the Bani Kainakaa was the smallest of the three tribes and ally of the less powerful Arab Khazraj tribe. Nonetheless, the Jews of this small tribe were doubtlessly the wealthiest inhabitants of Medina. Their territory was near the center of Medina and, unlike the other two tribes, they were not farmers but smiths and craftsmen. Therefore, the astute pretend-prophet chose the tribe of Bani Kainakaa as the first victim of a policy aimed at the eventual complete removal of the Jews from Medina and the confiscation of their properties.

With this goal in mind, a month after of his victory in the battle of Badr, Mohammed assembled the Jews of the Bani Kainakaa in their bazaar in the south of Medina and warned them not to call down upon themselves the anger of Allah such as that which had fallen upon the Quraysh. The Jews of Kainakaa listened to him in mutinous silence and replied, "O Mohammed, you seem to think that we are like your people. Do not deceive yourself because you have encountered a people at Badr with no knowledge of war and got the better of them; for by God, if we fight you, you will find that we are real men to be feared."[545] After this threat, Mohammed withdrew and bade his time. The Jews thought for the moment that they had triumphed.

After a few days, in the same market-place, an incident occurred which gave Mohammed a pretext to again confront the Kainakaa Jews. A Muslim woman went to the market of the Bani Kainakaa to sell milk, and sat in front of a goldsmith's shop. She was veiled but a Jewish prankster contrived to fasten the back of her skirt with a thorn in such a way that, when she stood up, a large part of her unveiled body was exposed. This so annoyed the woman that she screamed with shame. The Jewish bystanders laughed, but a Muslim who was present regarded the trick as an insult, came to her rescue and killed the offender. The Muslim, however, was out numbered by the Jews who owned the market; they attacked the Muslim and killed him.

This incident caused turmoil in Medina. The Muslims, indignant over the affair, called their fellow Muslims to arms and thus began the war between Muslims and the Jews of the Bani Kainakaa tribe. Though supposedly bound by a treaty to amicably arbitrate all disputes with the Jewish tribes, Mohammed made no attempt to do so in this instance nor was he satisfied to punish only the murderer(s). He pretended that Gabriel had brought him verse 58 of *Sura* VIII of the Koran mentioned above and set out to attack the Jewish tribe of Bani Kainakaa saying, "I fear not the Bani Kainakaa."

In 624 CE (2 A.H.), Mohammed put Abu Lubaba ibn Abdul-Mundhir in command of a large party of Muslims and they surrounded the stronghold of the Bani Kainakaa. The Jews retired within and locked the gates. The Muslims laid siege to their stronghold, cutting off all supplies. Mohammed settled down outside to starve them out; the siege continued for fifteen days.

---

[545] Ibn Ishaq, *Sira* 543, quoted by Guillume, *The Life of Mohammed*, p. 363.

The Jews of the Bani Kainakaa expected the Arab Khazraj tribe, with whom they had long been allied, as well as the other Jewish tribes to intervene on their behalf, but none of these fair weather friends took any action to help. They had about 700 fighting men at their disposal and if their supposed allies had come to their aid, they could have defeated Mohammed. When they realized there was no prospect of outside help, the Jews of Bani Kainakaa tribe decided to surrender and they did so unconditionally, so as not to further irritate their implacable enemy. As, one by one, they came out of the stronghold, Mohammed wishing to make an example of them, ordered their hands tied behind their backs in preparation for their execution.

Abdullah ibn Ubey, whose attachment to Islam was not very strong, wanted to help his former allies, but dared not openly join their ranks. The only thing he dared to do was to insist that Mohammed spare the lives of the captives. Mohammed first failed to answer and Abdullah ibn Ubey grabbed him by the collar, pressing his demands. Mohammed went white with anger but finally granted the Bani Kainakaa their lives, provided that they instantly leave the oasis. In this manner their lives were spared, but their houses, lands, slaves, goods, including their armor, were seized as booty and divided amongst the victors; debts owed to them by Muslims were cancelled.

Mohammed took his choice of arms—three bows, three swords, and two coats of mail. Then, he told Abdullah ibn Ubey to escort the vanquished tribe out of Medina. The Bani Kainakaa left the oasis without protest knowing that they were lucky to have escaped with their lives. They took refuge with a kindred Jewish settlement to the northwest in Wadi al-Qura, and, with their assistance, moved further north, to finally settle on the border with Syria.

The Bani Kainakaa was the first Jewish tribe to be thrown out of Medina by Mohammed. This event occurred in 624 CE, closely after the Battle of Nadr. After Mohammed's defeat at Uhod (625 CE), it was the turn of the Bani Nadhir to be banished.

Expulsion of Bani Nadhir from Medina

Obeida ibn al-Harith was Mohammed's cousin who died in combat at the beginning of the Battle of Badr leaving a young widow named

Zainab, daughter of Khuzaymeh, of the Bedouin tribe of Bani Amir. Mohammed married her a year after she became a widow. The Bani Amir, and their neighbors the Bani Suleim, belonged to the great Hawazin tribe living in Najd that had fought against the Quraysh. They were under the leadership of two chiefs, Abu Bara and Amir ibn at-Tofail. In May or June of 625 CE at Zainab's wedding, Abu Bara brought Mohammed a present of two horses and two riding-camels. Mohammed refused to accept the presents unless Abu Bara would embrace Islam. Abu Bara declined to personally accept Mohammed's religion but suggested that some Muslims be sent to Najd to instruct the whole tribe and possibly convert them to Islam.

Mohammed was hesitant to do so because he had already sent six Muslims to Al-Raji[546] for the same purpose. Three of them had been killed and the other three taken prisoner and sold. Moreover, some of the people of Al-Raji were in close alliance with the Quraysh. However, Abu Bara promised that he would be responsible for the Muslims safety. Trusting in this pledge, according to Ibn Ishaq, Mohammed sent forty (Tabari gives the number seventy) of the best of the Muslims under the command of Mundhir ibn Amr with a letter to Amir ibn at-Tofail.

After four days, the putative evangelists reached a spring called Bir Ma'una that lay some fifty miles southeast of Medina between the tribes of Bani Amir and Bani Suleim. At this place they halted and dispatched a messenger to take Mohammed's letter to Amir ibn at-Tofail. Before setting out from Medina, they had not known that Abu Bara's leadership had been challenged. His nephew, who aspired to be chief in his place, without looking at the letter, put the messenger to death and called upon his fellow rebels to slaughter the other envoys, but they refused to break Abu Bara's promise of safe conduct. Amir ibn at-Tofail then sent a message to the Bani Suleim, who had

---

[546] Two months after the battle of Uhod, in May 625, a group of tribesmen from a place called Al-Raji, about thirty miles between Mecca and Medina came to Mohammed, asking him to send some of his associates to instruct them in Islam. Mohammed accepted the invitation and sent with them six Muslims. When the group reached Al-Raji, they were ambushed by the Bani Lihyan, a clan of the Hudhail. Of the six Muslims three died in the fighting and three were taken prisoners, one of whom also was killed trying to escape. The two survivors, Khubaib ibn Adi and Zaid ibn al-Dathinna, were sold to Quraysh.

lost some of their clansmen at the Battle of Badr and had been involved in other hostilities against Mohammed, encouraging them to attack the Muslims. The Bani Suleim immediately sent out a detachment of horsemen and cut Mohammed's delegation to pieces. Two of the Muslims, Amr ibn Omeiya and Amr ibn Auf, however, had taken the camels out for grazing while their comrades rested at the well and, as a consequence, were not involved in the fight. When they returned from the pasture, they were dismayed to see the ground strewn with their dead comrades and large numbers of Bani Suleim close by.

Amr ibn Omeiya's was all for escaping back to Medina and reporting to Mohammed, but Amr ibn Auf said that he could not bring himself to leave the spot where their leader al-Mundhir had been slain nor could he bear the thought that people might think him a coward, so he fought the attackers until he joined his slain colleagues, presumably in Paradise. The Arabs ordered Omeiya to tell them the names of his dead companions and set him free. Then, when he was leaving, the Bani Suleim told him that the massacre had been instigated by the Bani Amir.

On his way back to Medina, Amr ibn Omeiya met two men belonging to a branch of the Bani Amir. That night, Omeiya waited until they fell asleep whereupon he slit their throats, thinking that he had taken some vengeance for the killing of his companions. But when he told Mohammed the story, it turned out that these men were loyal to Abu Bara and were returning to him, having just entered into terms with Mohammed. Therefore, Mohammed, instead of praising him, rebuked him and ordered that blood-money be paid to their nearest kin. The news of the Massacre of Bir Ma'un cast a pall over Medina and deeply affected Mohammed. It was obvious that he could not rest until he redressed his lost prestige.

The Jewish tribe of Bani Nadhir lived near the Bani Amir and they had been confederates for a long time. So, Mohammed thought because he had received ill-treatment from the Bani Amir, the Jews should help him pay the blood-money for the two men murdered by Omeiya. Under this pretext, in August of 625 CE (a year after he instigated the assassination of Ka'b ibn al-Ashraf's), Mohammed, accompanied by a small group of his followers including Abu Bark, Omar and Ali, visited the settlement of the Bani Nadhir and laid the matter before their chiefs. They agreed to comply with his request, and invited him and his men to stay until a repast could be prepared for them. The Jews' invitation was accepted and after sitting for a while, Mohammed rose and left the company without a word, as though answering a call of nature.[547] Everyone assumed that he would soon rejoin them. His companions waited patiently, but when some time had passed and he had not returned, Abu Bakr suggested to his companions that they leave the Jewish settlement and return to Medina.

Upon returning to Medina, they found, to their surprise, that Mohammed had returned directly to the mosque. He explained to them that his hasty departure was due to a revelation received from Gabriel: The chiefs of Bani Nadhir were planning a treacherous attack to kill him as he sat by their house by throwing down great stones upon him from the roof. Obviously, this was merely a deceitful pretext to justify the expulsion of the Bani Nadhir from Medina, as he had done to the Bani Kainakaa tribe.

He immediately dispatched Mohammed ibn Maslama (the Assassin of Ka'b), a chief of Aws and ally of the Bani Nadhir, to give them an ultimatum: "Leave Medina within 10 days, otherwise I will be forced to fight against you." Since (according to the angel Gabriel) they planned to slay him, the treaty he had made with them was thereby nullified and they could no longer live in Medina after such treachery. Therefore, they should leave Medina within ten days or face war. They must take their goods and chattels with them, and would receive a part of the produce of their date-palm trees.

Such an ultimatum seems horrendously cruel since no offense had actually been committed and the grounds for such a terrible punishment were based on the warnings of an imaginary angel as revealed to a so-called Prophet.[548] In fact, it was but a flimsy pretext for Mohammed to drive more Jews out of Medina and plunder their properties. The Jews were astonished that a member of the Aws tribe, a supposed ally, brought them such a message and, as did the Bani Kainakaa the year before, could not believe that Mohammed would ignore the covenants he had made with them. When they expressed surprise that a man allied to their tribe should have agreed

---

[547] Tabari, *Annales,* ed. Cit., 1,3, p. 1450; Ibn Saad, ed. Cit., vol. II, 1, 41.
[548] Watt, *Muhammad at Medina,* p. 211.

to carry such a message, Mohammed ibn Maslama answered them, "Hearts have changed now and Islam has wiped out old alliances.[547]

The Bani Nadhir were appalled at the prospect of leaving the home of their fathers with its fertile fields and exceptionally fine orchards of date-palms. Although he recalled the cruel actions of Mohammed against the Jewish tribe of Bani Kainakaa, Huyyay ibn Akhtab, the chief of Bani Nadhir was not inclined to submit to Mohammed. While Huyyay was hesitating, Abdullah ibn Ubey, one of the leaders of Medinians who was becoming increasingly disenchanted with Mohammed, sent a message to Huyyay advising him to resist. He promised to support the Bani Nadhir along with the remaining Jewish tribe in Medina, the Bani Qurayza, and indicated that his nomad allies, the Ghatafan, would also come to their rescue. Reassured by these promises, the Bani Nadhir resolved to hold fast and refused to comply with Mohammed's demand. Huyyay sent a message to Mohammed declaring that they would not leave their dwellings and their possessions and he could do whatever he wished. Upon hearing this, Mohammed delightedly cried, *"Allaho akbar, the Jews are going to fight."*

In 625 CE, Mohammed left Medina in charge of Abdullah ibn Umm Makhtum and marched against the Bani Nadhir in force. The Jews withdrew to their strongholds, watched the Muslims surround them, and waited for ibn Ubey and the other promised rescuers to come to their assistance. The cavalry never arrived. The siege lasted about two weeks and reduced the Jews to such a state of utter exhaustion that they decided to capitulate and give Mohammed what he wanted.[550]

In the meanwhile, Mohammed became impatient and, to hasten their surrender, committed an unusual and unwarranted action that was in violation of all laws and traditions of Arabic warfare. He gave the order to cut down and burn the fine date-palm trees, the tribe's chief source of income, in order to force the issue. The Jews remonstrated strongly against this since it was not merely a senseless, barbaric and cruel act, but was specifically forbidden by the Law of Moses (Deut. XX: 19) as well as Arab tradition. The destruction of the

---

[549] Rodinson, *Mohammad,* p. 192.
[550] Tabari, *The History of al-Tabari,* vol. 7, p. 86.

date-palm trees, and the despotic conduct of Mohammed towards the Bani Nadhir, resulted in much criticism against him. But he knew how to silence every objection. As usual, he justified it as the command of Allah[551] and, as always, Allah was conveniately waiting in the deserts of Arabia to send a vindicating revelation to Mohammed:

> "Whether you cut down the tender palm-trees, or you left them standing on their roots, it was by leave of Allah, and in order that he might cover with shame the rebellious transgressors." (Koran, LIX: 5).

The unfortunate Jews were devastated and Hayyay sent word to Mohammed that they were prepared to fulfill his original demand and leave their land, but now Mohammed's terms had grown much harsher; he decided that he would not allow them to take all their possessions with them into exile. Rather, they were to leave their armor and weapons plus any wealth they had accrued and the only goods they might take with them were those that could be carried on their camels. The wretched Jews were left with no option but to submit to Mohammed's inhumane demands.

They loaded six hundred camels with all that they could bear, even dismantling their houses and breaking down the lintels of their doors. They departed from the oasis under the leadership of Huyyay ibn Akhtab and set out for Khaibar, some seventy miles to the north, proudly defiant but glad to have at least saved their lives from the bloodthirsty Muslim Arabs. Sallam ibn Abu'l Huqayq and Kainakaa ibn Rabi' were prominent by their absence from the caravan of refugees. The people of Khaibar welcomed them wholeheartedly. Some of the Bani Nadhir who had estates in Khaibar stayed there and the rest departed the north toward to Syria.

Following such a cruel raid Allah, as usual, came to the assistance of His beloved Prophet and, to justify his terrorism, took the blame by revealing the following verse:

> "It was He that drove the unbelievers among the people of the Book out of their dwellings into the first exile. You did not think that they would go; and they, for their part, fancied that their strongholds would protect

---

[551] Muir, *The Life of Mohammad*, p. 282.

them from Allah. But Allah overtook them whence they did not expect it, casting such terror into their hearts that their dwellings were destroyed by their own hands as well as by those of the faithful. Learn by their examples, you that have eyes." (Koran LIX: 2)

The Bani Nadhir tribe had rich and extensive agricultural lands, all of which were appropriated by Mohammed. Their weaponry, including 340 swords, 50 cuirasses, and 50 helmets, all went to Mohammed to be used to slaughter his future victims. The whole affair of the Bani Nadhir passed without any fighting or bloodshed. Therefore, all the plundered booties went to Mohammed. The rationale for this "just" procedure was a revelation issued by Allah saying:

"What Allah bestowed on His apostle (and taken away) from them—for this you made no expedition with either cavalry or camelry: to His Apostle over any he pleases: and Allah has power over all things." (Koran, LIX: 6)

Sahih Muslim also writes:

"It has been narrated On the authority of Omar, who said, 'The properties abandoned by Bani Nadhir were the ones which Allah bestowed upon his Apostle for which no expedition was undertaken either with cavalry or camelry. These properties were particularly meant for the Holy Prophet. He would meet the annual expenditure of his family from the income thereof, and would spend what remained for purchasing horses and weapons for preparation of *jihad'*."[552]

The Massacre of the Bani Qurayza Jews

In 627 CE, two years after the expulsion of the Bani Nadhir from Medina, a great army of Meccans and Bedouins marched toward Medina, surrounded Mohammed's army and began what became known as the Battle of the Trench. The leader of the Meccan army, Abu Sufyan, was unsure of his numerical superiority so he decided

---

[552] *Sahih Muslim,* No. 4347, p. 954; *Sahih al-Bukhari,* vol. 4, p. 99.

to ally himself with the Bani Qurayza, the only Jewish tribe still living in Medina. At the same time, Huyyay ibn Akhtab came to the Bani Qurayza and told them that he had the support of the Quraysh and Ghatafan and together they could easily defeat Mohammed.

Ka'b ibn Asad, chief of Bani Qurayza, replied, "You have brought me shame for all the time; a cloud without water, all thunder and lightening, and nothing in it.[553]

The Bani Qurayza, although nominally subjects of Mohammed, were inclined disavow him because he had acted so barbarically toward the other two Jewish tribes of Medina. Therefore, they agreed to ally with Huyyay ibn Akhtab and Abu Sufyan and promised to attack Mohammed from the rear.

When Mohammed became aware of the alliance between the Bani Qurayza and Abu Sufyan, he invented an artful deception. There was a man named Na'im ibn Masoud, who had been employed by the Quraysh the previous year to in an effort to prevent Mohammed from advancing upon Badr, by exaggerating the Quraysh strength at Mecca.

However this year, as a believer in Islam, Na'im offered his help to Mohammed who decided to employ his services in an effort to break the alliance between the Bani Qurayza and the Quraysh. After giving him proper instruction, Mohammed told him, "War after all is a game of deception."[554]

Na'im ibn Masoud went first to the Bani Qurayza and, representing himself as their friend, artfully implied that the interests of the Meccan army were not necessarily theirs and they should be very careful about allying themselves with the Meccans. He told them that it would be wise to demand hostages from the Meccans, as a guarantee against betrayal by Quraysh. The Bani Qurayza's chief listened to him carefully and decided to carry out his seemingly logical advice.

Then, Na'im went to Meccan leaders and told them that he had received news indicating that the Jews of Bani Qurayza were going to remain faithful to Mohammed and that they were intending to ask

---

[553] Ibn Hisham, vol. II, p. 200; Martin Lings, *Muhammad, His Life Based on the Earliest Sources* (United Kingdom: George Allen & Unwin, 1983), p. 221.

[554] Ibn Hisham, vol. II, p. 313.

for hostages whom they intended to turn over to the Muslims. This insidious plot worked very successfully. When the Quraysh leaders asked the Bani Qurayza to fulfill their promise to attack the Muslim army on the following day, they declared that they could not possibly break the long-lasting laws of their fathers by fighting on the *Shabbat.*

The Muslim's siege lasted nearly two weeks, but nothing was ever achieved. Both sides were running out of provisions and their horses were dying of hunger or arrow wounds. The Meccans never were able to cross the trench that Mohammed had ordered dug to defend his position. They made several assaults, even some by night, but the trench was guarded too well. The alliance of Quraysh and their confederates dissolved and, while the Meccans struggled very hard to inflict a fatal blow upon the Muslims, everything worked against them. So Abu Sufyan decided to go back to Mecca. The failure of the Quraysh to defeat the Muslims in this battle was a great victory for Mohammed.

After the retreat of the Meccans, the day of reckoning had come for the last Jewish tribe in Medina, the Bani Qurayza. During the course of the siege by the Quraysh, Mohammed had ruminated upon the possible danger that he might face if he were to have a trouble-making enemy in Medina during a time of crisis. Mohammed was aware of the Bani Qurayza's attempted alliance with the Quraysh army and decided to get rid of them, once and for all. Now, he once again revealed that lack of honesty and moral courage which was so intrinsic in his character.[555]

According to Ibn Ishaq, on the morning following the withdrawal of the confederate army from Medina, Mohammed returned to the city with his army to rest. But about noontime, he pretended that Gabriel was bringing him a revelation from Allah. This revelation took the form of a reproaching query, "Have you already laid down arms, while the angels have not yet done so?" And then Gabriel continued, "Allah commands you to march against the Bani Qurayza, and I myself am going there to shake their towers."[556]

Following this cunning revelation, Mohammed left Medina in charge of Abdullah ibn Umm Mahtum and marched on the Bani

---

[555] Andrae, *Mohammed: The Man and His Faith,* p. 155.
[556] Quoted by S. W. Koelle, *Mohammed and Mohammedanism,* p. 175.

Qurayza. The Bani Qurayza possessed several fortresses a short distance southeast of Medina. When they heard that Mohammed was coming after them, they barricaded themselves in their fortresses. Before sunset all the fortresses were under siege by the same army that had opposed the Quraysh and their allies at the Battle of the Trench, three thousand Muslims (including 36 horsemen).

Mohammed besieged them for 25 days[557] after which the Jews sought to capitulate on condition of quitting the neighborhood empty-handed. But Mohammed, no longer having any other Jewish neighbors to worry about, refused their conditional surrender. The Bani Qurayza, remembering their ancient friendship with the Aws, and sent a message to Mohammed appealing him to allow them to consult with Abu Lubaba ibn Mundhir, who belonged to Aws tribe and had personal relations with Bani Qurayza. Mohammed granted their plea and bade Abu Lubaba to go to them. When Abu Lubaba entered the headquarters of the Bani Qurayza, he was touched by the weeping, trembling, wailing women and children who pressed round him and much of his antipathy toward the Jews was softened. They asked his advice as to whether they should surrender to Mohammed or resist him. He told them they had better surrender but at the same time, drew his hand across his throat, intimating that since there would be a massacre and death was inevitable, they should fight to the last drop of their blood.

Abu Lubaba's knew his advice to the Jews was against Mohammed's wishes because it would prolong the siege still further, so he went to Mohammed, confessed his guilt, and asked his pardon. Mohammed paid no attention to him. Then he went directly to the mosque and tied himself to one of the pillars by way of punishment. He remained there for several days until Mohammed at last relented and pardoned him. Thereafter, this pillar was called the "Pillar of Repentance" and became part of the formalities of the Muslims' superstitious worship.

Finally, the wretched Jews reduced to starvation and despite the hint of their eventual fate from Abu Lubaba, asked leave of Mohammed to allow them to depart the oasis on the same terms as the other two Jewish tribes (the Bani Kainakaa and the Bani Qurayza).

---

[557] *Ibid.* p. 255.

He refused and demanded unconditional surrender. The morrow of that night, the Arab tribe Aws sent a deputation to Mohammed asking him to forgive the Bani Qurayza since the latter had been their allies. They reminded him that he had done such with the Jewish tribe of Bani Kainakaa, for the sake of Abdullah ibn Ubey. This request put Mohammed in dilemma, because it was his intention to kill the Bani Qurayza Jews and yet he did not want to offend the Aws tribe. His cunning character asserted itself and he devised a way to extricate himself from the dilemma.

Lying in a tent pitched by Mohammed in the courtyard of the mosque was a prominent man of the Aws tribe, called Saad ibn Moaz. He had been gravely wounded during the Battle of Trench and had no hope of recovery. Mohammed had a talk with him and then went to the leaders of the Aws tribe and asked them if they would agree to arbitrate the matter if he appointed one of their own tribe as arbitrator.[558] As soon as they replied in affirmative, he appointed Saad ibn Moaz to arbitrate the case, knowing full well the final outcome.

Saad, being too ill to walk, he was brought to the arbitration table on a donkey. On the way, his Aws fellow tribesmen pleaded with him to be lenient with their former confederates, whose destiny had now been placed in his hands. He spoke not a word till he reached the place of judgment. As he approached, Mohammed received him with an unusual show of respect and commanded him to pronounce his decision. Saad first demanded that all parties concerned agree unconditionally to his terms of judgment. Following their assent, he pronounced:

"All adult males are to be slain, their women and children sold into slavery, and their property divided amongst the Muslims." The wretched Jews were completely shocked and disheartened, but there was no appeal. Upon hearing this cruel and barbarous judgment Mohammed was delighted and cried out, "You have judged according to the very sentence of Allah above the seven skies."[559]

---

[558] Koelle, *Mohammed and Mohammedanism,* p. 176; .Montgomery Watt, *Muhammad at Medina,* pp. 173–174.

[559] Rodinson, *Mohammad,* p. 213; Koelle, *Mohammed and Mohammedanism,* p. 177.

Mohammed now had fully indulged his hateful feelings toward the Jews. They were to lose their lives for denying Mohammed's pretension to prophethood. The women and children were separated from their husbands, brothers, and fathers and taken to the city. The men were manacled and spent the night in the camp, reciting their Scriptures and exhorting each other to faith and constancy in their beliefs. According to Tabari:

> "As they being taken in small groups to the prophet, they said to one another, 'What do you think will be done to us?' Someone said, 'Do you not understand. On each occasion do you not see that the summoner never stops? He does not discharge anyone. And that those who are taken away do not come back. By Allah, it is death! The affair continued until the Messenger of Allah finished with them all."[560]

The butchery of the men of the Jewish tribe began in the morning and lasted all day. A big pit was dug in the market place of Medina and the Jews, chained and manacled, were lined up. The able-bodied prisoners were brought in groups of five or six, seated in a row on the edge of the pit, beheaded in a leisurely manner, and their bodies cast into the pit.[561] According to the Arab historians, between 600 and 900 Jews of the Bani Qurayza tribe were cruelly massacred in cold blood, while Mohammed watched and delighted in the slaughter. Muir has mentioned the number of the slaughtered Jews as 800.[562] The land, houses, and chattels were distributed among the 3,000 Muslim soldiers and the women and children sold as slaves. There were thirty-six cavalrymen in Mohammed's army. Each horseman received three shares, two for the horse and one for the rider. A man without horse received one share. According to the Koran (*Sura* VIII: 41), Mohammed took a fifth of every share and this included two hundred women and children.

One woman was executed because she had killed Khallad ibn Suwayd by throwing a millstone on him[563] during the siege. When

---

[560] Tabari, *The History of al-Tabari,* vol. 8, p. 35
[561] Majumdar, *Jihad, the Islamic Doctrine of Permanent War,* p. 44.
[562] Muir, *The Life of Mohammad,* p. 319.
[563] Ibid., p. 318.

she heard that her husband had been executed, she loudly bragged at what she had done, and asked Mohammed to let her share her husband's fate. Mohammed was delighted to comply and ordered the wretched woman put to death. Ayesha has said about this woman, "By Allah, I shall never forget her cheerfulness and her great laugh when she knew that she was to be killed."[564]

Fully sated with butchery, Mohammed needed a break. No better break could be found than dalliance with a new member of his harem. This woman was Raihana, daughter of Simeon, a wealthy and powerful Jew, and the most beautiful female among the woman captives. Originally, she had belonged to the Bani Nadhir tribe but was now married to a man of the Bani Qurayza. Reyhana's husband and all her male relatives had just perished in the massacre. Mohammed invited Raihana to be one of his wives and enjoy the same privileges as his other wives, but she declined and chose to remain his slave or concubine. She told Mohammed, this would be better for both of them. Raihana also declined conversion to Islam, and continued in the Jewish faith, much to Mohammed's concern. It is said, however, that she finally succumbed and embraced Islam. She lived only five years in Mohammed's harem, dying at the age of 25 in 631 CE, one year before Mohammed's death. Almost certainly, she led a tortured life in the harem and probably died of grief.

The accomplice of Mohammed, namely the Almighty Allah did not leave him to solely bear the blame for the barbaric massacre of the Bani Qurayza. After the bloody savagery, Allah, the most gracious and the most merciful revealed the following verse to His beloved Prophet:

> "Allah made the Jews leave their homes by terrorizing them so that you killed some and made many captive. And He made you inherit their lands, their homes, and their wealth. He gave you a country had not traversed before." (Koran, XXXIII: 26)

By such unscrupulous means, a man who called himself the Prophet of God achieved wealth and power for himself and his followers.

---

[564] *Ibid.*

With the massacre of the Bani Qurayza tribe, Medina now was clear of Jews: two of the tribes had been banished, their lands and their properties confiscated, and the third massacred. Those few Jews who remained professed to accept, at least outwardly, Mohammed and his new religion. Now, finally, Mohammed had become ruler over the rich city of Medina. By putting into practice the cruel, brutal and terrorist precepts of Islam, he had achieved, under the guise of religion, his goal of power. Allah caused the triumph of the satanic forces over the righteous ones. The butchery of the Bani Qhoriza tribe casts an indelible blot upon the character of Mohammed.[565]

Many writers, including William Muir, Sprenger, Weil, and Wilson have likened the barbarity of Mohammed to bloody Nero. The author of this book does not accept this corollary. Nero was a secular emperor, whereas Mohammed pretended to be a Prophet. Nero did not share the blame for his atrocities with anyone else; Mohammed introduced himself as the Apostle of God and made Allah his accomplice. Moreover, under blatantly false pretenses, Mohammed tried to legitimize systematized murder.

The Torture and Extortion of the Khaibar Jews

After the final pogrom of the Bani Qurayza, Medina became a city unified under the banner of Islam with Mohammed as governor. Having consolidated his power in the city by trickery and bloodshed, Mohammed now turned to more spiritual matters. He sensed a feeling of homesickness in those followers native to Mecca who had fled with him to Medina and in order to appease them, he decided to lead a mass pilgrimage to Mecca. Rather than calling down a revelation from above to command this journey, he instead pretended to have had a dream in which he saw himself circumambulating Ka'ba, sacrificing, and completing other rituals associated with a pilgrimage. He described this dream to his followers and they all became enthused that they live it in reality.

---

[565] *Ibid.*, p. 335.

Therefore, in February 628 CE, the sixth year following his flight from Mecca to Medina, Mohammed, accompanied by fifteen hundred Muslims, set out for the holy city, to perform a pilgrimage. Mohammed invited some of his allied Bedouins to join him, but seeing no prospect of booty, they refused, much to Mohammed's disappointment. Covertly, the Bedouins suspected that the Muslims might not return safely.[566] Because of this perfidy, the Bedouins were to be denied a share in the spoils of the next plundering by the Muslims.

By Arab tradition and usage, every Arab has the right to make a pilgrimage to Mecca. The Muslims went practically unarmed, taking with them animals destined for the sacrificial altar. Mohammed, a heretic to the traditional Arab gods; one who had violated the sanctity of the sacred months; and who had fought this holiest of cities for years, now appeared as a contrite penitent, returning to the gates of the holy city that had exiled him six years previously. The freebooting war-like Arabs remained in Medina—a holy pilgrimage held no promise of booty or women slaves and therefore was of no interest to them.[567]

When the news of Mohammed's proposed return reached the Meccians, they thought the impostor prophet intended to wage war against them in which case the month of pilgrimage and the annual fair would be disrupted and desecrated.

A troop of two hundred fighting men was immediately raised in Mecca and, let by Khalid ibn al-Walid, sent to the desert to confront Mohammed and deny his approach to Mecca. Over the objections of his fellow Muslims, Mohammed obeyed the Meccan's injunction and camped at the oasis of Hudaibiya, in an open tract of land some 10 miles northwest of Mecca. After a period of mistrustful waiting, he proposed making a peace treaty with the Quraysh. Mohammed's offer of a peaceful solution was accepted and a deputation from each of the two parties—Othman on behalf of Mohammed and Soheil ibn Amr on behalf of the Quraysh—entered into negotiation and signed a treaty. The treaty is mentioned in verses 10 and 18 of *Sura 48* of the Koran. Verse 10 says:

---

[566] Montgomery Watt, *Muhammad at Medina,* p. 49.
[567] Essad Bey, *Mohammed* (London: Cobden Sanderson, 1938), p. 239.

"Those who plight their fealty to you, plight fealty to Allah. The hand of Allah is above their hands. He who breaks his oath breaks it at his own peril, but he that keeps his pledge to Allah shall be richly awarded."

Verse 18 says:

"Allah was well pleased with the Faithful when they swore allegiance to you under the tree. He knew what was in their hearts. Therefore, He sent down tranquility upon them and rewarded them with a speedy recovery and with the enemy spoils which they will take."

Under the terms of the Hudaibiya treaty, a truce was declared between Mohammed and the Quraysh for a period of ten years and the intended pilgrimage would be postponed until the following year. It further provided that any inhabitant of Mecca going to Medina without first obtaining permission from the authorities would be returned to Mecca by the Muslims. On the other hand, if one of the Mohammed's followers went over to the Quraysh, they were not required to deport him. The only concession Mohammed and Muslims could obtain was a long armistice and the promise that next year they might make a pilgrimage for three days, unarmed.

To compensate his followers for such an ignominious treaty and disappointment, Mohammed promised them other victories and spoils in abundance elsewhere. Each time Mohammed failed or disappointed his followers, he compensated for it by an attack on the Jews. So, after his return from Hudaybiya, to console his followers for their unfulfilled pilgrimage to Mecca, Mohammed planned a raid on the Jews of Khaibar.[568] Mohammed and his followers returned to Medina to prepare for the promised expedition, the spoils of which would only be shared by those who had taken part in the aborted pilgrimage. Several tribes that had refused to join Mohammed in the pilgrimage to Mecca offered to participate in the Khaibar raid, but Mohammed refused to accept their offer. He said that since they

---

[568] Margoliouth, *Mohammed and the Rise of Islam,* p. 355; *Washington Irving's Life of Mohammed,* p. 127; Muir, *The Life of Mohammad,* p. 319; Koelle, *Mohammed and Mohammedanism,* p. 180.

were not willing to participate in an unprofitable expedition to show their faith, they should not share in the profits from lucrative raids.

Khaibar is a word meaning "a fortified place." The town of Khaibar lay some one hundred miles northeast of Medina on the way to Syria and was inhabited by Jews who had grown wealthy by commerce as well as agriculture. The area about the town grew grain and was planted with groves of palm trees. Part was devoted to pasture and these fields were covered with flocks and herds. It was claimed to be the richest town in Hijaz and it was fortified by several castles. An army from Medina could march there within five days.

Khaibar had become a place of refuge for the fleeing Jews driven out of Medina by Mohammed as well as many others whom he had victimized for some reason or another. The teeming wealth of the region and the prospect of plundering same attracted the frustrated Muslims who had returned from Hudaibiya chagrined and empty-handed. Now the time had come for Mohammed to honor his promise to enliven his followers with new plundering and fresh spoils.

On his return from Mecca, Mohammed stayed for twenty days in Medina and then, leaving Numaylah ibn Abdullah in charge of Medina, he set out for Khaibar. He started the raid of Khaibar in September 628 CE. Anticipating valuable booty from the raid, many eager volunteers stepped forward in answer to Mohammed's call to arms. As noted above, various accounts state that Mohammed only accepted men who had been at Hudaibiya since this raid was to be compensation for their disappointment.[569] To take the Jews by surprise, Mohammed contrived to arrive near Khaibar during the night with 1600 soldiers, about the same number who had accompanied him on his pilgrimage to Mecca.

Early the next morning, when the Jews went forth to their fields, the Muslims army was quickly upon them and they hastened back to their strongholds. No one had had the least suspicion of an impending attack. The Jews of Khaibar had made an alliance with the Ghatafan Bedouins, to secure their help in such an emergency, but the rapidity of the raid cut off all hope of getting aid from them and the Jews became an easy prey for the merciless plundering of Mohammed and his followers.

---

[569] Bagot Glubb, *The Life and Times of Muhammad,* p. 280.

Mohammed besieged and overran the strongholds of Jews, one after another, taking them all into his possession. To strike terror into the Jews and neutralize their resistance, Mohammed mercilessly and barbarously butchered all the armed Jews who fell into his hands. Ninety-three Jews were thus slain, whilst Muslim casualties were only nineteen throughout the whole campaign.[570] After the capture of the minor strongholds of Na'm, Mohammed proceeded to capture al-Khamus, the main fortress of Khaibar; then the castles al-Watih and al-Sulaim were conquered after ten days siege. Several of the proud warrior Jews of Khaibar fought valiantly but, out-numbered, they were eventually overpowered. Then the Muslims poured through the breach like a torrent in flood and the inhabitants took refuge in their homes. Those who did not surrender were put to sword. The other Jewish colonies in the region, such as Fadak, Wadi al-Qura and Tyma, after learning of the barbaric behavior of Mohammed toward their brethren in Khaibar submitted without argument and were given the same terms as Khaibar.

Mohammed had first intended to expel all the Jews from Khaibar but the Jews suggested that, since they were skilled in the management of their farms and their orchards, they should allow them to remain in their homes and pay him an annual rent of half the produce. Mohammed agreed to this with the stipulation that they should give up all their property and, if in the future he decided to expel them from the city, they should obey his decision.

The first Islamic historian Tabari writes:

> "The Prophet conquered Khaibar by force after fighting. Khaibar was something that Allah gave as booty to His Messenger. He took one fifth of it and divided the remainder among the Muslims. The inhabitants who surrendered did so on condition that they should be expelled.[571] After the Messenger had finished with the Khaibar Jews, Allah cast terror into the hearts of the Jews in Fadak which they received news of what Allah had brought upon Khaibar. So they sent to Mohammed to make peace with him for a half share of Fadak's produce. Fadak became the exclusive property of Allah's Messenger."[572]

---

[570] Muir, *The Life of Mohammad,* p. 376.
[571] Tabari, *The History of al-Tabari,* vol. 8, p. 130.
[572] *Ibid.*

The spoils taken from Khaibar's wealthy Jews were tremendous. The booty wrested from Bani Qurayza, vast as it seemed at that time, was small compared to what Mohammed wrested from Khaibar. One-fifth of all moveable property was allocated to Mohammed and the remaining four-fifths divided among his warriors. Mohammed also appropriated fifty per cent of the lands of Khaibar and he gave the other half to his soldiers. Due to the fact that Fadak, Tyma, and Wadi al-Qura were not taken by actual fighting, but had been voluntarily surrendered, Mohammed claimed the entire spoil of those places for himself. (Koran, LIX: 6).

When the Muslims calculated their spoils they found that the conquest of Khaibar had yielded far more than any other blessing that Allah ever conferred on their impostor Prophet. Mohammed's one-fifth of the profits enabled him to enrich his wives and concubines, his daughters and their off-spring, his friends and acquaintances, even his servants. Fourteen hundred lots were portioned out for the infantry; two hundred horsemen got, according to custom, treble lots. Moreover, there was no fear of this wealth melting away as had former booty, for the Jews remained to till the land and remit fifty percent of the produce to the robbers.[573] This seems to be the first imposition of *Jizyah* in the history of Islam.

Sahih al-Bukhari writes:

> "Narrated Abdullah ibn Omar: 'When Allah's Messenger had conquered Khaibar, he wanted to expel the Jews from it as land became the property of Allah, His Messenger, and the Muslims. Allah's Messenger intended to expel the Jews but they requested him to let them stay there on the condition that they would do the labor and get half of the fruits. Allah's Messenger told them, <We will let you stay on the condition, as long as we wish.> So, they (i. e. Jews) kept on living there until Umar forced them to go towards Taima and Ariha.'"[574]

It was said that Kinana ibn Rabi', the chief of Khaibar had custody of the treasure of Ban Nadhir and that he had hidden it somewhere in the city. Therefore, after the city was captured by Muslims,

---

[573] Margoliouth, *Mohammed and the Rise of Islam,* pp. 361–362.
[574] *Sahih al-Bukhari,* vol. 3, No. 531, pp. 307–308.

every nook and cranny was ransacked in search of the treasure, to no avail. Mohammed questioned Kinana ibn Rabi' and his cousin about the location of the treasure. Kinana declared that it had all been expended on the subsistence of his troops and defense preparations. However, one of the Jews betrayed him and divulged to Mohammed where the treasure was concealed. Mohammed sent his people to search; they discovered the hidden place and brought the treasure to Mohammed. It was not what Mohammed expected, so he asked Kinana about the rest. Kinana refused to produce it. So, Mohammed gave orders to al-Zubayr ibn al-Awwam, to put him to torture until he revealed the location of the presumed balance of the treasure. Al-Zubayr kindled a fire with flint and placed the hot, glowing embers on Kinana's chest until his breath almost stopped. Mohammed then ordered the heads of both the chief and his cousin to be severed from their bodies.[575]

Tabari explains this tragic incident as the following:

> "Kinana ibn al-Rabi' ibn Abi al-Huqayq held the treasure of the Bani Nadhir. He was brought to Allah's Messenger, and he questioned him. But Kinana denied knowing where it was. So the Prophet questioned the other Jews. One said, 'I have seen Kinana walk around a ruin every morning,' Mohammed had Kinana brought to him and said, 'Do you know that if we find it, I shall kill you,' 'Yes,' Kinana answered. The Prophet commanded that the ruin should be dug up. Some treasure was extracted. Then Mohammed asked Kinana for the rest. He refused to surrender it; so Allah's Messenger gave orders concerning him to Zubayr, saying, 'Torture him until you root out and extract what he has.' So Zubayr kindled a fire on Kinana's chest, twirling it with firestick until Kninana was near death. Then the Messenger of God gave him to Mohammed ibn Maslamah, who beheaded him to avenge his brother Mahmud ibn Maslamah."[576]

After extorting the treasure from Kinana and killing him, Mohammed committed a scandalous act that further stigmatized his already tarnished character. Among the women made captive was Safiyyah, daughter of the executed chief of the Bani Nadhir, Hayyay

---

[575] Guillume, *The Life of Muhammad,* p. 515.
[576] Tabari, *The History of al-Tabari,* vol. 8, pp. 122–23.

ibn Akhtab, and widow of Kinana ibn Rabi', the newly slaughtered chief of the Khaibar Jews. Safiyyah was a strikingly good-looking girl, seventeen or eighteen years of age, whose beauty was renown in Medina. She, along with two of her cousins, was brought to Mohammed and, passing their slain husbands and relatives on the way, they burst out in tears of grief. Mohammed, upon seeing them in this state, said, "Take these demons away from me;" but he kept Safiyya, and cast his mantle over her, indicating that she was going to be added to the women of his harem (actually she became his tenth wife). Dahya ibn Khalifa al-Kalbi had asked Mohammed for Safiyya as part of his share of the booty of Khaibar but Mohammed refused. Instead, he gave him two of her cousins. *Sahih Muslim* recorded this scandal as told by Anas, Mohammed's personal attendant:

> "We took the territory of Khaibar by force, and there were gathered the prisoners of war. There came Dahya and he said, 'Messenger of Allah, bestow upon me a girl out of the prisoners.' He said, 'Go and get any girl.' He made a choice of Safiyya. There came a person to Allah's Apostle and said, 'Apostle of Allah, you have bestowed Bint Huyy ibn Akhtab, the wife of the chief of Bani Qurayza and Bani Nadhir, upon Dahya and she is worthy of you only.' . . . When Allah's Apostle saw her, he said to [Dahya]: 'Take any other women from among the prisoners . . .' He then granted her emancipation and then married her . . . On the way Umm Sulaim embellished her and then sent her to the Holy Prophet at night. Allah's Apostle appeared as a bridegroom in the morning."[577]

According to the rules of the religion Mohammed preached to his followers, such captives may not be married till the expiration of four months and ten days after capture, but Mohammed's carnal passions were more important than the "sacred" rules of his religion. When the feasting was over, Mohammed brought his camel and made it kneel before Safiyya. Then, offering her his own bended knee, he helped her mount the camel.[578]

One of the most ardent followers of Mohammed, Abu Ayub, with drawn sword voluntarily patrolled around the nuptial tent where Mohammed and his new wife spent the first night together. When in the

---

[577] *Sahih Muslim,* No. 3325, pp. 720–721.
[578] Koelle, *Mohammed and Mohammedanism,* p. 183.

morning, Mohammed asked him for the reason for his zealous guarding, he replied," I felt anxious for you on account of this woman, whose father, husband, and relatives you had slain, and who herself has been an unbeliever till quite lately." Mohammed's cruel disregard for the feelings of a woman whose nearest relatives he had just put to death was typical of his evil character and carnal nature.

When the fighting was over, a Jewish woman called Zainab invited Mohammed and his close companions for dinner. According to Mohammed's biographers, Zainab had asked what portion of a roast sheep he liked best and had been told that it was the shoulder. She then slaughtered and roasted a lamb, inserting a dose of poison in the shoulder. Mohammed took a mouthful of meat from the shoulder but spat it out before swallowing it, saying that he believed it to be poisoned. Zainab was brought before Mohammed and asked if she had poisoned the meat. She readily admitted that she had done so and excused her actions by saying,

"You know what you have done to my people. I said to myself that if you were just a tribal chief, we would get rid of you, but that if you were truly a prophet you would know what I had done."[579]

According to Ibn Ishaq, Mohammed pardoned her. One of Mohammed's companions, who was sitting beside him, swallowed a mouthful of the meat and died shortly afterwards. Mohammed, at the time of his death, three years later, attributed the agonies of his last illness to that poison, thereby winning for himself the title of martyr, as having been killed by an unbeliever.[580]

The chronicles of the early years of Islamic history all indicate that Islam became prosperous by destroying, one by one, the Jewish settlements around Medina and stealing their lands, properties, women and children.[581]

Raiding and Plundering Bani Mustaliq

At this juncture it is appropriate to describe Mohammed's atrocious behavior *vis-à-vis* his fellow Arabs as well as his pogroms against the Jews.

---

[579] Bagot Glubb, *The Life and Times of Muhammad,* p. 283.

[580] *Ibid.*

[581] Majumdar, *Jihad, The Islamic Doctrine of Permanent War,* p. 32.

Bani Mustaliq, a branch of Khoz'ah, was powerful tribe, Qurayshite in origin and non-Jewish. To the northwest of Mecca, within five miles of the Red Sea and between Medina and Kudaid., lie the wells of al-Muraysi. In December 626 CE, the sixth year of Hijra, Mohammed heard rumors that the Bani Mustaliq was preparing to raid Medina, under their chief Harith ibn Dhirar. Having verified these reports through a spy, Mohammed immediately decided to make a preemptive strike before they could move against him. By overthrowing them, Mohammed hoped to discourage their allies and at the same time safeguard the roads to Mecca. Mohammed was well supported by all Medinians and had a large army and thirty horsemen at his disposal. The Bani Mustaliq had a small army and was out-matched by the Muslims.

Mohammed left Medina in charge of Zaid ibn Harith and, by moving his army rapidly, soon engaged the Bani Mustaliq. Their chief, Harith ibn Dhirar, was killed at the onset and his troops fled in confusion after a brief resistance. Ten Bani Mustaliq soldiers were killed; Mohammed lost but one man, called ibn Subaba, by friendly fire from an erring Muslim. The booty that fell into the hands of the Muslims included the whole tribe, some two hundred families, with all their goods, five thousand sheep, and one thousand camels. It was divided in the usual manner; one-fifth being allocated to Mohammed.

One of the captives was Juwairiya, a beautiful young woman about twenty years of age, the daughter of Harith ibn Dhirar, the chief of the tribe. She was the wife of a young Arab and so beautiful that she captivated every man who saw her. When Mohammed was distributing the captives, Juwairiya fell to the lot of Thabit ibn Qays, who fixed a high price for her ransom. She came to Mohammed to ask his help in freeing her. As Mohammed was talking to Juweiriya, a sense of misgiving seized Ayesha as she perceived that the conqueror had become the captive of the prisoner. Ibn Ishaq was right when he wrote that Ayesha hated Juwairiya from the moment she first set eyes on her. Mohammed could not resist her charm, and without delay, paid her ransom to Thabit ibn Qays and added her to the number of his harem wives. Later on, Ayesha said, "By Allah, I had scarcely seen her in the doorway of my room before I detested her. I knew Mohammed would see her as I saw her."[582]

---

[582] Ibn Ishaq, *Sira* 729, p. 493; Tabari, *The History of al-Tabari,* vol. 8, p. 56.

It was Mohammed's custom to take one or more of his wives with him on his various expeditions from Medina, chosen either by rotation or by lot. On that expedition, Mohammed had taken Umm Salma and Ayesha, the latter being the infamous child bride whom Mohammed had married at age six and consummated the marriage when she was but nine years old. At the time of this expedition, she was still very young, about thirteen years old, but well versed in carnal pleasure due to Mohammed's assiduous tutelage. The choice of a child as his wife was scandalous even in the eyes of his own followers, and still more so in those of his countrymen in general.

The Scandal of Ayesha and Safwan

After Mohammed completed the successful raid against the Bani Mustaliq tribe and acquired his eighth wife, Juwairiya, he traveled back to Medina with his loot, halting in various places. During his last halt before Medina, Ayesha slipped off to satisfy a call of nature. The clasp on her precious necklace was insecure and, on her return to her *howdah,* she found that her necklace was missing. Without telling anyone, she went back to look for it. She found her necklace but when she came back to remount, she was astonished to find both the *howdah* and tent gone and no one anywhere in sight.

When they marched with him, each of Mohammed's wives, traveled on a camel in a *howdah,* carefully covered from public gaze by a veil. Ayesha's attendants had evidently assumed that she was in her *howdah* and behind the veil, so they lifted it and placed it on the camel's back. Since Ayesha was small and very light, no one would have noticed that she was not inside.

Although she was alone and deserted in the desert, Ayesha was not particularly worried because she thought the mistake soon would be discovered. Therefore, expecting the attendants to return for her, she lay down on the ground and fell fast sleep. Toward morning, Safwan ibn al-Mo'ttal Sahmi, who had dallied behind the raiding party, passed by and recognized Ayesha. He was quite surprised to find Mohammed's wife in such a predicament, so he offered his dromedary to Ayesha to ride to Medina. Ayesha gratefully accepted the offer so Safwan helped her mount, and together they ambled forth to Medina.

When the army returned to Medina from the expedition against the Bani Mustaliq, Ayesha's *howdah* was set down at the door of her house near the mosque. When it was opened, everyone was astonished and dismayed to find that she was not inside. Some hours afterward, Safwan, a young, attractive man, who had known Ayesha quite well before, appeared leading his camel, with Ayesha sitting upon it.

The incident soon became the beginning of a scandal that was to shake Medina. The usual scandal-mongers, sensing a juicy adulterous affair, loosed invectives against Ayesha. It was said that she had been seen talking with Safwan on several occasions before that. Chief among her accusers was Abdullah ibn Ubey, followed by her own cousin Mistah (a relative and dependant of Abu Bakr), Hamna, a favorite member of Mohammed's harem who rejoiced over the dishonor of a rival, and Mohammed's poet for propaganda, Hassan ibn Thabit. Hamna insinuated that Ayesha and Safwan had clandestinely met on several occasions and that the loss of the necklace was merely a pretext for a more private tête-à-tête.[583] The general consensus was that Ayesha been stricken by a fit of jealousy by Mohammed's marriage to Juwairiya and adding her to his harem. When these rumors reached Mohammed, he was deeply distressed for he loved his child-wife. Even so, he was not entirely convinced of her innocence.

Ayesha noticed Mohammed's change in behavior and fell sick. She asked her husband's permission to move to her parent's house where she could be looked after. Mohammed was at a loss and too embarrassed to turn to his usual companions for help and advice. He could not consult Abu Bakr about the man's own daughter. According to Sahih al-Buchari[584] Mohammed, being perturbed by the situation, finally called Ali ibn Abi Talib and Usma ibn Zaid and consulted them about divorcing Ayesha. Usma said that he knew the fine reputation of Mohammed's wives and advised him to keep Ayesha because he knew nothing but good about her. Ali, who was unsympathetic toward Ayesha, told his father-in-law bluntly,

---

[583] Emile Dermenghem, *The Life of Mahomet* (London: George Routledge & Sons Ltd., 1930), p. 279.

[584] *Sahih al-Bukhari,* vol. 3, pp. 504–512.

"Women are plentiful and you can easily change one for another, however, you should ask Ayesha's woman-servant, Buraira who will tell you the truth." This remark was brought to Ayesha who never forgot it. [Thirty years later when Ali's candidacy for the Caliphate came up, she opposed it so violently that it culminated in the first bloody civil war among the Muslims.]

Mohammed called Buraira and asked her whether she had ever seen Ayesha commit any suspicious activities. Buraira said, "I have never seen anything faulty about her except that she is a girl of immature age and when I am kneading dough and tell her to watch it, she neglects it and falls sleep and the sheep come and eat it."[585]

On that day Mohammed ascended the pulpit and requested that somebody volunteer to punish Abdullah ibn Ubey ibn Salul who had hurt him by slandering the reputation of his family. Usayd ibn Huydar got up and said if the slanderer is from the tribe of Aws, he will chop his head off, and if he is from Khazraj tribe, then he will order that he be done away with. Hearing this, Saad ibn Ubada, chief of the Khazraj and a Muslim got up and, motivated by loyalty to his tribe, said that he would never let any harm befall Abdullah ibn Ubey. The Aws and the Khazraj were at loggerheads and about to fight each other, but Mohammed, with some difficulty, cooled them down.

Finally, Mohammed realized that the longer he vacillated, the worse scandal would grow. Therefore, he went to Abu Bakr's home and, in front of her parents, told Ayesha,

"If you are guilty, then confess and repent to Allah, because he will accept the repentance of his servants."

Ayesha burst into a passionate flood of tears, and exclaimed, "There is nothing that I should repent, because Allah knows that I am innocent; therefore, I shall follow the example of Joseph's father and remain patient."

Even if Mohammed believed Ayesha guilty, it was not politic to make an issue over the matter since any discredit falling on Abu Bakr would have a deleterious affect on his own cause and risk the alienation of a hitherto faithful ally.[586] Therefore, Mohammed reverted to his usual means of obtaining his ends and fell into a

---

[585] A. Guillume, *The Life of Muhammad,* p. 496.

[586] Margoliouth, *Mohammed and the Rise of Islam,* p.342.

cataleptic fit. They covered him with a blanket and placed a pillow under is head. When his paroxysms subsided, he slowly opened his eyes and a smile appeared on his face. He rose up and said,

"Ayesha, good news for you, Allah has recognized your innocence." He went on to pretend that Gabriel had revealed verses 4 and 23 of *Sura* XXIV of the Koran concerning the innocence of his beloved child-wife.

> "And those who launch a charge against chaste women and Produce not four witnesses. . . . .Flog them with eighty stripes and reject their evidence. . . ." (Koran, XXIV: 4)
> "Those who slander chaste women, indiscreet but believing Are cursed in this life and in the hereafter. . . ." (Koran, XXIV: 23)

Ayesha simply replied, "I shall neither thank him (Mohammed), nor will I thank the both of you (alluding to her parents), who listened to the slander and did not deny it. I will only thank Allah alone, praise be to Allah."[587]

Then Mohammed walked out of the Abu Bakr's house, and standing before the Mosque, he announced the so-called revelation he had received from heaven which forms the Islamic law covering slander to the present day (see above *Sura* XXIV: 4).To carry out Allah's command, Mohammed ordered the so-called heavenly ordained punishment to be inflicted upon Hassan ibn Thabit, Hamna, and a friend of Abu Bakr named Mistah. Abdullah ibn Ubey, who was really the cause of the whole trouble, was spared because Mohammed was still not powerful enough to challenge him.

Was Ayesha really guilt of adultery or innocent? Bodley has elucidated the weak points of her claim of innocence as follows:

1. How was it that Ayesha, knowing that the caravan was preparing to move, ran off without telling anybody and spent a long time looking for the necklace? The time element here is important.
2. An Arab raiding force requires quite a while to pack up and move, especially a large one. Even when the main group of

---

[587] Armstrong, *Muhammad, A Western Attempt to Understand Mohammad,* p. 202.

camels is on its way, there are some who lag behind. Nor does a camel train move fast; two miles an hour is a good average. Therefore, to return to the camp and find no sign of the caravan, no sign of any laggards, no sight of the hundreds of men and animals in a country where there is little cover to the horizon, must have meant that Ayesha looked for her necklace for several hours.

3. Ayesha says that after she was left behind, she went to sleep. Let us assume that her nap did not exceed one hour; from where did Safwan appear over three hours after Mohammed and his troops had departed?

4. Ayesha was heard to say in later years that it was well known that Safwan was impotent. How could she have known that? Doesn't this statement prove her guilt rather than her innocence?[588]

5. Why didn't Ayesha simply tell her attendants to help her find her lost necklace thus avoid putting herself into such a miserable predicament?

Rodinson in his book, *Mohammed* quotes the author Carlo Levy who says, concerning the Lucanian[589] peasants:

"Love or sexual attraction is regarded by the peasants as a force of nature of such power that no will is strong enough to fight it. When a man and a woman find themselves alone together without witnesses nothing can keep them from each other's arms. No amount of resolution, chastity or any other obstacle can restrain them and if by any chance they do not actually make love, they might just as well have done. Simply being together amounts to making love."[590]

If Ayesha were really guilty of having an affair with Safwan that night in the desert, then she must have realized that when her husband produced a putative verse from God absolving her, he was lying and hence not a prophet.

---

[588] Bodley, *The Life of Mohammed,* pp. 224–225.

[589] A district in ancient Italy between the Tyrrhenian Sea and the Gulf of Tarentum (Toranto).

[590] Carlo Levy, *Crist se e fermato a Eboli,* French trans. Jeanne Modigliani (Paris: Gallimard, 1948), p. 93, quoted in Rodinson. *Mohammed,* p. 200.

Chapter Ten

The Intimidating
Character of the Koran

It was fear that first brought gods into the world.
Arbiter Petronius, *Satyricon*, c. 50.

Why does a person read a book and why does an author write a book? The purpose of both is to generate a change. Moreover, this change should be definitely "positive and constructive," and not "negative and destructive." The author writes to generate change in his readers and the reader reads a book to bring about change in his self. Some people think that the purpose of reading a book is to learn something new. This may be true, but certainly the learning process does not stop at the final chapter of a book. A book should act as an intellectual bulldozer, clearing the way for the discovery of new horizons and, eventually, leading to positive change. But this intellectual discovery will transcend the literal meaning of "discovery," and should be called "real discovery." The real act of discovery lies not in finding new lands, but in seeing with new eyes.

However, neither more than the 62,000 verses of the Koran nor the *Hadith* ever teach the reader anything new. They never broaden the mentality of the reader; rather they stultify the brain, filling it with boring senseless details, misleading superstitious absurdities, and threats of barbarous punishments *ad nauseam*.

Throughout the Koran we find warnings and threats that Allah's power is hanging over one's life like Damocles' sword and any deviation from His path will bring merciless punishment or death to the backslider. Allah warns His Muslim servants to be afraid of him and His harsh punishments 235 times in the Koran. The following are few verses with which Allah tries to instill fear in the mind of the believers.

" . . . Do not fear them; fear me. . . ." (Koran, II: 150)
"He sends down the angels with the spirit by His command upon whom He pleases of His servants, (saying): There is not God but me, therefore, fear me." (Koran, XVI: 1)

"O you who believe! Fear Allah as He should be feared and do not die except in a state of Islam." (Koran, III: 102)

" . . . And fear Allah: because Allah is swift in taking account." (Koran, V: 4)

" . . . Have fear of Allah. . . ." (Koran, V: 7, 8, 11)

"Those who reject faith and deny Our revelations, they shall become the people of Hell." (Koran, V: 10)

"Can they not see how many generations We have destroyed before them, whom We had made more powerful in the land than you, sending down for them abundant water from the sky and giving them rivers that rolled at their feet? Yet because they sinned, We destroyed then all and raised up other generations after them." (Koran, VI: 6)

"Are the people of the towns feeling secure from the coming of Our wrath upon them as a night-raid while they are sleep?" (Koran, VII: 97)

"Or are the people of the towns feeling secure from the coming of Our wrath upon them in the day time when they play?" (Koran, VII: 98)

"Are they then secure from Allah's artifice? But no one can feel secure from the artifice of Allah, except the lost people." (Koran, VII: 99)

"The true believers are those whose hearts are filled with fear at the mention of Allah . . . . ." (Koran, VIII: 2)

"O you, who believe, fight the unbelievers who are near you and let them find themselves in you. Know that Allah is with those who fear them." (Koran, IX: 123)

"How many towns We have destroyed while it was sinful, so that it lies in ruins, and how many a deserted well and lofty place!" (Koran, XXII: 45)

"Surely they are in doubt about my reminder (this Koran). But they have not tasted my torment yet!" (Koran, XXXVIII: 8)

"The unbelievers shall have layers of fire above them and layers of fire below them. By this Allah puts fear into His servant's hearts. Fear me then, my servants" (Koran, XXXIX: 6)

Tabari quotes the sermon of Mohammed at the first Friday prayer as the following:

"Allah says, 'Fear me, then, in this world and the next, in secret and in public. He who fears me will have his evil deeds forgiven and his reward magnified; he will achieve a great success. The fear of me will ward off my hatred and retribution and wrath. The fear of me will make people blameless in the sight of me, will please me and will raise their degree.'"[591]

Islam is a phobic religion whereas Buddhism, Zoroastrianism, and Confucianism that do not promise a heavenly Paradise may be considered didactic ameliorative religions. Only a few injunctions in the Koran are free of Allah's threats of severe punishments for disobedience to his wishes. We know that there was never a Divine authority in the sky called Allah issuing preposterous threatening injunctions to his servants in order to secure their obedience; rather it was the fantasies of an ambitious, cruel and rapacious human being (Mohammed) who made up the god and his decrees in order to further his own ends and attain power.

Mohammed was a product of the primitive Bedouin tribes of the early 7th century. In that era humanism, defined as the "inalienable rights" of the individual, was a concept never dreamed of and obedience enforced by fear and brutal terrorism was a norm of life. Brutal use of force applied sufficiently and well, will foster concurrence with any principle or order in most people. Of course, there is always the principled martyr but, by definition, he is soon eliminated from the equation.

Being a canny individual, Mohammed knew that religious fervor was one of the easiest and most effective ways to secure dominance over most people. The Prophets of Judaism and Christianity had already used the instrument of faith to induce others to acknowledge God and follow the path of righteousness, now it was Mohammed's turn to subvert the religious faith of the Arabs and use it as an instrument to achieve power and authority.

Mohammed recognized that religious faith had to be conceived and nursed by fear and terror of an unseen authoritative source and that he should make himself the representative of such source. In this way, fear of that unseen divinely authoritative source could in turn engender obedience to himself as its representative. Fear serves Islam the same way it serves all the totalitarian societies—it forces obedience. Throughout time, selfish despots like Mohammed have risen to infamy and fortune through fear and intimidation. Fear

---

[591] Tabari, *The History of al-Tabari,* vol. 7, pp. 2–4.

is the reason for the blind obedience characteristic of every Muslim society.[592]

Mohammed found it profitable to frighten his followers with a hateful God who was eager to torture them. His terrible description of hell is an example of such a strategy. Nowhere in the paraphernalia of Mohammed's bag of tricks was there a more suitable appellation for God than Allah. The idol of Allah was historically the greatest idol of Ka'ba and the Arabs were already conditioned to worship him. Therefore, it would serve Mohammed's cause better than any thing else.

An old Chinese proverb says, "Kill one, and [you will] frighten ten thousand." Also, Seneca said, "It is, as a rule, unseen terrors that have the most powerful effect on men's minds."[593] Fear and intimidation have long been instrumentalities of human coercion. In particular, hidden, silent fears have a great impact on human thoughts and behavior. Once fear has penetrated the minds of the people, it will fill their thoughts and, involuntarily, mold their behavior.

Mohammed was not a psychologist, but he was smart enough to base his self-made faith on the fear of an unseen authority which he called Allah, after the largest of the idols of Ka'ba. Throughout the preposterous injunctions of the Koran, this Allah intimidates his servants by threatening the most excruciating punishments that any cruel and barbarous human being could think of. Other than retribution, the object of punishment is to coerce others into obedience by demonstrating the fate of the disobedient. Obedience is what Islam hopes to attain by its threats of Divine punishment as written in the Koran. All rulers or governing bodies, from pre-historic times to date, have resorted to punishment in one form or another in order in ensure obedience to law or sovereign decree. This is true whether it be a destructive tribal chieftain, an emperor or an enlightened democracy.

In the beginning, Mohammed did not have the power to inflict punishment personally and directly upon disobedient Arabs, so he called himself Allah's Messenger and summoned Allah's punishment down upon those who did not obey him.

---

[592] Winn, *Muhammad, Prophet of Doom,* p. 206.

[593] Seneca, *Epistolae,* LVI., 10.

James Freedman Clarke writes, "Islam saw God, but not man; saw the claims of destiny, not the rights of humanity; saw authority, failed to see freedom—therefore hardened into despotism, stiffened into formalism, and sank into death."[594]

Furthermore, as it was mentioned before, in the Koran Allah characterizes himself as deceitful, an avenger, a subduer, a compeller, proud, dominating, and so on. In most of the verses Allah says he is omnipotent and omniscient; therefore, everyone should fear him. The punishment of infidels, according to the Koran, does not begin only in the life hereafter; it includes punishments of all kind in the present life. Naturally, such a draconic god does not have the attributes of a humanitarian or benevolent mentor. That is why the Koran is an intimidating hodgepodge of absurdities rather than a handbook of moral, uplifting guidance.

Paradise

According to the Koran and Islam, Muslims in the next world live either in everlasting physical torture or physical and sensual joys. The sinful Muslims will be tortured to death in hell, but faithful Muslims, the virtuous, the devout, the martyrs, the repentant souls, those who have suffered in the cause of Allah will enjoy, as the Allah has promised, the sensual delight of paradise, a place of bliss and perpetual happiness (II: 25). The word "paradise" occurs only twice in the Koran; on one occasion in conjunction with gardens "*Jannat*" (XVII: 107) and the second time by itself (XXIII: 11). Therefore, it is the word "garden" which is generally used to indicate the abiding place for the righteous. These "gardens" or paradise extends over the whole of the heavens and the earth, i.e., the whole universe (III: 132, LVII: 21).[595] Vivid pictures of Heaven and Hell are painted in colors of material joy and torment; which however absurd and childish to

---

[594] James Freedman Clarke, *Ten Great Religions,* 2 vols. (New York: Houghton, Mifflin and Company, 1886), vol., I, p. 86.

[595] Maulana Muhammad Ali, *The Religion of Islam* (Lahore, Pakistan: Ahmadiyya Anjuman Isha'at-i-Islam, 1983), p. 282.

our conceptions, were well calculated to affect a deep impression on the simple Arab mind.[596] The sensual delights of Mohammed's paradise are proverbial and on the basis of the Koran it can be said that the Islamic paradise is a lecher's dream.

What the Islamic chronicalers say on these texts is often unbelievable for a sound person. The *hadith* give minute particulars of the sanitary laws of heaven, as well as of its sexual delight. Al Ghazzali (A.H. 450), one of the great theologians of Islam whom no Muslim would dispute, wrote that Mohammed said, "The believer in paradise will marry five hundred houris, four thousand virgins and eight thousand divorced women." Ghazzali continues, "things which eye saw not and which did not enter the heart of man."[597]

The Muslim paradise in the words of the Koran is a garden of delight, "underneath which rivers flow interminably" (II: 25 etc.), "purifies spouses" (II:25, III: 15), "God's good pleasure" (III: 15 etc.), "a shelter of plenteous shade" (IV: 57), with cushions set in rows, and rich carpets, (LXXXVIII: 13–16, "forgiveness and a generous provision" (VIII: 4 etc.) wherein the believers clothed in green garments of fine silk and brocades recline on jeweled green couches in the shade of thornless trees with gushing fountains all around (XV: 4, XVIII: 31, XLVII: 17 etc.). They drink from the sweet waters of a fountain, from rivers of milk forever fresh, and rivers of clearest honey (XLVII: 15–17). Silver cups full of delectable aromatic wines dipped from ever-flowing rivers are placed before them by beautiful youths. They eat from clusters of fruits whose season is not limited, especially dates, grapes and pomegranates. All that the soul of man could desire or the eye could delight in are there in abundance and within easy reach. (LVI: 10–24, LXXVI: 19)

The consumption of alcoholic beverages is forbidden to the faithful in their earthly lives but Mohammed shrewdly includes the promise of endless rivers of wine after death as a reward to conversion to Islam. Omar Khayyam, the great Persian poet, satirist, mathematician and astronomer, often extols the pleasure of a glass or

---

[596] Muir, *The Life of Mohammad,* p. 74.

[597] Ghazzali, IV, 338, quoted by Samuel M. Zwemer, *Islam: A Challenge to Faith* (London: Darf Publishers Limited, 1985), pp. 94–95.

two of wine and, in one of his famous quatrains, lampoons this nebulous promise:

> *Of Paradise, they talk of angels sweet;*
> *The juice of grapes I hold no better treat;*
> *Ah, take the cash and let the credit go;*
> *Sweet sounds the drum when distant is the beat.*

In the often described shady garden "with fruits and meats, and beakers of wine causing not the head to ache, neither disturbing the reason," (LXIX: 21–24, LXXXIII: 25, LXXVI; 17) are those damsels of paradise described as "lovely large-eyed Houris [girls] resembling pearls hidden in their shells with swelling bosoms whom neither man nor jinns have touched before them. . . . .of equal age and remain virgins who are different from the daughters of men and all that your souls desire (LV: 46–56; XLIV, 54; LXI: 35–38, LII: 21ff; LVI: II ff.), (XLI, 31 etc.)

The foregoing paragraph again illustrates the low position of women in the Islamic community. All of the sexual fantasies promised are to satisfy the male lusts; not even a show with the Chippendale dancers is promised to female believers!

According to Bayazid Bastami (d. ca. 261/874), all the faithful will see Allah once in the paradise, but after that only the elect will continue to see Him. Because, in Paradise is a market where there is no buying or selling, only the forms of men and women, when a man desires a form, he enters into it. Those who enter a form will never again visit God: "God misleads you in this life as to the market, and also in the next; you will always be enslaved to the market."[598]

In view of all the nonsensical imageries conjured by the descriptions of the paradise awaiting the faithful, it seems that not only in

---

[598] William C. Chittick, "Escathology," In *The passion of al-Hallaj: Mystic and Martyr of Islam,* L. Massignon, trans. H. Mason (Princeton, New Jersey:Princeton University Press, 1982), 3: 166–67, quoted in *Islamic Spirituality Foundations,* Seyyed Hossein Nasr, ed. (New York: Crossroad, 1991), p. 405.

our earthly world Allah misleads His servants; he will continue this deception in paradise as well!

Hell

No human being, no matter how cruel he might be, could imagine such a place as the Islamic Hell. Hell in Islam is a fiery place where sinners are subjected to continual agonizing torture. The Koran equates Hell with fire. *Jahannam,* the Arabic word for "Hell," is mentioned at least thirty times in the Koran. Of all the world's religions, Islam is the most uncompromising in its conception of Hell. The concept is crude and barbarous; the torments are brutal and bear no relation whatsoever to the sinner's alleged faults.[599]

"Mohammed really let his otherwise limited imagination go wild when inventing the macabre place and the torments of Hell: boiling water, running sores, peeling skin, burning flesh, dissolving bowels, and crushing of skulls with iron maces. Verse 69 of *Sura* XIX, confirms that unbelievers will roast forever."[600]

According to the Koran:

"There is not one of you who shall not pass through it (Hell). Such is the absolute decree of your Lord which must be accomplished. We will deliver those who fear us, but the wrongdoers shall be left there on their knees."

The above verse does not say that the Lord Allah will save those who are righteous and faithful to him, rather it states that only those who **fear** him will be saved from His punishment. In Islam even children are not immune from the fires of Hell. There is a *hadith* that says

---

[599] Stanely Lane-Poole, *Studies in A Mosque* (London and Sidney: Eden, Remington and Company, 1983), p. 310.

[600] Ibn Warraq, *Why I am not A Muslim,* p.125.

infants at birth possess a primordial conformity[601] with truth; then their parents turn them into Jews, Christians or Muslims; that is, they acquire a way of life. From this one might assume that children who die before the age of reason are saved by virtue of their innate knowledge.[602] However, the theologian al-Ashari quotes the following *hadith* from Mohammed:

> "A fire will be kindled for all children on the Day that Death shall rise; and they will be commanded: 'Leap into the fire!' And every child who leaps in the fire will I bring into Paradise. But every child who will not, I shall cause to enter Hell."[603]

In other words, according to this doctrine, children who die before they have had the opportunity to be responsible for their own salvation are saved if, in their essential [predestined?] nature, they are truly innocent.[604] One *hadith* also reports that there are more women in Hell than men. As narrated by Usama, "the Prophet said, 'I stood at the gate of Fire (Hell) and found that the majority of the people entering it were women.'"[605]

When traditional Muslims mention hell in conversation, by reflex they invoke God's protection, for themselves and for the listener, because the portent of the word is frightening and its enunciation may be taken as a dreadful omen.[606] Below is an anthology of the barbaric punishments of Allah in the Koran:

> "Those who reject our revelations, we shall soon cast into fire; as often as their skins are roasted through, we shall change them for fresh skins, that they may taste the penalty: for Allah is exalted in Power and Wise." (Koran, IV: 56)
>
> "Thus Allah will separate the wicked from the just. He will heap the wicked one upon another and then heap them together and cast them in Hell. Such are those that shall be lost." (Koran, VIII: 37)

---

601 In Arabic, this "primordial conformity" is called *"fitrat."*

602 Quoted by Cyril Glasse, *The Concise Encyclopedia of Islam* (London: Stacey International, 1989), p. 86.

603 *Ibid.*

604 *Ibid.*

605 *Sahih al-Bukhari,* vol. 8, p. 363.

606 *Ibid.* p. 153.

"Are they not aware that the man who defies Allah and his Apostle shall abide for ever in the fire of Hell?" (Koran, IX: 63)

"Who is a better man, he who founds his house on the fear of Allah and His good pleasure or he who builds his foundation on an undermined sand-cliff, ready to crumble to pieces? And it does crumble to pieces with him, into the fire of Hell. And Allah does not guide the wrongdoers." (Koran, IX: 109)

". . . I will fill Hell with jinns and men all together." (Koran, XI: 119)

"For those who obey, Allah is good. But those who disobey him—if they possessed all that the earth contains, and as much besides, they would gladly offer it for their ransom. Theirs shall be an evil reckoning. Hell shall be their home, a dismal resting-place." (Koran, XIII: 18)

"In front of every sinner is Hell, and he is given for drink, boiling stinking water. He takes it in portions, but he cannot swallow it. Death will come to him from every quarter, yet he shall not die. A dreadful torment is before him." (Koran, XIV: 16, 17)

"He that desires this fleeting life, we readily grant him such things, but in the end we provide Hell for him; he will burn in it despised and helpless." (Koran, XVII: 18)

"So, by Lord, without doubt, we shall gather them together and also Satan with them; then we shall bring them forth on their knees round about Hell." (Koran, XIV: 68)

"And we shall drive the sinners to Hell, like thirsty cattle driven to water." (Koran, XIV: 86)

"Verily, he who comes to his Lord as a sinner, for him is Hell: therein shall he never die or live." (Koran, XX: 74)

"You and all those that you worship besides Allah shall be the fuel of Hell; there you surely come." (Koran XXI: 98)

"The unbelievers are entertained in the Hell with the Tree of Zaqqum. We have made this tree a trial for the wrongdoers. It is a tree that grows in the bottom of Hell, bearing fruit like devil's heads: on it they shall feed, and with it they shall feel their bellies. On top of that they will be given a mixture made of scalding water. Then to Hell they shall return." (Koran, XXXVII: 62–68)

"They shall burn in the fire of Hell, a dismal resting-place." (Koran XXXVIII: 56)

"Who does more wrong than the man who invents a lie about Allah and denies the truth when it comes to him? Is there not a home in Hell for disbelievers?" (Koran, XXXIX: 32)

"On the day of Resurrection, you shall see those who uttered falsehood about Allah—their faces will be turned black. Is there not in Hell a home for the arrogant?" (Koran, XXXIV: 60)

"Those in the fire will say to its keepers: "Implore your Lord to relieve our torment for one day!" (Koran, XL: 49)

" . . . But those who disgrace me shall enter Hell disgraced." (Koran, XL: 60)

"The sinners will be in the punishment of Hell. Their punishment will never be lightened and they shall be speechless with despair." (Koran, XLIII: 74, 75)

"And that He may punish the hypocrites and the idolaters, men and women, who think evil thoughts concerning Allah. A turn of evil shall befall them, and Allah's wrath is on them. He has laid on them His curse and prepared for them the fire of Hell: an evil fate." (Koran, XLVIII: 6)

"Have you heard of the overwhelming event? On that day there shall be downcast faces, broken and worn out, burnt by a scorching fire, drinking from a seething fountain. Their only food shall be bitter thorns, which will neither sustain nor satisfy hunger." (Koran, LXXXVIII: 1–7)

"(Then a voice will cry): 'Cast into Hell every hardened unbeliever, every opponent of good works, and every doubting transgressor who has set up another God besides Allah. Hurl him into terrible doom.'" (Koran, L: 23, 24)

"On that day, we will ask Hell: 'Are you full?' And Hell will answer: 'Are there any more?'" (Koran, L: 30)

"For a disbeliever is entertainment with boiling water and burning in Hell-fire." (Koran, LVI: 94, 95)

"Do you not see those who were forbidden secret counsels, and then they return to that which they are forbidden and hold secret counsels for inquiry and hostility and disobedience of the Messenger? When they come to you they salute you in words not as Allah salutes you and ask themselves: 'Why does not Allah punish us for what we say?' Enough for them is Hell: They shall burn in its flames, a wretched fate.'" (Koran, LVII: 8)

"But those that do wrong shall become the fuel of Hell." (Koran, LXXII: 15)

"Those who disbelieve, among the people of the Book (Jews and Christians), and the pagans shall burn for ever in the fire of Hell. They are the worst of creatures." (Koran, XCVIII: 6)

"On the day when they are dragged into the fire on their faces, (We shall say to them): 'Feel the touch of Hell.'" (Koran, LIV: 48)

The above verses are only a few out of more than one hundred and fifty verses wherein the Koran mentions Hell and the excruciating pains that the disbelievers are supposed to suffer as a result of the Hell-fire. In addition to those, there are also more than 360 verses in the Koran that talk about the various tortures that Allah inflicts upon his servants in the hereafter. Some of the verses mentioned above require comment:

In verse 56 of *Sura* IV, Allah threatens that if his servants reject his revelations, he will cast them into fire and roast their skins. There is a point in this verse that needs elucidation. When Allah speaks about his revelations, which of his revelations does he mean? The ones that he dictated to Moses and are written in the Old Testament; those that he revealed to his son, Jesus Christ; or the verses of the Koran, which he had sent down via Mohammed? Is this not a crazy, inconsistent God who first sends Prophets with certain instructions for human behavior, then sends a Messenger with new injunctions that tell him to kill those who follow His previous injunctions and His first Prophets?

In verse 68 of *Sura* XIX, Allah swears to himself that without doubt he will bring the sinners forth on their knees round Hell. It can be asserted that no person in this world has sinned against God as much as Mohammed. In Islam and the Koran, Allah is a plastic entity that Mohammed shapes to meet his needs, i. e. to further his ambitious goals. It is actually the voice of Mohammed that is purportedly issuing from Allah's mouth. That is why Allah seems a multidimensional entity in the Koran, an obedient servant that Mohammed uses for any occasion from managing the harem affairs of his wives to swearing to punish mercilessly whosoever disagrees with his beloved Messenger.

The tenor of verses 32 and 60 of *Sura* XXXIX mentioned above is so interesting that it really begs a logical commentary. Both verses say there is no greater sin than promulgating a lie about Allah and the place for anyone who dares commit such a sin is Hell. How does this verse relate to Mohammed? The verse specifies "those who invent a lie concerning Allah," but what about an impostor who invents a God? If Hell is to be the abode of a sinner who invents a lie concerning Allah, undoubtedly an Impostor, who invents a God and forges a whole book of superstitious scripture allegedly from his tongue, should be consigned to that place the transcendent genius of Dante Alighieri designed for him. In Dante's everlasting masterpiece, Mohammed is assigned to the eighth of the nine ditches of the Inferno, that series of gloomy trenches surrounding Satan's stronghold in Hell.

Thus before Mohammed reaches Hell, he passes through circles containing people whose sins are of a lesser order; the lustful, the avaricious, the gluttonous, the heretics, the wrathful, the suicidal, and the blasphemous. After Mohammed there are only the liars and the treacherous, before one arrives at the very bottom of hell, where Satan also is to be found. Mohammed thus belongs to a rigid hierarchy of evil, in the cateloge of evils. Mohammed's punishment, which is also his eternal fate, is a peculiarly disguising one.[607]

In this ditch, he is overwhelmed by the sight of mutilated, bloody shades many of whom are ripped open with the entrails spilling out. These are the purveyors of scandal and schism, and among them are Mohammed, Ali, Pier da Medicina, Gaius Scribonius Curio, Moca De' Lamberti, and Bertran De Born. All bemoan their painful lot, and Mohammed and Pier da Medicina relay warnings through the pilgrim to certain living Italians who are soon to meet terrible ends.[608]

Dante's encounter with Mohammed is explained as follows:

No wine barrel burst apart with scattered planks gaped wider than the soul I saw split down from where his chin was down to where he farts.

Between his legs his guts spilled out, with the heart and other vital parts, and the dirty sackshit whatever the mouth gulps down.

While I stood staring into his misery, he stared straight at me and with both hands he opened his chest and said: "See how I tear myself!" See how Mohammed is deformed and torn!

In front of me, and weeping, Ali walks, his face sliced from the hairline to his chin.

The souls that you see passing in this ditch were all sowers of scandal and schism in life, and so in death you see them torn asunder.

A devil stands back there who trims us all in this cruel way, and each one of this mob receives anew the blade of the devil's sword each time we make one round of this sad road, because the wounds

---

[607] Edward W. Said, *Orientalism* (New York: Pantheon Books, 1978), p. 68.

[608] Dante Alighieri, *Inferno,* trans and ed. Mark Musa (Bloomington and Indianapolis: Indiana University press, 1995), p. 13.

have all healed up again by the time, each one presents himself once more.[609]

The gist of the discussion of this section and the verses mentioned above, not only shows that the Koran is an intimidating book, void of any ameliorating or didactic character, it seems to have been produced by a sadistic individual. Instead of teaching moral values to the Muslims and guiding them to a better life, the contents of the Koran mostly threaten that Allah will roast the skin of the sinners in fire; that He will fill out Hell with *jinns* and humans; that Allah will crumble the sinners to pieces and cast them into fire; that they are given scalding stinky water to drink; that death will come from every quarter to them, yet they shall not die or live; that they are used as the fuel of Hell; that He will bring the sinners forth on their knees round about Hell; that He shall drive them to Hell, like thirsty cattle driven to water; that He will fed them with bitter thorn; that they are dragged into the fire on their faces, and so on.

Bertrand Russell brilliantly says, "I really do not think that a person with a proper degree of kindliness in his nature would have put fears and terrors of that sort into the world."[610] And Gibb said, "Man must live in constant fear and awe of [Allah], and always be on his guard against Him—such is the idiomatic meaning of the term for 'fearing God' which runs through the Koran from cover to cover."[611]

Thus, it seems safe to say that the contents of that book called the Koran introduces into the hearts and minds of Muslims a fear, rather than love, of God and no shred of compassion toward fellow humans.

Is Allah "Just"

If we believe there is a *"just"* god in the world then the theory of "prophethood" is not only disparate with the justice of God, it is

---

[609] Dante Alighieri, *Inferno,* trans and illust. Tom Phillips (United Kingdom: Thames and Hudson, 1985), p. 226.

[610] Bertrand Russell, *Why I am not A Christian* (London: National Secular Society, 1970), p. 19.

[611] Gibb, H. A. R. *Islam* (Oxford: 1953), p. 38, quoted by Ibn Warraq, *Why I am not a Muslim,* p. 127.

even against it. To substantiate the authenticity of this idea, we have but to glance at the theory of *"justice"* and the *"just"* action. Among the different meanings of the adjective *"just"* listed in the *Oxford English Dictionary* are: morally right or righteous; that which is equitable; what confirms to the standard of right, proper or correct, in accordance with reason, truth or fact; appropriate or suitable; exact; equal, even or level; complete in amount or character, proper or regular.

Most authors who have dealt with this topic believe that *justice* is defined by equality of treatment with regard to the weighing of differing considerations and claims, followed by a dispassionate judgment rendered in accordance with law. Even the utilitarian concept requires that justice be aimed at achieving the greatest usefulness for the greatest number and that judgmental results be evaluated from the viewpoint of equality of treatment.[612] Justice is based on the premise that there is a contractual consent by all parties to accept a fair and unbiased rendering of a decision and abide by it. The significance of this theory is that a just state of affairs is one that people can accept not merely in the sense that they cannot reasonably *expect* to get more but in the stronger sense that they cannot reasonably *claim* more.[613]

The motive for behaving justly is the desire to seek an agreement with others without the use of morally irrelevant bargaining advantages and disadvantages. This characteristic of justice is called by Brian Barry "justice of impartiality," in contrast to what might be called "justice as mutual advantage." The significance of "justice as impartiality" is that it requires that people should not look at things merely from their own viewpoint but should seek to find a basis of agreement that is acceptable from all points of view.[614]

The purpose of the above discourse about *"justice,"* is to show that a God who chooses an individual from among millions of his ser-

---

[612] John Chapman, "Justice and Fairness," in *Justice,* eds. Carl J. Friedrich and John W. Chapman, (New York: Atherton Press, 1963), pp. 158–59.

[613] *Ibid.*

[614] Brian M., Barry. *Theories of Justice* (Los Angeles: University of California Press, 1989), pp. 7–8.

vants (in particular one who is a lecherous cameleer) and requires all peoples of the world and future generations to comply with his selfish ambitions is not merely an "*unjust*" God, but a deranged one.

How could a God who picks a cruel, rapacious Arab from among all His other creatures and requires His angels to bless him and whom He Himself salutes (Koran, XXXIII: 56), be called "*just?*" Why didn't this caricature of a God choose his Messenger from one of the many brilliant philosophers who have contributed so much to the promotion of human ethics and the well-being of society?

When the Koran gives Mohammed the unique privilege to possess any woman who offers herself to him so that he does not have any difficulty in satisfying his sensual desires, is this compatible with the principle of "equality of treatment" explained above? When, in the same verse Allah clearly says that he grants this privilege *exceptionally* to Mohammed and not any other believer, is he following the principles of a *just* entity, much less that of an Omniscient, Wise, and All-Knowing God?

The content of verse 12 of *Sura* LVIII orders the people to pay a fee to Mohammed before they start talking to him. Verse 1 of *Sura* 8 and verse 41 of *Sura* VIII assign one-fifth all the spoils of war to Mohammed when physical combat took place but, in the absence of actual combat, all captured lands and chattel become the property of His Prophet. Are these pronouncements of Allah consistent with the principles of "justice of impartiality" explained above?

The contractual theory of justice requires that people not turn a bargaining power into an advantage and not unreasonably claim more than is proper and moral, but Mohammed's Allah ignores these humane ethical principles and orders his creatures to give alms and charity to Mohammed and abandon their shares of booty to him. What a *just* Allah!

If, on the basis of the basis of the above discussion, it is not possible to find any reason to believe in the *justice* of Allah as revealed in the Koran, then it is easy to prove by that same book that Islam teaches sedition and conspiracy. There are many verses in the Koran to prove this idea; but only a few verses will be mentioned as follows:

> "O believers, when you encounter the infidels gathered (for battle) do not turn your backs to them in flight. Unless it be in a stratagem of war, or to join another band, he shall incur the wrath of Allah and Hell shall be his home: an evil fate." (Koran, VIII: 16)

In verse 183 of *Sura* VII and in verse 45 of *Sura* LXVIII, Allah says, "My guile is strong," and in verse 54 of *Sura* III and verse 30 of *Sura* VIII he brags that he is a "conspirator" and "a very bad one."

When several times Allah himself emphasizes in the Koran that he is a "conspirator," "guileful," an "avenger," "misleading," and the like, how can any Islamic apologist—no matter how ingenious he is—talk about the *"justice"* of Allah?

The indiscriminant *"justice"* of Allah is shown in the following verse wherein he predestines his human creatures as well as his invisible creatures (*jinns*) to the fires of Hell:

> "We have *predestined*[615] for Hell many jinns and many men. They have hearts, yet they cannot understand; eyes, yet they cannot see; and ears, yet they cannot hear. They are like cattle—indeed, they are the most misguided. . . ." (Koran, VII: 178)

Furthermore, in this verse, Allah has given his servants heart, but not understanding, eyes but not vision, and ears but not hearing! What a *just* and humanitarian Allah! Above all, this *just* Allah is so polite that he calls his human creatures "cattle." Speaking about the Allah's courtesy, it is not only in this verse that he calls his human creatures "thirsty cattle," in verse L of *Sura* 74, he calls them "frightened asses" and in verse 57 of *Sura* XXI, he addresses his human creatures and says' "fie upon you." The Islamic hooligans and terrorists are justifiably proud of such an Allah and blindly follow his instructions for annihilation of human civilization.

---

[615] The word has been italicized by the author.

CHAPTER ELEVEN

PSYCHOLOGY OF MOHAMMED

Man is a strange being; he cannot make a flea, and yet he will make gods by dozens.
    Essays (1580–88), tr. Charles Cottonj and W. C. Hazlih

Allah does not like exultant.
    (The Koran, XXVIII: 76)

Detailed analysis of Mohammed's biography leads one to conclude that he suffered from some form of psychosis and probably a neurological disorder, as well. Any person who, among other atrocities, orders and watches 700 innocent people beheaded and beds the wife of a man whom he had tortured to death that very night cannot be considered psychologically normal. In the first chapter of this book we noted that Mohammed's father died before he was born and his mother passed away when he was only six years old. The latter incident had a big impact on the psychological make up of Mohammed and this will be analyzed in this chapter in addition to other factors that perverted his thinking, his behavior and his personality.

Epilepsy

Koelle speculates that the early death of both his parents may have been due to some type of genetically transferable defect and Mohammed inherited it from them.[616] Mohammed twice claimed hallucinatory episodes, once in the desert as a child under the care of a

---

[616] S. W. Koelle, *Mohammed and Mohammedanism*, p. 37.

Bedouin wet-nurse and the other time when he took his so-called sky trip. On both occasions, he insisted that two men clothed in white came down from the sky, seized him, threw him down and opened up his body from his throat down to his private parts.[617] According to his biographers, these hallucinations indicate that Mohammed suffered from epilepsy.

Sahih al-Bukhari, collected many *hadith* describing Mohammed's attacks and attributed his symptoms to epilepsy or some other brain disorder. As an example, Sahih al-Bukhari writes that "Mohammed would sometimes fall down on the ground" (vol. 5, p. 303); "he fell unconscious on the ground with both his eyes toward the sky. When he came to his senses, he said, 'My waist sheet! My waist sheet!' Then he tied his waist sheet (round his waist)." (vol. 5, pp. 108–109). When he would lie down on the ground, his lips would tremble (vol. 1, p. 5). He used to hear and see things no one else would hear or see (vol. 1, p. 2; vol. 4, pp. 302–303; vol. 6, p. 420).[618] One of his symptoms was that he would sweat profusely (vol. 1, p. 2, p. 315; vol. 3, pp. 504–505; vol. 4, pp. 67–68; vol. 5, pp. 319–29).

Epilepsy is a neurological disorder which manifests itself in the form of recurrent seizures. Seizures are sudden attacks of a convulsive nature due to abnormal cortical activity of the brain. The seizures may take a variety of form ranging from mild paroxysms to major convulsions, even to attacks so insignificant that they would never be noticed and are only known to individual experiencing them. Epilepsy is a definite indication that, at least at the time of a seizure, the brain is not functioning normally. One researcher maintains that epilepsy is associated with loss of inhibitions and leads to the reckless satisfaction of the sexual drive and in many epileptics this impulse very intense.[619] "It has been claimed," writes Patricia Smith, "that Mark Anthony was touched by God, though he evidently suffered from epilepsy. Epilepsy has also been suggested as the ac-

---

[617] Look at chapter one of this book.

[618] This is the symptom of schizophrenics that at the time of paroxysm, they will hallucinate.

[619] Martin G. Blinder, *Psychiatry in Everyday Practice of law* (Rochester, New York: Lawyers Co-operative Pub. Co., 1973), pp. 469–70.

tual basis for the conversion of St. Paul."[620] On another occasion, the same writer explains that a handful of epileptics say that cataleptic fits make them feel connected with an overwhelmingly powerful being; that they feel a great presence nearby. Some even say that during a seizure, they come into intimate contact with an invisible God. Ramachandran's subject did claim exactly that.[621]

The fact that Mohammed showed signs of epilepsy whenever he claimed he had a revelation, negates his whole claim of the divine origin of the Koran. Solomon Talbure's idea in this regard is conclusive. He writes: "People did not know very much about seizures in Mohammed's day, but we do know today that certain types of seizures, particularly when they are recurring, may cause both visual and auditory hallucinations. Rather than the Koran being the word of a god named Allah, it is much more likely that the revelations, as well as Allah, originated in the imagination of a man suffering from a kind of epilepsy-induced psychosis, and that Mohammed occasionally changed or abrogated verses based on the comments from his closest friends."[622]

Mohammed's Inferiority Complex

The reader will recall from previous chapters that, shortly after his birth, Mohammed's mother, Amina, delivered her infant to a Bedouin woman named Halima, to raise him through infancy in the healthy climate of the desert. According to Guillume, when Amina reached Mecca in search of a wet-nurse, baby Mohammed was offered to all the women who were looking for infants to nurse, but every woman refused him because they were not sure that they would be paid for the care of a fatherless child. Therefore, Halima and her husband at first declined Amina's offer. Finally, Halima and her husband decided

---

[620] Patricia Smith, *Brain-Wise* (Churchland, Massachusetts: Institute of Technology, 2002), p. 382.

[621] *Ibid.,* p. 385.

[622] Solomone Talbure, *Islam Exposed* (Coral Springs, Florida: Metier Books, 2002), p. 382.

to accept Mohammed because every lactating woman who had accompanied them to Mecca had procured a suckling to nurse and Halima and her husband did not like the idea of returning to their friends in the desert without one.[623]

The wet-nurse took care of Mohammed until he was about five years old and then returned him to his mother because, due to his abnormal behavior, she thought he was plagued by evil spirits. Shortly thereafter, Mohammed's mother passed away and he was entrusted to his eighty-year-old grandfather, Abd al-Mutallib. His grandfather died two years later when Mohammed was eight years old. Thereafter, his impecunious paternal uncle Abu Talib took charge of the orphan and he lived in poverty and deprivation. This was certainly an ill-fated beginning and may, in part, explain how his life evolved into a continual pursuit of power and carnal pleasure characterized by acts of cruelty and profligacy. From boyhood, up until he was hired by Khadija at the age of 25, he was merely a goat herder in the employ of the citizens of Mecca.

Mohammed suffered from an "inferiority complex" and this impaired his personality. According to the Austrian psychiatrist Alfred Adler, an inferiority complex is a combination of feelings and thoughts of inadequacy, insecurity, helplessness and insignificance associated with real or imagined inferiority, which prevent the individual from coping with the demands of life.

Alfred Adler distinguished between feeling *inferior* and an *inferiority complex.* "Inferiority feelings," Adler stated are not in themselves abnormal. They may, in fact, be a stimulus to improvement and discovery. However, if a person who is suffering from an inferiority complex is pressured into find a vent for his repressed feelings, he will resort to aggressive and brutal behavior if not otherwise dissuaded. The individual afflicted with a feeling of inferiority channels his reactions in constructive ways. Normal inferiority feelings impel a person to solve his problems successfully, whereas an inferiority complex prevents him from doing so.[624] A feeling of inferiority originating in childhood, according to Adler, "betrays itself throughout life" and may

---

[623] Guillume, *The Life of Mohammed,* p. 71.

[624] *Encyclopedia of Psychology.* 1984 ed., s. v. "Inferiority feelings," by "D. N. Lombardi."

lead to a neurosis. On the other hand, those with an inferiority disorder either withdraw from competition or seek to "overcompensate" by becoming excessively competitive and aggressive.[625] Numerous factors may contribute to low self-esteem: physical defects, parental factors, teasing, defeat or failure, poverty, lack of group acceptance.

One might easily believe that Adler and the other scholars derived the concept of "inferiority complex" by an analysis of Mohammed's character! The lack of parental affection and influence as well as the deprivation of a sound nurturing environment most certainly had a profound impact on Mohammed's psyche and personality.

Piaget, the noted child psychologist, and Freud both believed that prior to the twelfth year of their lives children are limited to thinking in concrete or non-symbolic terms. In other words, the conscious mind or "critical sensor" of children prior to the age of twelve is not mature. Children generally are not dominated by the rational thought derived from experience that influences adult thinking and, therefore, their unconscious mind is more accessible than that of adolescents or adults, allowing them to accept ideas uncritically and indiscriminately. Psychodynamic psychologists[626] also believe that although we, as adults, may think that we have free choice over what we think and do, critical dynamic forces developed during the early years of childhood influence our thinking and behavior throughout our lives. Other researchers suggest that when parents fail to give their children the loving nurture that healthy growth requires, the child's emotional growth is stunted and this may result in so-called "emotional poverty." There is also substantial agreement that this disorder develops out of some mix of four principal elements: early family relationships and parenting practices; defects in learning; biogenic factors, both genetic and psychological; and sociocultural factors.[627]

---

[625] *Longman Dictionary of Psychology and Psychiatry.* 1984 ed., v. s. "Inferiority compleax."

[626] Those psychologists who deal with the interaction of the psychic forces and processes developed during childhood which influences adult thinking, motives and behavior.

[627] Timothy W. Costello and Joseph T. Costello, *Abnormal Psychology* (New York: Harper Collins Publishers, Inc., 1992), p. 174.

If we relate the above psychological theories to the facts that we know concerning Mohammed's childhood: suffering from epilepsy; reared in the desert by a Bedouin woman until the age of five; deprivation of parental affection; lack of education and probably Halima's favoritism of her real son over him, we begin to understand their profound influence on his psyche. It would not be surprising if mental instability resulted from a childhood spent under such miSurable conditions. As noted above, "the lack of loving nurturing that healthy growth requires, leads to the breakdown of the child personality" and we know that Mohammed was indeed deprived of love and nurture. As a result of such an up-bringing, a child would feel unwanted and inadequate. His life would seem futile and empty and compensatory strivings for power and dominance would lead to a megalomaniac complex. The above-mentioned psychological theories help us understand the psychological profile of Mohammed and the atrocities that he committed during his lifetime.

Moral Insanity

The psychological theory called antisocial personality, sociopath or psychopath described by the British psychologist J. C. Prichard theorizes that the intellectual abilities of psychopaths remain unimpaired, but their morals are perverted and depraved and their self-control is lost or greatly impaired. These individuals are articulate and capable of reasoning with great shrewdness and intelligence, but they are unable to control their impulsive antisocial behavior.[628] It has been also shown that the level of violence exhibited by any given psychopath correlates to a remarkable degree to the amount of overt physical abuse suffered in childhood as well as with the level of violence in the psychopath's immediate social milieu.[629] No doubt, Mohammed's life was subject to both of these destructive conditions. In childhood he suffered, at the very least, from

---

[628] *Ibid.*, p. 171.

[629] Robert W. Rieber, *Manufacturing Social Stress* (New York and London: Plenum Press, 1997), pp. 54–56.

a lack of love and affection and, at the time of his self-annointed prophethood, his social milieu among Bedouin tribesmen was characterized by violence.

Psychopaths show no pity or sympathy for the victims of their crimes. Although intellectually able to recognize right from wrong and even preach about the principles of ethical behavior, they lack any sense of conscience and exhibit no remorse or guilt about their own unprincipled behavior. Their only emotional reaction might perhaps be a mild unhappiness about being caught.[630] But Mohammed was never troubled by such feelings because by fashioning his own God with whom only he could communicate, there was no earthly power above him to catch him or blame him, much less punish him for his criminal activities.

Each of the psychological flaws mentioned above are reflected in Mohammed's personality and explain his cruel and depraved treatment of his fellow citizens. As noted, psychopaths are often quite intelligent and a study of the various ruses and strategies Mohammed employed as he sought to attain power shows that his intellect was quite sharp and he was able to apply it very effectively. He was a charismatic leader and knew how to capture the minds of his fellow Arabs and foment them into war against his enemies. He was able to pretend for twenty-three years that, via the angel Gabriel, he was in communication with an unseen all-powerful entity that he called Allah. Whenever he committed an atrocity against his opponents, he would justify it with an injunction that he would bring down from his Allah in heaven. He definitely knew what was right and what was wrong, but whenever he would perpetrate an immoral and dreadful act, his conscience would never be touched and he would never exhibit any remorse. The following atrocities of Mohammed show his lack of a conscience as well as his callousness toward the victims of his barbarous behavior.

On the field of Badr, Mohammed exulted over the severed heads of several opponents with undisguised and ruthless satisfaction and several prisoners—accused of no crime other than skepticism or political opposition—were deliberately executed at his command.[631]

---

[630] Costello and Costello, *Abnormal Psychology,* p. 172.

[631] Muir, *Mahomet and Islam,* p. 513.

Two days after the battle of Badr, about half way to Medina, Mohammed ordered one of the prisoners, called Okba to be executed. Okba dared to expostulate why he should be treated more rigorously than the other captives.

"Because of your enmity to Allah and his prophet," replied Mohammed.

"Who is to be guardian of my little girl?" anguished Okba, "Who will take care of her?"

"Hell-fire!" exclaimed Mohammed heartlessly.[632]

On another occasion, when Abdullah cut off the head of Abu Jahl, Mohammed's arch enemy, and brought it to his master,

"The head of the enemy of Allah," exclaimed Mohammed. "Allah! There is none other Allah but Him!"

"There is no other!" responded Abdullah, as he cast its gory head at the Mohammed's feet.

"It is more acceptable to me," cried Mohammed, "than the choicest camel in all Arabia."[633]

As mentioned in previous chapters, the chief of Khaibar, after being subjected to cruel torture in order to extract the hiding place of his tribe's treasure, was put to death along with his cousin, and his wife led captive to Mohammed's tent, whereupon he bedded her. With rigorous severity, Mohammed forced into exile two of the Jewish tribes residing in Medina. The women and children of the third tribe were sold into captivity and the men, six to eight hundred in number, were butchered in cold blood before him. Then he took the wife of Kanana ibn Rabi' to his bed.[634]

In another incident, when the thieves who stole his camels and killed his herdsmen were captured, he ordered their arms and legs cut off and their eyes gouged out. When the mutilated, sightless trunks begged for water, it was not given to them before they died.[635]

---

[632] Muir, *Mahomet and Islam,* p. 230; Koelle, *Mohammed and Mohammedanism,* p. 151.

[633] Muir, *Mahomet and Islam,* p. 227.

[634] *Ibid.,* p. 514.

[635] Look at chapter two under the title "Was Mohammed a Bloodthirsty Individual?"

The above instances are sufficient to prove that Mohammed was a full-blown psychopath totally lacking in morality, conscience or compassion.

Megalomania

Megalomania is the delusion of greatness or importance. It is a type of delusion manifested by a feeling of great superiority. Common delusions include the belief that one is a quasi-God or a great personality, such as Napoleon. The afflicted may believe he is everything and everyone, omnipotent and omniscient.[636]

Another of Mohammed's abnormalities was that he was suffering from *megalomania*. As the author of the Koran, Mohammed unconsciously emerges in many verses of this book as a megalomaniac. The following examples support this thesis:

> O believers, say not (to the Prophet) words of ambiguous import, but words of respect. (II: 104)
> They can have no faith, until they make you (Mohammed) judge in all disputes, and find in their souls no resistance against your decisions, accepting them with complete submission. (IV: 65)
> He that obeys the Apostle obeys Allah Himself. (IV: 80)
> He that disobeys the Apostle after guidance has been made clear to him and follows a path other than that of the faithful shall be given what he has chosen. We will cast him into Hell: a dismal end. (IV: 114)
> The believers are only those who have faith in Allah and His Messenger and who, when gathered with him upon a grave situation, do not depart till they have begged his leave. The men who ask your leave are those who truly believe in Allah and His messenger. When they ask your leave to go away on some business of their own, grant it to whomever you please and implore Allah to forgive him. (XXIV: 62)
> You have had a good example in Allah's messenger; surely for him who hopes for Allah and the Last Day and remembers Allah often. (XXXIII: 21)

---

[636] *Baker Encyclopedia of Psychology and Counseling,* 1999 ed., s. v. "Megalomania."

No Muslim has any choice after Allah and His Apostle have decided a matter. (XXXIII: 36)

O you who believe! Enter not Prophet's chambers until leave is given you for a meal. But, when you are invited enter; and, when your meal is ended, then disperse. Do not engage in familiar talk, for this would annoy the Prophet and he would be ashamed to bid you go; but of the truth Allah is not ashamed. (XXXIII: 53)

Those who speak negatively of Allah and His Apostle shall be cursed by Allah in this life and in the life to come. He has prepared for them a shameful punishment. (XXXIII: 58)

Those who swear allegiance to you [Mohammed], indeed swear their allegiance to Allah. (IXVIII: 10)

O believers, do not advance hastily before Allah and His messenger, and fear Allah. (LXIX: 1)

Those who shout out to you from behind your chambers have no sense. (LXIX: 4)

Truly, Allah and His Angels send blessings on the Prophet: O you who believe, send your blessings on him, and salute him with all respect too. (XXXIII: 56)

The above collection of Koranic verses shows the megalomaniacal aspect of Mohammed's personality; the *hadith* are also full of similar allusions and the following is a synopsis of a few of them:

Mohammed said, Allah has given him five things that he had never given them to any one else before him.[637]

Allah addressed His believers and said, "In Allah's Apostle you have a fine example for anyone who hopes to be in the place where Allah is."[638]

Allah's Messenger said, "I have given five names: I am Mohammed And Ahmad, the praised one; I am al-Mahi, through whom Allah will eliminate infidelity, by killing every infidel; I am al-Hishr who will be the first to be resurrected, the people being resurrected thereafter; and I am also al-Aqib, because there will be no prophet after me."[639]

---

[637] *Sahih al-Bukhari,* vol. 1, p. 199.

[638] *Ibn Ishaq,* p. 467.

[639] *Sahih al-Bukhari,* vol. 4, pp. 483–84; at-Tabari, *The History of at-Tabari,* vol. 9, p. 156.

Mohammed said, "Whoever obeys me will enter paradise, and whoever disobeys me will not enter it."[640]

Mohammed was holding the hand of Omar ibn al-Khattab. Omar said, "O Allah's Apostle! You are dearer to me than everything except my own self." The Prophet said, "No, by Him in whose hand my soul is, you will not [have] complete faith till I am dearer to you than your own self." Then Omar said to him, "However, now by Allah, you are dearer to me than my own self." The prophet said, "Now, Omar you are a complete believer."[641]

Said, "It is obligatory for one to listen to and obey me. He, who obeys me, obeys Allah, and he who disobeys me, disobeys Allah. He, who obeys the chief, obeys me, and he who disobeys the chief, disobeys me."[642]

Mohammed said' " I have been given the keys of eloquent speech and given victory with awe cast into the hearts of enemy, and while I was sleeping last night, the keys of the treasures of earth were brought to me till they were put into my hand."[643]

Allah's Apostle said, "By Him in whose hands my life is, none of you will have faith till he loves me more than his father and children." The prophet said, "None of you will have faith till he loves me more than his father, his children and all mankind."[644]

> Said, "When we arrived at the Temple in Jerusalem, we found Abraham, Moses, and Jesus, along with a company of prophets. I acted as their imam in prayer."[645]

Each of the above-mentioned verses and *hadith* are sufficient to prove that Mohammed was a megalomaniacal charlatan who believed he was superior to others and plotted to gain power over them in order to rule in Arabia. This megalomania and hyperbolic ego were deeply rooted in his subconscious mind and, as a result, he

---

[640] *Sahih al-Bukhari,* vol. 9, p. 284.

[641] *Ibid.,* vol. 8, p. 408.

[642] *Ibid.,* vol. 4,.128.

[643] *Ibid.,* vol. 9, p. 127.

[644] *Ibid.,* vol. 1, p. 20.

[645] *Ibn Ishaq,* p. 182.

wanted his fellow-Arabs to acknowledge him as a quasi-God. When he first began his theological scam in Mecca, instead of respecting him, they scoffed at him because they viewed him as a sick-minded Arab, who ranted about speaking with *jinns* and roaming the seven skies to visit with Allah in the seventh heaven,

Naturally, when he was ridiculed and insulted by his fellow citizens, his ego was wounded but he temporarily suppressed his megalomania. As long as he was not in power and the Arabs did not respect him, he would struggle to garner their respect and obedience and satisfy his megalomania by "revealing" verses from Allah, such as those mentioned above and at the same time he would repress his feelings against those who humiliated him.

It can be fairly said that all the Koranic verses in which the so-called Allah recommends that people respect and obey Mohammed were fabricated by him when he had no power and could not force the compliance of his fellow Arabs. For the most part, these injunctions are found in the *Suras* "revealed" while he was still in Mecca. To illustrate how he used Allah to achieve his immediate goals, consider how he employed one of the verses of the Koran, namely (LVIII: 11). On one occasion he was talking with his followers in the mosque and a group of Badr veterans entered. Since the battle of Badr had a great impact on the consolidation of his power, Mohammed regarded Badr veterans very highly and ordered the people who were already in the mosque to make room for them to sit, but no one paid him any heed. So, he went into his usual fit, conjured down the angel Gabriel from heaven and "revealed" the following verse:

> "O you who believe! When you are told to make room in the assemblies, spread out and make room: ample room will Allah provide for you. And when you are told to rise up, rise up: Allah will rise up, to high rank those that have faith and knowledge among you." (IXVIII: 2)

Throughout various *Suras* of the Koran and also in the *hadith* Mohammed tries to use Allah to persuade the Arabs that he is a super human being, that they should regard him most highly, and subordinate themselves to him. When he talks about Allah (God), he tries to put himself on the same level, if not above Him. As noted above, when talks with his fellow Arabs, he boldly tells them that they should love him more than their family, themselves, and the whole of mankind. On another occasion, when he was ranting about his travels to the seven heavens and had visit with Allah, he was so blatantly impertinent that he boasted that he had led Abraham, Moses, Jesus, and other prophets as Imam in prayer at the Temple of Jerusalem.

Although he possessed a preposterously exaggerated ego and a native cunning and intelligence, Mohammed was quite ignorant. That is why the contents of the Koran look so ridiculous. As we see in *Sura* four, he totally lacked any knowledge of astronomy. On another occasion, he would say a mountain gave birth to a she-camel (VII: 73, 77; LIV: 23, 27, 29, 30, 31; XCI; 11, 13, 14) and, on yet another, he declared that Allah transformed Jews into pigs and rats (Sahih al-Bukhari, vol. IV, p. 333). He substituted superstition for morality; talked about invisible *jinns* (Chapter LXXII), *gog* and *magog,* and tried to explain teratological legends such as those that grandmothers fabricate to amuse their grandchildren. Despite such a backward and childish mentality, his megalomania would sustain him in his efforts to seek mastery over his fellow-Arabs.

The Combination of Inferiority Complex and Megalomania

Either a sense of inferiority or megalomania can turn a person into a psychopath (sociopath). But the combination of the repressed urges of an inferiority complex and megalomania may numb the conscience of the individual and drive him to unethical and vicious behavior. This is true in the case of ordinary run-of-the-mill psychopaths, but if one holding absolute power suffers from such a personality disorder, their behavior becomes unconscionable and may lead to carnage. Mohammed was a perverted individual who was suffering from a combination of both inferiority complex and megalomania. Psychologists Costello and Costello in their textbook state: "The common characteristics of all personality disorders are the development early in life of personality traits that are persistent, maladaptive, and that cause either significant impairment in social or occupational adjustment or extreme personal distress."[646]

---

[646] Costello and Costello, *Abnormal Psychology,* p. 179.

An inferiority complex is a learned psychological disorder, but megalomania is almost inborn. What makes an inferiority complex worse is the existence of inborn feelings of grandeur (megalomania), such as were deep seated in Mohammed's psyche. As Mohammed grew up into adulthood, he faced two alternatives: withdraw from competition and surrender to helplessness or *compensate.* This psychological phenomenon is a defense mechanism by which feelings of conscious or unconscious inferiority or insecurity are covered up by substitution. People often compensate for blocked goals by engaging in alternate behaviors that achieve a similarly desirable feeling or state.

To cope with his psychological deficiencies, Mohammed chose the latter alternative. As soon as Khadija married him and he found himself financially secure in the house of a wealthy woman, he started to compensate. Mohammed chose, as his psychological defense mechanism, the pretension of prophethood so as to acquire a social status above his peers and thus satisfy his megalomania and compensate for his inferiority complex. The initial contemptuous rejection of Islam by his fellow Arabs did not deter him from striving toward his final goal.

Mohammed had many predisposing psychological flaws and, as soon as he began to gain some power after the battle of Badr, these developed into an antisocial personality. Antisocial personalities are also called psychopaths or sociopaths and their behavior is characterized by truancy, delinquency, promiscuity, theft, vandalism, fighting, and violation of common social rules, poor work record, impulsiveness, irrationality, aggressiveness, and reckless behavior. The particular pattern of behavior varies from individual to individual.[647]

Scientific surveys indicate that psychopaths are unaffected by emotional or noxious stimuli that would horrify a normal individual. There is physiological evidence to suggest that the threshold of response of their autonomic nervous system is high, thus lowering the level of fear and anxiety they experience.[648] Punishments that most people would fear seem meaningless to them. Their needs are im-

---

[647] *Dictionary of Psychology,* rev. ed. (1985), s.v. "antisocial personality."
[648] Costello and Costello, *Abnormal Psychology,* p. 175–76.

mediate and memories of past punishments have little if any influence on what they will do today or tomorrow.[649] For them, the penal system is like a revolving door; in and out, without any change in behavior.[650] Many sociopaths are highly intelligent and are frequently able to escape arrest or punishment by their persuasiveness and deliberately projected air of candor and sincerity.[651]

The psychopath unconsciously perpetrates antisocial activities to rid himself of the frustrations of blocked goals and satisfy his inferiority feelings. The psychological rationale behind this subconscious sociopathic behavior is that by committing such, the psychopathic individual no longer feels himself inferior to others; he is aggressively damaging them and revenging fancied wrongs. A sane criminal commits a crime for a purpose, usually monetary, but the antisocial behavior of the psychopath is purposeless and spur of the moment: the crime is committed, often a heinous one, simply because the individual felt like doing it. A wanton impulsiveness and a compulsive need to seek thrills and excitement may comprise the only motivation.[652]

After Mohammed escaped to Medina and attained political power in that city, his psychological defense mechanism changed. Up until that time he had used fabricated commands of Allah to make Arabs submit to his power, but when he became the governor of Medina, he found it very easy to give vent to his repressions by applying his secular powers aggressively and barbarously. When an individual acquires high command and pretends to be the messenger of God, taking every step as God so orders, there will be no authority above him to admonish or punish his antisocial wrongdoings. Such a person then feels free to commit all kinds of atrocities and heinous crimes under the pretext of law and order and, in the case of Mohammed, obedience to the word of God.

Numerous incidents in the life of Mohammed show that he committed atrocities because he was suffering from serious psychological disorders, and by doing so he was unconsciously trying to

---

[649] *Ibid.*, p. 173.
[650] *Ibid.*, p. 178.
[651] *Ibid.*, p. 173.
[652] *Ibid.*

alleviate his suppressed aggression. As an example, in the Battle of Badr, Mohammed commanded that many of the innocent captives be murdered. One of them was An-Nadr, who was a captive of a Muslim soldier whose name was Mikdad. He had kept his captive unharmed, expecting to receive a rich ransom for his freedom. But the day after the battle, Mohammed saw the captive in the hands of Mikdad and cried, "Strike off his head" and adding, "O Lord! Do thou of thy bounty grant unto Mikdad a better prey than this." An-Nadr was immediately beheaded by Ali.[653]

Mohammed was the perfect personification of a psychopath in power. If he were an ordinary citizen and not in a commanding position with the authority to kill others by ordering, "Strike off his head," he might have stabbed one of his fellow-citizens to satisfy his repressions, then been caught and punished for breaking the law. But having power, he was immune from punishment by higher authorities and he could order someone to be killed and, being a psychopath, think nothing of it. Such an atrocity would temporarily allay the psychological forces which were seeking relief in his unconscious mind. "In his prophetical career," writes Muir, "political and personal ends were frequently compassed by *divine* revelations which, whatever more, were certainly the direct reflection of his own wishes . . . And what is perhaps worst of all, the dastardly assassination of political and religious opponents, countenanced, if not in some cases directed, by Mohammed himself, leaves a painful reflection upon his character."[654] Muir evaluates the personality traits of Mohammed under the rubric of "cruelty toward his enemies," but the psychological interpretation of what Muir is talking about is that by being cruel and unscrupulous against his enemies, Mohammed is trying to satisfy his repressed inferiority complex and at the same time realize his megalomaniac desires. These psychological disorders had desensitized his conscience and he was not only cruel and devious toward his enemies but also toward innocent people.

When Mohammed ordered all the men (at least seven hundred) of the Jewish tribe of Bani Khoraiza to be slaughtered and their women and children to be taken captive, he no longer saw himself

---

[653] *Ibn Hisham,* p. 458., quoted by William Muir, *Mahomet and Islam,* p. 230.
[654] Muir, *Mahomet and Islam,* p. 514.

as a poor orphan tending sheep in the scorching deserts of Arabia, but as a Prophet King who ruled Arabia and lorded over his fellow Arabs. By committing so many atrocities consciously, Mohammed was unconsciously trying to assuage the forces of his repressions, in addition to butressing his power in Arabia.

One may think that if he were driven by an "inferiority complex," "megalomania" and other psychological disorders, Mohammed should not be held legally responsible for his antisocial and perverted behavior. Psychiatrists consider most crimes committed involuntarily as acts of insanity and the perpetrator a candidate for treatment rather than legally responsible. They believe that a variety of uncontrollable forces and internal compulsions drive the individual to commit an antisocial act rather than a freely chosen alternative.[655] Generally, the law does not concern itself with the question of why a man commits a crime. It simply assumes the crime to be, by and large, the volitional act of a person who is doing wrong (disobeying the law) when committing the offence. Therefore, it holds the perpetrator of the act responsible and deserving punishment unless it can be proven by psychiatric evaluation that the offender cannot distinguish right from wrong.

A psychopath is legally liable for any criminal act that he does because he can fully differentiate between "right" and "wrong" and therefore is considered fully responsible for his behavior. A person suffering from a psychosis is not the same as a psychopath. Psychosis is a state of severe mental and emotional disorganization characterized by distortion of reality leading to delusions and hallucinations. For example, a psychotic may imagine that he hears or see things directing him to commit a heinous crime, temporarily deluding him into believing that he is performing a socially approved act. When he has recovered from his psychotic episode, he will usually have little recollection of what he has done and, when informed of his crime, finds his action as unacceptable as a sane person would.[656]

Mohammed was a "psychopath," because he was able to differentiate between "right" and "wrong," and had the ability to use winning ways to manipulate or exploit others, make friends easily, and

---

[655] Blinder, *Psychiatry in Everyday Practice of Law,* pp. 87–88.

[656] *Ibid.,* p. 96.

deliberately pretend candor and sincerity. All the atrocities that he committed were done just to satisfy his repressed feelings. When he was committing those savage crimes, he did not know why he was doing them, he just felt like it. To understand the psychology of Mohammed, it is helpful to refer to Gary Gilmore, a sociopath whose criminal behavior and life history are now a matter of public record,. His criminal behavior will illustrate two of the most prominent characteristics of the antisocial personality: purposeless, irrational and remorseless antisocial behavior. In his own words, Gilmore describes the murder that led to his death sentence:

"I pulled up near a gas station. I told the service station guy to give me all his money. I then took him to the bathroom and told him to kneel down and then shot him in the head twice. The guy didn't give me any trouble, but I just felt like I had to do it."[657]

Mohammed was a Sex Maniac

Recent systematic study of sexual behaviors by social scientists has revealed the relationship between a man's personality and his sex drive. No Islamist apologist can defend the sex life of Mohammed and an analytical study of same clearly shows that he was sexually perverted. Common sense alone tells us that a 51 year old man, who marries a six year old girl, is abnormal. The Diagnostic and Statistical Manual of Mental Disorders (1994)[658] describes such perversions as "paraphilia." According to DSMD-IV (1994), one of the essential features of paraphilia is sexual behavior involving "children or other non-consenting persons, that occurs over a period of at least 6 months." In some perverts the paraphilia occurs only episodically, and the individual is able to function sexually at other times without paraphiliac stimuli. Paraphilias can range from sexual fantasies that are never acted out to behavior that is considered

---

[657] Costello and Costello, *Abnormal Psychology,* p. 171–72.

[658] *Diagnostic and Statistical Manuel of Mental Disorders, 4th* ed (Washington, D.C.: American Psychiatric Association, 2005).

criminal, e.g., sexual contact with children, rape, exhibitionism and voyeurism.[659]

The DSMMD (1994) divides paraphilia into eight categories, one of which is pedophilia. Pedophilia involves sexual interest and activity with a prepubescent child. To be diagnosed as a pedophiliac, the offender must be 16 years of age or older and at least 5 years older than the victim. Statistically, it is reported that more pedophiles are interested in girls than boys.[660] We know that when Mohammed married Ayesha, she was only 6 and Mohammed was 51 years old. Ibn Ishaq also writes, "The Apostle saw Ummul when she was a baby crawling before his feet and said, 'If she grows up, I will marry her.' But he died before he was able to do so."][661] Can any of the Islamic apologists, no matter how equivocal they may be, defend Mohammed's behavior and deny that he was a pedophile? "Pedophilia, incest, and rape," writes Craig Winn, "are all perverted manifestations of a thirst for power and control. Insecurity is the cause."[662]

Let us now take another case of Mohammed's perverted sexual behavior. At a point in his life when he already had nine wives and numerous concubines, Allah gave him special permission to collect as many women as he wished. Verse 50 of *Sura* XXXIII of the Koran is articulate in this regard:

> "Prophet, we have made lawful to you the wives to whom you have granted dowries and the slave-girls whom Allah has given you as booty; the daughters of your parental and maternal uncles and of your parental and maternal aunts who migrated with you; and any other believing woman who gives herself to you and whom you wished to take in marriage. This is only for you and not any other believer."

Tabari writs:
"Layla approached the prophet while his back was to the sun and clapped on his shoulder. He asked her who it was and she replied,

---

659 Alan E. Kazdin, editor in chief. *Encyclopedia of Psychology* (Oxford: Oxford University Press, 2000), s. v. "Sexual Disorders," by Karen M. Donahey.

660 Winn, *Mohammed, Prophet of Doom,* p. 291.

661 Ibn Ishaq: 311.

662 Winn, *Mohammed, Prophet of Doom,* p. 245.

<I am the daughter of one who competes with the wind. I am Layla. I have come to offer myself to you.> He replied, <I accept.> Layla scampered back home and shared her story with mommy and daddy. They said, <What a bad thing you have done! You are a self-respecting girl, but the Prophet a womanizer.>"[663]

The above incidents and evidences leave no doubt that Mohammed was perverted sexually. But some Islamic apologists such as Amir Seyyed Ali and Hosein Nasr, defenders of Islam and Mohammed, maintain that Mohammed's marriages "are not at all signs of his lenience vis-à-vis the flesh. During the period of youth, when the passions are stronger, the Prophet lived with only own wife who was much older than he and also underwent long periods of sexual abstinence. And as a Prophet many of his marriages were political ones which, in the prevalent social structure of Arabia, guaranteed the consolidation of the newly founded community."[664] Another author writes: " . . . Almost all matrimonial unions of the Prophet were diplomatic and political, rather than lustful."[665]

There are ample reasons to reject these attempts to justify the sex life of Mohammed; among them are the following:

1. How would divine sanction of sexual access to the daughters of his uncle and aunts, as well as to "any believing woman who gives herself to the Prophet and who the Prophet wishes to take in marriage," guarantee "the consolidation of the newly founded Muslim community?"[666]
2. The above authors should know that Mohammed owed his entire support to Khadija and while she lived, this very powerful woman would not permit him to act out his perverted sexual desires, even if he had the courage to attempt it.

---

[663] At-Tabari, *The history of at-Tabari,* vol. 9, p. 139.

[664] Hosein Nasr, *Ideals and Realities of Islam* (ABC International Group, 2000), p. 61, quoted by Robert Spencer, *Islam Unveiled* (San Francisco: Encounter Books, 2000), p. 43.

[665] Fida Hussain Malik, *Wives of Prophet* (Lahore, Pakistan: SH. Muhammad Ashraf, 1983), p. 145.

[666] Spencer, *Islam Unveiled* (San Francisco: Encounter Books, 2002), p. 43.

3. The authors have not mentioned how they have found out that Mohammed went through a long period of sexual abstinence?
4. One should ask the above-mentioned Islamic apologists, isn't the tenor of verse 50 of *Sura* XXXIII of Koran which says, " . . . it is lawful for Mohammed to have any woman who gives herself to him . . . ," a reflection of Mohammed's lustful nature? Or could his sexual intercourse with various women have a consolidating effect on the newly founded Muslim community?"
5. How would the above authors justify killing al-Harith, Kinana ibn Rabi' and al-Hakam the husbands of Juwayria, Safiyyah, and Reyhana and taking the wives to bed the very same night that he had killed their husbands? Did this deplorable and cruel act help to consolidate the Muslim community?

Mohammed was a satyr who filled his Suraglio with the most beautiful women of Medina for no other reason than pure lust. Excerpts from the writings of two prominent authors prove this contention. Professor Muir writes: . . . . . Safiyyah, daughter of a chief, a beauty who was probably well known in Medina; and . . . . . because, immediately upon Kinana's execution Mohammed sent for her and cast his mantle over her, he is not free from the suspicion of arrainging the destruction of her husband in order to obtain his wife.[667]

Also, Koelle writes about Safiyyah, "At the first halting-place, six miles from Khaibar, he wished to consummate the marriage with her; but as she was unwilling, and refused, he became very angry with her."[668]

6. Other evidence proving the perversion of Mohammed's sex life was his marriage with Zainab Bint Jahsh, the wife of his adopted son, Zaid ibn Haritha. One day when Mohammed went to visit Zaid, he was not at home. His wife Zainab was dressing and half-naked, but she invited him in. Mohammed declined, but he had seen her body through the half opened door while she was hurriedly dressing. Mohammed was smitten and fell in love with the spectacularly beautiful Zainab. However, he left their home

---

[667] Muir, *The Life of Mohammad,* p. 377.
[668] Koelle, *Mohammed and Mohammedanism,* p. 504.

saying, "Praise be to Allah the Most High! Praise be to Allah who changes men's heart." According to Rodinson, the Arabic histories and *hadith* texts stress Mohammed's disturbed of mind after his glimpse of Zainab in a state of undress and describe her remarkable beauty.[669] When Zaid came home, Zainab told him about the incident. Zaid, knowing Mohammed and his lecherous taste for women, went to him and told him he would like to divorce Zainab so that Mohammed could marry her.

Fearing the tongues of the people, lest they would say, "He has married his adopted son's wife," Mohammed rejected Zaid's proposal and told him, "Keep your wife and fear Allah." Arabs regarded marriage with the wife of an adopted son as illegal as that with the wife of a natural son, but the lust-filled heart of Mohammed was pounding for Zainab and finally Zaid divorced her. Then, as always in times of difficulty, Allah came to his Apostles's rescue. Verses 3 to 40 of *Sura* XXXIII were sent down to him that not only permits him to marry Zainab; they even admonish him for having concealed the sentimental emotions that he had developed for her. Did Mohammed marry Zainab, the wife of his adopted son, to consolidate the newly founded Islamic community or was it for some diplomatic or political reason? Those Islamic apologists, who defend Mohammed's sexual perversions, should indeed feel shame for so deceiving the people.

7. *Kashfolasrar* commentary states, "Today, it has become the rule of Islamic canonical law that every man may marry one to four free women, not more. But the Prophet of Allah was given the exceptional privilege to marry more than four and he was permitted to do so without any witness or dowry, and he also was given the right to ignore all the rules and regulations ordained for others. If Mohammed showed interest in a married woman, it was incumbent upon her husband to divorce her and the prophet could marry her without observing the traditional period of prohibition for a divorced or widowed woman to re-

---

[669] Rodinson, *Muhammad,* p. 205.

marry. These were all privileges that Allah bestowed exclusively to Mohammed and no one else."[670]

The tenor of the above point is that Mohammed was permitted by Allah to possess any woman that he wished and, if the woman were married, her husband would be expected to divorce her. Moreover, when Mohammed took a woman into his possession, he was exempt from all the religious requirements ordained for other Muslims, such as a marriage contract specifying payment of dowry and alimony, attendance of witnesses, or observation of the waiting period before a divorced or widowed woman could marry another man, and so on.

Arabs have an axiom which says: "Contrary to one's belief, his inner characteristics will become manifest to the public." While Mohammed was alive, he was able to hide his proclivities under the cover of an assumed prophethood and commit all kinds of shameful atrocities against his opponents under the guise of Allah's revelations. Over the years, scholarly research has stripped aside the veil of deceit woven by that lying, lascivious and pretentious weaver of fallacy (the Koran) and today his true nature has became manifest to those who seek the realities of history. Only that segment of humanity that is content to vegetate in the depths of ignorance and superstition can accept one of the greatest impostors of history as the Prophet of God and that preposterous book, the Koran, as the direct words and revelations of God.

---

[670] *Tafsir Kashfolasrar,* vol. 2, p. 409.

CHAPTER TWELVE

EVALUATION OF MOHAMMED'S PERSONALITY IN HISTORY

The truths of religion are never so well understood as by those who have lost the power of reasoning.
Voltaire, *Philosophical Dictionary*

Every religion has its dogma. Sometimes, one faith will share its beliefs with another, e.g., the Judeo-Christian religions. Generally speaking, religious dogma is benign and spiritually uplifting but, on the basis of the more than 6200 verses of the Koran and other Islamic writings, it can fairly be said that none of the organized religions of the world can match the despotism of Islam. Since Islam considers politics and government part of religion—two sides of the same coin—Islamic dogma will find expression in all polity resulting in a despotic theocracy. The rulers will claim that the governing laws are divinely acquired and every citizen should blindly abide by them; dissention or criticism is not tolerated. Anyone against the government policies is guilty of heresy and a menace to society. Because of this despotism, Islamic scholars have not had the liberty (or courage) to evaluate and write about the personality of Mohammed and Islamic principles. Those who challenged Islam or Mohammed were ruthlessly persecuted and executed.

In the very last years of the seventeenth century, the so-called period of Enlightenment, the atmosphere of freedom permitted a just evaluation of Mohammed's personality. In the first *Encyclopedia of Islam,* the most important source of reference in Islamic and oriental studies under the entry for Mohammed, Barthelmy d'Herbelot describes Mohammed's ideological and doctrinal values as follows:

"This is the famous impostor Mahomet, author and founder of a heresy, which has taken on the name of religion, which we call Mohammedan. The interpreters of the Alkoran and other Doctors of Muslim or Mohammedan Law have applied to this false prophet all

345

the praises which the Arians, Paulicians or Paulianists, and other Heretics have attributed to Jesus Christ, while stripping him of his Divinity . . . ."[671]

The English Orientalist Humphrey Prideaux's evaluation of Mohammed's character:

"For the first part of his life he led a very wicked and licentious course, much delighting in Rapine, Plunder, and Blood-shed, according to the usage of Arabs, who mostly followed this kind of life, being almost continually in arms one tribe against another, to plunder and take from each other all they could . . . .

His two predominant fashions were *ambition* and *lust.* The course which he took to gain Empire abundantly shows the former; and the multitude of Women which he had to do with, proves the latter. And indeed these two run through the whole frame of his *Religion,* there being scarce a chapter in his *Alcoran* which doth not lay down some law of war and blood-shed for the promoting of the one; or else give some liberty for the use of women here, or some promise for the enjoyment of them hereafter, to the gratifying of the other."[672]

In 1741 in his drama *Mahomet or Faniticism,* Voltaire took advantage of the current prejudice against organized religion and used Mohammed as an example of all the charlatans who have enslaved people by religious trickery and lies; finding some of the old legends insufficiently scurrilous, he had blithely made up some of his own. Even Gibbon had little respect for Mohammed, arguing that he had lured the Arabs to follow him with the bait of loot and sex. As for the Muslim belief in the divine inspiration of the Koran, Gibbon loftily declared it an impossible position for the truly civilized man.[673]

---

[671] Quoted in Armstrong, *Mohammed, A Bibliography of the Prophet,* pp. 35–36.

[672] Humphrey Prideaux, *The True Nature of Imposture, Fully Displayed in the Life of Mahomet* (London: 1708), p. 80.

[673] Armstrong, *Mohammed, A Bibliography of the Prophet,* 37.

Dagobert Runes writes:

"The real character of Mohammed became evident only after the death of his first wife Khadija . . . . In true Bedouin fashion, he raided caravans and attacked villages, either massacring the inhabitants or carrying them off into captivity. According to Bedouin law, a fifth of the entire boot went to Mohammed. Runaways were left in the desert with amputated hands and blinded eyes, and it was forbidden even to give them a drink as they perished under the sizzling desert sun. The stories of his brutal conduct are endless. 'Drive all the unfaithful out of Arabia,' he ordered, 'and slaughter every Jew who comes into your hands.'"[674]

"At this period of his mission, Mohammed appears to us little more than a barbaric Bedouin chieftain. A disorderly mob, of whom the old writers say that they clutched their rags about them to hide their nakedness, rallied beneath his banner to fight for the self-proclaimed prophet of God . . . . At the age of forty-five he married the nine-year-old daughter of his friend Abu Bakr. From year to year his harem grew. When his wife-stable could no longer accommodate the influx of wives, he disposed of the excess among the faithful. "Women are your ploughs," he said. "You can order them as you will." No woman was safe from his demands. "The prophet needs more women than other men," the angel Gabriel had revealed to him. Gabriel had made still another concession: "If a married woman offers herself to the Prophet, the prophet may take her, but that is forbidden to other Muslims."[675]

Professor Muir's evaluation of Mohammed is:

"Magnanimity or moderation is nowhere discernible in the conduct of Mohammed towards such of his enemies as failed to tender a timely allegiance. On the field of Badr he exulted over the dead, with undisguised and ruthless satisfaction; and several prisoners, accused of no crime but that of skepticism or political opposition, were deliberately executed at his command. The Prince of Khaybar, after being subjected to cruel torture for the purpose of discovering the treasures of his tribe, was, with his cousin, put to death for having concealed them, and his wife led captive to the conqueror's tent. Sentences of exile was

---

[674] Ibn Hisham, 553, quoted in Dagobert D. Runes, *Philosophy for Everyone* (New York: Philosophical Library Inc., 1968), p. 67.

[675] Dagobert Runes, *Philosophy for Everyone* (New York: Philosophical Library, Inc.1968), pp. 67–68.

enforced by Mohammed with rigorous severity on two whole Jewish tribes residing at Medina; and a third, likewise his neighbors, the woman and children were sold into captivity, while the men, amounting to six or eight hundred, were butchered in cold blood before his eyes . . . . In later years, however much sincerity and good faith may have guided his conduct in respect of friends, craft and deception was not wanting towards his foes . . . . When Medina was beleaguered by the confederate army, Mohammed sought the services of Na'im a treacherous go between, and employed him to sow distrust amongst the enemy by false reports; 'for,' said he, 'what else is War but a game of deception?' . . . And what is perhaps worst of all, the dastardly assassination of political and religious opponents, countenanced, if not in some case directed, by Mohammed himself, leaves a painful reflection upon his character."[676]

Koelle one of the most renowned scholars of Islam, writes:

"Some episodes of the raid of Khaibar (the settlement of the Jewish tribe of Bani Nadhir), are recorded which likewise show up Mohammed in the light of a common, rather unscrupulous, conqueror, and as glaringly wanting in the characteristic of the true, heavenly-minded prophet. Among the women made captive in one of the first Khaibar strongholds taken, was *Safiyyah* daughter of the chief of Bani Nadhir tribe, and hence probably known to Mohammed by sight. Her husband, Kinana,[677] was accused by Mohammed of concealing part of his treasure, and was cruelly tortured to death. Safiya and some other females, on being taken to Mohammed, passed their newly slain husbands and relatives on the way, and naturally burst into a paroxysm of grief. The prophet, seeing them in this state, said, 'Take these demons away from

---

[676] Muir, *The Life of Mohammad,* pp. 513–514.

[677] At the Khaibar's raid, the citadel of al-Khamus was surrendered to Mohammed, on condition that the inhabitants were free to leave the country, but that they should give up all their property to Mohammed. Then, Mohammed accused Kinana, chief of Khaibar, and his cousin of keeping back in contravention of the compact, some part of the treasure, and notably the marriage portion Kinana had obtained with his bride Safiyyah, whose father was slaughtered in the massacre of the men of Bani Quraiza's tribe. Since neither Kinana, nor his cousin revealed the place of hidden treasure, Mohammed ordered to torture them to death and then the heads of both of them were severed from their bodies.

me;' but he detained Safiyyah casting his mantle over her, thus making her destined for his own harem.

According to the rules of his religion, such captives may not be married till at the expiration of three months; but this prophet's carnal passions were so strong that he could not brook delay, and he actually made her his wife, almost within sight of the place where her husband and friends had been slaughtered only a few days before . . . Mohammed's cruel outrage of the feelings of a woman whose nearest relatives he had just put to death, casts so unfavorable a light upon his character, that, to screen him, his biographers tell a story, obviously invented for the purpose, which represents Safiyyah as a willingly consenting party.

Ibn Ishaq favors us with another story, which is a sad illustration of the want of truthfulness in early Islam, and shows how unscrupulously Mohammed himself authorized the circulation of untruths. We are told that, as soon as Khaibar was conquered, *Hajjaj ibn Ilat* one of his followers, asked permission of Mohammed to leave the army and go to Mecca, in order to collect some debts which were owing to him there. Having obtained the permission asked for, he added, 'But I shall have to tell lies.' Mohammed not only abstained from expressing any displeasure, but he approvingly replied, 'Say what you want.'"[678]

David Frawley in *Arise Arjuna* writes about Mohammed:

"The founder of the religion of Islam was a camel driver named Mohammed, who himself a most violent man, who killed hundreds of people personally, and who taught his followers to do the same. He was prone to violence with those who criticize Allah . . . He saw the value of promoting his religion by force, if necessary, during more than eight battles that he fought. After his exile from Mecca, Mohammed organized numerous raids on caravans to Mecca. He fought as the leader of his army, in both offensive and defensive conflicts, and was once severely wounded. He took and ransomed hostages. He had a group of seven hundred Jews of the Bani Quraiza tribe massacred after they surrendered to him and became his prisoners, when he determined that he could not trust them.

He at times approved of his followers performing assassinations to eliminate enemies of the faith (for example Asma a woman poet of

---

[678] Koelle, *Mohammed and Mohammedanism,* p. 182–84.

Mecca, who was killed by Umayr one of the Mohammed's followers for criticizing Mohammed.)

Mohammed is credited with introducing Islamic law codes, which like most medieval codes, contain much that the modern world regards as unnecessary cruelty, including cutting off of the hands and feet of criminals for certain offences."[679]

Wilson Cash writes about Mohammed as the following:

"Mohammed had many faults, and they were the common faults and failings of his day. They were shared by his people as a whole, though at times he did succeed in shocking even the Arab's sense of propriety, as, for example, when he married the divorced wife of his adopted son. This was contrary to all Arab tradition, but the Prophet did not allow this to stand in his way. His action was right, he declared; and though he caused no small scandal at the time, yet he silenced it by a divine revelation in which God is made to say, "When Said had settled the matter of his divorce, we did wed her to thee that it might not be a crime in the faithful to marry the wives of their adopted sons." (Koran, XXXIII: 37)

. . . Mohammed must be judged relatively to the violence, indifference to bloodshed, and loot of the people among whom he lived . . . In aggressive warfare Mohammed gave to his followers a strong lead. Muslim authorities give case after case where Mohammed attacked tribes and was aggressor. The attack on the tribe of Khaibar is a good and authenticated example. In intertribal wars the Arabs, by general agreement, always spared the date palms, but Mohammed on his attack on the Bani Nadhir had the date palms burned or cut down. The authority for this is Ibn Ishaq, the oldest biographer of Mohammed, and a Muslim. The treatment of women in the warfare has been the subject of much adverse criticism of Mohammed; and there is no doubt, if Muslim authorities are to be relied on, that he sanctioned and took part in atrocities very similar to those reported from Armenia in recent times. Turkey, in fact, has simply copied what Mohammed and his followers did. He laid down the rule that the capture of women in battle did *ipso facto* dissolve previous heathen marriages. The times were certainly barbarous and cruel, for Muslim tradition tells of the slaughter of pris-

---

[679] David Frawley, *Arise Arjuna: Hinduism and the Modern World* (New Delhi, India: Voice of India, 1955).

oners of war in cold blood, the torture of captives to make them reveal the secret of their hidden treasures, and the slaying of men traveling to Medina under safe-conduct."[680]

Ernest Renan, the brilliant French historian and essayist, has said:

"Muslims are the first victims of Islam. Many times I have observed in my travels in the Orient that fanaticism comes from a small number of dangerous men who maintain the others in the practice of religion by terror. To liberate the Muslim from his religion is the best service that one can render him."[681]

Craig Winn writes:

"Mohammed was the most evil man who ever lived. Allah was the most demonic god ever conceived. The Koran was the nastiest book ever written. Islam was the most hateful and violent fraud ever perpetrated on humankind . . . . And as evil as the Islamic "god" is, his prophet was worse. His resume reads: demon possession, suicidal, bearing false witness, hate speech, taking and offering bribes, pedophilia, piracy, slave trading, incest, rape, torture, genocide, warmongering, plagiarism, womanizing, sexism—well, you know the list."[682]

Mohammed Confesses Duplicity

The following is a verbatim quote of Sahih al-Bukhari:

Narrated Zahdam: We were in the company of Abu Musa al-Ashari and there were friendly relations between us and this tribe of Jarm. Abu Musa was presented with a dish of chicken. Among the people there was sitting a red-faced man who did not come near the food. Abu Musa (said to him), "Come on (and eat), for I have seen Allah's apostle eating of it (i.e., chicken)." He said, "I have seen it eating something dirty

---

[680] Wilson Cash, *The Expansion of Islam,* pp. 17–19.

[681] Ibn Warraq, *Why I am not a Muslim.*

[682] Winn, *Prophet of Doom,* pp. V–VI.

and since then I have disliked it." Abu Musa said, "Come on, I will tell you (or narrate to you). Once I went to Allah's Apostle with a group of al-Ashariyin, and met him while he was angry, distributing some camels of Zakat. We asked for mount but he took an oath that he would not give us any mounts, and added, "I have nothing to mount you on.' In the meantime some camels of booty were brought to Allah's Apostle and he asked twice, "Where are al-Ashariyin?" So he gave us five white camels with big humps. We stayed for a short while (after we had covered a little distance), and then I said to my companions, "Allah Apostle has forgotten his oath. By Allah, if we do not remind Allah's Apostle of his oath, we will never be successful." So we returned to the Prophet and said, "O Allah's Apostle! We asked you for mounts, but you took an oath that you would not give us any mounts; we think that you have forgotten your oath.' He said, 'It is Allah who has given you mounts. By Allah, and Allah willing, if I take an oath and later find something else better than that, then I do what is better and expiate my oath.'"[683]

This *hadith* clearly shows that Mohammed lacked any integrity and possessed no ethical values. He confesses that he is a liar and not trustworthy. Therefore, how can anyone believe Mohammed's claim that he and his Koran were divinely inspired? His character, as we saw in the different discussions of this book, was sadly deficient and "his life as despicable, as anyone who has ever lived."[684]

---

[683] *Sahih al-Buchari*, vol. VII, pp. 308–309.
[684] Winn, *Muhammad, Prophet of Doom*, p. 1.

BIBLIOGRAPHY

A Dictionary of Islam. 1965 ed. s. v. "Slavery."

———. S. v. "Zimmi."

Abdul Rauf, Mohammed. *al-Hadith.* Washington, D. C.: The Islamic Center, 1974.

Abu Davud, Suleiman. *Sunan.* 4 vols. Cairo: 1935.

Adamec, Ludwig W. *The A to Z of Islam.* Lanham, Maryland, and Oxford: 2002.

Ali, Sayed Amir, *A Short History of the Saracens.* 2n. ed. London: Macmillan and Company, 1953.

———. *The Legal Position of Women in Islam.* London: and Stroughton, 1912.

Alighieri, Dante. *Divine Comedy.* Translated by Lawrence Grant White. New York: Pantheon Books, 1948.

———. *Inferno.* Translated by Michael Palma. New York: W. W. Norton & Company, 2002.

American Encyclopedia, 2003 ed., s. v. "Thirty Years' War." by H G. Koenigsberger.

American Heritage Dictionary, 4th ed. (2000), s. v. "Terror."

Amnesty International. *Iran, Violations of Human Rights,* 1987–1990. London: 1991, 12.

Andrea, Tor. *Muhammed: The Man and his Faith.* Translated by Theophil Menzel. New York: Harper & Brothers, 1960.

Anwar Ali, Seyyed. *Qur'an, the Fundamental Law of Human life.* Karachi, Pakistan: Hamdard Foundation Press, 1994.

Arberry, A. J. *The Holy Koran* (An Introduction with Selections). London: George Allen and Unwin, 1953.

Archer, John Klark. *Mystical Elements in Mohammed.* (dissertation). New Haven: Yale University Press, 1924.

Armstrong, Karen. *Muhammad.* London: Victor Gollancz Ltd., 1991.

Ayoub, Dr.Mahmoud. *The Qur'an and its Interpreters,* 2 vols. Albany: State University of New York, 1984.

Baghdadi, Abu Mansur Abd al-Qadir. *Al-Farq Bayn al-Firaq.* Cairo, 1328/1910.

Baker Encyclopedia of Psychology. 1999 ed. s. v. "Megalomania."

Baladhuri, Ahmad ibn Yahya. *Futuh al-Buldan.* Cairo: 1318 A. H.

Barry, Brian, M. *Theories of Justice.* Los Angeles: University of California Press, 1989.

Bay, Essad. *Mohammed.* London: Cobden–Sanderson, 1972.

al-Baydawi, Abdullah ibn Umar. *Anwar al-Tanzil wa Asrar al-Ta'wil.* Cairo: 1344/1924.

Becker, C. H. *Die Kanzel im Kultus des Alten Islam.* (Islam Studien), Leipzig: 1923.

———. *Christentum und Islam.* Leipzig: 1907.

Blackmore, Susan. *The Meme Machine.* Oxford: Oxford University Press, 1999.

Blinder, Martin G. *Psychiatry in Everyday Practice of Law.* Rochester, New York: Lawyears Cooperative Pub. Co., 1937.

Bodley, R. V. C. *The Messenger: The Life of Mohammad.* New York: Doubleday Incorporation, 1964.

Boisard, Marcel A. *Jihad: A Commitment to Universl peace.* Indianapolis, Indiana: American Trust Publication, 1979.

Brockelmann, Carl. *History of the Islamic Peoples.* New York: G. P. Putmann's Sons, 1947.

al-Bukhari, Muhammad ibn Isma'il. *Kitab al-Jami' al-Sahih.* Leiden, Holland: Brill, 1986.

———. Translated by Muhammad Muhsin Khan, 9 vols. Cambridge: Cambridge University, 1975.

Caetani, Leon. *Annalli dell'Islam.* 5 vols. Milano, 1905–13.

Carl J. Friedrich and John W. Chapman, eds. *Justice.* New York: Atherton Press, 1963.

Carlyle, Thomas. *On Heroes, Hero-Worship and the Heroic in History.* Lincoln: University of Nebraska Press, 1966.

Cash, William Wilson. *The Expansion of Islam.* London: Edinburgh House Press, 1928.

———. *Christendom and Islam.* New York and London: Harper & Brothers Publishers, 1937.

Chirol, William. *Foreign Affairs.* Vol. I, No. 3.

Clarke, James Freedman. *Ten Great Religions.* 2 vols. New York: Houghton, Mifflin & Company, 1948.

Collier's Encyclopedia, 1994 ed., s. v. "Stanislavsky's Method," by Rodolph Goodman.

Costello, Thimoty W. and Costello, Joseph T. *Abnormal Psychology.* New York: Harper Collins Publishers, Inc., 1992.

Cottrell, Alvin and Olson, William. "Jihad: The Muslim View of War," *Middle East Insight,* 39.

Daniel, Norman. *Islam and the West.* Edinburgh: Edinburgh University Press, 1960.

Dashti, Ali. *Twenty-Three Years: A Study of the Career Prophetic of Mohammed.* London: 1958.

Dawkins, Richard. *The Selfish Gene.* Oxford: Oxford University Press, 1999.

Delgado, Roman. *Acting With Both Sides of the Brain.* New York: Holt, Rinehart and Winston, 1986.

Dermenghem, Emile. *The Life of Mohammed.* Great Britain: Stephen Austin and Sons, Ltd., 1930.

Diagnostic and Statistical Manuel of Mental Disorders, 4th ed. Washington, D. C. American Psychiatric Association, 2005.

Dibble, R. F. *Mohammed.* New York: The Viking Press, Inc., 1926.

al-Dinawari, Ahmad ibn Dawud. *al-Akhbar al-Tiwal,* 2 vols. Leyden: 1888.

Dolman, John Jr. and Knaub, Richard K. *The Art of Playing Production.* New York: Harper & Row Publishers, Inc., 1973.

Donner, Fred McGraw. *The Early Islamic Conquest.* Princeton, New Jersey: Princeton University Press, 1981.

al-Dowry, Abdolaziz. *Moghaddamah fi Tarikh Sadre Islam.* Beirut: Catholic Press, 1960.

Emadzadeh Esfahani, Hossein. *A Detailed History of Islam.* Farsi edition. Tehran: Islam Publications, 1991.

Encyclopedia Britanica, 15th ed. s. v. "Jihad."

———. 15th ed. "Crucifixion."

Encyclopedia of Islam. ed. Hamilton Alexander Rosskeen Gibb *et al,* s. v. "Abd."

The Encyclopedia of Islam. New ed. s. v. "Hadjdj."

Encyclopedia of Psychology. 1984 ed. s. v. ""Inferiority feelings," by "D. N. Lombardi."

The Encyclopedia of Religion. 1987 ed. s. v. "Hadith," by "L. T. Librande."

Encyclopedic Dictionary of Religion. 1979 ed. s. v. "Sacred and prophane," by V. T. Johnson.

Exodus. XXI: 20.

Fakhri, Maid. *An Introduction of the Qur'an.* New York: New York University Press, 1994.

Farah, Caesa E. *Islam: Beliefs and Observations.* New York: Barron's Educationl Series, Inc., 2003.

Fazlul Karim, Alhaj Maulana. *Mishkat-ul-Masabih.* Calcutta, India: Mohammadi Press, 1938.

First Encyclopedia of Islam 1913–1936 ed. s. v. "Harut and Marut," by A. J. Wensinck.

Forward, Martin. *A Short Biography.* Oxford, England: A One Publications, 1997.

Frawley, David. *Arise Arjuna: Hinduism and the Modern World.* New Delhi, India: Voide of India, 1995.

Fregosi, Paul. *Jihad in the West.* Amherst, New York: Prometheus Books, 1998.

Funk, Von S., Neumann, W. A., and Wünsche, A. *Monumenta Talmudica, unter Mitwirkung Zahlreicher Mitarbeiter hrsg.* Vienna, Leipzig and Orion, 1914.

al-Ghazali, Abu Hamid Muhammad. *Ihya' Ulum al-Din.* 4 vols. Cairo: 1348 A. H.

Ghomshei, Mehdi Elahi. *Koran al-Karim.* Ghom, Iran: Osweh Publications, 1991.

Gibb, Hamilton Aexander Rosskeen. *Islam.* Oxford: 1953.

Glasse, Cyril. *The Consise Encyclopedia of Islam.* London: Stacey International, 1989.

Glubb, John Bagot. *The Life and Times of Mohammad.* New York: Stein and Day Publishers, 1970.

Goldziher, Ignaz. *Introduction to Islamic Theology and Law.* Translated by Andras and Ruth Hamori. Princeton: 1981.

———. *Muslim Studies.* 2 vols. Translated by C. R. Barber and S. M. Stern. London: Allen and Unwin, 1967–1968.

Gosh, A. *The Koran and the kafir (Islam and the Infidel).* Houston, Texas: 1983.

Graetz, Heinrich. *History of the Jews.* Philadelphia: The Jewish Pubication of Society of America, 1894.

Guillume, Alfred. *The Traditions of Islam.* Salem, New Hampshire: Ayer Company Publishers, Inc., 1987.

Hekmat, Anwar. *Women and the Koran.* Amherst, New York: Prometheus Books, 1997.

Ibn Hisham, Abu Muhammad Abd al-Malik. *Kitab Sirat Rasul Allah.* Based on the Chronicle of his teacher ibn Ishaq. 4 vols. Edited by Wüstenfeld. Gottingen: 1858–1860.

Hitti, Philip K. *History of the Arabs.* 5th ed. London: 1953.

_____. *The Origin of the Islamic State.* New York: 1916.

The Holy Koran. Revised and edited by the Presidency of Islamic Researchers, IFTA. Medina, Saudi Arabia: undated.

The Holy Koran. Saudi Arabia: undated.

Hoodbhoy, Pervez. *Islam and Science.* New Jersey: Zed Books, 1991.

Hook, Sidney. *From Hegel to Marx.* Michigan: The Michigan University Press, 1966.

Houtsma, M. Th., Rasset, H., and Hartman, R., eds. *The Encyclopedia of Islam.* London: Luzac & Co., 1913.

Huart, Clement. *A History of Arabic Literature.* London: William Heinemann, 1903.

Humphrey, Prideaux. *The Life of Mohammed.* London: 1723.

Irving, Washington. *Washington Irving's Life of Mohammed.* Edited by Charles Getchell. Massachusetts: Ipswich Press, 1989.

Ibn Ishaq. Muhammd, *Sirat Rasul Allah (The Life of Muhammad)*. English translation by Alfred Guillume. New York: The Viking Press, Inc., 1926.

Jones, V. R. and Jones, L. Bevan. *Women in Islam: A Manuel with Special Reference to Conditions in India.* Westpoint, Connecticut: 1981.

al-Jumahi, Muhammad ibn Sallam. *Tabaqat al-Shura,* Edited by Joseph Hell. Leiden, Holland: 1916.

Ibn Kathir, al-Qurayshi al-Dimashqi, Imad al-Din Abi al-Foda Isma'il. *Al-Bidaya wa'l-Nihaya,* 14 vols. Cairo: 1351/1932.

Ispahani, Abul-Faraj. *Kitab al-Aghani.* 21 vols. Cairo: 1927–1936.

———. *The Life of the Prophet Muhammad.* Traslated by Professor Trevor Le Gassick. United Kingdom: Garnet Publishing limited, 2000.

———. *Tafsir al-Qur'an al-Azim.* 7 vols. Beirut: Dar al-Fikr, 1389/1970.

Katib, Dr. M. M. *The Bounteous Koran.* London: MacMillan Press, 1948.

Kazdin, Alan, E., editor in chief. *Encyclopedia of Psychology.* Oxford: Oxford University Press, 2000. s. v. "Sexual disorders," by Karen M. Donahey.

Kazi, Dr. Mazhar U. *A Treasury of A Hadith, Introduction.*

Khadduri, Majid. *War and Peace in the Law of Islam.* Baltimore: John Hopkins Press, 1955.

Ibn Khaldun, Abd al-Rahman ibn Muhammad. *The Muquddimah: An Introduction to History.* 3 vols. Translated by Franz Rosenthal. Princeton: Princeton University Press, 1967.

Khoje, Abdullah Muhammad. *The End of the Journey.* Washington, D. C.: The Islamic Center, 1987.

Ibn Khordad Beh. *Almasalik valmamalik.* Edited by. M. J. de Goege, 1889.

Koelle, S. W. *Mohammed and Mohammedanism.* London: Rivingtons: 1972.

Lane-Poole, Stanely. *Studies in A Mosque.* London and Sydney: Eden, Remington and Company, 1983.

Levy, Carlo. *Crist se e fermato a Eboli.* Translated from French by Jeanne Modigliani. Paris: Gallimard, 1948.

Lewis, Bernard, ed. and tras. *Islam From the Prophet Muhammad to the Capture of Constantinople.* 2 vols. London: The MacMillan Press LTD., 1974.

Lings, Martin. *Muhammad: His Life Based on the Earlier Sources.* New York: Inner Traditions International, Ltd., 1983.

Longman Dictionary of Psychology and Psychiatry. 1984 ed. s. v. "Inferiority complex."

Macdonald, Duncan Black. *Aspects of Islam.* Freeport, New York: Books for Libraries Press, 1943.

Machiavelli, Niccolo. *The Prince and Discourses.* New York: Ransom House, Inc., 1950.

al-Majlesi, Mulla Mohammed Baqer. *Bihar el-Anwar fi Akhbar el-Aemmatel Athar.* Farsi text. 110 vols. Tehran: al-Maktabah al-Islamyah, 1387–1392/1956–1972.

———. *The Life and Religion of Muhammad, Hyat-ul-Kuloob.* Translated by James L. Merrick. San Antonio, Texas: The Zahra Trust, 1982.

Majma'-al-Bayan, vol. 10.

Majumdar, Suhas. *Jihad: The Islamic Doctrine of Permanent War.* New Delhi, India: Voice of America, 1994.

Malayeri, Dr. Mohammed. *The History and Culture of Iran.* Farsi edition. 5 vols. Tehran: Tus Publicaion, 1379.

Malik, Fida Hussain. *Wives of Prophet.* Lahore, Pakistan: SH. Muhammad Ashraf, 1983.

Marghinani, Ali ibn Abi Bakr. *The Hedaya (Guide: A Commentary on the Mussalman Law).* Translated by Charles Hamilton. Delhi, India: Islamic Book Trust, 1982.

Margoliouth, David. *Mohammed and the Rise of Islam.* New York: Books for Libraries Press, 1972.

Massignon, Louis. *The Passion of al-Hallaj: Mystic and Martyr of Islam.* Translated from French by Herbert Mason. Princeton, New Jersey: Princeton University Press, 1982.

Masudi, Abul-Hassan Ali. *Muruj al-Dhahab.* (The Meadows of Gold). 2 vols. Cairo: 1303, 1346 A. H. and 1885.

Maududi, Seyyed Abul Ala. *The Meaning of the Qur'an.* Lahore: Islamic Publications, 1982.

―――. *Towards Understanding the Qur'an.* English version of *Tafhim al-Qur'an.* United Kingdom: The Islamic Foundation, 1993.

Maulana, Muhammad Ali. *The Religion of Islam.* Lahore, Pakistan: Ahmadiyya Anjuman Isha'at-i-Islam, 1983.

Mernissi, Fatima. *Beyond the Veil: Male-Female Dynamic in Modern Muslim society.* Bloomingdale and Indianapolis: Indiana University Press, 1987.

Mohajer, N. "The Mass Killings in Iran," *Aresh* 57(August 1996): 7.

Moor, Thomas. *The Soul's Religion.* New York: Harper Collins Publishers, 2002.

Morey, Robert. *The Islamic Invasion.* Eugene, Oregon: Harvest House Publishers, 1992.

Moujudi, Hassan. *Ezdevaje Daem va Ezdevaje Movaqqat.* Farsi text. Tehran: Moujudi Publication, 1370.

Mufti, Abdullah IBM. *Shah al-Azhar.* Cairo: 1358 A.D.

Motavval. *Tarikh al-Arab.*

Muir, Sir William. *Mahomet and Islam.* London: Darf Publishers Limited, 1986.

―――. *The Life of Mohammad.* Edinburgh: John Grant. 1912.

Murdoch, J. *Arabia and its Prophet.* Madras, India: The Christian Literature Society for Inda, 1992.

Muslim, Imam. *Sahih Muslim.* Translated by Abdul Hamid Siddiqi. 4 vols. Beirut, Lebanon: Dar al-Arabia, 2000.

―――. *The Life of Mohammad.* Edinburgh: John Grant, 1923.

al-Muttaqi. *Kanz ul-Ummal.*

Nasr, Hosein. *Ideals and Realities of Islam.* ABC International Group, 2000.

Nicholson, Raynold A. *A Literary History of the Arabs.* Cambridge: University of Cambridge, 1941.

al-Nisaburi, Nizam al-Din al-Hasan ibn Muhammad ibn al-Husayn al-Qummi. *Ghara'ib al-Qur'an Wa Ragha'b al-Furqan.* Edited by Ibrahim Atwah Awad. 5 vols. Cairo: Mustafa al-Babi al-Halabi, 1381–1384/1962–1964.

Nöldoke, Thedore. *Gechichte des Qorans.* 2nd. ed. Revised by F. Schwally. Leipzig, 1909–38.

―――. ed. *The Origins of the Koran.* Amherst, New York: Prometheus Books, 1998.

Nubakhti, Abu Muhammad al-Hassan. *Kitab Firaq al-Shi'a.* Edited by Ritter. Istanbul: 1931 and al-Najaf: 1936.

O'brien, Conor Cruise. *The Times,* 11 May 1989.

Payne, Robert. *The History of Islam.* New York: Dorset Press, 1987.

Pickthal, M. *The Meaning of the Glorious Koran.* London: 1930.

Pochmann, Henry A. and Feltskog. E. N., eds. *Mahomet and his Successors.* Madison, Milwaukee: The University of Wisconsin Press, 1970.

Polisensky, Josef, V. *The Thirty Years War.* Translated from the Czech by Robert Evans. California: California University, 1971.

Prideaux, Humphrey. *Mahomet: The True Nature of Impostor.* London: 1708.

Random House Unbridged Dictionary, 2nd ed. (1987), s. v. "Terror."

al-Razi, Fkhr al-Din. *Al-Tafsir al-Kabir.* 32 vols.Cairo: al-Matba'ah al-Bahyah, n.d.

Rieber, Robert. *Manufacturing Social Stress.* New York and London: Plenum Press, 1997.

Rihani, Ameen. *Arabian Peak and Desrt.* London: Constable & Co., Ltd., 1903.

Robinson, Neal. *Islam: A Concise Introduction.* Surrey: Great Britain: Curzon Press, 1999.

Rodinson, Maxim. *Mohammad.* New York: The New Press, 1980.

Roppin, Andrew, ed. *Approaches to the History of the Interpretation of the Qur'an.* Oxford: Clarendon Press, 1988.

Rowdell, J. A. *Koran.* London: J. M. Dent & Sons Ltd., 1953.

Runnes, Dagobert. *Philosophy for Everyone.* New York: Philosophical Library, Inc., 1968.

Runciman, Steven. *The Fall of Constantinople 1435.* Cambridge: 1990.

Russell, Betrand. *A History of Western Philosophy.* New York: Simon & Schuster, 1945.

————. *Why I am Not A Christian.* London: National Secular Society, 1970.

Ibn Sa'd, Muhammd. *Kitab al-Tabaqat al-Kabir.* 8 vols. Edited by E. Sachau. Leyden: 1322 A. H.

Sahih Muslim. Translated by Abdul Hamid Siddiqi. 4 vols. Beirut, Lebanon: Dar al-Arabia: 2002.

Said, Edward W. *Orientalism.* New York: Pantheon Books, 1994.

Sale, George, trans. *Koran,* London: 1986.

Sarakhsi, Muhammad ibn Ahmad. *Kitab al-Mabsut.* Cairo: 1324 A.H.

Seneca, *Epistolae,* LVI., 10.

Servier, Andre. *Islam and the Psychology of Musulman.* Translated by A. S. Mose-Blundell. London: Chapman & Hall ltd., 1924.

Sheikh Muhammad as-Saleh al-Uthaimin. *The Muslim's Belief.*

Sheriff, Faruq. *A Guide to the Contents of the Koran.* United Kingdom: Reading, 1995.

Shorrosh, Dr. Anis A. *Islam Revealed.* Nashville, Tennessee: Nelson Publishers, 1988.

Smith, Patricia. *Brain-Wise.* Churchland, Massachusetts: Institute of Technology, 2002.

Smith, William Cantwell. *Questions of Religious Truth.* New York: Charles Scribe's Sons, 1967.

Spencer, Robert. *Islam Unveiled.* San Francisco: Encounter Books, 2000.

Sprenger, Aloys. *The Life of Mohammad from Original Sources.* Allahabad: Printed at the Presbyterian Mission Press, 1851.

Stanislavsky, Konstantin. *An Actor Prepares.* Tanslated by Elizabeth Raynolds Hapggod. London: Mathews, 1984.

————. *Building A Character.* New York: Theatre Arts Books, 1949.

Stoll, Otto. *Suggestion und Hypnotismus in der Völkerpsychologie.* 2 umgearb und verm aufl. Leipzig: Veit & Co., 1904.

Swarp, Ram. *Understanding the Hadith.* Amherst, New York: Prometheus Books, 2002.

al-Tabari, Muhammad ibn Jarir. *The Histopry of at-Tabari (Ta'rikh al-rusul wa'l muluk).* 33 vols. Translated and annotated by different scholars. New York: New York State University, 1991.

Taheri, Amir. *The Spirit of Allah: Khomeini and the Islamic Revolution.* London: Adler and Adler, 1986.

————. *Holy Terror.* London: Sphere Books Ltd., 1987.

Talbure, Solomon. *George Bush Is A Moron, Islam Is Not Peace.* U. S. A.: Xlibris Corporation, 2002.

al-Tirmidhi, Abu Isa Muhammed. *al-Jami',* 3 vols. (The Collection), Cairo: 1938.

————. *Islam Expoesed.* Coral Spring, Florida: Metier Books: 2002.

Tisdall, W. St. Clair. *The Original Sources of the Qur'an.* New York: E. S. Gorham, 1905.

De Tocqueville, *Democracy in America,* 2 vols. New York: Vantage Books, 1954.

Torrey, Charles Cutler, *The Jewish Foundation of Islam.* New York: KTAV Publishing House, Inc., 1968.

Vander Leeuw, Gerardus. *Religion in Essence and Manifestation.* 3 vols. New York: Harper & Row, Publishers, 1963.

Vigor, P. H. *A Guide to Marxism.* New York: Humanities Press, 1966.

Vroom, Hendrik, M. *Religion and the Truth.* Michigan: Grant Rapids, 1989.

al-Waqidi, Muhammad ibn Umar. *Kitab al-Maghazi.* 1966.

Ibn Warraq, ed. & trans. *What the Koran Really Says?* Amherst, New York: Prometheus Books, 2002.

————. *Why I am not A Muslim.* Amherst, New York: Prometheus Books, 1995.

Watt, Montomery, William. *Muhammad Prophet and Statesman.* Oxford: Oxford University Press, 1961.

Webster's Third New International Dictionary, 2nd ed. (1993)), v. s. "Terror."

Weldon, Fay. *Sacred Cows.* London: 1989.

Wensick, A. *A Handbook of Early Muhammadan Traditons.* Leyden: 1927.

"Where Two World Collide." *Washington Post,* 25 February 2002, sec. AI, p.1.

Winn, Craig. *Muhammad, Prophet of Doom.* Canada: Cricket Songs Books, 2004.

Ya'qubi, Ahmad ibn Abi Ya'qub. *Tarikh al-Ya'qubi.* 2 vols. Edited by Houstma. Leyden: 1883.

Yusuf Ali, Abdullah. *The Holy Koran.* Brentwood, Maryland: Amana Corporation, 1989.

Zwemer, Samuel. *Across the World of Islam.* London: Fleming H. Revell Company, undated.

———. *Islam: A Challenge to Faith.* London: Darf Publishers Ltd., 1985.

———. *Studies in Popular Islam.* London: The Sheldon Press, 1939.

INDEX

ABOUT THE AUTHOR

Masud Ansari, B.A., M.A., PH.D., D.C.H., F.C.H., holds a B.A. in law, M.A. is International Relations from the University of London, and three doctorate degrees, two in political science, one from the Tehran University, the second from the George Washington University, and the third in hypnotheraphy from the American Pacific University.

He is the author and translator of 33 books on psychology, law, political science, philosophy, theology and hypnotherapy—in addition to two works of fiction. One of his books, *Nationalism*, won critical acclaim in 1968.

The outcome of his teaching and research in the London University, American University of Beirut, UNAFI (Japan), and Iranian and American Universities has been: Phi Beta Kappa and three President awards—one from the National Guild of Hypnotists (1991) and two from the Eastern Institute of Hypnotherapy (1995).

BY THE SAME AUTHOR

Nationalism and Anti-Colonial Campaigns of the East European Countries (Winner of the best prize of the year, 1967)

Political Tensions after the Second World War

67 Massacres

The Impact of Mullahism on the Iranian Contemporary History

Legal Immunities

New Frontiers in Psychology

Psychology of Sexual Crimes and Deviations

Psychology of Gambling and the Treatment of Gamblers

Golden Bunches

The Resurrection in Islam

Cyrus the Great and Mohammed ibn Abdullah

Shi'ism and Mahdi'ism

A Re-Evaluation of the Koran

The Greater God

A New Perspective on Islam

Broken Decision

Human Calamities

New Method in English Grammar

Tenses in English

English at Home (28 Volumes)

The Court of People's Justice

International Terrorism: Its Causes and How to Control It

Modern Hypnosis: Theory and Practice

Hypnotherapy for Smoking Cessation with Ease

Alcohol Addiction and Its Successful Treatment by Hypnotherapy
Hypnotherapy, the Treatment of Choice for Weight Control
Treatment of Sexual Deviations and Sexual Dysfunctions by
    Hypnosis

Translations

The Autobiography of Bertrand Russell
Guilty Land
Islam and Mohammadanism
Blood Money
Countdown to Terror
Koran and Hadith in Picture